# ZERO POINT FOUR

## How U.S. Leadership in Maritime Will Secure America's Future

Rear Admiral James Watson (USCG, Ret.),
Carleen Lyden Walker, Rich Mason, Jonathan Kempe,
Nishan Degnarain, Captain Anuj Chopra

Published by the Maritime Accelerator for Resilience ("MAR") New Castle, Delaware, 19720, United States of America

**A Maritime Policy Accelerator**
The Maritime Accelerator for Resilience ("MAR") is a U.S.-based maritime organization, operating as a Maritime Policy Accelerator, at the forefront of innovation and industry leadership. Collaborating with influential figures in shipping, ocean policy, and innovation, MAR aims to catalyze transformative change. Our vision is to motivate the U.S. maritime industry to global competitiveness, navigating challenges and embracing opportunities in the next decade.

www.maritimeresilience.org

Published by The Maritime Accelerator for Resilience –
New Castle, Delaware, 19720, United States of America

www.maritimeresilience.org



Manufactured in the United States of America

Drafting by Jonathan Kempe

Editing by Nishan Degnarain

Cover design by Jonathan Kempe

Graphics by Thomas Harris

Printed by Amazon Kindle Direct Publishing

Library of Congress Number:

ISBN Hardback: 978-1-963153-47-7

ISBN Paperback: 978-1-963153-46-0

Thanks for your dedication to the maritime industry

# DEDICATION

Dedicated to the men and women of the United States Merchant Marine

*"The maintenance of a merchant marine is of the utmost importance for national defense and the service of our commerce."*

**President Calvin Coolidge,** Message to Congress (1925)

NYHS
Together we will right this ship!
5/22/05

# ACKNOWLEDGEMENTS

*ZERO POINT FOUR* contains research from a wide range of sources and has been compiled from the input of a diverse array of skillful, passionate, apolitical, and globally recognized contributors - without the use of generative artificial intelligence.

The authors also wish to acknowledge the long list of supporters and tireless advocates working to support seafarers and promote the U.S. and international maritime sectors.

*This page is intentionally left blank.*

# CONTENTS

# FOREWORD

Admittedly, over my 34-year career in the U.S. Coast Guard, the dwindling number of U.S.-crewed ships and the strategic implication of my country being so reliant on foreign crews and foreign control of international trade and logistics did not seriously concern me. I could see there were hundreds of U.S. merchant mariners and sea-going U.S.-flagged ships routinely coming and going in every port where I served. It didn't readily occur to me that the activity I saw were people and ships transiting only within the United States.

The domestic-only merchant marine, which includes tugs, barges, supply boats, ferries, dredges, research ships, fishing vessels, and about 100 deep draft coastal ships, is appropriate for a country the size of the United States. But I rarely saw ocean-going U.S.-flagged ships importing or exporting cargo to and from U.S. ports. Deep-sea capable U.S. registered commercial ships are essential for national security and prosperity, however the overall numbers are stark: 99.6 percent are foreign-flagged, whereas 0.4 percent, less than 200 ships, fly the stars and stripes. Out of around 50,000.

During 2022, there were about 80,000 foreign vessel port calls into the United States. The U.S. Navy, Coast Guard, and Customs and Border Protection (CBP) Service have an entirely different role policing foreign vessel activities compared to supporting and serving tax-paying U.S.-registered vessels and mariners. I was required to screen and board foreign ships as part of U.S. border security. However, my visits to U.S. ships were friendly. U.S. merchant mariners and Coasties have a mutual appreciation for a Coast Guard certificated ship and the safety of our ports and waterways.

It wasn't until I retired and felt the impact of the post-COVID supply chain crisis that I began to question the severely lopsided ratio of foreign to U.S. ships. I realized the magnitude of everyone's dependence on international trade and how little we control it.

My focus as a contributor to this book is on the U.S. deep-sea international trading fleet. Currently there are less than 200 ships engaged in these activities. Most are built in foreign shipyards and currently depend on government stipends or cargo preference. At least 75% of the crews of these ships are U.S. citizens. This fleet might cover the needs of military sealift, when combined with the U.S. Military Sealift Command and Maritime Administrations reserve fleets, however I believe National Security is greatly at risk for a variety of other reasons related to Economic, Energy & Food, Climate and maritime Workforce Security.

This book provides a useful framework for questioning the adequacy of U.S. dependence on assets that are not entirely within our control. After reading it, I hope readers will want to study maritime security the way I have recently. Like me, you might have assumed that the Navy, Coast Guard and CBP are in control of what occurs at the waterfront and beyond. Why should we care that so few Americans are skilled seagoing mariners? Is the world so interdependent that foreign-controlled ships are of little concern? Are we really energy and food independent? What opportunities are we missing when we have so little involvement in an industry that is so critical to the world's climate, political stability, and orderly technological advancement?

I believe our national well-being demands action. This book offers solutions. Acting now will help assure a resilient future for our maritime industries and the United States in general.

I'm very proud of the team who helped author this book. We are a diverse group with very different perspectives who all have come to similar conclusions about maritime security. Read our bios; you may fall within or between the spectrum of backgrounds and interests we represent. If so, I hope you will join us to seek a stronger, resilient and more forward-leaning U.S. merchant marine.

RADM James Watson (USCG, Ret.)

December 31, 2023
Lusby, Maryland

# PREFACE

Weaving through waterways, twisting across the sky, and crisscrossing the land, sprawling arterial networks convey life-sustaining cargo around an increasingly fragile planet. Five distinct, yet interconnected domains - sea, air, land, cyber and space - facilitate the movement of global trade. The transportation modes associated with these domains have been subjected to growing scrutiny: Clogged ports, choked expressways, derailed trains and shipment delays have all grabbed headlines, amidst a disruptive pandemic, and the looming threats posed by geopolitical tensions and a rapidly changing climate.

The maritime supply chain has garnered increased attention in recent times. The world was transfixed by a large vessel stuck in the narrow Suez Canal. Feverish commentary followed the growing congestion off the California coast, as hundreds of large ships waited to discharge cargo. Iran-backed Houthi militants in Yemen used drones, helicopters and missiles to target the global shipping industry passing through the Red Sea and Gulf of Aden. Wildly fluctuating freight rates foisted abnormal cost pressures on suppliers, manufacturers, retailers, and ultimately the public. And, through the analysis of talk show pundits and arm-chair experts, the world suddenly became more aware of the tumultuous journey of shipping containers as they traversed beleaguered supply chains; contending with equipment shortages, warehousing woes, labor disputes, abandoned seafarers, natural disasters, war, and the ravaging effects of a global pandemic.

An uncomfortable truth was magnified in the chaos: The United States lacks a discernible strategy to adequately control, manage or profit from most forms of commercial maritime activity. With shrinking influence over the construction and ownership of ships, the operation of ports, and the flow of goods through intermodal means, the U.S. has been relegated from maritime world leader to reluctant participant; trailing allies, and dangerously lagging behind adversaries. While continued investment has solidified the superiority of the U.S. Navy, the U.S. commercial fleet is in rapid and precipitous decline. This is epitomized in one percentage:

***Zero Point Four***

There are over 50,000 commercial, ocean-going vessels currently operating around the world, yet only 180 fly the U.S. Flag. This represents a diminutive *Zero Point Four* percent (0.4%) of the global fleet, or about 0.57% of total tonnage. By contrast, in 1950, the United States owned and operated over 1,000 private and 2,200 Government vessels, commanded 50% of the world's total tonnage, and carried nearly 80% of global trade. From half of all, to half a percent. To put this more starkly: The United States has the largest economy in the world, and yet around 98% of all U.S. imports and exports are transported on vessels controlled by foreign countries and operated by foreign mariners. This striking imbalance exposes the U.S. economy to undue external influence, introduces complex security risks, and diverts billions of dollars away from U.S. businesses and citizens every year. For clarity, while there are thousands of smaller pleasure craft, barges and fishing vessels registered within the United States, the scope of this book covers the large, ocean-bound commercial ships that is used for international trade, and which we refer to as commercial or ocean-bound vessels. They typically carry over 1000 containers (to as many as 24,000 containers), liquid or dry bulk goods (such as oil, fuels or grain), or specialty ships such as ice-breakers, vehicle transporters, sub-sea cable laying ships, or heavy lift vessels (e.g., to transport heavy maritime infrastructure or damaged vessels). These are the 180 vessels that fly the U.S. flag and can be used for international shipping, of which around 100 are required for domestic trade purposes (e.g., to Alaska, Hawaii, Puerto Rico, U.S. Virgin Islands, the Great Lakes Region).

History yields many informative lessons, but this book does not seek to restore old glories. Times have changed and new strategies are required to influence the global narrative and solidify U.S. maritime leadership. To that end, an examination is conducted on sobering present realities through an impact analysis on five 'Principles' of Maritime Security:

I. National Security

II. Economic Security

III. Energy & Food Security

IV. Climate Security, and

V. Workforce Security

Each Maritime Security Principle is analyzed in four steps:

- The context through which each Principle represents an important security issue for the U.S.;
- How this security issue is inextricably linked to the shipping industry;
- Why the current state of U.S. maritime represents particular security risks to each Principle;
- Proposals for creative and pragmatic solutions that would reverse the decline, increase national resilience, and deliver profitable outcomes to the U.S. economy, U.S. citizens, and ultimately, the world.

This book's authors have their own perspectives on this multi-faceted industry. However, they all gravitated to the same conclusion: Where is the U.S. maritime industry today, and where does it need to be? Each author recognizes the important role that the U.S. maritime industry could play in maintaining a rules-based international order, introducing technologies that could revolutionize the industry, and ensuring fair and safe navigable passages around the world. The authors additionally recognize the opportunities, economic growth, and assurance of security by American leadership in maritime - and particularly by Americans investing in careers, ships, infrastructure, skilled workers and emerging technologies.

As the U.S. cultural anthropologist Margaret Mead has said, *"Never doubt that a small group of thoughtful committed individuals can change the world. In fact, it's the only thing that ever has."*

# INTRODUCTION

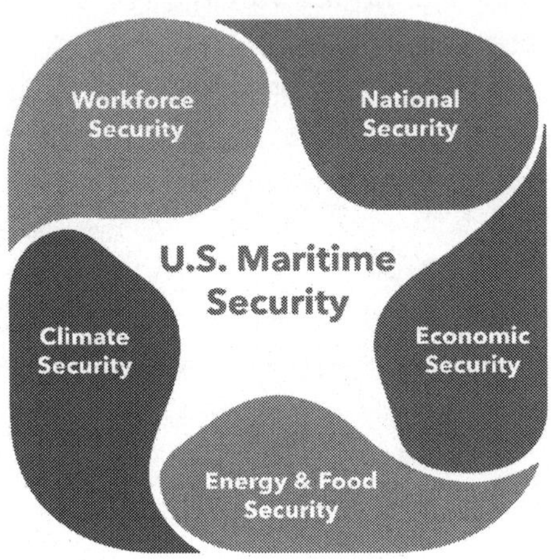


The United States is a maritime nation. It has always been highly dependent on a well-functioning international shipping system. One could say that the U.S. maritime industry is the blue in the Stars and Stripes. It is the glue that keeps the union strong and secure. Shipping is essential to every aspect of U.S. life, in particular, National Security, Economic Security, Energy and Food Security, Climate Security and Workforce Security. A dollar invested in the U.S. maritime sector should yield over five times this amount back in return in terms of greater security across each of these five domains.

However, today, the U.S. maritime sector is at its weakest point than at any point in U.S. history. From a peak of over half the world's ocean-crossing vessels being U.S.-flagged after World War 2, today that number is less than *Zero Point Four* percent (0.4%). This presents a significant threat to five key domains for the United States: Military, Economic, Energy and Food, Climate, Workforce. Anyone caring about these five domains should find this book essential reading to understand the importance of the U.S. maritime sector to each. It is through this lens that this book and the ZP4 ("*Zero Point Four*") Framework evaluates the importance of the U.S. maritime industry to America today.

This book is not just about identifying vulnerabilities, but proposing actionable solutions. The concluding chapter of this book identifies a 57-point Action Plan to turn around the fortunes of the U.S. maritime sector within a decade. These are solutions that have been vetted by experts and industry leaders, and present several 'no-regret' proposals for leadership at the highest levels of the country to consider as part of a new and holistic National Maritime and Blue Economy Strategy.

By way of comparison, the solutions proposed in this book represent a fraction of the $17 billion of taxpayer funds allocated for U.S. ports in 2021 as an emergency measure to alleviate the supply chain crisis, much of which supports foreign-owned port infrastructure, vessels and containers, and very little of which addresses the root-cause vulnerabilities in the U.S. maritime sector that continues today.

With the world in an increasingly volatile and uncertain state, the U.S. needs a reliable and robust maritime sector unlike any time in recent history. The COVID-19 pandemic, European migrant boat crisis, growing number of extreme weather events, conflicts in Ukraine, Israel, Gaza and the Red Sea, and rising tensions in Asia represent considerable concerns for stability in the near future with the probability of unexpected 'Black Swan' events rising.

This is why the ZP4 Framework matters to the United States' security, preeminence and viability.

# I. NATIONAL SECURITY

The weak state of the U.S. maritime industry risks National Security in five major ways:

- **Significant shortfall of military support vessels from the commercial fleet**. The U.S. requires up to 1120 commercial vessels in the event of a prolonged international conflict around the world, without losing its economic competitiveness or harming domestic energy or food security. This is over six times more vessels than it currently has access to today (180 vessels). These vessels would be commercially operational in peacetime, and not be a drain on the public purse. Specifically, of these 1120 vessels, the U.S. military may need access to 1000 militarily-useful commercial container and vehicle transport (RORO) ships in a major conflict, but currently only has access to 180. Not all of these 180 vessels are considered 'militarily-useful' (i.e., can be used to support military operations). There is also a need to include enough commercial vessels to backfill essential domestic transport needs that would have been redirected to support military forces in times of war. In addition, the U.S. would require 100 tankers to meet its refueling needs during a conflict, but can only access fewer than 10 today. With an increasingly ice-free Arctic, more icebreakers are needed to escort vessels or rescue vessels (e.g., around Alaska). The U.S. needs at least 5 icebreakers but has fewer than 2 available today. The U.S. economy and military are dependent on subsea internet cables and infrastructure, but the U.S. has only three cable-laying and repair ships should this infrastructure be attacked. Hence, the U.S. may need access to around 15 other specialty ships (such as cable laying and repair ships, heavy lift ships, salvage ships). In essence, the U.S. needs to radically scale up its access to U.S.-owned commercial vessels by 600%. This would benefit the U.S. both during peacetime and in the event of a major and sustained conflict around the world. This does not necessarily mean these new vessels should be built in the U.S. or purchased by the U.S. Government, but could include creative measures and incentives to "re-flag" suitable commercial vessels.

- **Wasteful Government support programs creating 'Zombie Assets.'** The U.S. has 3 major support programs that are wasteful and have led to vessels that cannot be used in the event of a conflict, but which the U.S. military assumes they can rely on. One program includes the Ready Reserve Force (RRF), which has declined from 2,277 vessels at its peak in the 1950s to fewer than 100 today. Recent military exercises revealed that of these, fewer than 40% could depart port and operate effectively with the military. Most of the RRF vessels are over 45 years old, spend their time idle in storage, are barely operational, and are operated by skeleton crews. Another program, the Maritime Security Program (MSP) costs over $300 million a year to provide 60 vessels to the Department of Defense for Emergency Sealift operations, but these vessels do not meet military requirements, nor does this program support U.S.-built, owned or operated vessels. Yet another program, the Voluntary Intermodal Sealift Agreement (VISA) Program where commercial vessels support national programs (such as U.S. defense department cargo and food aid) is insufficient to provide the right type and number of vessels to the U.S. On top of this, none of these programs meaningfully address the serious shortfall of U.S. mariners required to operate commercial vessels that can support the U.S. military during a time of conflict or national emergency, forcing the U.S. to rely heavily on non-U.S. vessels and mariners.

- **Significant foreign ownership of the U.S. maritime sector.** For such a strategic sector, the U.S. is highly dependent on non-U.S. owned and operated vessels, non-U.S. mariners, and non-U.S. owned port infrastructure (such as terminals and cranes). This represents a major vulnerability to National Security in the event of a conflict. In addition and as a result, the U.S. military and commercial fleet have reduced their collaboration at a time when other countries are blending commercial and military interoperability, in the advent of conflict. The U.S. military has assumed that in the event of a conflict, it can simply appropriate commercial vessels from the domestic supply chain for military purposes, (for example vessels servicing Hawaii, Alaska, Puerto Rico, U.S. Virgin Islands, Guam, Mississippi river, around the Great Lakes). This would cause significant domestic economic harm, and such vessels would need to be rapidly backfilled (e.g., tankers, container vessels, bulk carriers), which may not be possible if such assets are not easily accessible to the U.S. Government. We refer to this as the U.S. maritime "Double Counting Conundrum." The result of significant foreign ownership of the U.S. maritime sector is an anemic commercial maritime industrial base that is unable to drive the next generation of maritime innovation.

- **Growing vulnerabilities from emerging technologies.** New technologies such as cyber-security Artificial Intelligence bots, satellites and space technologies, modern critical infrastructure (such as ship-to-shore container cranes), and the rise of asymmetric warfare (e.g., the rise of unmanned aerial and maritime vehicles) has altered the balance of power. New capabilities are required to defend against these threats, but such capabilities are being built too slowly, and with insufficient engagement of the private sector despite some of the leading emerging technologies being pioneered in Silicon Valley and implemented in other adjacent transportation sectors in the U.S. such as automotive, aviation and private space flight.

- **Rise of China as a maritime power.** China has rapidly increased its influence in the international maritime sector. While some policy objectives may be aligned with U.S. interests (e.g., on reducing the impact of climate change), others are not (e.g., human rights and questions of sovereignty over Taiwan). This represents an unstable relationship upon which very high stakes depend, and where a weak U.S. maritime industry exposes several major vulnerabilities. China's rapid rise raises important questions for U.S. National Security in 8 domains: relative strength of each country's naval power; strength of each country's commercial maritime fleet; operational readiness of each respective country's commercial mariners; each country's shipbuilding capabilities; access to shipping containers; influence over international ports, terminals, and waterways; domestic maritime industrial capacity; use of each nation's fishing fleets.

## II. ECONOMIC SECURITY

A small U.S. commercial maritime industry weakens U.S. Economic Security in the following five ways.

- **Threats to U.S. dollar denominated international trade.** Every year, goods valued at over $25 trillion are transported across the world, with over 90% of all foreign exchange transactions involving the U.S. dollar (USD). Vessel owners and shipping companies have a high degree of influence over the currency used for global trade transactions. While USD-denominated trade appears largely impregnable today, the U.S. share of global output has fallen from 40% in 1960 to 25% in 2022. The rise of China and demands for trade to be denominated in Renminbi (RMB) could pose a threat to the stability of the U.S. dollar. In recent years, several large trading nations (such as China and Saudi Arabia) have made overt policy statements to reduce their dependence on U.S. dollar denominated trade in light of growing U.S. use of economic sanctions. A USD-denominated global trading marketplace gives the U.S. one of its most powerful international policy levers in the form of U.S. economic sanctions. Economic sanctions have been imposed at various times against regimes such as Iran, Iraq, North Korea, Russia, Venezuela, Afghanistan to prevent U.S. dollars held by these countries from being traded, and crippling their economies. New alliances such as the China-backed 155-nation Belt and Road Initiative provide credible alternative trading blocks to USD-denominated trade. A decoupling of global trade from the U.S. dollar could significantly impact the ability of the U.S. to wield such influence, and conversely reveals a vulnerability to the U.S. if a hostile nation decided to impose economic sanctions against the U.S. in a currency over which they hold significant influence. This could prevent trade with the U.S. in certain critical goods and would force the U.S. to seek alternative suppliers at short notice. This is why a large U.S. maritime industry active in critical trading nodes is essential to safeguard the U.S. dollar for international trade.

- **Shipping is a critical node in global trade that the U.S. is losing influence over.** A handful of influential shipping industry owners, operators, Flag-State Administrations, can dictate which ports are developed, what types of fuels are used, and what regulatory standards are adopted. Without a strong U.S. commercial presence in the sector, decisions may be taken that go against U.S. national and economic interests at the risk of trillions of dollars. For example, without a strong U.S. maritime sector, decisions on emission standards, labor safety standards, cybersecurity protocols may be taken that could harm U.S. economic security, and leave the U.S. absent from international strategic initiatives as new trade routes start to open up around the Arctic and along the Belt and Road Initiative. Oscillating U.S. leadership has meant that politically-driven initiatives, such as President Obama's Trans-Pacific Partnership with 12 Pacific Rim economies, was never ratified, but may have survived with a stronger U.S. maritime presence and economic stake across each of these nations.

- **Growing foreign influence over U.S. critical infrastructure sectors.** Foreign investors - rather than U.S. investors or the U.S. Government - have invested across the entire U.S. shipping value chain, from vessel registrations, shipbuilding, cargo carrying vessels, port infrastructure, to seafarers. As a result, over 99% of vessels carrying containerized cargo into the U.S. are foreign-flagged, over 98% of mariners involved in carrying U.S. cargo are from other countries, and a significant proportion of port terminals are foreign controlled. At any point, a foreign entity could raise prices, cease offering a service, or disrupt operations, significantly impacting U.S. economic security. Such a disruption could occur for non-malicious reasons if a foreign operator has less transparent and more risky business practices than a U.S.-owned business, leading to its collapse (as seen recently across several maritime organizations in Asia). Similarly, such risks extend internationally. Foreign investment in strategically located ports (e.g., around maritime chokepoints) have increased risks to U.S.-bound shipping at the same time as U.S. financial institutions, development and aid organizations have reduced such investments in strategically located ports abroad.

- **Missed $6 trillion Blue Economy opportunities.** One of the biggest growth opportunities in the next decade will be the growth of the sustainable Blue Economy. This comprises sectors such as the emergence of greener international shipping, offshore fish farms (aquaculture), offshore floating wind farms, short sea shipping and autonomous maritime systems. The U.S. has much of the technology and financial system needed to lead a sustainable Blue Economy globally but lacks a coherent national plan or set of institutions to drive this forward even domestically. As a result, foreign firms have taken a leadership position in key niches of the Blue Economy such as in aquaculture, offshore windfarms, autonomous vessels and even 'Blue Finance.' In the same way, large foreign-owned shipping companies like Maersk generated over $80 billion revenue in 2022, compared to the largest U.S. shipping company which generated just over $4 billion revenue in 2022, a 20X difference. Maersk's profits alone over the past three years were over $60 billion, which would have been a significant source of corporate tax revenue that could have supported re-investment and modernization of U.S. port infrastructure. Without strong domestic maritime operators, the U.S. will continue to have a weak and fragmented innovation economy around the maritime sector, even though the U.S. leads the world in breakthrough technological innovation in almost every other domain. One of the roadblocks to faster growth is misaligned taxes that penalize more efficient shipping operations (e.g., the $500 million a year Harbor Maintenance Tax that has held back Short Sea Shipping operations). Much of this revenue has not been invested to modernize port infrastructure or operations as it was intended. Another strategic disadvantage of a weak domestic maritime sector has meant that the U.S. has not effectively exerted its influence globally over the trade in illicit goods. Trade in illicit or counterfeit goods are estimated to harm the global economy by between $2-4 trillion a year, and U.S. firms could be setting global standards on relevant data, technologies and protocols to eradicate such harmful business practices through its own fleet.

- **Shipping as a catalyst for an inflationary crisis.** Following the COVID-19 pandemic, inflation spiked to 5.2% in 2021 (almost double the average of 2.9% the decade prior), partly driven by a global supply chain crunch. The recent Houthi-Yemen Red Sea crisis in January 2024 has seen ship insurance rise 70-fold since December 2023, with the premium to insure a $100m container ship jumping from $10,000 to $700,000. Over $17 billion of taxpayer funds was allocated to immediately alleviate congestion around ports, but many of the structural economic risks remain. For example, U.S. ports remain highly dependent on only a handful of very large ports that are able to receive the very largest cargo vessels (U.S. ports and vessels are the wrong size for economic security). There has not been an attempt to move the U.S. toward smaller, more agile vessels that could open up many more ports across the U.S., nor has there been much effort made to introduce floating port infrastructure and cranes to avoid a repeat of the supply chain crisis that cascaded into a macroeconomic inflationary crisis. The current port configuration suits large vessels operators, who are largely foreign-owned, and in fact weakens U.S. economic security. This is known as the "*A380 Problem*" in aviation, where tens of billions of taxpayer dollars were spent upgrading airports around the world to accommodate the needs of one company Airbus' double-decker, wide body A380 airliner, only for the aircraft to end production after just 14 years in 2021 with no equivalent replacement.

## III. ENERGY AND FOOD SECURITY

A small and weak U.S. maritime sector represents significant risks for U.S. energy and food security in the following areas, given the particular requirements of moving energy and food around in specially adapted vessels (primarily tankers and bulk carriers).

- **Lack of consensus over future U.S. energy mix.** The U.S. is at a crossroads over its future energy mix and the timing for the phase out of fossil fuels. By weight, 40% of all cargo carried on ships around the world today consists of either oil, gas, coal and other fossil fuels on their way to be burned, or of products derived directly from fossil fuels, making shipping a major cog in the decision-making and economics around the global energy transition. Power generation and secure transportation of America's future energy mix are closely intertwined. Trillions of dollars of infrastructure have been invested in liquid- and gas- based energy transportation for the oil and gas industry (e.g., oil and LNG tankers), with close proximity to coasts for pipelines, refineries, offshore rigs and oil storage depots. There is a major operational difference between the transportation of a fuel that is solid, liquid or gas. A key determinant in the roadmap to Net Zero is to understand how alternative fuels can be safely transported, processed and placed in strategic locations around the U.S. and the world to avoid energy price spikes and power outages. The U.S. has a strategic opportunity to build shipping capacity in a future energy mix that offers the U.S. a competitive 'leapfrog' advantage, rather than being burdened with a large legacy fleet. A vibrant U.S. shipbuilding and maritime industry could rapidly form a consensus around a sustainable global energy mix and future vessel design for its efficient and safe transportation. For example, if the U.S. has a strategic advantage in small, modular nuclear reactors or particular biofuels such as methanol, this could help shift the balance. Either way, the shipping industry needs to be at the table when discussing the national energy transition (and not having a strong domestic sector will impact decisions).

- **Shortage of U.S.-controlled vessels risks U.S. Energy and Food Security.** Despite being home to some of the world's largest oil and gas companies, most oil companies charter non-U.S. flagged oil tankers (there are only a few dozen U.S.-flagged oil tankers, and these are mainly involved in domestic trade). Despite record LNG production in 2022 and 2023, the U.S. does not have any LNG tankers in the U.S.-flag fleet. LNG tankers are incredibly specialized vessels that require complex engineering to operate and maintain. The U.S.

will be dependent on foreign-built LNG vessels for many years to come under current plans. With food security, of the 12,700 dry bulk ships in the world, the U.S. has direct access to just 4. The U.S. is projected to export 66 million tons of grain in 2023, with over 99% of this grain being shipped on foreign-flagged vessels. Large U.S. agriculture firms like Cargill operate over 500 vessels that move over 200 million tons of commodities a year. Yet most of these vessels are foreign-flagged. Fertilizer is critical to agricultural production and is shipped in bulk bags or the holds of bulk carriers. Over 300 million tons of the three most common fertilizer ingredients (ammonia, phosphoric acid and potassium chloride) are produced each year, with the U.S. importing around 50 million tons of fertilizer a year (17% of the global total). There are no U.S.-flagged ships dedicated to the fertilizer trade. Refrigerated shipping containers are critical to the transportation of fresh food products around the world (the cold supply chain). The three largest shipping lines, MSC, Maersk and CMA-CGM have a combined total of 1.5 million capacity for refrigerated shipping containers on their vessels, which requires an independent power source for refrigeration. U.S.-flagged vessels have a combined total of just 22,000 (70 times fewer). In the event of a major global energy or food crisis, the U.S. would not easily have access to such vessels.

- **Weak U.S. leadership over future fuels in shipping.** There are several key alternative fuels for shipping: Liquefied Natural Gas (LNG), Hydrogen, Ammonia, Methanol, Electrification, Nuclear and Biofuels. Each has strategic pros and cons for U.S. Energy Security - both for general power grid usage and for shipping propulsion. Without a strong U.S.-controlled maritime sector, U.S. energy producers remain dependent on foreign flagged vessels to dictate the pace of transition to zero emission maritime fuels.

- **Vulnerability to foreign ownership of key food security assets.** A weak U.S. maritime sector creates major domestic and international food security vulnerabilities.

    - ***Rising complexity of domestic food security risks***: domestically, the U.S. imports around $190 billion of food and exports around $180 billion, much of which relies on foreign-flagged vessels for transportation. With the impact of climate change being increasingly felt - such as droughts in the Mississippi region - the costs of transporting agricultural goods along parts of the U.S. inland waterway system has increased 5X in the last 12 months alone. In the event of further extreme weather conditions, there is no U.S. maritime agricultural fleet to ship food from international markets to the U.S. as an insurance hedge for the U.S. food supply chain. The U.S. food supply chain remains vulnerable to cyber-security threats and aging infrastructure, posing significant food security risks. At the same time, the U.S. is falling behind on new Blue Economy food security opportunities such as aquaculture and algae production.

    - ***Emerging international food security risks:*** In 2022, USAID provided almost $3 billion in-kind Food Assistance, totaling 1.8 million tons to support around 60 million people around the world. According to USAID conditions attached to this Food Assistance, 50% of food aid must be shipped on U.S.-flagged vessels, but the U.S. only has access to 4 of such dry bulk vessels suitable for food assistance programs. Food exports are increasingly used as a tool for soft power, such as Russia's exports of 65 million tons of wheat to sympathetic countries such as Turkey, Egypt, Iran, Saudi Arabia, Sudan and Algeria amidst the conflict with Ukraine. It is critical that the U.S. is seen as a reliable trade and food security partner for its allies in the same way, by having stronger influence over its agricultural maritime fleet. For example, during the Russia-Ukraine conflict, as one of the world's largest food producers, Ukraine's monthly grain exports fell by 87% in 2022, with 20 million tons of grain trapped in its ports unable to be exported. A sizable U.S.-controlled maritime agricultural fleet would have been able to provide assistance and a policy option to decision-makers should such a scenario arise again, but which is unavailable today. Rising food insecurity in many parts of the world that are strategically important for international stability (such as across West Africa / Sahel region) may require strategic interventions by an operationally ready U.S.-controlled agricultural maritime fleet.

- **A small U.S. fleet creates risks for a Rules-based International Order for energy and food security.** It is estimated almost 1000 tankers are involved in moving sanctioned oil to and from Iran, North Korea, Russia and Syria, with Lloyd's List claiming around 10% of this fleet is controlled by China. Poorly regulated ships present a major environmental threat. Similarly, the U.S. remains reliant on non-U.S. flagged vessels around key maritime chokepoints (such as the Panama Canal, Suez Canal and Red Sea, Straits of Malacca, Niger Delta, Taiwan Straits, and increasingly the Arctic). Hostile actions by state and non-state actors present a risk to food and energy security, as witnessed in the ongoing attacks by Houthi rebels on vessels transiting the Red Sea. Such actions are more likely against non-U.S. flagged vessels where there is a lower chance of intervention. As the U.S. increases its dependence on non-U.S. flagged vessels, it is increasing the risks of such hostile activities on U.S.-critical international food and energy supply chains.

## IV. CLIMATE SECURITY

The shipping industry is at the mercy of a changing ocean and is an important driver of environmental change. Without a strong U.S. commercial fleet, the transition to less harmful shipping operations is likely to be slower at the very time when the pace of change needs to accelerate to avoid irreversible planetary tipping points. A strong U.S. maritime industry could be a powerful catalyst for change.

- **The changing state of the ocean.** The biology, chemistry and physics of the ocean are changing at a faster rate than at any time in modern history. Melting ice-caps, mass coral reef bleaching, rising sea-levels, collapsing air and sea currents, increased acidification, and plummeting marine life will have a significant impact on all life on Earth. Yet, this represents the biggest opportunity to transition to alternative ways of operating vessels safely at sea. Without a strong maritime fleet, the U.S. domestic fleet remains a laggard in the transition to green shipping operations, relative to the pace of change in other regions such as Scandinavia, the EU, and even China who can dictate the pace and way in which the transition will take place.

- **All aspects of maritime operations will be altered by climate change.** The climate crisis presents a unique opportunity for U.S. shipping to leapfrog industry incumbents. Over the next forty years, the entire global fleet of shipping will be replaced. At the same time, every aspect of a ship's design, operations, propulsion and navigation systems will be altered. Just as the electric and self-driving car company, Tesla, has reinvented how automobiles are powered, controlled and built over the past decade, the U.S. has a unique opportunity to redesign ocean-bound ships from a blank slate and with modern technologies. Climate change will also lead to changing trade patterns. A prolonged drought around the Panama Canal that has led to 30% less rainfall, has reduced the capacity of the canal by 20%. Similar challenges are being faced in inland waterways such as the Mississippi Delta and Rhine River. But at the same time, new trade routes are opening up across the Arctic that will reduce the Asia-Europe transit by 40%, but will require a different vessel build and design to adapt to new navigation conditions and challenges. Climate change will also force almost all major ports and naval bases to upgrade their infrastructure as tidal surges and extreme weather become more common, and which could significantly disrupt shipping operations. So it is critical that the U.S. is able to both mitigate the impact of climate change, but also adapt as needed over this period of transition and unstable weather conditions. A strong U.S.-controlled maritime industry could help drive this change, and U.S. climate mitigation investments should also be driving a better return for U.S. owned infrastructure.

- **Climate Security and National Security increasingly intertwined.** The U.S. Department of Defense has identified the climate crisis as one of the biggest threats to National Security the U.S. will face between now and 2040. This is due to both the impact on U.S. military and economic operations around the world, but also the increasing instability climate change will bring to many regions. For example, one of the main drivers of Somali Piracy over the past two decades has been the collapse in tuna fisheries due to overfishing by EU trawlers in the Indian Ocean. Rising sea levels will soon lead to lost nations as low lying states like Kiribati become a nation of climate refugees. The loss of coral reefs in tropical regions around the world will destroy both an important source of fish protein as well as a critical coastal protection. The U.S. has an opportunity to start developing new Blue Economy technologies and solutions to support such nations facing these crises as they adapt to new climate realities. A strong U.S. maritime fleet would develop a better understanding of the ocean to complement the investments being made by U.S. research agencies such as NOAA and NASA.

- **Climate change as a driver of new business models**. A newer generation of consumers and investors are significantly altering corporate behavior. The rise of metrics such as Environmental, Social, Governance (ESG) indicators, Central Bank regulations through the Task Force on Climate-Related Financial Disclosures, and stronger consumer and shareholder activism has forced businesses to respond with more stringent environmental disclosure and action. Many U.S. firms and industries have become global leaders in sustainability as a result. It is only a matter of time before such scrutiny extends to the maritime sector and how goods are transported around the world. A new, clean, green U.S. maritime fleet could present a new and attractive business opportunity that could catalyze a global revolution in green international shipping.

- **Absence of critical U.S. Blue Economy Institutions.** Although the U.S. has the largest territorial waters in the world (an Exclusive Economic Zone of 3.4 million square miles), it does not have the right institutional setup to capture the full potential of the Blue Economy and to successfully transition to cleaner ship fuels. Current institutions are poorly resourced and ineffective. A holistic National Blue Economy Strategy with critical new institutions is required to govern the ocean in a more effective way than how land is governed. Other competitor nations have established such institutions such as China's Belt and Road Initiative and OBOR ('One Belt One Road') Annual Summit, supported by the Asian Infrastructure Investment Bank and New Development Bank. In the same way, a stronger U.S. maritime fleet would enhance the position of the U.S. in international climate negotiations and other international bodies such as the UN specialist agency, the International Maritime Organization (IMO).

# I . WORKFORCE SECURITY

There is no U.S. maritime industry without U.S. mariners – both a shoreside workforce and on vessels. The shortage of U.S. mariners presents a major threat to U.S. security. Here are U.S. mariner requirements under three scenarios.

- **'Minimal Needs in Peace:'** The minimum number of commercial ships required during peacetime to serve commercial routes and for basic security of the United States is 250 vessels, implying access to at least 15,000 suitably credentialed U.S. mariners. Currently, there are just over 11,000 qualified U.S. mariners available to crew either commercial or government support ships, implying a shortfall of 4000.

- **'Minimal Needs in War:'** However, during a prolonged conflict, the U.S. would need around 500 commercial vessels and, hence, 31,500 U.S. mariners (assuming a 5% buffer for casualties) to ensure minimal security cover for the U.S. Navy and to support the war effort. This implies an estimated shortfall of over 20,000 U.S. mariners to cover for the war effort and domestic vessels that need to be backfilled for those who are serving in a conflict zone even to assure the U.S. minimal security. These numbers only take into account what would be required to ensure stability and security during times of war.

- **'Future Competitive Fleet:'** As will be explored in the Principle of Economic Security, to increase international competitiveness and to sustain operations during a prolonged conflict, the U.S. would need access to 1120 large commercial vessels. This number of vessels would offer substantial competitive and security advantages to the U.S. during peacetime, too. At two crews of 30 each (taking into account crew rotations and training), this would require around 70,000 U.S. mariners (assuming a 5% buffer during conflict for casualties) who have unlimited tonnage and unlimited horsepower credentials. This is the size of the British Army. Such a U.S. mariner workforce does not exist today, and would need to be 6X greater than current resources.

Today, the U.S. has access to just over 11,000 suitably qualified U.S. mariners, implying a shortfall of 59,000 credentialed U.S. mariners if 1120 U.S.-flag ships were in operation. Licensed officers take at least four years to train in maritime colleges at a cost of $300,000 each. The current primary training colleges do not have the capacity or instructors to train this many mariners in such a short space of time (around 1,400 U.S. citizens are admitted to the United States Merchant Marine Academy, and State Maritime Academies each year). More radical solutions are needed to address the Workforce Security issue and scale up recruitment, training and retention by 6X.

- **Addressing the critical shortage of U.S. mariners.** The U.S. remains heavily dependent on foreign crew during peacetime (e.g., imports of goods, food and energy security). Currently there are just over 11,000 qualified U.S. mariners available to crew either commercial or government reserve ships. However, during a prolonged conflict (the "Minimal Needs in War" scenario), the U.S. would require 500 commercial vessels and 31,500 U.S. mariners - a shortfall of over 20,000 U.S. mariners. For full security coverage and to ensure economic competitiveness (the "Future Competitive Fleet" scenario), the shortfall is 59,000 suitably qualified mariners. There are several approaches to address this shortfall by looking at fast-tracking visa and naturalization procedures for non-U.S. citizens for critical maritime roles (e.g., maritime engineers and officers), enlisting suitably experienced retiring military personnel, and expanding recruitment and training efforts. However, all of this requires a holistic U.S. maritime workforce preparedness plan and bold leadership.

- **Revitalizing U.S. maritime training and education institutions.** The U.S. requires an overhaul of its recruitment, training and education institutions. If the U.S. is to expand recruitment, training and retention by 6X from today's numbers, a radical step-change in how training institutes are certified, regulated, resourced and incentivized is needed. This includes Vocational and Technical Schools as well as Merchant Marine Academies. This is critical to attract high-potential mariners, offer them a fulfilling career path, and ensure they are equipped with the latest thinking to become pioneers and help the U.S. assume a leadership position in maritime once more.

- **An inclusive U.S. maritime workforce.** At the same time as U.S. maritime institutions need to be overhauled, so too does the mariner talent pipeline, in order to hit the 6X objective. There needs to be a well-resourced effort to define an attractive career path in the merchant marine for all communities, and then attract, equip and retain talent along this path especially for new opportunities in the blue economy (e.g., offshore windfarms). Such long-term workforce planning initiatives are critical in professions where it takes multiple years of training to play an important role in a key industry (e.g., in healthcare with medical professionals). The U.S. maritime workforce can have a significant multiplier effect in some of the poorest areas of the U.S. around major ports, especially among historically underrepresented communities.

- **Partnering with forward-thinking U.S. maritime Unions.** The Blue Economy presents a strong and attractive opportunity to expand the workforce in U.S. maritime. Important safety standards will need to be set. Maritime unions have played an important role in the industry for decades. Sometimes adversarial, other times forward-thinking to ensure appropriate safety and environmental standards. With the maritime industry in such rapid transition given the pace of technological change, there is a unique opportunity for the maritime trade unions to work in partnership with the public sector and key actors in the maritime sector to define what a robust and reliable U.S. maritime sector could look like, and work together to build it.

- **Overdependence on foreign influence and international partners.** There is likely to be a global shortage of mariners and subsequent war for talent. With the U.S. dependent on foreign-crew for maritime operations, it may not be possible to attract, recruit and equip sufficient numbers of U.S. mariners in time to meet security needs. Non-U.S. mariners fill around 97% of the positions required to sustain the vast majority of U.S. commercial, peacetime trading activity. This represents a security risk to the United States, particularly if conflict or war arises, as the required personnel may not be available, or may be restricted by their country of origin to assist the U.S. war effort. A dependence on foreign crew who have not been vetted or credentialed by U.S. organizations presents a significant risk to the U.S. Innovative new programs may be needed to vet, credential and recruit non-U.S. nationals into critical maritime roles until a sufficient number of U.S. mariners have been recruited into such roles.

## THE 57-POINT ACTION PLAN

This book lays out the five main ways in which a U.S. maritime industry is vital to National, Economic, Energy and Food, Climate and Workforce Security, and what the risks are today by having such a weak maritime industry.

The solutions are within our grasp. They are practical and implementable with relatively little public funding, much of which will be recouped by expanding U.S. economic activity in international maritime. These actions are listed clearly in the concluding chapters of the book.

What has been lacking has been leaders with the courage to take the time to understand how vital the maritime sector is to the U.S., why recent policies have failed so far, and to dedicate the time and resources required to rebuild the sector to the strength it needs to be at.

Within a decade, it is possible to strengthen the U.S. maritime sector from ***Zero Point Four*** to ***Four Point Zero***, an increase of over 1000 U.S.-flagged ocean-going vessels.

America's very security depends on it.

# CHAPTER 1 | PRE-EMINENCE

*We are tied to the ocean. And when we go back to the sea, whether it is to sail or to watch - we are going back from whence we came.*

- President John F. Kennedy (1962)

Our pale blue dot's life-emanating hue is distinctive in the cosmos. This unique coloring originates from the water covering over 70% of the earth's surface. Two percent of all water is locked up in glaciers and ice. One percent is fresh. The remaining 97% is found in the ocean.

The world has one ocean, divided into five parts: Pacific, Atlantic, Indian, Southern (Antarctic) and Arctic. The Pacific Ocean is particularly large, covering 30% of earth's surface. The Atlantic covers around 20%, the Indian 15%, the Southern 4%, and the Arctic Ocean, 3%. Ocean regions can be divided into two distinct areas: Exclusive Economic Zones (EEZs) extend 200 nautical miles - 370 kilometers - off a country's coastline. All other oceanic areas are classified as Areas Beyond National Jurisdiction (ABNJ), commonly called the 'high seas', that no individual nation has any responsibility over. More than 60% of the world's oceans fall within the ABNJ.

Oceans play a vital role in regulating global temperatures. Greenhouse gasses in the atmosphere trap heat from the sun, which either warms up land, or warms up the ocean. Given oceans cover nearly three quarters of the earth's surface, they absorb most of this heat; estimates are around 90% of earth's extra heat since the 1950's. Due to various factors including the sheer volume of water involved, changes in ocean systems occur over centuries, which is why the oceans have not yet warmed as much as the atmosphere. The atmosphere (air) would be significantly hotter if it wasn't for the immense heat-storage capacity provided by the ocean.

Currents are movements of water due to gravity, the earth's rotation (Coriolis effect), water density, water depth, wind patterns, the sun, and the position of the moon. Currents can flow for thousands of miles and are found in all major oceans of the world. Ocean currents are essential to the survival of most occupants of Earth. Ocean currents redistribute water, nutrients and oxygen, and play an important role in controlling the planet's climate by moving heat from the equator toward the poles. Through upwelling, currents play a key role in marine productivity by sweeping vital nutrients from deep water up to the surface. Downwelling acts like a conveyor belt, taking oxygen-rich surface water and moving it down into the deep sea. Without this renewal, dissolved oxygen at lower layers (in water, and locked in sediments) would quickly be depleted by decaying organic matter, which would rapidly eliminate any oxygen-dependent aquatic life. One of the more well-known ocean currents is The Gulf Stream: a warm, swift Atlantic current that originates in the Gulf of Mexico, flows through the Straits of Florida, traverses the eastern U.S. coastline, then veers east near North Carolina and moves on to Northwest Europe. Through water and air temperature differentials, the Gulf Stream influences the climate of the U.S. East Coast from Florida to southeast Virginia, and the intensity of storms and cyclones that often travel through that region.

Oceans occupy expansive areas of the planet, yet over eighty percent are unmapped and unexplored. Similarly, while 94% of earth's wildlife exists in the ocean, most of it - around 90% - is yet to be classified. Out of the unobserved comes abundance, out of the unknown comes life: Consider microscopic phytoplankton right at the bottom of the food chain. This prolific, mostly invisible resident of the ocean, along with other photosynthesizing agents - bacteria, algae and plants - produce around 50% of oxygen in the atmosphere. Further up the food chain, feeding on phytoplankton and algae, are microscopic zooplankton, krill. Although present in all five oceans, krill only swim in large swarms around Antarctica, in the Southern Ocean. Krill are plentiful: The total weight of the krill biomass is around 500 million metric tons, or nearly twice the combined weight of all human beings currently on the planet. Every wildlife species in the ocean either eats krill, or species that feed on krill, making krill vital to the world's food chain, particularly the 20,000+ species and estimated 3,000,000,000,000 (three trillion) fish that swim in the ocean.

Oceans are directly responsible for supporting the lives and livelihoods of hundreds of millions of people, every single day. Over one-third of the planet, around 2.4 billion people, live within 60 miles (100km) of an oceanic coast. Of those, over 260 million live in low-lying coastal areas - below 2m - with the majority (191 million people) located in the tropics, and 157 million (59%) in tropical Asia alone. Proximity to the ocean is essential for over 300 million people who rely on desalinated water, for some, or all of their daily water needs. Easy access also extends opportunities for sustenance and employment: Fish and seafood are important for nutrition, providing about 3.3 billion people around 20 percent of all protein at a global level, and more than 50 percent in less developed countries. Among a growing list of other benefits, the nutrients found in fish enhance neurological development in children and have been proven to positively impact cardiovascular health. About 97% of the world's fishermen live in developing countries, and rely on fishing as a major source of food and income. Secondary marine-related activities like fish processing and selling produce at markets, is a notable employer of women.

The ocean provides many unique recreational pursuits, from swimming and fishing, to boating, kayaking and tourism activities like whale watching. In the ocean: Swimming is one of the most popular forms of ocean recreation. Millions of people visit the beach every year to swim, deriving direct and indirect benefits from this enjoyable, and health-promoting pastime. Snorkeling and SCUBA diving have grown in popularity. The global Scuba Diving Equipment market was valued at USD $1.5 billion in 2022 and is on a trajectory to reach USD $2 billion over the next five years. On the ocean: Sailing, boating and yachting are common leisure activities, the world over. There are around 30 million recreational boats in the world. Yachting is experiencing a phenomenal period of growth: The global luxury yacht market is projected to grow from USD $8 billion in 2023 to $14 billion by 2030. Whale watching has also grown in popularity. Over 13 million people in around 119 countries enjoy whale watching every year, generating more than $2 billion in related revenues, and employing over 13,000 people.

The ocean is an essential facilitator of all forms of global economic activity. Between 80-90% of all produced or consumed goods traveled across the ocean in shipping containers, or the storage compartments and cargo holds of merchant vessels. The building blocks of entire economies and the essential ingredients to sustain modern life are regularly transported in this manner: commodities, machinery, agricultural products, vehicles, clothing, food, energy, military equipment and medical supplies, among many others. Merchant shipping provides direct employment to 1.89 million mariners globally, and many millions more in adjacent, supporting industries. The ocean-economy, which includes all work and related services provided directly by the ocean, generates between USD $3-6 trillion per year, or around 5-7% percent of global GDP. Fisheries and aquaculture alone contribute USD $100 billion per year and add around 260 million jobs to the global economy.

The ocean allows economic activity to be sustainable, by facilitating the efficient movement of many different forms of cargo. Ably assisted by winds, tides and currents, shipping is one of the most efficient forms of transportation. One gallon (3.8 liters) of fuel can transport 10 tons of cargo: 6 miles by truck, 1 mile by airplane, and over 50 miles on a ship. Shipping also generates the lowest amount of greenhouse gas (GHG) emissions per ton/mile; the measure of moving one ton of cargo, over one mile. Trucking emits 200-300 grams of $CO^2$ per ton-mile, air freight, over 2.6 pounds (800 -1200 grams). Shipping, offering flexible capacity across the entire world, emits just 35-40 grams of $CO^2$ per ton-mile; modern ships even less.

The preeminent ocean has been generous to many. The United States is no exception.

The United States shares a unique connection to the ocean. Geographically, the Continental United States (CONUS) is ideally situated, and enjoys unfettered access to two of the world's largest oceans; the Pacific on the West Coast, and Atlantic on the East. This enviable position extends effortless entry to the world's major oceanic trading routes, allowing the U.S. to utilize shipping's scale and efficiency for the export and import of manufactured products, commodities and raw materials - "*From Sea to Shining Sea*" as the lyrics to *America the Beautiful* goes. Considering shipping's integral role in global trade and positive impact on most forms of productivity, this one factor alone - unchallenged access to two of the world's largest oceans - has been the single greatest historical determinant of prosperity for U.S. citizens, and the domestic economy.

A large proportion of the U.S. populace live in close proximity to the ocean. 127 million people, around 38% of the population, live in coastal counties; as much as the entire population of Japan. If counted as their own nation, these coastal communities would rank third in the world in gross domestic product (GDP), bested only by China and the U.S. as a whole. Coastal areas are crowded: With only 10% of the total land in the contiguous United States, these areas have over five times greater density than the U.S. average. This means that any issue that affects the coasts, impacts a larger proportion of the U.S. population. These include increased risks from tidal variations, destructive winds, flooding, erosion, rising sea levels, hurricanes, and a range of other environmental effects that can be attributed to fluctuating temperatures and a changing climate. These and other risks directly affect many different groups of people, and the activities they might perform at sea. One obvious example is the use of sailing boats, fishing boats, yachts and other pleasure craft. The impact on this segment would be pronounced: U.S. citizens own around half of the 30+ million recreational boats in the world, an estimated 13 million vessels.

The ocean directly facilitates U.S. hard and soft power projection through military activity, and diplomacy, commerce and trade. The U.S. Navy and U.S. Coast Guard are predictably dependent on the ocean to maintain a rules-based order, and protect Freedom of Navigation (FON) of the seas. Over 50,000 merchant vessels, from around 120 Flag States operate within these protections; delivering essential supplies and cargo all over the world. A proportion of those ships deliver 40% of U.S. international trade by value, and nearly 70% of U.S. trade by weight, which represents around 20% of total U.S. GDP. Merchant ships regularly carry more tonnage and value than any other mode of transportation; around 1.5 billion short tons (1.36 billion tons), amounting to around USD $1.8 trillion in total value, during 2022. Ocean-dependent businesses, including ports, supply chain providers, and the cruise industry, employ almost three million people across the country.

The ocean: Pre-eminent, abundant, and life-sustaining.
And as we will discover, increasingly fragile.

*This page is intentionally left blank.*

# CHAPTER 2 | PROSPERITY

*The nation cannot prosper long when it favors only the prosperous. The success of our economy has always depended not just on the size of our gross domestic product, but on the reach of our prosperity, on the ability to extend opportunity to every willing heart -- not out of charity, but because it is the surest route to our common good.*

- President Barack Obama, Inaugural Address (2008)

## The Evolution of Industrial Revolutions

*Exhibit 1: Phases of rapid technological advancements have shaped our use of the oceans since the First Industrial Revolution on left of image, to the brink of the Fourth Industrial Revolution on right of image. (credit: Degnarain, McCauley 2017)*

The world has evolved through a series of significant developmental epochs, commonly referred to as 'Industrial Revolutions'. When paired together, the terms 'industrial' and 'revolution' convey a hope for human progress, freedom, wealth and a more utopian future. However, those terms can also carry a different connotation: uncertainty, oppression, exploitation, poverty. For people in developed nations, the Industrial Revolution occurred hundreds of years ago and conjures up images of iron foundries, steel mills, coal mines and railways; along with giant cities and choking smog. To many others, including the roughly two billion people who currently have no reliable access to electricity, it was a series of events that happened entirely to other people.

Each Industrial Revolution corresponds to a period of time, coupled to distinct technological advances, most noticeably in energy, transportation and communications. One after another, rapidly developed and inter-connected innovations transformed individuals, countries, and the world. The fuels used to power these revolutions changed first from wood to coal, then from coal to oil, gas and electricity, then to nuclear and renewables. Communications also advanced at a rapid pace: The postal and semaphore systems developed during the First Industrial Revolution were quickly replaced by the telegraph, telephone and radio, which would give way in subsequent eras to fiber-optics, cell phones and satellite communications.

Transportation has changed beyond recognition: from traversing on foot, to using horse and cart, to trains, cars, trucks, large aircraft capable of transporting hundreds of passengers, and now autonomous vehicles. Marine transport similarly transformed in scale and capability: from simple barges and steam-powered ships, to present-day supertankers, nuclear submarines, and Ultra Large Container Vessels able to haul 20,000 or more shipping containers at the same time. While in pursuit of profitability and progress, of equal significance has been the rapid rise in pollution, greenhouse gas emissions and environmental damage that accompanied each of these stages.

Time demarcations for each Industrial Revolution, along with the more significant advances and events in maritime can be largely seen around the following timelines:

- **First Industrial Revolution:** Sail to Steam | Whaling | Slavery | Naval Powers | Colonialism (1750 - 1850)
- **Second Industrial Revolution:** Steam to Oil | Electrification | Transocean Telegraph Cables | World Wars (1850 - 1950)
- **Third Industrial Revolution:** Electronics | Space | Nuclear | Plastics | Containerization | Multinational Corporations (1950 - 2020)
- **Fourth Industrial Revolution:** Synthetic Biology | Artificial Intelligence | Autonomous Systems | Renewable Energy | Decentralized Organizations (2020 - onwards)

The transition between one industrial revolution and another is often accompanied by major shifts of power and sources of value. For example, what may be valued in the First Industrial Revolution (e.g., access to coal) is less valuable in a Second Industrial Revolution driven by oil, or a Fourth Industrial Revolution driven by data and renewable energy. As the source of value shifts, so too does power structures. This has often led to conflicts around the edges of the industrial revolutions. For example, the European Revolutions of the mid-1850s, the World Wars around the end of the Second Industrial Revolution. The world is now on the brink of a Fourth Industrial Revolution, and global tensions are rising once more. Some of this is due to pressure on oil producing nations due to climate change. At the same time, new sources of power such as the ability to harness data and artificial intelligence is empowering other nations. What is also critical to note is that new institutions and ways of organizing have emerged with each transition of industrial revolution. For example, naval power and colonial institutions dominated the first industrial revolution, and gave way to joint stock companies from European trading nations, and then a state-based multilateral system built around the United Nations and Bretton Woods System, followed by the rising power of large, top-down multinational corporations. The Fourth Industrial Revolution is raising questions about the sorts of governance systems that are likely to thrive in the 21st century (e.g., more decentralized organizations that use different models and technologies to create 'Exponential Organizations,' as defined by Author Salim Ismail).

It is beyond the scope of this book to explore the background, progress and legacy of each Revolution in detail, other than to position them in the context of how they have been enabled by the ocean, and how the ocean has, in turn, been affected by them. The rest of this chapter reflects on each period and finishes by examining how to capitalize on presented opportunities in a structured and values-driven way.

## The First Industrial Revolution and U.S. Maritime: 1750s - 1850s

The First Industrial Revolution was characterized by the discovery of steam power and the transition from wood to coal as the fuel of choice for a variety of increasingly powerful machines. On land, this period saw workers in the West move from the field to cities, where they were put to work in new mills and factories. On the ocean, the transition from sail to steam signaled the emergence of an age of momentous exploration, accompanied by a noticeable rise in exploitation of the marine environment (and of people).

*Exhibit 2: World's fastest sailing vessel at the time, the US-designed and built 'Sovereign of the Seas,' 1852 (credit: Wikimedia Commons)*

The First Industrial Revolution was not all positive. This period coincided with an era colonialism, the destructive search for whale oil and dehumanizing slave trade. On the ocean, the First Industrial Revolution gave rise to a range of beneficial maritime innovations. The problem of accurately establishing one's longitude at sea was finally solved with the development of the marine chronometer. Loss of life, and the prohibitive cost of losing ships, was a very real and very urgent concern to those who wished to rule the waves. This prompted colonial powers like Spain, Holland, France and Great Britain to install a variety of navigational aids such as lighthouses and buoys, and to draw up detailed charts of safe harbors, including channels and approaches. As intercontinental seafaring became less dangerous and more widespread, international fleets and merchant navies formed the first regular, global system for communication. This global network meant that a distant colony or country could communicate on a regular (if infrequent) basis for commercial, personal and – most importantly for the colonial powers - imperial purposes.

In the United States, riverboat designer and operator Robert Fulton successfully employed steam engines which quickly became a favored mode of domestic travel and commerce. In 1819 the U.S. designed and built *SS Savannah* became the first trans-Atlantic steam-powered ship, ultimately steaming all the way to St. Petersburg, Russia. However, American designer, Donald McKay, and New England shipbuilders continued perfecting the famous China clipper ships into the 1850s. So by 1852, McKay's clipper, *Sovereign of the Sea*, reached the fastest sailing speed ever at 22 knots.

*Exhibit 3: The SS Savannah, the first ocean steamship in 1819 (credit: Boston Public Library)*

## The Second Industrial Revolution and U.S. Maritime: 1850s - 1950s

The noticeable step-change during this period centered around two incredible innovations: The first, electricity, led to a huge surge in innovations including the invention of

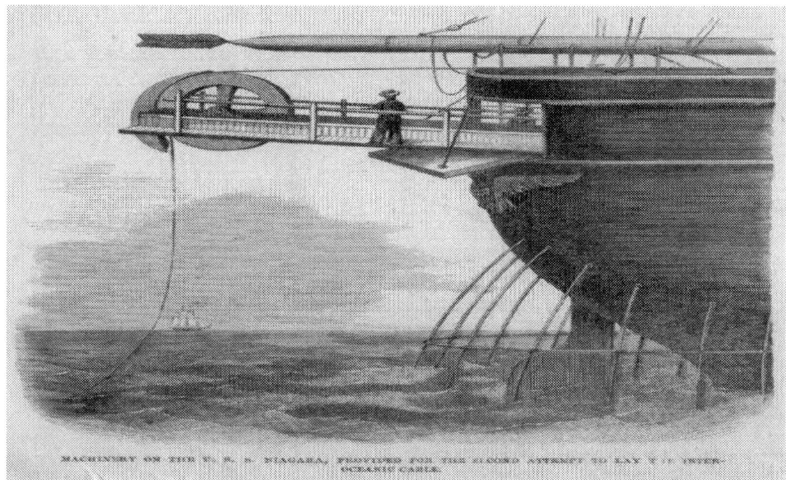

*Exhibit 4: USS Niagara attempting to lay a trans-Atlantic telegraph cable in 1858 (credit: U.S. Library of Congress)*

electro-mechanical machines and mass production, to advancements in communications like the telegraph, telephone and radio frequency transmission. The second innovation was the change in the fuel of choice: Coal gave way to oil, which was later complemented by gas as the preferred way of generating the power needed to run factories, power lighting and drive ships across (and under) the sea.

One of the greatest achievements during this era was the laying of subsea communication cables, a process that began in the 1850s and culminated in the trans-Pacific cables installed in the early 20th century. This endeavor required new technologies, new techniques, and advanced engineering, along with unprecedented levels of coordination and cooperation. For those with access to them, these cables allowed for instant, secure communication with other people across the world; a feat unimaginable in the days of sail. A new era of global connectivity had begun. For better or worse, individuals, industries, nations and cultures were now closer together than they had ever been before.

*Exhibit 5: Western Marine & Salvage Co in 1925 destroying hundreds of federally-ordered excess vessels (credit: Library of Congress)*

Over this period, on a much wider scale, the ocean was embraced and exploited. This applied to a range of different activities including food production, transportation, trade and warfare. Just as communications were revolutionized by technological progress, so too were the whaling and fishing industries. This was achieved by the invention of drag-net fishing, oil-powered turbines and electric motors that were installed on new, powerful factory ships. These New England-style boats had so successfully exploited the depths that, by around 1850, the stocks of the whales they targeted had been depleted. Demand for whale oil subsided at the same time, as fossil fuels became more easily and cheaply refined at scale.

During this era, American magnate, J. P. Morgan, financed the British *White Star Line* and other non-US flagged fleets. John D. Rockefeller, Standard Oil tycoon, owned 80% of the world's international tanker fleet until 1911. The sinking of *RMS Lusitania* in 1915 marked the beginning of unrestricted naval warfare. The U.S. Shipping Board ordered 734 steel, concrete and wooden ships, but only 98 were delivered when WWI ended in 1918. Another 166 ships were delivered by 1919. On November 7, 1925 the *Western Marine & Salvage Company* torched the excess ships that could not be sold or scrapped.

Advances in oil-powered and mechanized marine transportation throughout the first half of the 20th century, allowed developed nations to conduct wars on a global scale; building submarines, aircraft carriers and fleets of destroyers. The two World Wars waged during this period prompted targeted investments in a range of technologies that greatly impacted maritime operations: Hydraulics, radar, electronic navigation, long-range radio communications and new discoveries in material science were all beneficial byproducts of these major conflicts.

*Exhibit 6: One of over 2700 Liberty Ships launched during WW2 (credit: U.S. National Park Service)*

President Franklin Roosevelt, anticipating the Second World War, made Joseph P. Kennedy first chairman of the US Maritime Commission. Industrialist Henry J. Kaiser, was commissioned to build assembly line ships on a massive scale, eventually launching 2,710 WWII *Liberty Ships*. ADM Wasche, USCG and VADM Land, USN founders of the U.S. Maritime Service established the recruiting and training institutions necessary to crew this massive number of sealift ships. Meanwhile, Andrew Higgins of New Orleans, built 23,398 WWII *Higgins landing craft* for amphibious combat.

*Exhibit 7:*
*One of over 23,000 Higgins landing craft credited with successful D-Day landings during WWII (credit: The National WWII Museum)*

The end of this era also saw the birth of the Inter-Governmental Maritime Consultative Organization (IMCO), the precursor to the International Maritime Organization (IMO). IMCO was established in 1948 to build a regulatory framework for ship safety to govern the actions of the international community. The fledgling organization's first task was to update the convention of Safety Of Lives At Sea (SOLAS), originally adopted in 1914 after the sinking of the Titanic.

## The Third Industrial Revolution and U.S. Maritime: 1950s – 2020s

*Exhibit 8: Containerization revolutionized global shipping in the twentieth century, with the first container ship being the SS Ideal X in 1956, seen here invented by American Malcom McLean.(credit: U.S. Navy)*

The Second World War unleashed the awesome and awful potential of the atom, endowed with the power to destroy cities and even whole civilizations. The ferocity of weaponized nuclear energy dominated global ideological conflict for the fifty years that followed, however it was harnessing the atom's potential as a power source that was truly revolutionary; not only as a fuel to generate electricity on land, but to drive ships and submarines at sea. This potent energy source allowed nuclear-powered fleets to be submerged for weeks and even months, during the silent, unobserved games of cat and mouse that played out all across the world. The 'Cold War' made ocean exploration more than simply a line of academic enquiry or a military endeavor; it made it an existential necessity.

Following on from the trends of the previous two, the Third Industrial Revolution was characterized by new inventions like nuclear weapons and reactors, megaships and supertankers, mobile phones and the internet, but it at its heart, discreetly making them all possible, was another new innovative technology: The microchip. The microchip, and other newly invented electronic technologies would go on to radically change the world, and at a rapidly accelerating pace. Consider how many machines (and appliances) are now highly dependent on small bits of silicon for creation, control and computation. The disruptive impact of the global chip shortage that began in 2020, provides a clear indication of just how reliant humanity has become on semiconducting materials, transistors and integrated circuits.

*Exhibit 9: Edward Reilly Stettinius, 48th Secretary of State and founder of a U.S. company to register ships under the Liberian flag. (credit: U.S. Navy)*

The industrialized world at the end of the Second World War could be crudely divided up into U.S. and Soviet spheres of influence. Harry Truman dissolved the U.S. Maritime Commission to establish MARAD. Edward R. Stettinius, Jr., the US Secretary of State and first US Ambassador to the UN, established International Registries Inc., a U.S. company to administer registration of ships under the Liberian flag. After WWII American and foreign owners acquired hundreds of excess U.S. ships and registered them under foreign flag administrations. MARAD went on to commission the first nuclear powered commercial ship, the NS Savannah, but generally oversaw the U.S. merchant marine continually shrink over this period.

As the century drew to a close and the Cold War subsided, 'Group of 5' (G5) countries grew to prominence; the five largest emerging economies at the time, which in 1974 included

France, Germany, Japan, the United Kingdom, and the United States. The G5 evolved over time into the G7, the G8 and eventually the G20, with members added or removed as influence and wealth increased, or fell. The so-called Asian Tigers - Taiwan, Malaysia, Hong Kong, Japan, South Korea - grew rapidly in this post-Cold War era too, adopting new technologies and heavy industries of their own, along with populations that required more and more natural resources to support increasingly western lifestyles. The end of the Third Industrial Revolution saw the rise of other economies. Two notable examples are BRICS - Brazil, Russia, India, China, and South Africa - and the faster-moving 'global South' that includes countries like Indonesia, Morocco, Nigeria, and Argentina.

In just forty years, from 1950 to 1990, the global population doubled; from 2.5 billion to 5 billion people. Megacities swelled and increasingly consumption-heavy lifestyles made new and ever-increasing demands on the ocean. In the two decades following the Second World War, fishing fleets caught as many fish as they could, regardless of species. It wasn't until the 70s that a noticeable change occurred. There were fewer fish to be found and it took more effort to catch them. Though felt almost everywhere in some form or another, the symptom was most spectacularly shown by the sharp, sudden and catastrophic collapse of North Atlantic Bluefin tuna and cod.

After nearly a decade of negotiation, the United Nations Convention of Law of the Sea (UNCLOS) was ratified in 1982. Article 57 stated "*The exclusive economic zone shall not extend beyond 200 nautical miles from the baselines from which the breadth of the territorial sea is measured."* One by one, countries started claiming their own 200-mile-wide sovereignty over the ocean. Whatever lay within these waters, including the life that was in it and whatever was of value on and under the seafloor, was now able to be either preserved, or exploited. The ocean's bounty had become something to own, along with all of the problems that accompanied it.

UNCLOS introduced another key concept of how the oceans can be used by all countries, regardless of geographic access. Article 87 stated that *"The high seas are open to all States, whether coastal or land-locked"* and lists "Freedom of Navigation" (FON) as the first of several rights for those operating on the high seas. Article 87 officially codified the principles U.S. President Woodrow Wilson had spoken about during the First World War: *"Absolute freedom of navigation upon the seas, outside territorial waters, alike in peace and in war, except as the seas may be closed in whole or in part by international action for the enforcement of international covenants."* The list of other freedoms included in UNCLOS are freedom of overflight; freedom to lay submarine cables and pipelines; freedom to construct artificial islands and other

*Exhibit 10: Capable of drilling wells in water up to 40 feet deep, Kerr-McGee's mobile rig, 'Mr. Charlie,' was the first mobile offshore drilling platform in 1954 (credit: Murphy Oil Corporation)*

installations permitted under international law; freedom of fishing; and freedom of scientific research, with each freedom followed by guiding principles to encourage compliance, and curtail exploitative behavior. It should be noted that the United States is still not yet a signatory to UNCLOS.

Humanity's insatiable desire to secure new fuel sources during this period, placed new and strenuous demands on the ocean. Kerr-McGee's 1954 mobile offshore drill rig, *Mr. Charlie*, established U.S. leadership in offshore technology and exponential offshore oil and gas exploration and production world-wide. Over the course of a few short decades, 70% of the world's energy would be extracted from the seabeds off Nigeria, Brazil, Brunei, Malaysia, the UK and Mexico. Burgeoning off-shore oil and gas operations led to the introduction of supertankers for transportation, along with coastal refineries to process the raw inputs into finished products. *SS Methane Pioneer* was the first LNG ship commissioned in 1959. Later, with U.S. demand for natural gas imports General Dynamics built spherical tank LNG carriers to import gas from Algeria. Traffic volumes across the oceans, and through the mighty Panama and Suez canals, increased dramatically. Ports were inundated, then

*Exhibit 11: U.S. pioneer and billionaire Howard Hughes' Golmar Explorer vessel used a cover story of pursuing Seabed Mining to recover a Soviet submarine from 3 miles depth in 1974 (credit: U.S. Government)*

expanded, then were inundated again.

U.S. innovators were active throughout the Third Industrial Revolution. William F. Gibbs of New York designed the ocean liner *SS United States*. In 1952 Gibb's *SS United States* made the fastest Atlantic crossing ever, over 38 knots. The first ice-strengthened oil tanker, *SS Manhattan*, traversed the Northwest Passage in 1969. And when the Soviet diesel-electric submarine *K-129* sank in the Pacific Ocean 1,560 miles from Hawaii, 8 March 1968, billionaire Howard Hughes built the *Hughes Golmar Explorer* in 1971 and 1972 for a secret CIA mission to recover the sub. The forward part of *K-129* was successfully recovered from a depth of 3 miles in 1974.

*Exhibit 12: The first ice-strengthened oil tanker, the SS Manhattan, crossing the Northwest Passage through Canadian, U.S. and international waters in 1969 (credit: U.S. Government)*

Reliably, affordably, and scalably moving cargo became progressively more important during the Third Industrial

*Exhibit 13: The container, pioneered by American Malcolm McLean led to a revolution in global shipping. His company, Sealand, was eventually acquired by Maersk. (credit: creative commons)*

Revolution. Enter the humble shipping container; the most globally impacting innovation produced during this era, and some would argue, in all of human history. Prior to the development of these now-ubiquitous oblong boxes, products and goods were individually loaded and unloaded onto trains and trucks, and then again onto cargo ships; a slow, inefficient and expensive process. The shipping container, with its standardized size and fittings designed to accommodate ships, trains and trucks, was a simple, technological masterpiece. American Malcolm McLean, pioneered containerized cargo and established the *Sealand Shipping Company.* McLean's 1970s US-built *Sealand SL7* fast container ships achieved speeds of 33 knots and led the revolution in shipping.

*Exhibit 14: The 2010 Deepwater Horizon disaster was the largest marine oil spill in history and revealed the risks of going bigger, deeper and faster without sufficient oversight. (credit: U.S. Coast Guard)*

Shipping containers saved time and effort and made it possible to move commodities and consumer goods at volume, and at a price and speed that met the growing demands of the global market. In 1956, most cargo were loaded and unloaded by hand by longshore workers. Hand-loading a ship cost $5.86 a ton at that time. Using containers, it cost only 16 cents a ton to load a ship, 36-fold savings. Containers opened up entirely new mechanisms for the distribution of wealth, by greatly enhancing local, regional and international trade. Refrigerated containers vastly improved the efficient distribution of food, allowing a variety of seasonal delicacies to be enjoyed all year round. Shipping containers made it possible to move products from anywhere to everywhere, prompting a range of inventions including supermarkets and megastores; the early forerunners of a future activity that would be known as online shopping.

The Third Industrial Revolution produced ever-larger ships, with more and more containers, that navigated a veritable spider's web of shipping routes along which 90% of all the goods in the world traveled. The acceleration in the velocity and scale of trade presented considerable challenges to those managing inventories, procuring products and handling logistics. Computers were built and purposefully deployed to assist: Factories, plants, power stations, rigs and docks were automated, inventories, cargo paperwork and delivery schedules digitized, and transport systems streamlined and optimized. Circling high above, advanced satellite systems neatly synchronized these activities.

## The Fourth Industrial Revolution: Present Day to the Future

The edges of the Fourth Industrial Revolution (4IR) are messy and overlapping, and where exactly it may lead is not entirely clear. As with previous revolutions, the 4IR is founded on new innovations that converge physical solutions (3D printing,

*Exhibit 15: offshore floating windfarms are just one of the technologies that the Fourth Industrial Revolution can usher in for the next phase of the U.S. maritime industry. (credit: U.S. Department of Energy)*

nanotechnology, drones and autonomous vehicles) with digital systems (Big Data analytics, AI, Natural Language Processing and robotics) and biological advances, like genome sequencing, the bio-economy and synthetic biology. Potent combinations of these and other solutions, when coupled with exponentially increasing processing power, operate at a greater scale, scope and complexity than anything that has been witnessed in human history. Entirely new business models are also being created, bringing innovation, wealth and disruption to workplaces, marketplaces and communities.

Transformational technologies are clearly visible in every facet of daily, modern life. Consider the following changes that have taken place over (just) the last ten years: Anyone with a mobile phone and a modest line of credit can call a car to an exact location for transport; reserve a table at a restaurant; book a room in a private residence; order any one of a million physical products; listen to almost any music ever recorded, watch any film ever made, and access most of the knowledge humanity has ever created. This can all be done instantly, without exerting much energy, and in most instances, without speaking or even standing up. This rapid state of change affects both sides of the marketplace; consumers on the one, and those supplying goods and services on the other. In many industries, large, centralized, monolithic corporations have been supplanted by nimble, distributed, internet-powered enterprises. The changing nature of business is perfectly captured in a quote from author and social commentator, Tom Goodwin: *"Uber, the world's largest taxi company, owns no vehicles. Facebook, the world's most popular media owner, creates no content. Alibaba, the most valuable retailer, has no inventory. And Airbnb, the world's largest accommodation provider, owns no real estate."*

'Sharing' is a new catchphrase that has entered common vernacular, and is liberally applied to ideas, data, technology, expertise, or when organizing a ride to work. 'On demand' is another, referring to the ability of consumers and businesses to access people, energy, products, food and services wherever and whenever they want them; and in a way that is as close-to-instant as possible. Businesses that adapt to these new conditions, thrive. Others that cannot, or will not, fall by the wayside. Most individuals are now more connected than ever before; yet, many would argue they've never felt more alone. And while it's never been easier to share ideas and collaborate, it's also never been easier to spread extreme or destructive thinking. On a national and international level, governments now have at their disposal, powerful systems of insight that can be used to guide (or manipulate, and control) the populations they lead. And yet, thanks to the democratizing power of shared information via the internet, the ruling classes have also never before been so vulnerable to those they hope to govern.

The Fourth Industrial Revolution promises to enhance, and also threaten what is known, or thought about everything; from energy production, patterns of consumption, transport, communication and manufacturing, to governance, ethics, privacy, work and even what it means to be human. Along with the promise of peace, prosperity and equality, the next era of advancement also has the potential for war, poverty and inequality. Whether agreeable or not, this Revolution is destined to alter existing hierarchical structures, disrupt businesses and government, erode long-held and traditional values, and transform humanity's relationship with the environment; and will do so, at current trajectory, over the course of decades, not centuries.

## The Way Forward

As humanity navigates this Revolution and beyond, and regardless of what solutions are proposed or chosen, there is a great need for a shared set of values, deep collaboration, systems thinking and new forms of governance to be explored and established. These characteristics set the tone for the analysis and conclusions that are explored throughout the rest of this book.

**Values:** A common set of shared values - 'What we will collectively fight for' - will be needed to guide all potential ocean-based endeavors that are to be undertaken. These values must be grounded in reality, and reflect what is collectively required (as a species, and for the planet) to protect the valuable natural assets that have been entrusted to all of us. These values must directly inform the activities and behaviors that will ensure the ocean remains healthy for generations to come. Positive values alongside thoughtful design principles will also manage any unintended consequences of new technologies, bending the arc of ocean health beyond sustainability, to restoration. And, unlike attempts in the past, these values must be actively enforced from the outset, rather than overturned, at the end, in response to failure.

**Collaboration:** Secondly, a highly collaborative approach must be pursued to discover and establish these values. Competing and/or complementary goals of a range of stakeholders will emerge as this occurs, as will the need for clear, and definitive leadership. The thoughts, aspirations and concerns from each participant must be understood, then worked into the overarching frameworks and solutions that follow. Any new platform, policy, technology or determination can be explored in the same way, with decisions made in an inclusive yet purposeful manner. New partnerships will be forged with governments, the private sector, the scientific community and NGOs, to empower those who are affected the most by increasing ocean fragility, while connecting a wider range of citizens more deeply to the ocean. Thankfully, a range of existing and emerging technologies are available to facilitate these activities: Highly-scalable, cloud-based platforms that capture and analyze shared information - using emerging AI tools and Natural Language Processing - can accurately document sentiment and encourage faster decision-making.

**Systems Thinking:** Thirdly, systems-thinking must be employed, in a data-rich and technology-augmented way. Systems thinking makes sense of the complexity of the world, by considering the relationships between various elements, rather than focusing on separate or individual parts. To that end, any solution or technology proposed for ocean conservation should not be regarded in a compartmentalized fashion, but rather designed with the broader context in mind; assessing the impact, both positive and negative, to all identified participants, groups, and stakeholders. Systems thinking allows for a pragmatic exploration, while acknowledging that implementing any given solution is rarely simple, and will likely have unexpected flow-on effects even from the earliest stages of discovery. Readily available technologies - from chat platforms and task management tools, to sensor-based hardware - can be used as systems-thinking processes are implemented, to centralize thoughts and capture data, and present desired outcomes in visibly engaging and easily digestible ways.

**Governance:** And finally, a more proactive approach to ocean governance is required. Historically, during periods of transition between Industrial Revolutions, value systems tended to lag behind progress, rather than actively supporting proposed and emerging technologies. A new approach, where governance is championed and implemented right from the outset, will sharpen the focus on areas of critical concern, and provide a guiding framework for solution delivery. This style of governance will likely require new organizations to be created, audacious leaders to emerge, and new decision-making strategies to be employed; specifically designed with the complex, interconnected nature of the world's oceans in mind. Practical governance ensures that those employing new technologies do not just accept the current systems, but instead, proactively build complementary systems so that better stewardship can occur.

* * *

The prosperity of each previous Industrial Revolution has been largely attributable to the sea that gave so generously and was exploited in return. Now increasingly fragile, the world's oceans require immediate, measurable and effective solutions in order to prosper once again. Through a creative, values-driven strategy, the United States can boldly lead the global mission to solve some of the most complex problems humanity has ever faced while pursuing opportunities that are both sustainable and profitable. The U.S. has led industrial revolutions before, with breakthrough innovations, bold entrepreneurs and new institutions. Such bold leadership is not just a temporary administrative need and is needed once more; the very future of the ocean, and indeed the world, depends on it.

*This page is intentionally left blank.*

# CHAPTER 3 | PRINCIPLES

*It is a national humiliation that we are now compelled to pay from twenty to thirty million dollars annually (exclusive of passage money which we should share with vessels of other nations) to foreigners for doing the work which should be done by American vessels, American-built, American-owned and American-manned. This is a direct drain upon the resources of the country of just so much money, equal to casting it into the sea, so far as this nation is concerned. A nation of the vast and ever-increasing interior resources of the United States must one day possess its full share of the commerce of these oceans no matter what the cost.*

- President Ulysses S. Grant, Message to Congress (March 23, 1870)

*To speak plainly we have grossly erred in the way in which we have stunted and hindered the development of our merchant marine . . . It is necessary for many weighty reasons of national efficiency and development that we should have a great merchant marine . . . It is high time we repaired our mistake and resumed our commercial independence on the sea.*

- President Woodrow Wilson, Message to Congress (1915)

*The complex task of creating and maintaining a merchant marine adequate to our needs for peacetime commerce, and sufficient for defense purposes, requires the efforts of government, management and labor and the support of all Americans.*

- President Lyndon B. Johnson, National Maritime Day (1966)

Shipping is considered by many to be *the engine of global trade*. As described in the opening chapters, the movement of cargo on ships that cross the ocean has underpinned most forms of economic and social progress. The pattern from history is clear: Strong maritime nations exercise significant economic and military dominance, and conversely, complacency about maritime strength has often been accompanied by a significant fall in influence. Examples include Portugal, Venice, Spain, Netherlands, France, and Great Britain. The precedents of the past provide helpful guidance during the exploration, formation and application of future strategies. A brief examination of select theory from Alfred Mahan sets the scene.

Born in West Point, New York in 1840, Naval Officer and historian Alfred Thayer Mahan gained prominence as a leading military theorist during the late 19th and early 20th centuries. His detailed depictions and thoughtful analysis garnered public accolades from foreign officials and heads of state from all over the world. English military historian, lecturer, and author Sir John Desmond Patrick Keegan described Mahan as *"the most important American strategist of the nineteenth century."* Mahan's theories have been translated into many different languages, and greatly influenced the naval strategies employed by emerging naval powers - the U.S., Japan and Germany - and legacy naval nations like Britain, France and Russia. It is possible that the present-day activities of China's People's Liberation Army Navy (PLAN) have also been guided by Mahan's doctrines. Former U.S. Navy surface warfare officer and the Chair of Maritime Strategy at the Naval War College, James R Holmes, claims that Chinese officials "hybridize Mahanian and Maoist theory."

Mahan's seminal work 'The Influence of Sea Power Upon History: 1660–1783' was published in 1890. This book outlined Mahan's philosophy about the interdependence of military and commercial control of sea lanes and how such control determines the outcome of conflict. Mahan argued that a nation must possess the following six characteristics to establish and maintain naval dominance: Geographical position, physical conformation, extent of territory, size of population, character of the people, and character of the government. These six characteristics coexist alongside the Five Principles that will be examined in greater detail in subsequent chapters.

- **Geographical Position:** Geographical position directly impacts a nation's maritime capabilities and potential sea power. The strategic advantage offered by geographical location influences a country's access to trade routes and resources, ability to project power and to protect its interests on the seas. Countries favorably situated - those with extensive coastlines, multiple natural harbors, and close proximity to international shipping lanes - are naturally better equipped to build and maintain naval assets.

- **Physical Conformation:** Physical conformation relates to those natural characteristics associated with a country's land. Countries with diverse geographical features - extensive coastal plains, fertile soil, and ample resources - have greater potential for stronger and more diverse economies. Increased economic power can, in turn, support a robust and expansive naval force. However, a country's topographical vulnerabilities - low-lying areas prone to flooding or narrow straits susceptible to blockades - can negatively affect a country's sea power.

- **Extent of Territory:** Extent of territory affects a nation's ability to support a powerful navy in a range of different ways. Large nations, especially those with extensive coastlines, have more resources and advantageous locations to use for the construction, supply, and defense of naval forces. This may also mean more land to cultivate, which can translate into increased economic prosperity, which, in turn, provides the means to maintain and expand a powerful navy. Territory can also be extended in a distributed fashion - e.g, in islands, atolls or remote territories - which greatly improves geostrategic reach.

- **Size of Population:** Scale begets scale. The size of a nation's population is an important factor in building and sustaining sea power. A larger population provides a larger pool from which to recruit sailors, shipbuilders, and naval officers. Further, a larger population usually means a larger economy, which can provide the necessary resources to maintain and develop a substantive navy. A large, industrious population can also contribute to a nation's resilience during conflict.

- **Character of the People:** This element is less tangible but no less important. The character of the people refers to their collective values, attitudes, and societal norms, which greatly influences their propensity for maritime endeavors and resilience during maritime conflicts. A nation with a history of seafaring and naval tradition, for example, is more likely to be adept at utilizing sea power. Equally, a population willing to innovate, take risks, and adapt as circumstances change, will be more likely to maintain sea power, even if faced with threats or periods of extended conflict.

- **Character of the Government:** The character of the government greatly influences a nation's sea power. A government with a detailed understanding of the importance of naval power will be committed to investing in naval infrastructure, education, and research and more likely to build a powerful navy and merchant marine. A government's strategic decision-making, diplomatic skill and commitment to the rule of law influences a nation's relationships with other countries and its ability to navigate international conflicts and alliances. Government stability is another critical factor, as it ensures consistent support for naval policies and strategies; both of which can take many years to form, and to come to fruition.

When taken in totality it is clearly evident why the United States is uniquely positioned to be a dominant naval - and therefore, maritime - nation.

- **Geographical Position:** As per the commentary in the opening chapter, the U.S. is unparalleled in its geographic location. The continental United States is exceptionally well positioned to take advantage of global oceanic trade; spanning two oceans, and with safe passage via the Gulf Coast through the Panama Canal. The U.S. also has very supportive neighbors to the North and South. Both Canada and Mexico are active trading partners and supply goods and labor into the U.S. domestic market.

- **Physical Conformation:** The U.S. is endowed with diverse geographical features - extensive coastal plains, fertile soil, and ample resources - that support a thriving internal economy, and extend opportunities to export produce, commodities, manufactured goods and food to trading partners across the world. The U.S. also has a sprawling domestic waterway system, the 4th largest in the world at over 25,000 mi (40,000 km), to facilitate the efficient movement of food, produce and cargo from inland areas to the coast.

- **Extent of Territory:** The U.S. has an extensive coastline, which supports many different maritime activities. This coastline is well defined, uncontested, and is relatively easy to access from most inland areas. Geo-strategic influence is expanded through U.S. control over multiple non-contiguous areas and islands; Alaska to the northwest, Hawaii in the North Pacific, and a handful of islands in the Pacific, including the Marshall Islands, Northern Mariana Islands and Guam. The U.S. extends this even further, through an established presence in many allied countries; operating around 1,000 military and naval installations in locations all over the world.

- **Size of Population:** The U.S. is home to over 330 million people; the third most populous, and 4.23% of the world's total. This population base provides a strong foundation for many industrious activities, including the potential to build naval and maritime assets. The U.S. population can supply personnel for maritime activities, and improve economic resilience by sustaining high levels of industrial output. The U.S. population also has a diverse range of skills, and has proven - many times throughout history - to be resourceful, adept and hard-working during times of conflict or crisis.

- **Character of the People:** The U.S. has a long history of seafaring and naval tradition that stretches all the way back to the earliest days of settlement. The U.S. also has a culture that rewards innovative thinking and risk-taking. The presence of Silicon Valley and Wall Street, renowned organizations like NASA, and industry leaders like Tesla, Walmart and Apple, testify to the spirit of entrepreneurship that has been encouraged in U.S. businesses and academic institutions. Furthermore, the universally applicable values enshrined in the

Declaration of Independence, notably "Life, Liberty and the pursuit of Happiness" are reflected in domestic policies, and embodied in the majority of U.S. endeavors at a global level.

- **Character of the Government:** The U.S. is a stable democracy, and exercises a strong commitment to the rule of law, both at home and abroad. U.S. administrators have demonstrated an understanding of *naval* affairs, and guided by precedent and Mahan's theories, focused on increasing the capability, lethality and size of the U.S. Navy. This has come at the expense of *commercial* maritime endeavors, and the U.S. Merchant Marine. Mahan himself saw the need for interdependence and balance between naval and commercial activities, as evidenced in the quote at the start of this chapter: "Control of the sea, by maritime commerce and naval supremacy together, means predominant influence in the world." Even though Mahan is commonly regarded as being more focused on military affairs, he also espoused the notion that "Armed might is simply accessory and subordinate to the other greater interests, economical and commercial."

If the United States is to maintain control of the sea, an understanding of the nuanced, overlapping and interwoven nature of naval *and* commercial maritime activities is essential. Over the last 50 years, a focus on the operations of the Navy has led to diminished interest and investment in the U.S. merchant fleet, and subsequently U.S. merchant mariners. The evidence is clear: While the U.S. Navy is universally ranked 1st in lethality and capability, the U.S.-flagged merchant fleet is ranked 70th by vessel count, and 22nd by tonnage. This decline has accelerated in a precipitous manner, compared to allies and near-peer competitors. For example, in the last five years, the U.S. commercial fleet decreased in size (Deadweight Tonnage) by 12%, while the fleet size of the People's Republic of China increased by 55%.

Today, there are 180 commercial oceangoing ships flying the U.S. flag of the world's 50,000 vessels. This is a diminutive *Zero Point Four* percent (0.4%) of the global fleet, or about 0.57% of total tonnage for the world's largest economy. By contrast, in 1950, the United States owned over 1,000 private and 2,200 Government vessels, commanded 50% of the world's tonnage, and carried nearly 80% of global trade. Of the 180 vessels flying the U.S. flag today, around 100 of these vessels are used for essential ocean route domestic trade (e.g., to Alaska, Puerto Rico, Hawaii, U.S. Virgin Islands, Great Lakes Region, and U.S. territories abroad such as Guam). This means just 80 vessels are flagged to the U.S. and are responsible for transporting goods internationally. Most of these vessels are certified for safety by the American Bureau of Shipping (ABS) and are insured by the American P&I Club, one of 13 P&I (Protection and Indemnity mutual insurance for shipping risk pooling) that insures the global shipping industry around the world. In the global context, while not a signatory to the United Nations Law of the Sea (1982), the U.S. participates in the International Maritime Organization, a U.N. specialist agency that is responsible for global shipping. When a Government accepts an IMO Convention, it agrees to make it part of its own national law and to enforce it just like any other law.

The U.S. possesses great depth across the six characteristics described by Mahan at the start of this chapter, but lacks a comprehensive, all-encompassing *maritime* strategy. For a nation that has clear advantages in so many areas and a long history of naval excellence, it is rather surprising that a detailed, modern strategy does not currently exist. This U.S. Maritime Strategy must be a whole-of-Government, whole-of-nation strategy that balances military execution and commercial excellence: A strategy purposefully built around enduring qualities, that can increase prosperity and provide gainful employment, while being fiscally responsible and environmentally sustainable. A strategy that builds sovereign capability, while collaboratively involving global partners, lending effectiveness to any maritime endeavors being pursued across the world. And, a strategy that honors the sacrifice of the men and women in the U.S. armed forces, by providing the support, technologies and resources they need.

Where to begin?

## First, Principles

A 'principle' is defined as "a fundamental truth or proposition that serves as the foundation for a system of belief or behavior, or for a chain of reasoning." Five 'Principles' have been identified: National Security, Economic Security, Energy & Food Security, Climate Security and Workforce Security. These Principles provide the framework for the analysis and commentary that follows. There is overlap between the Principles, and while each Principle has unique qualities, they are all, in many ways, heavily interconnected; impact in one, has a cascading effect on another, and in some cases, all others.

*The ZP4 'Star' Framework for Maritime Security ©*

## I. National Security

National Security, sometimes called National Defense, involves the deployment of assets, infrastructure, and personnel to protect a nation's interests, sovereignty, industries, and people. For reference, the simply-worded mandate of the U.S. Department of Defense is to "provide the military forces needed to deter war, and to protect the security of the United States." The phrase 'to deter war' explains why it is called the Department of *Defense*, and not the Department of *Offense*.

National Security is almost always considered a duty of government and involves military and non-military dimensions. Non-military functions include combating terrorism, reducing organized crime, and minimizing the impact or effects of natural disasters. Non-military strategies include establishing international partnerships, exercising diplomacy, implementing tariffs, or enacting foreign policy. National Security requirements can be found in a variety of domains; aviation, transport, trade, cyber (digital), space, and maritime, including the subsea environment, among many others.

On an international level, protecting U.S. National Security involves establishing and maintaining a rules-based order, and specific to the maritime domain, protecting Freedom of Navigation (FON) of the sea. Performing these functions is highly complex, due to large geographic distances, most of which are in Areas Beyond National Jurisdiction (ABNJ), the presence of merchant vessels sailing under 'Flags of Convenience' (FOCs) and the emergence of a global dark/gray/opaque fleet involved in illegal trade.

The need for a rules-based order and to protect FON illustrates how the role and function of National Security is increasingly defined around activities that occur in a regional and global context. The positioning of U.S. armed forces across the world, the evolving nature of international commerce, and the rise of globalization have also contributed to the convergence of domestic and international security operations. Of equal importance is how modern conflicts - for example between Ukraine and Russia, and Israel and Hamas, and the Iran-backed Houthi militant attacks in the Red Sea - challenge and redefine the theories and strategies being employed by U.S. and global National Security practitioners.

The Principle of National Security assesses the risks and opportunities associated with U.S. domestic and international security activities, and proposes creative solutions to enhance military and diplomatic effectiveness. Pertinent questions: How can the U.S. exercise hard and soft power projection in an effective, yet sustainable way? What role does maritime play in the nation's National Security posture? How will the U.S. adapt to emerging threats, and the changing nature of warfare? What National Security assets, processes, investments, or priorities need to change or evolve?

## II. Economic Security

The definition of Economic Security is commonly informed by the contextual perspective, mandate, or operational responsibility of an individual, organization or group. The United Nations (UN) relates Economic Security to the assurance of a basic income. The definition from the International Committee of the Red Cross reads "the ability of individuals, households, or communities to cover their essential needs sustainably and with dignity." The U.S. Department of Defense (DOD) defines it as "the ability to protect or advance U.S. economic interests, shape international interests to American liking, and possess material resources to fend off non-economic challenges." And, the U.S. Department of Homeland Security (DHS) defines economic security as "the increasing dependence on the flow of goods, services, people, capital, information, and technology across borders."

In May 2023, the Group of 7 (G7) nations - Canada, France, Germany, Italy, Japan, the United Kingdom and the United States, along with the European Union - formalized a definition of Economic Security, that includes the following seven dimensions:

- Building resilient supply chains
- Building resilient critical infrastructure
- Responding to non-market policies and practices
- Addressing economic coercion
- Countering harmful practices in the digital sphere
- Cooperating on international standard-setting
- Preventing leakage of critical and emerging technologies

The preamble to this definition states: "We affirm that our cooperation to strengthen economic resilience and economic security will be rooted in maintaining and improving a well-functioning international rules-based system." The United States is uniquely positioned to utilize each of these seven dimensions to drive positive Economic Security outcomes, while maintaining a rules-based order. The combination of these two activities directly informs the central thesis communicated in this Principle, that "Economic Security *is* National Security".

The Principle of Economic Security explores the risks and opportunities associated with U.S. domestic and international economic interests, and proposes novel ways to enhance prosperity by utilizing maritime assets and infrastructure. Pertinent questions: How has globalization affected U.S. and international shipping? How can the U.S. secure and profit from global commercial maritime trade? What is meant by "Economic Security *is* National Security?" And what future maritime activities might be the most productive and economically viable?

## III. Energy & Food Security

### Energy

The United Nations defines Energy Security as "the continuous availability of energy in varied forms, in sufficient quantities and at affordable prices" (World Coal Institute, 2005). The International Energy Agency (IEA) defines it as the "uninterrupted availability of energy sources at an affordable price", which is similar to the Organization for Security and Co-operation in Europe (OSCE) that defines Energy Security as "having stable access to energy sources on a timely, sustainable and affordable basis."

The energy blend required to sustain modern life and improve output and drive productivity, has markedly changed over time, and will continue to change over the coming decades. The fundamentals that underpin energy supply, and the needs of consumers have remained largely the same. The United States, along with all other countries across the world, will need to source and secure, continuous, varied, sufficient, affordable, and sustainable energy, to keep industries powered, and citizens productive. But how can this occur at scale? And how can the right forms of energy be generated and used without destroying the planet?

### Food

At the World Food Summit in 1996, the World Bank described Food Security as being "when all people, at all times, have physical and economic access to sufficient safe and nutritious food that meets their dietary needs and food preferences for an active and healthy life." Four common characteristics of Food

Security are: Availability. Access. Utilization, and Stability. When these are out of balance or absent, food *insecurity* eventuates, which can lead to malnourishment, starvation and eventually, death.

A lack of access to food, or if food-growing regions are continuously impacted by drought, flooding or other natural disasters, can prompt, or force, mass migration, which tends to generate tension that leads to conflict. Millions of people can also suffer if food is unable to be safely transported between producing countries and consumers. This happens if there is a failure to monitor and protect food as it transits dry or refrigerated supply chains, or if the movement of food is impacted by disruptions, delays, or as witnessed in recent times, war: Pertinent examples being the Black Sea grain blockades in Ukraine, and the impact on food exports and imports to and from the Middle East, due to the conflict between Israel and Hamas. Another example is the conflict in the Red Sea, which is one of the world's busiest shipping lanes. The movement of ships through the Red Sea has been severely disrupted by Houthi rocket, drone and missile attacks which impacts the Food Security of countries in the region, and those dependent on the food shipments that traverse through the Suez Canal.

The contribution of fish, as a percentage of total protein intake differs between countries. In developed regions like North America and Europe, it ranges from 7-11%. In small island developing states, it accounts for 50% or more. However, around 80 percent of the world's fish stocks are reported as fully exploited or overexploited, which has been driven by the explosive growth of Illegal, Unreported, and Unregulated (IUU) fishing. Overfishing, bycatch wastage, oil spills, toxic discharges, and plastic pollution, among a range of other alarming issues, all endanger our oceans, and subsequently the Food Security of millions of people.

The Principle of Energy & Food Security explores the risks and opportunities associated with energy generation, distribution and use, and food production, transportation and consumption. This includes an examination of historical examples, present realities, and future trends. Pertinent questions: How productive are current forms of energy and food production? What new fuels and propulsion technologies are available to improve shipping efficiency, and reduce emissions? What role does sustainability play, for energy use, and food consumption, in the maritime domain? How can the U.S. take a leading role, on a global level, to universally improve Energy & Food Security?

## IV. Climate Security

The United Nations Development Program (UNDP) defines Climate Security as "the impact of the climate crisis on peace and security, particularly in fragile and conflict-affected settings." The effects of a changing climate - observed by an increase in extreme weather events, temperature fluctuations, and increased impacts from natural disasters - can exacerbate water, food and livelihood insecurity, especially for those in developing countries. According to a recent report from the United Nations Intergovernmental Panel on Climate Change (IPCC), over 3.3 billion people - or over 40% of the world's population - already live in contexts that are highly vulnerable to climate change. And, as per the World Bank, by 2030, climate change could push up to 130 million more people into poverty, by exacerbating existing vulnerabilities, including food and water insecurity, and by increasing the likelihood of socio-economic fragility. Competition for scarce resources, mass displacement, and conflict are all potential outcomes from climate-related events.

While a changing climate poses obvious risks for securing food and water, it also has a direct impact on many other domains, and in particular, the operations of the military. The U.S.

Department of Defense (DOD) identifies climate change as "a critical national security issue", explaining that "Climate change will… amplify operational demands, degrade installations and infrastructure resilience, increase health risks to our service members and require modifications to existing and planned equipment needs." These are not recent observations. Intelligence reporting and estimates have been released by the DOD since 2008, while military institutions such as the Naval War College have been warning policy-makers about the impact of climate change since 1990. Identifying the threat is easy; adapting is not.

The Principle of Climate Security explores the risks and opportunities associated with rapidly accelerating climate change, with a particular focus on how changing weather patterns, amplified weather events, rising temperatures, and more extreme natural disasters will impact U.S. productivity, people and progress. Pertinent questions: What elements of Climate Security are relevant to the maritime sector? What National Security risks relate to climate change? How can the U.S. play a leading role in environmental protection and sustainability? What future endeavors or policies may assist to mitigate the risks of climate change, while also being economically profitable?

## V. Workforce Security

Workforce Security shares, in a collective sense, the same principles that underpin job security for any given individual. Job security is typically defined as a worker's perception that their job, or an important feature of their job, is secure i.e., the job they performed yesterday will be present, and largely unchanged, when they arrive at work the next morning. Job security includes access to employee entitlements that form part of continuing employment. These could be: health benefits, welfare support, insurance coverage, medical programs, leave and holiday arrangements, and any other entitlement or benefit generally made available across a term of employment. Another consideration is what access a worker may have to assistance from worker advocacy groups, including trade and industry unions.

Workforce Security weighs up the needs of the individual, but must also scale up to consider the requirements of entire industries and market segments. Two other elements that are relevant for shipping are national imperatives, and the state of the global workforce. A balanced perspective is required: Solutions that might offer some degree of benefit at a smaller scale, may not be relevant to the country as a whole. Conversely, decisions made nationally, may lead to local workforce volatility and instability; especially if contextual nuance is ignored.

The Principle of Workforce Security explores past, present and future risks and opportunities, particularly as they relate to the United States commercial maritime sector. Pertinent questions: How will the United States adapt to the changing nature of work, and increased labor force fluidity? What priorities need to be realigned now, so that workers are sourced for critical industries needed in the future? How can the U.S. assist those seeking employment in the U.S. Merchant Marine? And, how can the Maritime Administration (MARAD), and public and private maritime training colleges 'Attract, Equip, and Retain' mariners?

# NATIONAL SECURITY

**National Security**

- *Ships and assets*
- *Programs*
- *Ownership*
- *Technology*
- *China*

# I. NATIONAL SECURITY

*It is necessary for the national defense and for the proper growth of its foreign and domestic commerce that the United States shall have a merchant marine of the best equipped and most suitable types of vessels sufficient to carry the greater portion of its commerce and serve as a naval or military auxiliary in time of war or national emergency, ultimately to be owned and operated privately by citizens of the United States; and it is declared to be the policy of the United States to do whatever may be necessary to develop and encourage the maintenance of such a merchant marine...*

- President Franklin Delano Roosevelt, U.S. Congress, (March 4, 1935)

*In recent years, we have identified logistics as the "pacing function" for operations. Among the seven warfighting functions, logistics most dictates the tempo of operations and the operational reach of a unit. No other warfighting function more profoundly affects our ability to persist in contested spaces.*

- Installations and Logistics 2030 Plan, United States Marine Corps (2023)

## National Security Context

The United States maintains a unique position in the world - and sustains superpower status - through a number of mechanisms including military strength, economic capacity, and by protecting the universal values of democracy and freedom. The application of these mechanisms is enacted through hard or soft power projection. Hard power projection primarily relates to the use of military force or military intervention. Soft power projection via trade, diplomacy and other avenues, can also be used, but has limited effectiveness if not backed by able and available armed forces. The U.S. is in the enviable position of possessing ample amounts of both forms of influence, and must delicately balance the application of each; aggressive adversaries are emboldened when only soft power is used, and negative perceptions weaken partnerships and alliances, if hard power is used with impunity.

In the context of the United States, National Security includes:

- Preserving the safety of the U.S. homeland
- Protecting U.S. domestic institutions and systems vital to preserving domestic safety
- Maintaining a global balance of power that favors U.S. security and - economic, social, or political - interests, and those of aligned friends and allies.
- Exerting U.S. influence on an international level through various instruments of soft and hard power, including: Deploying armed or peace-keeping forces, foreign aid, intelligence sharing, financial support packages, public and private diplomacy, and humanitarian programs.
- Actively maintaining a global economy based on economic freedom (i.e., democratic capitalism), which includes essential features like reduced barriers of entry

between trading partners, and where possible, the establishment of Free Trade Agreements
- Guaranteeing Freedom of Navigation (FON) of the seas, which is critically important to U.S. global interests, stabilizes various international regions, and promotes harmonious world trade.

The last four points illustrate how U.S. National Security is heavily connected with international activity. Freedom of Navigation is particularly pertinent. The United States is in the extraordinary position of being one of only a handful of countries that possess a blue-water (deep sea) navy. Conversely, due to restraints of access or resources, most countries either possess a green-water navy - for patrolling coastal regions - or a brown-water navy, for rivers and estuaries.

The U.S. Navy (USN) with 11 Carrier Strike Groups, including 70 submarines, 72 destroyers and 17 cruisers, is a formidable fighting force. The USN Fleet is constantly forward-deployed, and operates from home ports in strategic positions in the United States and across the world. The 7 USN Fleet bases - Virginia, San Diego, Fort Meade (Fleet Cyber Command), Florida, Bahrain, Italy and Japan - were purposefully chosen to effectively distribute the Fleet across the greatest distance. The presence of the U.S. Navy, ably supported by the U.S. Marines Corps (USMC), and the U.S. Coast Guard (USCG), allows the United States to project hard and deterrent power into every corner of the globe. This extends the defensive perimeter of the United States from the domestic coastline to 'over the horizon'.

The United States dedicates a significant amount of time, resources and money to National Security, including domestic defense and intelligence activities, and protecting U.S. interests abroad. In FY2023, over $800 billion was allocated to the Department of Defense (DOD), along with $30 billion for national security programs within the Department of Energy

(DOE). U.S. Defense spending accounts for around 40% of the world's total; more than China, Russia, India, Saudi Arabia, United Kingdom, Germany, France, South Korea, Japan, and Ukraine, *combined.*

Defense spending is spread across a number of Departments and agencies: Army, Air Force (National Guard), Navy (Marine Corps, Coast Guard), Defense Logistics Agency, Defense Health Agency, Missile Defense Agency, Defense Information Systems Agency, United States Transportation Command (USTRANSCOM), and the U.S. Special Operations Command (SOCOM), among others. The U.S. military is one of the largest employers in the country: There are 452,000 active-duty personnel in the Army and 190,000 in the Army Reserve; 354,000 active-duty and 56,254 reservists in the U.S. Navy; 42,000 active-duty and 7,000 reserves in the U.S. Coast Guard (USCG); 321,848 active duty and 68,927 reserves in the U.S. Air Force; 177,000 active-duty, and 40,000 reserves in the U.S. Marine Corps; and, around 8,600 serving personnel in the United States Space Force.

### Current U.S. Maritime Logistics Programs

There are four Government programs that provide 'militarily-useful' maritime logistics and supply chain assets (and support) to the U.S. military:

- **Military Sealift Command (MSC)** - MSC reports to USTRANSCOM for defense transportation matters; to U.S. Fleet Forces Command (USFF) for anything Navy-unique; and to the Assistant Secretary of the Navy (Research, Development and Acquisition) for matters relating to procurement policy and oversight. From the official description: "Military Sealift Command is responsible for 125 commercial-crewed ships that replenish U.S. Navy ships at sea, conduct specialized missions, preposition combat cargo at sea, perform a variety of support services, and move military equipment and supplies to deployed U.S. forces around the world."

Acquisition: "MSC also charters commercial vessels as needed to meet government requirements. By law and policy, MSC must first look to the U.S.-flagged market to meet its sealift requirements. Government-owned ships are used only when suitable U.S.-flagged commercial ships are unavailable. Finally, during a national emergency, MSC can employ dozens of additional commercial vessels enrolled in the Voluntary Intermodal Sealift Agreement and the Maritime Security Program."

MSC also operates a fleet of 17 vessels in the Prepositioning Program (PM3). PM3 strategically places military equipment and supplies aboard ships located in key ocean areas around the world. These ships are deployed to ensure that capacity is rapidly available during war, humanitarian operations or other contingencies. MSC's PM3 ships support the Army, Navy, Air Force, Marine Corps and Defense Logistics Agency, and are equipped to discharge liquid, containerized or motorized cargo; pier side or while anchored offshore via floating hoses or shallow-draft watercraft (lighterage / barge). The PM3 fleet has declined by around 20 vessels since 2001.

- MSC has an annual operating budget of around $3 billion, and is funded only by purchases from its customers. The goal of MSC's 'Working Capital Fund' is to break even, i.e., charges paid by customers equal MSC's expenses.

- MSC is the largest employer of U.S. merchant mariners in the United States: 9,500 people worldwide, most of whom serve at sea.

- Over half of MSC's workforce are civil service mariners who are federal employees. The remainder includes contract U.S. commercial mariners, civil service personnel (ashore) and active-duty and reserve military members.

- Two labor models are used to manage crewing aboard MSC ships. The crew on government operated vessels are civil service mariners and employed directly by MSC. They are issued DOD identification cards and receive federal benefits. The crews on contractor-operated vessels are called contract mariners and are employed directly by the operating company of the ship (that is under contract to MSC). These crews are usually represented by a maritime labor union in a similar fashion to mariners in the civil service.

- MSC crew members are U.S. citizens and either licensed and unlicensed. Licensed personnel (e.g., ship's master or chief engineer) hold a USCG-issued license, obtained through a combination of sea time and completing relevant licensing exams.

- **Maritime Security Program (MSP) -** Established by the Maritime Security Act of 1996, and administered by MARAD, the "Maritime Security Program (MSP) maintains a fleet of commercially viable, militarily-useful merchant ships active in international trade. The MSP fleet is available to support U.S. Department of Defense sustainment sealift requirements during times of conflict or in other national emergencies. The program also provides DoD access to MSP participants' global intermodal transportation network of terminals, facilities, logistic management services, and U.S. citizen merchant mariners."

The Federal government's organic fleet of military sealift vessels is too small to sustain supply operations or provide support in a prolonged conflict, without being augmented by commercial ships. One of the mechanisms available to address this shortfall is through the Maritime Security Program. The MSP is a fleet of 60, relatively modern, U.S.-Registered, U.S.-flagged, congressionally-funded, militarily-useful ships that are commonly engaged in commercial trade. As of 2023, the MSP has access to approximately 130,000 TEUs of container capacity, 3.4 million square feet of RO/RO and heavy-lift capacity, and 666,800 Barrels of tanker capacity. The MSP fleet has a total capacity of 2,210,274 dwt.

At time of writing, the use and positioning of ships involved in the Maritime Security Program are being challenged, due to the evolving conflict in the Red Sea. For example, at the start of the conflict, there was confusion as to whether U.S.-Flagged vessels transiting the area were comprehensively protected, which led some industry commentators to express concerns about crew safety. The complicated nature of this conflict will be defining for the Maritime Security Program and may lead to changes to contractual arrangements and operational procedures in the future.

The annual MSP stipend is $5.3 million per vessel. The 60 vessels of the MSP supports around 2,400 mariners, and has a total program cost of $318 million / year.

- **Voluntary Intermodal Sealift Agreement (VISA) -** Authorized under the Defense Production Act of 1950, and administered by MARAD, the "Voluntary Intermodal Sealift Agreement (VISA) program is a partnership between the U.S. Government and the maritime industry to provide the Department of Defense with assured access to state-of-the-art commercial sealift and intermodal equipment when DOD deploys military forces during a national emergency or wartime operations."

The operating model for VISA is different from the MSP:

- There is no limit to the number of vessels that can be enrolled in VISA
- Enrollment is voluntary, but participation by an enrolled vessel in a VISA (military) activation is mandatory.
- Enrollment does not result in direct financial compensation, but enrolled vessels are offered DOD cargo contracting priorities i.e., qualified operators agree to volunteer time and intermodal capacity during wartime in exchange for priority access to DOD cargoes during peacetime.

Cargo preferences require the use of U.S.-Flag vessels to move cargo that is owned, procured, furnished, or financed by the U.S. Government. This also includes cargo being shipped under an agreement of the U.S. Government, or part of a U.S. Government program. Cargo preferences apply to a number of commercial and military agencies, and must be moved on U.S.-Flag ships in these ratios: Military Cargo - 100%. Commercial Agencies Cargo - at least 50%. Agricultural Cargo - at least 50%. Export Import Bank Cargo - 100%.

- **Tanker Security Program (TSP) -** Administered by MARAD, the "Tanker Security Program (TSP) will ensure that a core fleet of U.S.-based product tankers can operate competitively in international trade and enhance U.S. supply chain resiliency for liquid fuel products. The TSP will provide the Department of Defense with assured access to 10 U.S.-registered product tank vessels that may be used to supply the armed forces with fuel during times of armed conflict or national emergency."

Background: A study conducted for the 2020 National Defense Authorization Act examined how the U.S.-flagged tanker fleet met U.S. National Defense Strategy requirements. The report found that substantial risks existed with current tanker arrangements and a distinct need for U.S.-flagged assets; due to the location, timing, and specific mission requirements of certain military operations. The current lack of available tankers represented a critical risk to the DOD, and so a Tanker Security Program was recommended to increase capacity, and reduce the reliance on foreign-flagged tankers. The annual TSP stipend is $6 million per vessel. The TSP currently has 10 vessels enrolled and supports around 250 mariners, for a total program cost of $60 million / year.

Alongside these programs are the National Defense Reserve Fleet (NDRF) and Ready Reserve Force (RRF). Both are managed by MARAD. The NDRF are approximately 100 inactive, Government-owned, 'military-useful' ships that can be called upon to support national defense and emergencies. There are current 48 ships in the RRF: 42 roll-on/roll off (RO/RO) vessels, including 8 Fast Sealift Support (FSS) vessels, 7 LMSR (Large, Medium-Speed, Roll-on/Roll-off) 4 auxiliary crane ships, and 2 aviation repair vessels. These ships are located in a number of 'outports' around the United States, and are expected to be fully operational within an assigned 5 and 10-day window. The RRF supports the transport of Army, Navy and Marine Corps combat and support equipment, and provides initial resupply during surge periods. Once activated, command and control of the RRF is handled by Military Sealift Command.

## National Security and U.S. Shipping

Shipping plays a key role in the defensive and offensive posture and foreign policy objectives of the United States. Mission requirements, available Fleet blend and the geographic region of operation (military theater) influence the type of vessels being deployed. A visible demonstration of maritime power is achieved through aircraft carriers, destroyers or submarine-based nuclear deterrents; for example the 2023 deployment of the newly constructed USS Gerald R. Ford aircraft carrier to the Mediterranean Sea. Alternatively, the presence of support vessels projects a sense of readiness and resilience, especially if they are involved in maintaining long logistical supply chains spanning thousands of miles.

While the U.S. has a very strong maritime heritage, naval and merchant marine co-dependence has dramatically diverged. This decoupling, fueled by many factors including a lack of investment in critical infrastructure and key assets, leaves the U.S. militarily vulnerable, and represents several major risks to National and international Security.

The U.S. relies heavily on maritime assets to handle logistics through a process called Military Sealift. How dependent? While military personnel are now predominantly moved by plane, the DOD estimates that more than 90% of military equipment, supplies, and fuel travels by sea. Due to the volumes, weights and scale involved, this task cannot be easily assigned to other forms of transportation. Captain John Konrad (gCaptain) astutely points out that "The entire U.S. Air Force Heavy Lift Fleet has less carrying capacity than one ultra-large container ship." Due to a lack of suitable ships, the U.S. would be unable to reliably and securely transport the necessary cargo to sustain combat operations during a protracted conflict. This becomes significantly worse when operating in contested environments, i.e., if supply lines are actively targeted by adversaries. To solve for a lack of appropriate ships, the DOD is forced to charter vessels from the open market. The problems associated with this practice were identified in a 2010 report to Congress: "[Military Sealift] charters ships (from the commercial market) to meet the requirements of DOD components and respond to changes in the operational environment. Unfortunately, very few commercial ships with high military utility have been constructed in U.S. shipyards in the past 20 years. Consequently, when Military Sealift has a requirement to charter a vessel, nearly all of the offers are for foreign-built ships."

As will be explored throughout this Principle, supplying naval fleet operations is essential to any military strategy. As Army General John J. Pershing aptly put it: *"Infantry wins battles, logistics wins wars."* Fleet supply includes the acquisition and delivery of materiel, munitions, food and water, fuels and lubricants, vehicles, replacement parts and equipment, and personal effects cargo, as well as the movement of people. An efficient and secure supply chain increases Fleet reliability and robustness, allowing assets and personnel to dwell in remote theaters for extended periods of time. This is illustrated in the quote at the beginning of this Principle: Logistics most dictates the tempo of operations and greatly improves the ability of a unit to "persist in contested spaces." Over the coming decade, the world will face greater geopolitical risks than at any time since the end of the Cold War. Within this timeframe, the U.S. could potentially find itself engaged in major conflicts on opposite sides of the world; in Europe, the Middle East, or in the Pacific. These conflicts will consume significant resources, and require the establishment and security of multiple international logistics supply chains over a prolonged period of time i.e., greater than 1 month, and likely 6 months or more.

The construction, control and management of ports, along with appropriate support infrastructure - in the U.S. and distributed worldwide - is also critical for National Security. The potential for commercial port disruptions to create risks to National Security was most profoundly seen during the supply-chain crisis at the height of the COVID-19 pandemic. For various cascading reasons, the throughput of most major U.S. ports was dramatically impacted, which led to backlogs at the dock, and on the water. At the height of this disruption, in January 2022, 109 merchant ships were parked off the California coast, waiting to be processed through the Port of Los Angeles and the Port of Long Beach. This in turn, affected a variety of imports and exports, and introduced unpredictable strains on the U.S. economy and domestic production. This backlog took months to resolve, and created a significant amount of anxiety, frustration, and tension; and also panic buying when common consumer goods were unavailable. Foreign adversaries could well have taken advantage of this situation using commerce in a way that some have described as a 'Weapon of Mass Disruption.' Structural changes to prevent this from happening again have not taken place, which reinforced the view that maintaining control over key maritime assets and infrastructure is not a high priority, nor deemed important to U.S. National Security.

Further abroad, the U.S. has historically retained a strong military presence close to critical logistics choke points around the world, e.g., establishing bases and maintaining patrols around the Panama Canal (that connects the Atlantic with the Pacific), Suez Canal (connecting the Mediterranean Sea to the Red Sea), and Straits of Hormuz (connecting the Persian Gulf to the Arabian Sea). U.S. deployments in these regions strengthen strategic alliances, secures the movement of cargo and energy, protects Freedom of Navigation, and acts as a deterrent to hostile actors. However, this form of hard power projection is only credible if there is a realistic prospect of intervention. With a growing percentage of goods critical to U.S. supply chains transported on (non-U.S.) foreign-flagged vessels, with no U.S. mariners on board, this style of deterrence is rapidly losing effectiveness. Without U.S. citizens to protect, and with no formalized terms of engagement, the U.S. Navy or Coast Guard is less likely to defend a foreign-flagged vessel, even if that vessel is carrying cargo or commodities being exported or imported by U.S. companies. Similarly, the perception that hostile forces could attack any vessels with impunity, would increase the frequency of maritime violence, which would seriously affect the volume and velocity of world trade. The crisis in the Red Sea - that began in November 2023, and continued into 2024 - is an alarming representation of how this very scenario may play out, in a continuous and potentially cyclical fashion, in other regions, in the future.

## National Security Maritime Risks and Vulnerabilities

Asset deficiencies, wasteful support programs, a lack of domestic capacity, and the influence of foreign powers are all a direct threat to U.S. National Security:

**A. Contending with the wrong blend:** - How a lack of cargo-carrying ships, oil tankers, and specialized support vessels threatens National Security

**B. Unfit for purpose:** RRF, MSP and VISA - The risks associated with insufficient, inadequate, and overpriced ships, and how Zombie Assets detrimentally impact naval operations

**C. Diminished domestic control and productivity:** - The consequences of an excessive reliance on foreign participation and inadequate domestic capacity

**D. Emerging technologies, modern threats:** - Securing cyber/digital systems, automation and space and the threats posed by the changing nature of warfare

**E. China: Peer or Power?** - How the rising influence of China affects the United States

# A. Contending with the Wrong Blend

## I. Militarily-useful container, transport and RORO ships: The U.S. needs 1,000, but only has access to 180

*Exhibit 16: Shipping containers being offloaded from the Military Sealift Command ship MV Virginian in Kuwait in 2011 (credit: U.S. Army)*

The U.S. merchant marine includes around 200 vessels exceeding one thousand gross tons (gt). MARAD considers around 150 to be 'militarily-useful.' This number has dropped from around 320 strategically relevant ships since 1996; a dramatic halving of the available fleet over the last 20 years. The U.S. is estimated to need a strategic blend of around 1,000 vessels, to sustain major combat operations or for a large-scale Eurasian or Pacific war. Some commentators believe the real number is triple that figure (up to 3,000 ships) due to the heavy toll of combat operations, to account for repairs and maintenance, and when factoring in the losses that occur in heavily contested environments. A detailed breakdown for why 1,000 vessels are required for a 'Future Competitive' U.S. Maritime fleet is explored in the Principle of Economic Security (with a corresponding solution proposed as the 'Economic Security Program').

To comprehensively support naval operations, the correct support fleet blend would need to include container ships, ships to move troops (who aren't moved via Air Mobility Command), dry cargo vessels, bulk liquid transports, and Roll-On / Roll-Off (ROROs) for vehicles and heavy machinery. This fleet blend would also need to complement the Combat Logistics Force

(CLF), afloat prepositioning fleet (PM3), and other auxiliary ships that are engaged in support activities. Choosing the right blend is essential to sustain immediate, and long-term operations, particularly if conflict zones are contested, or if assets are spread out over a large geographic area.

Choosing the right blend is even more important if the Navy pursues a strategy of Distributed Maritime Operations (DMO). The nuance of DMO was succinctly defined in the tri-service maritime strategy 'Advantage at Sea' as a concept that combines "the effects of sea-based and land-based fires… [and] leverages the principles of distribution, integration, and maneuver to mass overwhelming combat power and effects at the time and place of our choosing." Chief of Naval Operations Admiral M. Gilday expanded this definition in a testimony to Congress in 2021: "By maneuvering distributed forces across all domains, we will complicate adversary targeting, exploit uncertainty, and achieve surprise." This statement echoed the sentiment of Secretary of Defense James Mattis who declared in a National Defense Strategy briefing in 2018 that "the United States must be strategically predictable, but operationally unpredictable."

Three core tenets of DMO are that military assets should be 'Hard to find, hard to kill and lethal'. Distributed warfare, operationally unpredictability and being 'hard to find' are potent concepts in theory, but are very difficult to implement in practice. While variability may increase the element of surprise, distributing military assets over greater distances requires a more comprehensive web of logistics support; a greater number of ships performing more frequent resupply operations, covering more expansive geographical areas, through a variety of contested environments. 'Operational unpredictability' is more complicated to coordinate and subsequently resupply. All of these challenges are magnified in complexity and scope if operators also have to contend with contested communications and digital (cyber) domains.

Being 'hard to kill' and 'lethal' is only possible if a warship has enough fuel to move, and enough stocked missiles and ammunition to attack others or defend itself. The five R's of Logistics are: Refuel, Rearm, Resupply, Repair and Revive; 'Replace' is added, when considering total loss. Military operations may have to stop entirely if the correct support is not available to complete these five critical activities. This can be illustrated using a recent example in a modern theater of war: In October 2023, while strategically forward deployed during the conflict between Israel and Hamas, the Arleigh Burke-class guided-missile destroyer *USS Carney*, shot down nearly 20 cruise missiles and drones over the Red Sea. Similar feats have been performed in the Red Sea, on multiple occasions, by a range of other U.S. Navy ships as the Iran-backed Houthi attacks on global shipping have continued. While exceptional and admirable, these defensive activities would be significantly more powerful, if they were highly repeatable, rather than requiring a one-off operation.

Repeatability can only be achieved if a warship has access to the correct blend of support vessels that can perform Refuel, Rearm and Resupply operations. Without easy access to fuel, armaments and stores (including food and other supplies to sustain the crew), the *Carney*, or any other warship would be unable to rapidly return to the fight. This applies to aircraft carriers; while the carrier itself can continue sailing due to its nuclear reactor, its entire air wing would be unable to fly. In that unfortunate position, these expensive assets transition into floating liabilities that are likely to be deliberately targeted by aggressive adversaries.

Similarly, Roll-On / Roll-Off vessels play an important role in moving equipment, machinery and weapons systems from storage and production to the front line. The U.S. Transportation Command has access to 50 ROROs, including 20 Large, Medium-Speed Roll-on/Roll-off (LSMRs), that were built between 1972 and 2002. The oldest RORO is 51 years old, the youngest, 21. As with other types of support vessels, if Government-controlled, militarily-useful ROROs are unavailable, commercial equivalents are supposed to be sourced from the open market. This poses two immediate problems: Commercial risk, and utility.

- **Commercial risk:** If a RORO is required in a short time frame, the first major problem would be convincing the (likely non-U.S.) shipowner to make their foreign-flagged, foreign-owned vessel available for U.S. military service. This is likely to be at odds with the owner's interests to exercise impartiality and pursue profitability through other less controversial means.

- **Utility:** Migrating a commercial RORO to military use is not always possible without heavy modifications. As observed in Defense News, in June 2022 "in some cases, more than half the space onboard is not militarily-useful. And decks aren't strong enough, ceiling clearances are too low, ramps are too steep and corners are too tight." A modern RORO can transport up to 6,000 commercial cars. That number is markedly reduced if hauling machinery, and reduced further still, if moving larger and bulkier military assets. For example, the average car weighs about 2 tons, whereas an Abrams tank weighs around 60. Assuming all slots are used

*Exhibit 17: M/V Honor RORO (credit: Crowley)*

> just for tanks, and assuming the RORO could handle the extra weight and size, a modern RORO could only shift 200 tanks at one time. The U.S. has 5,500 tanks. If a modern ground offensive required 1,000 tanks, then five trips (assuming no losses) would be needed, across thousands of miles of open ocean, to move just one military asset to the battlefield.

MARAD purchased two, used ROROs - *Honor* and *Freedom* - in late 2022, and revealed in the same press release that 37 (74%) out of these 50 vessels were due to retire in the next 10 years. It will be very difficult and expensive to replace 37 ROROs. Given the purchase of *Honor* and *Freedom* was the first time this portion of the fleet had been replenished in over 25 years, replacing 37 vessels may take decades to complete. This is made even more complicated as there is (as of November 2023) a worldwide shortage of RORO capacity; most are being built in China for their own purposes. To put this in perspective, China is slated to construct 25-50 ('dual-use' capable) ROROs to service a rapidly expanding automotive sector over the next 24 months (2024-2025). This will be a fleet of ultra-modern carriers, with increased capacity for transporting all types of equipment and therefore capable of 'dual-use' operations (a concept that will be explored in further detail later on in this chapter). This will dwarf the U.S.-controlled RORO fleet, and take a commanding lead globally.

Note: Notwithstanding the lack of present available domestic capacity to build these ships in the United States, constructing a support fleet with the correct blend of fit-for-purpose vessels, would take a very long time and would also be very expensive. Assuming a number of variables, and if the average price tag to build each ship was a conservative $30 million each (in a non-U.S. shipyard), 850 extra ships would cost $25.5 billion. In this thought exercise, we assume 850 extra ships as the U.S.

currently has 180 militarily-useful commercial vessels, that would make the total fleet 1000 vessels.

### II. Militarily-useful Oil Tankers: The U.S. needs 100, but has access to less than 10

*Exhibit 18: Strategic transfer of fuel to merchant tanker Empire State from the Red Hill Bulk Fuel Storage Facility in 2023 (credit: U.S. Army)*

The U.S. military doesn't just move personnel and equipment. A significant amount of fuel - marine oil, vehicle and jet fuel - is required to ensure naval, army and airborne assets can move and fight in geographically distant locations. Due to size and weight, most fuel cannot be transported by air, and must be carried by ship (tankers). Medium-range (MR) tankers - ships that carry roughly 300,000 barrels (12,600,000 gallons, or 48 million liters) of multiple types of refined product - are best suited to this task. These large, ocean-going tankers are critical for refueling operations, in particular if the Navy is engaged in continuous regional skirmishes, or travels long distances to a conflict zone.

The current method for naval resupply relies on larger tankers to deliver fuel to the edge of the battle space, which is then transferred to 'oilers' - smaller, more nimble vessels - that directly supply the Fleet. This approach is one of only a few available options, due to various factors such as the closure of centralized fuel supply depots; Red Hill in Hawaii being the most recent example. The U.S. has around 5-7 oilers capable of supplying the fleet in-theater. These vessels are not armed -

Kaiser-class oilers have the mounts for close-in weapons systems (CIWS) but lack the weapons - and would be prime targets for creative aggressors, which means they would need to be escorted. However, assigning a guided missile destroyer or equivalent for this task, may not be an option during times of furious conflict, which would leave these highly-valued assets vulnerable.

Current estimates indicate that around 100 tankers are required to replenish the existing U.S. Fleet, though some consider the real number to be 2-3 times higher, given the excess fuel burned by actively engaged vessels involved in evasive maneuvers. 100 or 300, the U.S. only has direct access to ten appropriately outfitted tankers through the Tanker Security Program (TSP). Another five have been identified but will take years to be fully integrated into the fleet, and will also need the correct equipment installed to perform fuel transfers at sea; a process known as consolidated cargo replenishment at sea (CONSOL).

While there are plans to eventually increase the total number to 20, progress to complete these acquisitions has been slow. Assessing, purchasing, checking compliance, and reflagging a tanker can take years to complete; a rate that does not match the operational cadence of a constantly-deployed U.S. Navy, who may suddenly be engaged in conflict at very short notice. Any of these estimated support fleet numbers must accommodate the potential that modern maritime conflict zones will include contested areas, and supply lines will be actively attacked. These estimates need to increase even further if the Navy distributes assets across a wider geographic area (DMO). Being unable to adequately supply the U.S. Navy (ships, support vessels and mariners), Air Force (planes, helicopters and aircrew), or Army (trucks, tanks, and warfighters) would lead to the devastating loss of people and assets. In short, this means that the availability of ships will be the single most important determining factor of the final outcome of any war that requires an international supply chain.

Note: Again, notwithstanding the lack of domestic capacity to build them, constructing 100 tankers is expensive and takes a very long time. Assuming a number of variables, one MR tanker costs around $50 million each, if built in a non-U.S. shipyard. 100 would cost 5 billion dollars.

### III. Icebreakers: The U.S. needs 5 icebreakers, but has "1.5"

The U.S. has significant interest in the Arctic and Antarctic, which may become major theaters of conflict. In the meantime, warming temperatures are likely to transform the Arctic into a major transportation route. Some industry analysts predict up to 80 million tons of cargo will traverse through the Arctic per year by 2030. The presence of U.S. icebreakers in these regions demonstrates an effective defensive capability and is useful for deterrent force projection.

Five heavy icebreakers operated by the U.S. Coast Guard, would allow two to be deployed in each polar region, with the 5th out of rotation for training, repairs or maintenance. Given the extended durations these vessels spend at sea, and the long distances they normally travel, heavy icebreakers are an ideal candidate for nuclear propulsion.

The U.S. currently has "1.5" icebreakers and an inability to construct required vessels on time, or on budget. The Coast Guard's only heavy icebreaker, *Polar Star,* is 46 years old, and is nearing the end of its useful service life; it relies on its out-of-service sister ship, *Polar Sea,* for spare parts. A next generation USCG polar icebreaker is due to be constructed in 2027. The acquisition of an existing commercial vessel, with a price tag of $150 million is being considered to fill the gap. While deliberations continue in the U.S. over where, when and how to complete the construction of heavy icebreakers, Russia has continued to strengthen its fleet of 40 nuclear, diesel-electric, and diesel-powered vessels; recently ordering the 6th and 7th nuclear-powered ships to complement the 5 that are currently being built. Russia is the only country that builds and operates nuclear-powered icebreakers.

*Exhibit 19: Ice breaker USCGC Polar Star (credit: U.S. Coast Guard)*

The commitment by Russia and other countries to build icebreaking ships is a clear declaration of intent. China currently has three icebreakers under construction, and recently (November 2023) sent two icebreaker vessels and a cargo ship - with more than 460 personnel on board - to build a new research station on Inexpressible Island near the Ross Sea. The lack of U.S. icebreakers in these regions leaves U.S. merchant and military vessels vulnerable and heavily dependent on foreign assistance. Unless dramatic changes occur, the Arctic and Antarctic may well be regions the U.S. has to cede to other countries; the only two regions in the world that will exist beyond the reach and control of the U.S. Navy's surface fleet.

## IV. Sub-sea cables and infrastructure: The U.S. has three cable-laying / repair ships

There are more than 500 active and planned submarine cables, that stretch over 750,000 miles, and transport over 97% of intercontinental data to and from 1,400 coastal landing stations across the world. Around $10 trillion in transactions and countless amounts of information are transmitted across commercial and government-sector assets every day. The United States is connected to around 88 subsea cables, with another 12-17 connections due for completion in the coming years.

*Exhibit 20: Cable-laying ship USNS Zeus (credit: Military Sealift Command)*

The U.S. economy, and the majority of U.S. businesses are heavily dependent on the global connectivity provided by these subsea cables. In parallel, as cables are being deployed, hostile actors are developing capabilities to significantly disrupt subsea infrastructure; as witnessed with the Nord Stream natural gas pipeline sabotage in September 2022, and the severing of an undersea fiber-optic cable in Norway, in 2021.

The United States needs advanced capabilities and purpose-built assets to inspect and protect critical subsea infrastructure. This may include repairing severed or sabotaged cables, constructing offshore or deepwater observation sites, or conducting search and rescue missions in deep-sea areas. The recent fatal disaster involving the *Oceangate Titan* tourist submersible demonstrated the ability of the U.S. private sector - ably assisted by the U.S. Coast Guard - to perform complicated recovery operations at great depths; an admirable display in incredibly trying conditions. Another accident that required highly specialized equipment and deeply skilled operators to resolve, was the deepwater *Macondo* explosion and oil spill, in the Gulf of Mexico that began on the 20th April, 2010.

The National Security mandates of the U.S. Navy and U.S. Coast Guard must extend to investment and construction, or the intelligent acquisition of a fleet of subsea vessels and equipment. The Maritime Security Program 'Cable Security Fleet' (CSF) has access to two cable laying ships, Transoceanic Cable Ship Co's Decisive and Dependable. A pathway to replace the other cable repair ship USNS Zeus, T-ARC-7 must be explored. Zeus was built in 1984 and is nearly 40 years old.

*Exhibit 21: Heavy lift ship MV Blue Marlin carrying USS Cole following October 2000 terrorist attack (credit: U.S. Navy)*

In total, the U.S. may require access to an additional 15 'specialty ships' from the commercial sector, such as cable laying and repair vessels, heavy lift ships, and salvage ships.

**Acquiring a 1120-vessel U.S. maritime fleet**

To be clear, this book is not advocating that the U.S. Navy (or any other public agency) builds and operates these vessels on a day to day basis. Such an exercise would be prohibitively expensive and take too long:

- As a thought exercise, the average cost to build a container ship in a U.S. shipyard today is around $300 million. So for a fleet of 1000 vessels, this would cost $300 billion in construction expenditure alone. This is just the CAPEX cost for the vessels - not the CAPEX and workforce to build the additional shipyard capacity needed, nor the operating expenses of around $12 billion of salary alone for the approximately 60,000 U.S. mariners needed to operate the vessels. Fuel and maintenance would add additional annual operating costs. There are just under 100 shipyard berths for shipbuilding and repairs in the U.S. today. Assuming half of these are devoted to building a new 1000 vessel fleet (and the other half kept aside for existing construction, maintenance and repairs), it would take 40 years to build a fleet of 1000 vessels, by which time some of these vessels would need to be retired. By way of comparison, this would be the equivalent of one quarter of the Bipartisan Infrastructure Law of 2021 signed by President Biden, which approved $1.2 trillion spending - one of the largest infrastructure budgets ever authorized.

- Similarly, purchasing 1000 vessels from foreign shipyards at a cost of $30 million each would cost $30 billion in total and would effectively be a direct subsidy to foreign shipyards. This is why more creative and cost-effective policy levers are proposed for the U.S. to access such vessels, which is explored in more detail in the U.S. Maritime National Action Plan in the concluding chapters of this book.

## B. Unfit for Purpose: RRF, MSP and VISA

Current maritime assets required for National Security are not fit-for-purpose or exist in a dilapidated state, and in most instances, would significantly hamper military operations if deployed.

### I. The Ready Reserve Force

The 'ghost ships' of the National Defense Reserve Fleet (NDRF), and 'zombie fleet' of the Ready Reserve Force (RRF) pose a distinct threat to naval support operations. At its peak in 1950, the NDRF had 2,277 ships in lay-up; now less than 100 exist, in various states of decay and disrepair. The RRF is a subset of the NDRF. The 48 ships of the RRF are younger - on average 46 years old - but nearly impossible to operate and maintain, present difficulties when sourcing replacement parts, and represent a backwards-step when training younger mariners. 27 of these 48 ships are steam-powered, which adds to operating complications, including longer spool up times, and a larger carbon footprint.

*Exhibit 22: The James River Ready Reserve Fleet in September 1990 (credit: U.S. Navy)*

A Sealift 'Turbo Activation' trial was completed in 2019. It did not go well. Former Administrator of MARAD, Rear Admiral

Mark Buzby shared his frustrations with the various failures that occurred:

- **Readiness:** Despite being (technically) manned by maintenance crews, and (supposedly) kept in a ready state, “only 60% of ships were considered ready, and less than 40% were able to depart port and act effectively in partnership with the military”. By comparison, there was an 80% activation rate for Desert Storm in 1990, and 92% in 2003 at the start of the Iraq War.

- **Responsiveness:** “Age is the main reason why the response was so troubling. The vessels are on average, 45+ years-old and they spend a lot of time sitting idle, maintained by skeleton crews. When they’re called upon to activate within 48 hours, the systems don’t always work.”

- **Resiliency:** “I’m finding myself in competition with the military sealift command for drydocking space,” We both have big ships and there are a certain number of dry docks that can take our ships. We’re both kind of fighting at times for space to get in there. When the ships do get into drydock, the maintenance often takes longer than anticipated because work crews discover more wear and tear problems than what was known.” He added “They’re more broken because they’re old”.

- **Retention:** 682 mariners were called up to flesh-out crews over the ten day Activation period. While that worked, “We got it, but the industry felt it,” Buzby said. His concluding remarks were sobering: “This was only a ten-day call. But if this was going to be an open-ended call, one has to wonder if there would be the same turnout.”

The RRF, along with other maritime assets are supposed to (directly and effectively) support the U.S. Army, Navy, and Marine Corps. If these vessels cannot even successfully steam out of port, how can they traverse the ocean, or exist for any duration in a contested environment? How can they be successfully crewed if the mariners are not available? And if requested mariners do report for duty, how are they expected to operate vessels that may well be older than they are? To reinforce this sentiment, in a March 2023 joint hearing of House Armed Services Committees, Administrator of the U.S. Maritime Administration (MARAD), Ann Phillips stated that she "was not at all confident" that all the ships in the Ready Reserve fleet could be crewed if called to duty in a crisis.

The limitations and failures of the RRF are worth exploring, as they are symptomatic of a lack of investment, strategy and understanding that is present across many other areas of the U.S. maritime sector. The RRF specifically demonstrates that:

- **Number of ships - rather than the usefulness of ships - does not encourage healthy outcomes:** The RRF's dysfunctionality and shortcomings have predominantly occurred because of poorly applied government capability assessments. This means the U.S. government continues to pay for outdated vessels that mostly sit idle and are maintained by skeleton crews, rather than replace them with more modern, fit-for-purpose ships. Put simply, in the minds of the current administrators, acquiring a certain number of vessels is more important than maintaining fully capable ones.
  Applying incentives in this fashion has not led (and will not lead) to positive outcomes that provide the necessary capacity to meet sealift obligations or benefit the U.S. military. In a highly probable worst-case scenario, U.S. armed forces would deploy overseas, and

then find themselves without the requisite ships to deliver critical stores, supplies, fuel, vehicles or replacement equipment. This lack of logistics support would severely slow the tempo of military operations, adversely delay the completion of strategic objectives and, most worryingly, endanger the lives of warfighters, aircrew, mariners and other serving personnel. Additionally, the preponderance of steam-powered engines reduces the pool of candidates qualified to service them, should that need arise.

- **The RRF's 'layup' management model is inefficient and ineffective:** Ask anyone who owns their own, and they'll likely express some variation on the saying "A boat is a hole in the water you throw money into." Idle ships are continually exposed to the elements, corrosive sea salt, and the impact and stresses of the wind and tides. Ongoing maintenance is required to remove rust, protect against corrosion, repair worn out components, and lubricate moving parts, among a long list of other activities. Keeping the 48 ships of the RRF in a perpetual state of semi-readiness is incredibly expensive; given that most of the RRF ships have been proven to be *un*ready, this is money that is not being well spent.
  A more superior 'engaged' model is used in the Civil Reserve Air Fleet (CRAF). As per official guidelines: "To participate in the international segments of CRAF, carriers must maintain a minimum commitment of 30 percent of its CRAF capable passenger fleet and 15 percent of its CRAF capable cargo fleet. Aircraft must be U.S.-registered, and carriers must commit and maintain at least four complete crews for each aircraft." This model utilizes aircraft that are already in active rotation and subsequently can be called upon without fear they aren't available or cannot activate in the

required manner. Maintenance, upkeep, properly trained crews and other responsibilities are handled by the (commercial) asset owner, massively reducing management costs and program overheads.

- **The model for vessel acquisition is inherently flawed:** Modern ships that were first selected for the Maritime Security Program (MSP) aged 15 years or less, usually end up in the Ready Reserve Force. They become RRF ships once they reach 25 years for a dry cargo ship and 20 years for a tanker, which means the RRF ends up with ships that are 20+ years old and subsequently require more expensive maintenance to maintain operational readiness. These aging ships are usually foreign-built, are less efficient (in fuel use and other consumables) and cannot be operated unless an older, suitably skilled crew is available. As previously mentioned, the two RORO's that were most recently purchased by MARAD for the RRF, *Freedom* and *Honor*, are both over 26 years old already.

In conclusion, the Ready Reserve Force is not fit-for-purpose. Due to reduced numbers, inability to activate, and an inappropriate fleet blend, it is neither Ready, nor much of a Reserve Force, either. Incentives do not encourage healthy outcomes, the layup management model is ineffective, and the selection process for ships entering the program is inherently flawed. A complete rethink of how the RRF is managed and incentivized is urgently required. To be clear: These problems will *not* be fixed by extending the life of the RRF to 60 years (or more), as was recently proposed. Doing so will exacerbate the long list of underlying problems associated with maintaining an aging fleet, while continuing to pose an unacceptable risk to the men, women and operations of the U.S. Army, Navy, Air Force and Marines.

## II. MSP and VISA

Reminder: The Maritime Security Program (MSP) is a fleet of 60, relatively modern, U.S.-registered, U.S.-flagged, congressionally-funded, militarily-useful ships commonly engaged in commercial trade. The MSP stipend is $5.3M per vessel, per year, has 60 vessels (2,400 mariners), and costs $318 million / year.

The Voluntary Intermodal Sealift Agreement (VISA) is a partnership between the U.S. Government and the maritime industry to provide the DOD with commercial sealift and

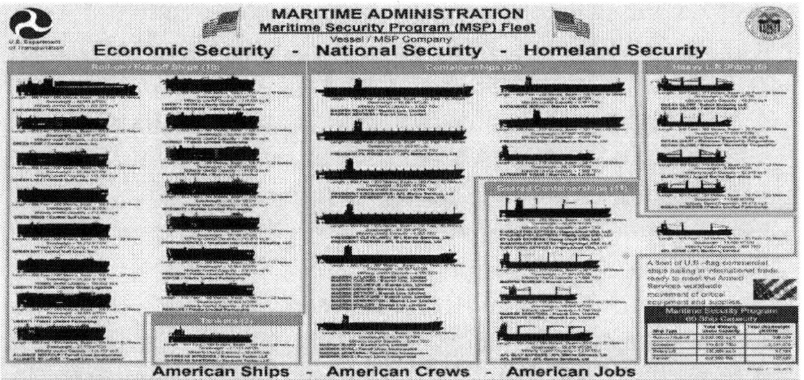


*Exhibit 23: The Maritime Security Program Fleet (credit: MARAD)*

intermodal equipment during national emergencies or wartime operations. VISA partners are not paid a stipend and are incentivized instead through preferential access to move DOD and other cargo.

There are several challenges that exist within the MSP and VISA programs. Far beyond being inconvenient, these complexities represent a significant risk to National Security:

- **The available fleet does not match military requirements:** The current fleet blend is entirely dictated by the ships that can be acquired, or the ships that commercial operators have made available. This blend may not (and, for the most part, does not) match the requirements of the U.S. military. Access to certain common types of vessels - e.g., container ships - is assured, but direct access to others is not. For example no enrolled vessels provide the means to lift and transport other ships on the water, which poses a challenge for the recovery and repair of damaged ships in wartime. The current model, particularly in the VISA program is a demonstration of 'the tail wagging the dog' - U.S. military requirements are subservient to the capabilities of available vessels, rather than the U.S. military actively choosing the best vessels that match the required Force posture, and that can sustain Fleet operations. And, unlike the rigid (U.S.-built, U.S.-controlled) standards that are in place for other branches of the U.S. military, many vessels in the MSP are made in China, and most contain Chinese parts.

- **The model for involvement and acquisition supports foreign interests:** The subcontracting, tendering, and approval processes for acquisition are fraught with delays and are uneconomical. Most MSP ships are foreign-built, and many participants in the VISA program operate under the influence of non-U.S., multinational companies. When an MSP ship reaches a pre-set age limit - MSP rules stipulate 25 years for a dry cargo ship and 20 years for a tanker - it is usually rotated into the RRF, and replaced by a younger equivalent. Due to a lack of U.S.-made ships, it is likely that the replacement MSP vessel is foreign-built. So in a rather perverse way, the U.S. Maritime Security Program directly supports the growth and profitability of foreign shipyards and companies. To make matters worse, this also means these programs indirectly support the political and military endeavors of the various countries associated with them; even if those regimes are at odds with U.S. values or geopolitical interests.

- **Program incentives are unsustainable:** Vessels enrolled in the VISA program are supported by U.S. Cargo Preference laws. This means the vessels receive preference to carry U.S. military and non-defense commercial agency cargoes, including food aid and Export Import (EXIM) Bank trade. However, changes in food aid preference requirements and a range of other factors have reduced the amount of cargo available to participating carriers. The drawdown in Afghanistan, and a general reduction in overseas military engagements has also reduced military cargo volumes.

  If cargo volumes decline beyond commercially sustainable levels, carriers will exit the program, further decreasing the availability of required vessels. This was confirmed in a 2015 analysis, where MARAD reported that "U.S. humanitarian assistance cargoes are the greatest source of preference cargo," and representing over half of all dry cargoes shipped by government agencies since 2002. The report detailed that since the year 2000, the U.S. fleet "had shrunk dramatically as U.S. food aid cargoes plummeted 77%", even though DOD cargoes "increased by 60% during the same period."

  Cargo preference requirements extend U.S. military and U.S. aid providers assured access to commercial maritime assets when required. However, there is a complete lack of transparency if the right (legal, allowable) assets are being used for these purposes. A review in 2022 by the Government Accountability Office (GAO) found the main reason for this was because MARAD had not taken any enforcement actions "because it had not developed the necessary regulations" to do so, "primarily due to challenges in reaching consensus with other agencies on how to implement cargo preference requirements". MARAD acknowledged that this lack of enforcement meant "federal agencies and their contractors are able to ignore and circumvent the cargo preference laws." This represents a fundamental flaw in how the program is administered, and introduces a range of covert and overt security risks into the U.S. military supply chain.

- **U.S. merchant mariner shortfall:** There is a shortage of skilled, certified U.S. citizen mariners to operate the surge and commercial fleets as they presently stand, let alone in an extended, major conflict. This means that even if the fleets associated with these programs were expanded, there would not be enough U.S. mariners to crew the supplied vessels. As will be explored in more detail throughout the rest of this book, there is an enhanced risk to military operations if foreign mariners are required. Non-U.S. citizens are unlikely to sacrifice their own safety to assist the United States in a time of conflict, and in many instances, might be personally, emotionally or politically aligned to the opposing regime or country.

## C. Diminished Domestic Control and Productivity

Foreign dominance, ownership and control over the U.S. maritime sector; diminished collaboration between Defense and the private sector; the potential for military activities to seriously disrupt the U.S. economy, and lagging domestic capacity all directly affect National Security.

## I. Dependence on non-U.S. vessels and mariners

Due to a distinct lack of U.S.-owned shipping companies, and a long history of underinvestment in the maritime sector, around 98% of all U.S. imports and exports are shipped on vessels wholly controlled by other countries. These vessels are commonly registered through 'Flags of Convenience' (FOCs). FOCs are commonly attached to nations that impose minimal tax and regulatory burdens, or have high levels of State participation and subsidies. Vessels operating under an FOC do not have U.S. beneficial owners, and are much less likely to have any U.S. crew.

While the use of cheaper foreign vessels provides some benefits during times of peace, it represents a serious National Security risk in times of war: Firstly, there is no guarantee that foreign-owned merchant ship operators, or foreign-flagged or FOC shipowners will comply with U.S. requests for support or assistance, during times of instability or war. How might this happen? Flag States may refuse to allow their vessels to enter a war zone so as not to offend an ally or compromise existing business interests.

Furthermore, vessel owners may not wish to charter vessels to the U.S. military because of the fear of public scrutiny that would lead to a decrease in market share. Secondly, carrying U.S. military cargo might also be detrimental to future business associations, which may mean some operators classify it as unviable, and wouldn't ever consider it as an option; even if they have been offered significant premiums. This distinct lack of control calls into question the mentality that the U.S. 'could buy their way out' of such a problem; if it is complicated during peacetime, then it will become almost impossible during times of war.

This problem first became apparent during World War One, when overseas combatants withdrew merchant vessels from U.S. trade routes in order to support their own war efforts. At the time, the U.S. domestic fleet was only capable of conducting around 10% of waterborne commerce, so the withdrawal of foreign vessels had immediate consequences for the economy. This was rectified during World War Two, when concern about the adequacy of the domestic fleet led the government to build a staggering 5,777 cargo vessels to support the war effort.

Dependencies on foreign-flagged vessels, carriers and crews are more pronounced today, because the United States is significantly more reliant on overseas trade and offshore sources for many essential items. A range of machinery and equipment, food products, critical minerals, spare parts, textiles, chemicals, medical supplies, and raw materials are all imported into the U.S. on a regular basis. For example, the U.S. imported $3.35 trillion dollars of goods from other countries in 2022, and over $516 billion from China alone. A large percentage (around 40% of all imports) are delivered by ship; around $1.8 trillion in total, during 2022. As has been articulated previously, around 99% of these ships are not under direct U.S. control, and do not have any U.S. crew.

## II. Diminished collaboration between Defense and the private sector

Collaboration between the military and commercial maritime partners in the private sector can yield a range of highly profitable, mutually-beneficial outcomes. One way collaboration is expressed between these sectors is through the development of 'dual-use' technologies. 'Dual-use' refers to any innovation, equipment, asset or technology that has both military and commercial applications. Dual-use innovations are usually first proven to work, scale and be saleable in the commercial domain; this means they can then be repurposed with less effort and expenditure into a military context.

The U.S. has lagged other nations in coordinating, resourcing or investing in the development of dual-use assets. The U.S. has also not established any formalized dual-use policies to encourage and grow partnerships between the two sectors. While some effort has been made in recent years, the impact and implementation of developed solutions remain largely unnoticeable and incomplete. Due to higher barriers to entry, the somewhat complex nature of naval operations, and a lack of investment, these types of innovations are even rarer in the maritime domain.

In order for dual-use technologies to remain viable in the open market, they must also be covered by adequate legal protections. These protections are also designed to make technologies more difficult to steal or be copied by others. Most countries use export control laws to protect innovation and military superiority, but these are often difficult to apply to technology. The U.S. International Trade and Arms Regulation (ITAR) is infamous for being too strict, which lowers the chance that newly developed technologies that are tested or developed in the U.S., can be shared with other countries. Reciprocally, this also makes it more difficult for other countries to introduce new technologies into the U.S. market. Recent discussions under the AUKUS agreements between Australia, the United Kingdom and the United States have led to increased scrutiny of ITAR and other export controls for various types of missile systems, weaponry, and unique forms of propulsion; for example, those required for the nuclear submarine program that is the cornerstone of the AUKUS agreement. The collective hope for these negotiations is that revised ITAR restrictions will allow for faster, mutually-beneficial transfers of military technologies, and trade secrets, to occur between allied countries.

Another method to encourage collaboration between the U.S. military and commercial maritime operators is through exercises, drills and simulations. While some exercises have been completed with overseas allies - e.g., with NATO forces stationed across Europe - they are often limited in scope as they don't involve creative or aggressive multi-domain adversaries, or a complete blend of commercial support partners. Another constraint is that information sharing between participants is (often deliberately) restricted. Multi-stakeholder virtual simulations and desktop wargaming offers an alternative. While simulations might be informative, they would be nearly impossible to practically apply in a U.S. maritime context, due to the diminished capacity of the 'real world' U.S. commercial maritime fleet.

The U.S. Air Force and U.S. Army regularly perform exercises, drills, and live-fire simulations; in many instances, in close collaboration with commercial support divisions. The Air Force's two-week advanced aerial combat training 'Red Flag' exercises attract hundreds of aircraft, and are held several times a year. Red Flag aims to offer realistic air-combat training for military pilots over a variety of realistic combat scenarios. Similarly, every year, about 1/3 of the Army's active-duty brigades regularly meet to strategize and run combat training at the National Training Center (NTC) at Fort Irwin, in the Mojave Desert.

The U.S. Navy does not have an equivalent to Red Flag or the National Training Center, and does not regularly conduct exercises with U.S. commercial maritime operators or the U.S.-Flag fleet.

The most common justification for this discrepancy is that the U.S. Navy relies on active deployment to hone tactical skills and develop new strategies. While being constantly deployed ensures that all core Navy assets are combat ready, it makes it extremely difficult to train alongside an appropriate blend of commercial ships, in a coordinated and realistic fashion; primarily because it would mean that commercial ships would need to abandon existing, profitable trades, and travel long distances to join the Fleet. The U.S. Navy may be presently vulnerable to a range of threats that might have been discovered during practice scenarios with the U.S. merchant marine. These risks could include equipment malfunctions, mismatches in procedures, misunderstandings about roles or how to cope with changing operational tempos, or an inability for personnel to communicate clearly when joining a formation, or when under fire.

These problems were highlighted by U.S. Merchant Marine Captain John Konrad in an opinion piece written in 2022. Despite many years of study and at-sea training in the Merchant Marine, Konrad asks: "How do I join a military convoy? How do I share information with Naval Intelligence? How do I contact a naval vessel on a secure line? How do I navigate a minefield? Will zig-zagging help me avoid modern submarines? What do I secure for radio silence? How do I darken my ship to naval standards? The answer to all these questions (and countless more) is… I don't have a clue."

The conflict in the Red Sea is providing an important opportunity for the U.S. Navy to work directly alongside U.S. commercial carriers in a live-fire environment. While safety is of critical concern, the convoy and escort operations being conducted in the Red Sea and surrounding area could also be used to hone and refine merchant marine and naval collaboration, and identify conflict-tested dual-use procedures or equipment.

## III. The U.S. Maritime 'Double-counting Conundrum' and the domestic economy

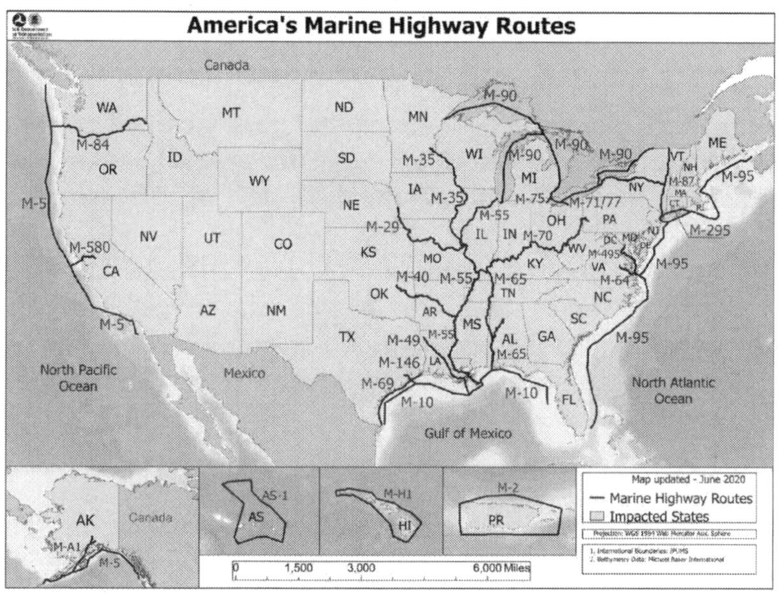


*Exhibit 24: The U.S. Marine Highways Program (credit: U.S. Department of Transportation)*

The existing U.S. commercial fleet is mostly dedicated to serving routes between domestic ports. The predominance of this fleet - barges, ferries, container ships and bulk carriers - perform an admirable job of moving cargo around the country both coastwise and via a network of 'marine highways' e.g., along the Mississippi and Columbia-Snake rivers, and around the Great Lakes. This trade must be performed by U.S.-registered vessels that cannot easily be migrated to military duty without severely impacting domestic economic production.

This presents a problem dubbed the 'Double-counting Conundrum.'

Many maritime commentators, analysts and even senior administrators tend to forget that once a maritime asset is removed from domestic trade and repurposed for the military, that it cannot simultaneously fulfill its originally intended purpose. For example, there are around 45 tankers engaged in U.S. domestic trade that some argue could be used to assist with international naval operations. While it is feasible to assume that *any* available domestic asset might one day be called upon to assist with the war effort, a pragmatic assessment reveals three serious flaws with this position:

- Firstly, domestic vessels would need to be deemed capable and ready to handle the more extreme conditions of the open ocean. Performing the necessary checks or conversions would take expertise, resources and some time to complete.

- Secondly, an appropriate crew is needed that has the experience to command the vessel across the ocean, and to safely join in with naval fleet operations. Even if the existing crew were retrained, this would take expertise, resources and some time to complete.

- And finally, and most critically, the removal of these 45 tankers - or any other similar vessel engaged in domestic supply - would have a negative impact on local transportation and manufacturing, cause a significant reduction in production and output, and hamper the operations of the very industries that would be desperately needed to support the war effort.

Right from the outset, the removal of tankers (e.g., to join or rejoin the TSP), container ships, bulk carriers, ROROs or other transport ships (e.g., to join or rejoin the MSP) from rotation would devastate regions that are dependent on domestic trade and transportation; this includes Hawaii, Puerto Rico, Alaska, the U.S. Virgin Islands, and Pacific territories such as Guam. Due to the distances involved and comparatively small cargo-carrying capacity, it would be unsustainable to supply these regions via plane for any protracted period of time. The removal of domestic ships would also force the following outcomes:

- A lack of fuel, oil or lubricants would lead to an inability to run the machinery required to produce arms, ammunition, missiles, military vehicles and equipment

- A reduction in transport capacity would mean this produced materiel could not be shipped around the country, or to the front line

- Without bulk carriers, there would be a noticeable drop in agricultural distribution (imports and exports), which would ruin the livelihoods of many rural towns and communities

- Without containerized imports, the output of the manufacturing and construction sector would be extremely impacted, due to an inability to source spare parts, chemical additives, or raw materials from international suppliers.

However, the most dramatic consequences might be seen if deliveries were deprioritized for the food and retail trading sectors. The psychological effect of reducing access to essential products could rapidly destroy consumer confidence, generating angst and social instability, which may lead to - local economy destroying - civil unrest or riots; a recent precedent being the 'Great Toilet Paper Crisis' of 2020.

## IV. Domestic commercial maritime industrial base

Examples of domestic partnerships capable of producing highly scalable commercial maritime solutions, are few and far between. The small number of private companies in operation are mostly focused on building for the U.S. Navy, or vessels that ply domestic trades. More work needs to be done to increase the number and capabilities of companies involved in the commercial maritime sector, and in a way that allows these providers to competitively cater for the needs of the international market. When solidified through strong alliances, increased maritime capacity carries noticeable benefits during peacetime - e.g., increased productivity leads to a net increase in GDP - and during times of war; as the industrial base resiliently adjusts output to replace, replenish and repair damaged or destroyed vessels and equipment.

As previously mentioned, one third of the U.S. Navy's ~300 ships are constantly deployed at any one time; the other two thirds are either preparing to deploy, or being repaired or rested. Roughly half of the surface and subsurface Fleet is deployed throughout the Atlantic, and the other half in the Pacific. The sheer volume of personnel and assets involved in a modern Naval operation was witnessed in late October 2023, when the USS Dwight D. Eisenhower Carrier Strike Group joined the USS Gerald R. Ford in the eastern Mediterranean. These vessels were deployed for deterrent power projection, and to ensure the Israel-Hamas conflict did not expand into a wider regional conflict. The two Carriers - along with eight armed escorts, submarines, and support vessels - shifted over 12,000 U.S. Navy personnel (and support crew) into the region. Any sudden increase in operational tempo places a strain on the domestic resources that are required to keep forces deployed. Ships returning from the battlefield require repairs and upgrades, while the crews rotate and rest. New ships might be needed if older ones are retired, or to meet strategic objectives. The

United States needs a highly-efficient, domestic maritime industrial base that can match the operational tempo of the U.S. Navy.

The United States does not possess a highly-efficient, domestic maritime industrial base.

While improvements have happened over the last 5 years, naval shipbuilding and repairs have been more expensive, and taken longer to complete than expected. Naval Sea Systems Command (NAVSEA) is responsible for coordinating these three functions for the U.S. Navy. NAVSEA employs 80,200 personnel, and with an allocation of almost $30 billion, accounts for nearly one quarter of the Navy's entire budget. Referencing shipbuilding performance in an interview in early 2023, NAVSEA Commander Vice Admiral Bill Galinis stated "We're seeing on time delivery rates in the 40% range… and to deliver a ship on the committed date, we're averaging around 40% ... which clearly does not meet Fleet requirements." Navy repairs have experienced similar delays. A January 2023 report from the Government Accountability Office (GAO), found that since 2011, the U.S. Navy's warships have been spending less time at sea and more time under costly and lengthy repairs. The GAO review was conducted on 151 surface warships, and discovered lengthy maintenance delays, an increase in breakdowns requiring repairs and an escalation in part 'cannibalization' due to shortages in the industry supply chain. For example, the USS Connecticut was damaged in 2021 and will likely not be repaired for at least another 5 years. The Ticonderoga-class guided missile cruiser USS Vicksburg has been undergoing conversion and repairs that have cost over $300 million dollars, so far; plans to retire Ticonderoga-class vessels, may mean the Vicksburg may not ever reenter active service. The Los Angeles-class nuclear-powered attack submarine USS Boise (SSN-764) has been in dry dock for 8 years, and has so far cost over $250 million in repairs. Attack submarines USS Albany's maintenance was completed 570 days late, and USS Asheville 670 days late.

The sole responsibility for these delays cannot be leveled at the Navy: Lagging construction, repair and conversion times are symptomatic of much wider problems within the U.S. maritime sector. Time to commit, time to complete and time to repair would markedly drop if the U.S. *commercial* maritime industrial base was operating at a complementary size and scale, and if dual-use, dual-purpose policies were employed for construction and repairs. This technique has been witnessed overseas - most notably in China - where the same (or twinned) shipyards build, repair and deploy naval and commercial vessels; in the same shipyard and often at the same time. A dual-purpose, dual-use approach speeds up builds for both naval and maritime assets, by leveraging economies of scale, and utilizing similarly-skilled teams to oversee and complete the work. The U.S. has not invested in increasing domestic commercial maritime industrial capacity to match the operational tempo of the U.S. Navy, and does not currently have shipyards configured for dual-use construction. Modern policies have not considered or encouraged investment in this capability, either. The recently proposed 'U.S. Shipyard Act' (May, 2023) was almost entirely focused on boosting the Navy's capacity, but devoid of any plans to increase the capacity of the U.S. domestic commercial maritime industrial base.

The deficiencies present in the U.S. domestic commercial industrial base confirm an unpalatable truth: The result of the next major global conflict may be entirely determined by the presence, or absence of shipping, with any given nation likely to have no more ships to support a war effort than whatever was owned on the first day of hostilities. This means the possibility that even though the United States greatly outspends countries like Russia and China: "For want of a sail…the empire was lost."

## D. Emerging Technologies, Modern Threats

### I. Cybersecurity

The U.S. Cybersecurity and Infrastructure Security Agency (CISA) defines "16 critical infrastructure sectors whose assets, systems, and networks… are considered so vital to the United States that their incapacitation or destruction would have a debilitating effect on security, national economic security, national public health or safety, or any combination thereof." Shipping is directly involved in 10 of these sectors: Chemical, Communications, Critical Manufacturing, Dams, Defense Industrial Base, Energy, Food and Agriculture, Government Facilities, Transportation Systems, and the Nuclear Reactors, Materials, and Waste Sector. Given the high degree of exposure each of these sectors has to shipping, there is a clear need to protect all participants and assets in the U.S. maritime sector, to stop 'incapacitating, debilitating or destructive' events from occurring.

Subsequently, maritime cybersecurity threats pose a significant National Security risk to the United States, especially as the size of vessels, and the velocity of trade increases. Cyberattacks take many forms, but are commonly performed by criminals or malicious individuals to illegitimately access digitally connected systems to steal data, intellectual property, or money; disrupt internal activities or operations; or damage an organization's brand or reputation. State-sponsored attackers act on behalf of a country's military or political leaders and often use cyberattacks to cripple an adversary's critical infrastructure, make political or social statements, or spread chaos and confusion.

The global maritime domain is subject to increasingly complex cybersecurity threats and disruptions. Almost all major shipping lines, and a number of service providers suffered significant outages from cyberattacks over the last six years: Port of Rotterdam (2017), Port of Long Beach (2018), San Diego (2018), Vancouver (2018), Kennewick, Washington (2020), and Houston (2021). Maritime service providers Maersk (2017), COSCO (2018), CMA-CGM (2020), MSC (2020), Saudi Aramco (2021), Tokyo MOU (2022), DNV Norway (2023), and when pro-Russian attackers targeted the websites of Rotterdam, Amsterdam, Den Helder and Groningen Ports in 2023.

Maritime cyberattacks are occurring with greater frequency, because of the steady convergence of OT (Operational Technology), and IT (Information Technology) systems. OT systems are usually manually operated, and while some have electronic components, are not commonly connected to any external networks; examples include levers, motors, steering components and hydraulic pumps. Information Technology systems come in many different form factors, are digitally-enabled and data-driven, and usually connected to a network, or the internet; examples include sensors, cameras, monitoring devices, wireless access points and printers.

While IT components have been integrated into the maritime domain for many years - GPS was introduced in the early 90s - the convergence of IT and OT is much more pronounced today, as most ships carry equipment that is connected to a local network, broadcasting to an external network, or connected to the internet. Some OT equipment may be operating in this fashion, without the express knowledge of support staff, or a ship's crew. This makes securing a maritime system or vessel difficult, as complex security vectors (holes) can now exist at every level of operational activity.

A modern connected asset is the ‘smart’ shipping container. From place of procurement, through to final delivery, global supply chains are heavily dependent on maritime links, and various forms of containerized transportation. Smart containers contain an array of sensors that monitor location and report on the condition of the cargo, via cellular or satellite connectivity. These containers are becoming more ubiquitous; it is expected that around 30% of worldwide inventories, some 10 million units, are expected to be fitted with some form of telemetry or monitoring hardware over the next five years. Securing these assets, and the data they accrue and transmit, will prove difficult; these containers already exist in a hostile physical environment, and will now also be exposed to an array of potent cybersecurity threats as they traverse the world.

Attacks can also impact sectors necessary to support key maritime activities like energy and transportation. The *Colonial Pipeline* attack in May of 2021, was the largest cyberattack against critical infrastructure ever to be publicly disclosed. The 5,500 mile long *Colonial Pipeline* starts in Texas and crosses through New Jersey, delivering refined oil for gasoline, jet fuel and home heating oil. It supplies nearly half of the fuel for the U.S. East Coast of the United States. The *Colonial Pipeline* attack started with data exfiltration (extraction via a digital channel) on May 6, 2021. This progressed to a full ransomware attack on May 7, which forced staff to take the Pipeline offline to reduce the risk of damage to the internal OT network. This followed on May 9th, when the attack was deemed a national security threat, prompting President Joe Biden to declare a state of emergency.

The *Colonial Pipeline* shutdown dramatically affected consumers along the East Coast, including the airline industry; there was a jet fuel shortage for many carriers, including American Airlines, and some disruption at nearby airports, including Atlanta and Nashville. Gas stations in northern South

Carolina and southern Virginia were hit the hardest; 71% of stations in Charlotte ran out of fuel on May 11 and 87% ran out in Washington, D.C., by May 14. Neighboring states, including Florida, Georgia, Alabama, Virginia and the Carolinas experienced panic-buying and long lines at the pumps, due to a fear of a gas shortage. The average price of gas spiked in the aftermath of the shutdown; in some areas, topping $3/gallon. While the pipeline resumed operations on May 12th - 6 days after the attack started - it took many weeks for calm to be restored.

The *Colonial Pipeline* attack had a dramatic impact on critical infrastructure and the U.S. public. This attack should be a wake-up call to the maritime sector, which has historically lagged other sectors in areas like technological readiness and securing connected systems. Disruptions at scale that often continue for some time past the initial attack - as witnessed on multiple occasions in the maritime domain - reflects an under investment in appropriate technologies, systems, protocols, and training at every operational level. Maritime assets along with all other forms of critical infrastructure must be carefully monitored for a range of emerging threats, especially from financially-motivated activists, or politically-motivated, state-sponsored attackers.

Even though these facts are well known, most participants in the supply chain (including vessel, port, and critical infrastructure operators) have not kept pace with emerging cybersecurity risks, and do not regularly invest in mitigation strategies to minimize potential threats. As witnessed with the *Colonial Pipeline*, a reluctance to protect vulnerable systems can quickly escalate from being an annoying business disruption, to a crippling National Security threat in the space of 24 hours. Similar risks exist across all critical infrastructure providers, in particular at U.S. ports, where ships from a range of foreign countries arrive and dock every day; potentially carrying cybersecurity threats in OT or IT equipment, or on devices owned by the crew.

Note: The Department of Energy (DOE) 2022 budget included a request of USD $201 million for the Office of Cybersecurity, Energy Security and Emergency Response to "advance policies, technologies and initiatives to increase the visibility of physical and cyber threats in the operational technology environment."

## II. Satellites and space

Satellite coverage has fundamentally changed the world by enabling global connectivity to anything, anywhere, at any time. Satellites provide coverage at the GEO (Geo-stationary Earth orbit), MEO (medium Earth orbit), HEO (Highly elliptical orbit) and, increasingly, the LEO (Low Earth orbit) layers. Connectivity to the internet and/or external private networks has become integral to the operations of a ship on the open ocean: improving positioning and navigation at sea; assisting with collision avoidance and emergency and disaster response; performing intelligent supply-chain and onboard system monitoring; and through personnel support, by connecting the crew with family and friends, or education, medical, and mental health services.

Two common maritime services reliant on satellite communications are Global Positioning Systems (GPS) and Automatic Identification Systems (AIS). GPS has significantly enhanced safety at sea, allowing vessels to perform route tracking, and avoid hazards like shoals, reefs, and coastlines. GPS also assists with efficient voyage planning, by optimizing routes that can minimize fuel consumption and reduce travel times. AIS was introduced by the IMO in 2000, and became effective for all ships at the end of 2004. AIS transponders provide automatic position and identification information to other ships and to coastal authorities at set intervals. AIS regulations include mandatory reporting for different types of information, and apply to ships of 300 gross tonnage or more, engaged on international voyages; cargo ships of 500 gross tonnage and upwards, not engaged on international voyages; and all passenger ships, irrespective of size.

GPS and AIS are very important to both naval and merchant shipping operations. By connecting different parties and transmitting actionable information, secure communications are now essential to maritime safety and security; including maintaining a rules-based order, and protecting Freedom of Navigation of the sea. Recent examples involving GPS spoofing dramatically highlight why this is so: AIS systems receive location data from the ship's GPS unit, which is then broadcast to other parties. A broad-scale GPS spoofing attack displaces the GPS location a ship is broadcasting, and replaces it with a false equivalent that can produce bizarre or erroneous results. For example, in 2017, more than 20 ships transiting the Black Sea reported their GPS positions were relocated 25 nautical miles inland to an airport in Novorossiysk. In mid-2021, three NATO warships - Royal Navy's USS Defender, the U.S. Navy's USS Ross and a Royal Dutch Navy vessel - had their locations spoofed to positions off Russian-occupied Crimea. GPS spoofing and jamming (blocking the signal) have been common throughout the Ukraine-Russia war.

While only used on a Navy ship in a supplementary role alongside other navigational systems, GPS and AIS are still important tools to monitor and maintain control of the ocean. For example, without accurate AIS signatures, tracking where vessels are can be made significantly more difficult. This is especially evident with the increased number of ‘dark,’ ‘gray,’ or ‘shadow’ fleet vessels traversing the world that deliberately disable their AIS transponders, in contravening the international laws governing the sea. These ships are commonly involved in illegal activities, such as fishing in protected areas or marine sanctuaries, smuggling guns, drugs or people, or shipping sanctioned oil.

Shadow Fleets are largely invisible to the U.S. Navy and other maritime enforcement agencies. Historically, such ships were only able to be spotted visually, or within the range of radar and other localized detection technologies. New space-based, optical, thermal, and emissions sensors - usually operating at the LEO layer, and at affordable prices - are opening up a range of previously inaccessible options for global enforcement. These new systems make what was previously invisible, visible, and across a global coverage area, with greater granularity and accuracy than has ever been seen before. The proliferation of these, and other space-based technologies means that within the next 10 years, it will be impossible to hide in the open ocean.

## III. Critical infrastructure

The technology challenges facing U.S. maritime gateways are many and varied, but escalate in complexity with the use of automated assets in the port environment. Over the last 10 years, a large number of container terminals have implemented some form of automation; digitally-enabled or remotely operated ship-to-shore (STS) container cranes, automatic straddle carriers, or equipment to weigh, scan or monitor containers and cargo. Once these assets are working at optimal levels, most ports experience noticeable improvements with container throughput and handling times, which generally leads to a decrease in vessel turnaround times.

While the benefits may seem obvious, there are also a number of risks associated with automated assets, particularly when it comes to cybersecurity. Nearly all automated equipment requires an active connection to a network, or the internet, so they can be monitored, checked, or remotely-controlled. This immediately imposes a requirement to protect the (converged) OT and IT systems used during normal operations, from attack, exploitation, or manipulation from an external adversary. The potential for the digitally-enabled and remotely-monitored STS cranes at U.S. ports to be attacked or compromised has been fiercely debated over the last two years in particular. Increased scrutiny has been applied largely because of the high percentage of cranes supplied into the U.S. market by one foreign company.

A report conducted by the Foundation for American (FoA) Innovation in August 2023 found that roughly 43 percent of ship-to-shore cranes in operation across major U.S. ports had been sourced from Shanghai Zhenhua Heavy Industries Company Limited (ZPMC), a subsidiary of China Communications Construction Co. The FoA report followed an earlier Pentagon review in March 2023, that found "up to 80%" of STS cranes at certain U.S. terminals were made by ZPMC. This is somewhat predictable, as ZPMC supplies 75% of all container cranes globally, however the presence of a high percentage of these cranes on the frontline of U.S. supply chains, however poses multiple risks to port operations, U.S. supply chains and therefore National Security.

The Pentagon, Department of Homeland Security (DHS) and a range of U.S. Senators all voiced their concerns about the possibility the cranes could be shut down with very little warning or recourse available to U.S. operators. Some commentators expressed concerns about the potential for espionage and spying. Several proposed solutions have been tabled, aimed at mitigating disruptions, should an adversary decide to disable, or remotely control the cranes via internet-connected interfaces. While the debate rages on, the dependency on ZPMC's cranes continues unabated in the background; with no near-term solution in sight.

## IV. Asymmetric Warfare: The new normal

The U.S. State Department defined the term 'asymmetric warfare' in the early 2000's as "Using an adversary's strength against him, while exploiting his weaknesses" and "Warfare in which belligerents are mismatched in their military capabilities or their accustomed methods of engagement". These concepts have appeared with greater frequency in recent times, but are essential military strategies that have been around for thousands of years. For example, in 500 BC, Sun Tzu wrote, "If the enemy is superior in strength, evade him. If his forces are united, separate them. Attack him where he is unprepared. Appear where you are not expected". In essence, Sun Tzu was arguing that "Exploiting an adversary's weaknesses while exploiting one's own strengths" is at the heart of the 'art of war'.

The potential to overlook the core principles of asymmetric warfare, and initiate a series of events that threaten U.S. military operations and endanger National Security was addressed by Franklin B. Miles, in a paper entitled 'Asymmetric Warfare: An Historical Perspective', written for the U.S. Army War College in 1999. Miles poses this thought: *"The critical question is whether U.S. military and government leaders are aware of the history of asymmetric warfare and are using that knowledge to adequately prepare our nation and soldiers, or to tailor our force structure, to successfully engage and defeat asymmetric enemies in future conflicts."*

Various forms of asymmetric warfare have been on display in the war between Ukraine and Russia. Examples include: Unmanned Aerial Vehicles (UAVs), Unmanned Surface Vessels (USVs), and the use of data and AI.

- **Unmanned Aerial Vehicle (UAV):** UAV's, or more commonly, drones, are aircraft that do not have any human pilot, crew, or passengers on board. UAVs vary in size, shape, range, dwell time, payload capacity and capability. Ukraine has deployed a range of drones since the beginning of the war; one of the most popular brands is the Mavic range of quadcopters from China's DJI, which can cost between $400-$2,000. According to recent estimates, the Ukrainian military and allied partners are buying around 60% of DJI's global output of Mavic drones.

  Whether for reconnaissance, dropping bombs or exploding on impact, drones are cheap and highly effective against a wide range of targets: personnel, tanks, other drones, parked aircraft and any asset in an open, outdoor, unprotected location. Cost and convenience are key factors in their continued use, making drones simultaneously dispensable, and indispensable. For example, a $400 drone may do the same amount of damage as a conventional projectile (e.g., a standard 155mm howitzer round) that can cost 10 times as much. Odds are still favorable even if multiple drones are required to take down a larger target, such as a tank or an expensive Russian military spy plane. The Ukrainian government wants to spend more than $1 billion to upgrade its drone-fighting capabilities over the coming years; 10,000 new drone pilots have been trained in the country since 2022.

- **Unmanned Surface Vessels (USV):** Drones are not just flying aircraft. There has been increased use of drones in the maritime domain as well. USVs (or autonomous ASVs) are fast, versatile and comparatively cheap to build and operate. The operations of the Russian surface fleet have been seriously impacted by the use of armed Ukrainian unmanned surface vessels on several occasions. Ukrainian USVs attacked Russian ships docked in Sevastopol, in October 2022. No ships were sunk, however the Ukrainians managed to damage two Russian ships, including the Admiral Makarov, the replacement for the sunk Black Sea Fleet's flagship guided-missile cruiser, *Movska.* Additional attacks using USV's have been conducted by Ukrainian forces as the conflict has continued, most recently in Crimea, in late January 2024. It's impossible to deny the effectiveness and lethality of USVs, especially given their low cost. The use of USVs in Ukraine should serve as an example for any country that may lack budgetary resources and need a credible presence at sea. For example, one of Ukraine's armed unmanned surface vessels costs around $274,000, which is extremely cheap when compared to even a small naval attack boat like Ukraine's Ada-class corvettes (with a price tag of over $236 million).

The U.S. Navy has recognized the importance of USVs and other unmanned systems, and factored them into the future Navy Fleet blend. This was confirmed by Capt. Scot Searles, program manager for unmanned maritime systems, at Sea Air Space in 2023: "By the middle of this century … up to 40 percent of the [U.S. Navy] fleet will be unmanned."

- **Data and AI:** Ready access to data, in a form that is easy to read, digest, and action can be the determining factor between winning and losing a skirmish; or, as is currently occurring in Ukraine, potentially an entire war. U.S. technology provider Palantir has played a key supporting role to the Ukrainian military through the deployment of '*MetaConstellation*', a software package that helps users find objects in real time. The system can request and capture data from radio signals, infrared light images and aerial photographs taken by satellites flying over conflict areas. The data captured and analyzed by *MetaConstellation* is augmented by an artificial intelligence (AI) system. This software package, and others like it in use by modern militaries around the world, illustrate the convergence of signals intelligence (SIGINT), satellite imagery and high-level data processing. No human is capable of performing accurate analysis on the sheer volume of data, images, or intercepted communications captured by these types of systems, which is why AI, along with Natural Language Processing (NLP) is commonly required.

The application of data and AI into a military context has become of heightened interest (and concern) for many governments around the world. The U.S. DOD requested $1.8 billion dollars for FY2024 for AI and machine-learning (ML), which will be used to "support efforts to deliver and adopt responsible AI/ML-enabled capabilities on secure and reliable platforms". The DOD budget request also includes $1.4 billion for Joint All-Domain Command and Control (JADC2) initiatives - including The U.S. Navy component, Project Overmatch - which aims to better connect sensors, shooters and networks. JADC2 will require the integration of AI and ML components if it is to match the capabilities of similar platforms that already exist in a commercial context.

The U.S. is familiar with asymmetric techniques in the maritime domain: Q-Ships or "Mystery Ships" were deployed during World War 2. These ships were generally heavily armed merchant ships and designed to act as a decoy, or perform some form of special service or offensive action. One method Q-

Ships employed was to lure in, and then sink the submarines that were assigned to perform commercial vessel inspections. While this has not been identified as a method the U.S. might use in future conflicts, other countries (and notably, China) have released graphical depictions of modern-day container ships equipped for warfare in a similar fashion to these historical examples.

Applying the lessons of asymmetric warfare and building rapidly, and at scale, U.S. company *Anduril* provides integrated solutions to the U.S. military, using modern technologies and techniques. For example, *Anduril's XL-AUV* - Extra Large Autonomous Undersea Vehicle - 'Dive-LD' uses advanced 3D printing to create a number of the vehicle's parts, including the outer hull. In May 2022, the Royal Australian Navy (RAN) ordered three of these underwater vehicles, at a cost of around $100 million dollars. While not directly involved in the same program, these three XL-AUVs will augment the other military surface and subsea systems involved in the - Australian, United Kingdom, and U.S. - trilateral security pact, AUKUS.

It is not possible to predict if the use of drones, ASVs, USVs, XL-AUVs, data or AI will be the deciding factor in future conflicts. However it is highly probable that these and related platforms will become increasingly interoperable, powerful, and prolific. Predictions aside, what can be determined with a high degree of confidence at this point in time, is that new forms of asymmetry demand a complete rethink of how maritime scenarios are fought (and won). In other words, an effective naval and maritime strategy must cater for the wars of the coming century, and not be built around the conditions, or context of the past.

## E. The Rise of China as a Maritime Power

*"We have, for too long, expected the world to play by our rules. In doing so, we failed to ask ourselves what would happen if these rules were incompatible with reality."* Army Gen. Stanley McChrystal, 2019, in the foreword to 'Goliath: Why the West Isn't Winning. And What We Must Do About It' by Sean McFate.

The global geopolitical landscape is rife with various forms of competition, counteractions, criminality and conflict. In parallel, there exists ample opportunities for collaboration, cooperation, co-dependencies, and congeniality. Whether interactions are perceived as positive or negative, largely depends on how two parties define or classify the relationship they share. Two classifications that can be applied in these situations are that of peers, or powers. Peers are friends. Powers are foes. Peers are affable rivals. Powers, hostile adversaries. Where peers overtly support, powers covertly oppose. Peers believe two entities can harmoniously coexist in the same place. Powers tend to displace others for sole occupation. Peers seek out win-win scenarios, while the contrasting lens of a power is win-lose; challengers must be forced into submission to maintain the correct hierarchical order. While peers consider mutually beneficial association, powers contemplate mutually assured destruction.

Designating a country, regime, or leader as a peer, or power, deserves careful and thoughtful consideration. Mislabeling carries dramatic consequences. Mistakenly believing an overt ally is supportive, when in fact they are not, can be just as disastrous as misjudging the actions of a covert opponent. Timing is also important: The early identification of a peer will likely lead to reciprocally profitable outcomes, while irreparable damage may occur if a power is identified too late.

The potential for one to transition to the other must also be regarded. This highlights the need for due diligence as partnerships are forged, and, equally, as they evolve over time. When considering all the peers and power associations that exist in the world today, the complex and complicated, evolving and evocative relationship between the United States and China commands the most attention.

## I. China and the Maritime Domain

China's influence has rapidly expanded across the world, at a scale and velocity that makes many U.S. commentators, administrators and military leaders uncomfortable.

### Context: How China views the world

China's geographic perspective on the world has been aptly described by Adjunct Professor at the U.S. Merchant Marine Academy, and host of the popular 'What's Going on With Shipping?' YouTube channel, Professor Sal Mercogliano. In a recent video, Sal encouraged viewers to visualize China's maritime position by spinning a world globe so it showed how sealanes and exits appeared from the perspective of mainland China. Placing the globe in this orientation clearly displays that China's only naval pathways are around Taiwan, up through Japan, or down through the Philippines; from 9,000 miles of coastline. Viewing it from this angle explains why regional actions by the U.S. and others are regarded as hostile, and also explains why China has taken specific steps to build and heavily invest in the maritime sector.

Secondly, to protect trading activity, and exert influence on regional and global affairs, China employs a multi-domain strategy that utilizes a broad spectrum of assets and techniques. The DIME (Diplomatic, Information, Military and Economic) model is often applied to these activities. DIME "seeks to avoid counter-productive and conflicting activities during tactical operations by considering these factors in a coordinated manner during mission planning and execution." A 2019 presentation by MARAD, referenced the DIME model to explain China's recent forays in the maritime domain:

*Exhibit 25: Shipping routes, as seen from China (credit: Economist, World Economic Forum, China Institute of International Studies)*

- **Diplomatic** - Includes government-to-government interactions; active involvement and advocacy at the United Nations; expressing and defending territorial claims

- **Information** - The use of propaganda, the media, internet, and academia to spread information (or disinformation) about China's agenda or activities

- **Military** - Deploying new combat ships or weapon systems; building and protecting artificial Islands; through coercion, or use of force, or area denial so that military intervention cannot occur

- **Economic** - Through the activities of the merchant fleet; port investment and development; by controlling trade; extending financial aid or assistance; and through Belt-and-Road Initiative

Thirdly, and most significantly: Across 2022, China imported around $177 billion from the United States, and exported around $581 billion. Total trade between the United States and China equaled $759 billion, less than that of the entire European Union ($847 billion) but greater than the totals of the next two countries - South Korea ($362 billion), and Japan ($357 billion) - *combined.* Furthermore, around 60 percent of all maritime trade passes through Asia, with the South China Sea (SCS) carrying an estimated one-third of the global total; around $5 trillion dollars' worth of goods annually. This means that approximately 15% of goods moving through the SCS are either moving from, or being sent to, the United States. These trade figures add commercial context to a complicated relationship that is often only characterized adversarially and militaristically.

## II. Eight Areas of Influence

The growth, and in some cases, outright dominance, of China's maritime capacity is clearly evident across eight different areas outlined on the pages that follow. Each of the eight areas contains a series of facts and figures, followed by a brief synopsis about how (and why) each might affect global maritime affairs, the United States, and U.S. National Security.

### 1. Navy

A comparison between the U.S. Navy and China's PLAN appears in the following table. Numbers have been gathered from an array of sources, confirmed through the 'World Directory of Modern Military Warships' (updated August 2023) and, where possible, via official press releases. If a data disparity exists, a range has been given.

| | China | United States |
|---|---|---|
| **Total Naval Battle Fleet size** | 355-425 | 243-293 |
| **Projected Fleet size (2030)** | ~440 | ~355 |
| **Battle Fleet tonnage** | 2,400,000 | 4,635,628 |
| **Median Hull Age (years)** | 13.8 | 23.3 |
| **Serving Personnel** | 240,000 | 438,000 |
| **Aircraft Carriers** | 2 | 11 |
| **Submarines** | 72-79 | 68 |
| **Naval Aircraft** | 437 - 712 | 4,012 |
| **Defense Spend (annual)** | \$300-\$700 billion | \$877 billion |

Comparing the numbers in each navy is thought-provoking, particularly when considering the current state and future trajectory of each Battle Force. China has a larger, younger fleet that will expand rapidly over the next 10 years, reaching an estimated 440 ships by 2030. By comparison, the U.S. has much higher tonnage - i.e., a smaller number of larger and more capable ships - and while lagging behind on total number, U.S. ships and submarines are generally regarded as superior to PLAN equivalents. Furthermore, U.S. spending may seem disproportionate to China (and indeed other world fleets) however must be taken in context: The U.S. has the only truly global blue-water fleet, and, due to higher standards and more advanced equipment, pays higher costs to maintain their fleet relative to most other countries.

A noticeable difference exists between aircraft carriers: With upwards of 5,000 sailors, and an attached air wing that is larger than the standing Air Force of many countries, the United States' nuclear-powered Carriers have unrivaled fighting capability. U.S. Carriers are deployed all over the world, and regularly used for hard power projection, and regional stabilization or peace-keeping duties; as is being witnessed with the presence of two carriers (USS Dwight D. Eisenhower and the USS Gerald R. Ford) that were recently deployed to the Mediterranean during the Israel-Hamas conflict. The United States has 11 Carriers, with a corresponding 11 Carrier Strike Groups. China has just two carriers that are smaller and much less capable, and have a fraction of the air power, fire power and experience of U.S. equivalents. A third carrier, the *Fujian,* has been built, and was due to complete sea trials at the end of 2023.

This comparative analysis brings into focus the pitfalls of comparing Fleet size and Fleet blend. Simply put, the total number of ships (or, vessels in a certain class) is not the best indicator of strength. For example, North Korea has one of the largest navies in the world, and eclipses the U.S. and China in certain categories. However real numbers are hard to verify, and many commentators describe the North Korean fleet as being “very old, and in poor condition”. Of greater relevance is the correct Fleet blend, which is why the U.S. Navy is regarded as the most lethal and capable in the world. With advanced technologies, highly trained personnel, and a sizable aircraft fleet (which is larger than the U.S. Air Force), the constantly-deployed U.S. Navy plays a critical role in maintaining global security and stability, and protecting Freedom of Navigation of the seas.

It should be noted that numbers do have *some* bearing on achieving certain tactical and strategic objectives. For example, a military planner with many ships at their disposal, can flexibly mix and match the fleet to cater for changing conditions. Additional assets also means a greater possibility for active-duty ships (and personnel) to be rested or rotated. Furthermore, being able to send a larger volume of ships into an active theater, even if many units are lost, may be the determining factor in winning or losing a skirmish or battle. This sentiment was recently conveyed by Pacific Fleet Commander Admiral Samuel J Paparo, when he channeled defense consultant theory from the 70-80’s, and stated: “Quantity has a quality, all of its own”.

**Implications:** China has purposefully directed, and will continue to invest a significant amount of money, resources and effort into Naval strategy and shipbuilding activities over the next decade. This will test U.S. naval dominance on the open ocean, and may even lead to a new status quo that involves sharing responsibility for policing the world’s oceans. As this happens, China's evolving Navy - with a growing Fleet size, differing Fleet blend and more frequent deployment schedule - will introduce unpredictable variables for the maintenance of Freedom of Navigation, and also challenge the U.S.-centric rules-based-order that has been a core component of global affairs over the past century.

## 2. Commercial Maritime Fleet

China controls the second-largest number of merchant vessels in the world; around 9,000 vessels if fleet numbers from connected territories are included. This growth has been relentless over the last two decades: China only controlled about one-twentieth of the global merchant ship fleet in the early 2000s, and now directly commands one-seventh (around 15%). China overtook Greece in total global commercial tonnage, in August 2023. China also maintains indirect influence over a large proportion of other ships and maritime assets, including visibility of around 65% of the world's shipping tonnage through strategic Flag State partnerships.

China is a dominant player in the global container shipping market. This is abundantly clear when assessing one company in particular; state-owned China Ocean Shipping (Group) Company (COSCO). As of June 2023, COSCO has the largest fleet in the world, comprising 1,372 vessels, with a total rated capacity of 111 million deadweight tons (dwt). COSCO's container fleet can carry 3.04 million TEU, and is ranked fourth overall in the world. To put that in perspective, this means that *one Chinese company* has 7.6x more ships, 13.5x the deadweight tonnage, and 10x the container carrying capacity of the *entire* U.S. ocean-going, commercial maritime fleet.

China's advantage in commercial maritime extends to other 'dual-use' capable vessel types as well; for example bulk carriers and ROROs. There are around 12,700 bulk carriers in the world that move large quantities of coal, grain, steel coils, cement and other items around the world. Around half of these bulk carriers are registered in Greece, Japan or China, with the majority of these registered in China. Secondly, a review conducted by military analysts 'War on the Rocks' found China's RORO ferry fleet weighed in at roughly 750,000 displacement tons, and vehicle carriers totaled 425,000 tons, or an additional "1.1 million-plus tons of potential transport capacity". Putting that in perspective, the Chinese RORO ferry fleet is "three times the tonnage of the PLAN's entire fleet of traditional amphibious assault ships (that weigh around 370,000 tons)".

**Implications:** China is clearly dominant in the commercial domain, and has invested heavily in ships and increasing Flag State influence over the last decade in particular. This means, among many other considerations, that vessels controlled by China carry the majority of U.S. commodities and cargo as they traverse the world. Rapid expansion of China's commercial fleet, alongside China's Naval fleet has been clearly evident in recent years. 'Dual-use' in other countries is 'Fit-for-Purpose' (single-use) in China. That is, China's commercial fleet is synergistically aligned to the PLAN's military operations, as evidenced by recent footage that showed Chinese RORO vessels loading and unloading military equipment. Noted author and strategist, and pre-eminent scholar on China's naval activities Toshi Yoshihara, states: "[China has] clearly invested in Defense / industrial infrastructure to build multiple ships, simultaneously... effectively outbuilding many of the Western navies combined".

## 3. Commercial Mariners

China also has a distinct advantage in the number of serving mariners in the international commercial maritime sector. Figures are difficult to confirm however if China controls around 15% of the world's commercial ships - and assuming 100% of those ships are crewed entirely by Chinese citizens - then China's commercial maritime workforce numbers somewhere between 300,000 and 400,000. This can be validated by multiplying the number of merchant ships controlled by China (around 9,000) with the average number of mariners required to operate them; if that is around 40 per vessel, it equates to 360,000 mariners. However this does not take into account Chinese seafarers serving on ships of other Flag states, which could add another 150,000 to that total. A statement released by the China Maritime Safety Administration in 2020 tells an entirely different story: Total numbers in that report were 808,183 serving on oceangoing ships, and 908,683 deployed on inland river ships, for a total of 1,716,866 mariners.

It is widely accepted that China is the largest supplier of officers, however official numbers are also difficult to confirm. Some estimates are as high as one third of the world's total. This suggests, if using the latest figures on the global mariner workforce, that China could have between 150,000 - 250,000 serving officers. This ranks China 1st in the world for maritime officers, and depending on what numbers are used, either 1st or 2nd (behind the Philippines) in the supply of ratings.

Only 11,768 qualified, experienced U.S. merchant mariners were available and ready for duty, according to an audit conducted by MARAD in 2017. The number of mariners COSCO employed in that same year? 13,000.

**Implications:** China has a distinct advantage over every other country in one of the most critical categories of maritime strategy: People. When considering just volume alone, China's 400,000 - 800,000 mariners (and 150,000 - 250,000 officers) represents a formidable number of personnel that have been trained in domestic and deep-water maritime operations. Such large numbers indicate that huge investments have been made to secure a maritime talent pipeline over a long period of time, and great emphasis placed on training and upskilling mariners into senior-ranked positions.

Furthermore, China's dual-use strategy suggests that many of these mariners are capable of participating in commercial *and* naval operations. Due to the wide distribution of China's commercial fleet, these mariners are deployed all across the world, granted access to geographic and geostrategic areas, and constantly being trained on different types and classes of vessel. These numbers should also be viewed in light of the 'Serving personnel' totals in the table that compares the U.S. and Chinese Navy. If using a conservative figure of 500,000 mariners, and assuming 50% are trained in dual-use operations, then the actual number of personnel available to the PLAN is 490,000; 52,000 more than the U.S. Navy.

## 4. Shipbuilding

Twenty years ago, Chinese shipyards had a market share of less than 10%. A massive capacity expansion during the 2000s propelled China to the number one spot by 2009. Between 2010 and 2018, China was estimated to have contributed $132 billion dollars to its shipbuilding sector. By comparison, through the 'Federal Ship Financing Program' shipbuilding loans scheme (commonly referred to as Title XI), the U.S. government provided the U.S. shipbuilding sector a paltry $77 million over the same period. If previous expenditure is indicative of present-day investment, the Chinese Government will spend around $16.5 billion on shipbuilding subsidies in 2023. In stark contrast, MARAD allocated just $3 million in FY23 "to support administrative costs necessary to manage the current loan guarantee portfolio of the Title XI program, as well as new loan agreements".

China, Japan, and Korea build about 94% of the world's ships. China builds more than Korea and Japan combined; about 47% of the world's vessels. Nearly half of all ships delivered in 2022 to new owners were made in Chinese shipyards: 14.6 million compensated gross tons (cgt) of the 30.8 million total. Japan and South Korea delivered 4.8 million and 7.8 million cgt respectively. Shipyards in China also dominate new builds: The 2023-24 global order book totals just over 100 million cgt, with 45% of those orders held by Chinese yards, 34% by South Korean yards and 10% by Japanese shipyards.

**Implications:** Given it provides the essential services for the 'means of distribution', shipbuilding is entirely necessary for the secure and efficient functioning of any economy. That being said, shipyards are on the decline the world over; down around 40% compared to a decade ago. This has been caused by shrinking orders, changing build techniques, and increasing complexity of vessel construction. This decline directly benefits China, who has captured increased market share, and can build a wider defensive moat around a traditionally capital-intensive industry, all while honing niche skills in efficient, dual-use ship construction. China leads the world, and is in an undeniably dominant position in relation to the United States. This lead is accelerating.

The United States, a global naval superpower, is a sideline participant to commercial shipbuilding activities: The U.S. builds around 0.05% of the world's commercial ships, and is highly reliant on China to meet the needs and demands of U.S. exporters, importers, producers and the domestic transportation sector. And, increasingly, to also meet the needs of the Department of Defense. A November 2023 Congressional Research Services summary, highlighted this disturbing dependency: "Three of the ten commercial oil tankers selected to ship fuel for DOD as part of the newly enacted Tanker Security Fleet are Chinese-built, 7 of the 12 most recently built ships in the Maritime Security Fleet are Chinese-built."

The United States will need to approach an expansion of domestic shipbuilding very carefully: Most foreign shipyards are heavily subsidized, and many run at a substantial loss. It has also been estimated that building commercial ships in U.S. shipyards may cost 3-4x more than foreign-built equivalents. Expanding U.S. shipbuilding is, and must remain a National Security imperative, and will require a significant degree of strategic thought to be completed in an economically viable way. This will not happen unless there is a concerted effort to establish a National Security-aligned agenda for the U.S. commercial fleet, and new techniques are employed to reduce the costs involved during planning and construction.

**5. Shipping Containers**

It is estimated that there are around 50 million shipping containers in active rotation around the world. Between 5 and 6 million are being moved at any one time. Each container may make around five voyages a year, implying there are around 250 million individual container voyages a year on around 6,000 container vessels internationally. New containers need to be constructed, and old containers are retired (after around 15-20 years of service) into secondary markets as they wear out. Supply chain bottlenecks increase the length of time containers are needed for. For major shipping lines, they may need an additional 20% more containers to compensate for such bottlenecks. Chinese companies build 96 percent of all shipping containers. A Drewry study conducted in 2021, found that just three Chinese companies account for 82% of the total global market: China International Marine Containers (CIMC) Group built 42.5% of all containers, Dong Fang International Containers, 25.5% and the CXIC Group, 14.1%.

**Implications:** This represents an extreme degree of consolidation involving a small group of companies in just one country. Price to build and purchase, throughput and innovation are all affected by this shift in supplier concentration. There is also the potential for National Security risks to be introduced into supply chains if constructed containers - particularly newer 'smart' containers - contain sensors or communications equipment that could be repurposed for espionage or unauthorized remote monitoring.

## 6. Ports and Terminals

Chinese companies own and operate ports and terminal assets in 96 ports in 53 countries. Recent investments include buy-ins into regionally significant ports in Greece, Germany, and Africa. 'Dual-Use' applies to ports as well: 10 of the ports where China has majority control have the right blend of physical characteristics to support naval activities. As of September 2023, China has signed 70 bilateral and regional shipping agreements involving parties from 66 countries and regions. Domestic ports are large and active: China hosts 6 of the 10 busiest commercial ports in the world. Regarding specific port infrastructure: Chinese companies build around 80% of all port cranes, with one company, ZPMC, responsible for around 75% of the global total.

**Implications:** Belt and Road (BRI) and other global trade expansion initiatives have brought about a significant increase in the number and value of investments in domestic and overseas ports. China's domestic ports are large, and increasingly turning to automation, digitalization and other modernization techniques to increase throughput and efficiency. China is constantly expanding its portfolio of overseas ports, most notably in Africa - an estimated 100 seaports since the year 2000 - and South America; one example being the $3.5 billion Chancay Multipurpose Port Terminal in Peru, that will be managed by China's state-owned COSCO Shipping. These investments mean that China is in charge of the method of distribution - through ships and shipping - *and* the infrastructure that processes goods across sovereign borders. The United States has not matched China's tempo with equivalent investment or involvement.

## 7. Domestic Maritime Industrial Capacity

An extreme degree of investment and resources have been injected into increasing China's domestic maritime industrial capacity. Just one Chinese shipyard, Jiangnan Dao, one of 19 in China, has the same capacity as all 7 major U.S. Navy shipyards *combined.* In terms of space, Jiangnan Dao is four times the size of the shipyards at Newport News, Virginia. A number of these yards are capable of (and actively employ) 'dual-use' construction.

**Implications:** The last three 'R's in the Five R's of Logistics are: Repair, Revive and Replace. China's naval shipyards are sizable, and grow larger with each passing year. This reduces overheads by leveraging economies of scale, which decreases costs and increases vessel throughput. It also means that vessels can be revived, repaired and replaced in a much faster and more efficient manner, too. An industry commentator recently estimated that if China's navy was completely destroyed, it would take 2-3 years to completely rebuild. By contrast "it would take the United States 20-30 years, and in reality, it might never recover".

## 8. Fishing Fleet

China's fishing fleet is considerable, with some estimates varying between 170,000 up to 500,000 vessels, of all different sizes. China's Distant Water Fleet (CDWF) operates all across the world. International Trade Commission (ITC) estimates for the CDWF range between 2900 - 3400 vessels. Others estimate the CDWF to be nearly 17,000 vessels, including observations between 2017-18 that discovered 12,490 ships outside internationally recognized Chinese waters. If an estimate of 10,000 vessels is chosen, and there are an average of 6 crew per vessel, then the CDWF adds 60,000 additional to the total count of Chinese mariners, operating in foreign waters and the ABNJ.

**Implications:** By operating for long periods of time, with massive hauls per vessel, the CDWF worsens already depleted global fish stocks. The sheer scale of this fleet makes responsible and sustainable sourcing of fish and seafood difficult. Furthermore, fishing, militia fleets, and other non-conventional forces have also played, and will continue to play a role in disrupting naval operations, and can be brazenly repurposed for conflict through blockades or 'Adverse Possession'.

There has been an increased appetite for interruption and interdiction, as witnessed throughout 2022 and 2023 in the South China Sea. China's fishing fleets are already impacting the lives and livelihoods of fishermen and the fishing industries attached to countries like Japan, the Philippines and Taiwan. Escalating CDWF numbers and regional geographic expansion - for example extending the 'Nine Dash Line' beyond Taiwan - highlights the need for an enhanced strategy that would contend with, as described by retired U.S. Navy Admiral Jim Foggo, "China's Great Wall at sea".

U.S. citizens are unwittingly contributing to these problems: The U.S. population eats around 14.6 pounds of fish per person per year, and spends an average of $102 billion each year on seafood, a large proportion of which is then used to fund China's commercial and naval fleets. Professor Ian Ralby, Non-Resident Senior Fellow at the Center for Maritime Strategy, states that China is "weaponizing fish" pointedly adding that "China is using its DWF globally in a manner that accrues tremendous benefits to the Chinese armed forces. The least that can be done is stop buying fish caught by the DWF and processed by enslaved Uyghurs and serving it on U.S. military bases."

## III. Defining China

The foundational premise of this book is clearly evident when assessing the disparities between the combined fleets of the United States and China: The U.S. ranks 1st in naval fleet lethality, but 21st in commercial vessel carrying capacity, and 70th by commercial vessel count. While China's Navy ranks 2nd to the U.S. Navy in firepower, the PLAN is far superior in every other perceivable category when combined with the high-ranking Chinese merchant fleet; in total number of ships, ship value, total tonnage, fleet blend, sailing frequency, and in many ways, geostrategic influence and geographic reach.

China's maritime strategy employs Mahanian theory, by directly aligning the objectives of the military with commercial activity; from shipbuilding through to daily trade. China has utilized this interdependency very successfully, as is clearly visible across each of the eight aforementioned categories. In turn, commercial profitability has been used to fund China's military expansion, a fact that led Isaac B. Kardon - Senior Fellow for China Studies at the Carnegie Endowment for International Peace - to posit that "the biggest threat to the United States may not be the PLA, but China Inc." Combining this with other facts previously presented leads to the awkward conclusion that the United States has funded (and continues to fund) the expansion of China's commercial maritime industry, and by extension, China's military.

With sobering irony, China has been the primary beneficiary of U.S. enforcement of Freedom of Navigation of the seas.

China's commercial ships are given safe passage under the watchful eye of the U.S. Navy on a daily basis. While outrage would ensue if one of China's aircraft carriers approached U.S. territorial waters, hundreds of Chinese commercial ships - potential 'Weapons of Mass Disruption' - freely and regularly navigate into U.S. ports, without any pause for thought. This illustrates the tension between commercial and military objectives, and why clearly defining China is important; one hand cannot be extended in friendship, while the other is being slowly balled into a fist.

In conclusion, the relationship between China and the United States is multi-faceted, multi-layered and complicated, and therefore difficult to neatly define. Is China a peer or power, or something entirely different? Does a relational redefinition need to occur? Can both nations advance their own agendas, and still peacefully coexist? One thing is certain, the U.S. and China must determine the nature of this nuanced association carefully and thoughtfully, using intuition, tact and diplomacy; three techniques that also happen to be essential to National Security, and the sustainment of secure and open global trade.

## National Security Maritime Solutions and Opportunities

The following solutions and opportunities are matched to the maritime risks and vulnerabilities explored throughout this Principle:

1. **Risk: A lack of understanding about the U.S. Maritime Sector**
   **Solution: Maritime Awareness Campaigns & Partnerships**
   Knowledge is power: As simple as it may sound, a general increase in the level of understanding about the importance of maritime and shipping activities will go a long way to reducing the overall (short and long term) risks that exist in these domains. Public awareness campaigns should be conducted with the coordinated support and buy-in of organizations, agencies, institutions, departments and commercial participants. The goal of these campaigns would be to elevate understanding about shipping; highlight the National Security risks that arise if shipping is absent, under-resourced or dysfunctional; promote career opportunities across society; and, communicate the details of a unified U.S. Maritime Strategy. Partnering with reputable academic institutions will directly support the cause, and also incubate a future naval, and merchant marine talent pipeline.

2. **Risk: Incomplete support fleet blend**
   **Solution: Dual-Use Capabilities Register (DUCR)**
   The needs of the DOD must be directly cross-pollinated with the capabilities and activities of commercial operators. Reciprocally, closer coordination, information sharing and training should be conducted so

commercial assets can be readily deployed in a Defense context. These requirements can be detailed in a Dual-Use Capabilities Register. A DUCR would include the formation of a set of specific dual-use parameters, for example, deck heights and weight limits for commercial ROROs, or the skills and equipment needed on cable-laying or subsea vessels.

Thought must be given to National Security parameters on the Defense side, and commercial realities, on the other. The intentional creation of a Dual-Use Capabilities Register will ultimately redefine the meaning of 'fit-for-purpose' for U.S.-controlled commercial vessels. Note: This is difficult if the U.S. does not have U.S.-flagged vessels, so a process to rapidly Flag-in appropriate (specifically mission-aligned) tonnage needs to be explored in parallel.

3. **Risk: Lack of subsea vessels and equipment**
   **Solution: Subsea Support Fleet (SSF)**
   Building or sourcing the expertise, vessels, and equipment to repair, recover and replace assets in subsea and deepwater environments must be given higher priority. The Subsea Support Fleet would be a collection of vessels, submersibles and Unmanned Underwater Vehicles (UUV's) that have been carefully selected and/or purpose-built to perform designated tasks, including inspecting and protecting subsea telecommunications cables. Upskilling personnel and sourcing (or building) the required vessels - including the replacement of the USNS Zeus - must be conducted in close collaboration with the private sector; a mutually-beneficial collaboration that will generate positive National and Economic security outcomes.

4. **Risk: Lack of appropriate tankers**
**Solution: Creatively reform the Tanker Security Program**
A range of new ideas should be considered and pursued to increase the number (and tonnage) of appropriate vessels into the Tanker Security Program (TSP). Flagging-in modern, allied-made foreign hulls using new incentives and benefits must be considered. This should be completed in collaboration with the commercial sector, so that the right blend of tankers is acquired (and at the right price). Cargo preferences and other incentives need additional thought so they are commercially viable, and lead to more predictable, longer-term benefits. A dedicated program should also be created that allows a vessel to be more quickly adapted for CONSOL duties at sea.

5. **Risk: The Ready Reserve Force**
**Solution: Redefine the role and management of the RRF**
National Security interests will only be assured with a marked increase in fit-for-purpose ships and mariners. The current RRF methodology is based around a 'lay-up' (paused) vs 'engaged' model, and is clearly not fit-for-purpose. If the RRF is modernized and used in an 'engaged' capacity (e.g., rotated out with the existing naval fleet, or employed in 'dual-use' roles), it will naturally build momentum in attracting investment to the U.S. maritime sector, while equipping U.S. mariners and retaining appropriately-trained talent. Furthermore, the personnel operating these ships should be given access to modern training technologies and incentivized with increased privileges (e.g., medical, leave, insurance and family support), as well as being actively trained on combat scenarios that match the future of

warfare; including the potential for rapid deployments, and the presence of asymmetric threats.

6. **Risk: Dysfunctional MSP and VISA**
   **Solution: Annual MSP/VISA Report Card**
   Annual reporting should be conducted and presented by MARAD on the status of the MSP and VISA programs. A 'MSP and VISA Report Card' should be made available every year, to increase accountability and transparency of both programs. Visibly representing program categories in an easy-to-understand format will allow for accurate mapping of progress and clear comparisons to occur between years. This must include cargo preference data and statistics (as stipulated by the Government Accountability Office in a hearing in September 2022); details about the suppliers of transportation and logistics support; a register of engaged vessels, including crew and carrying capacities; and, the statistics (including costs) about vessels that have been required to move Food Aid and other forms of government-impelled cargoes.

7. **Risk: Excessive dependencies on non-U.S. entities**
   **Solution: Foreign-Interest Impact Record (F-IIR)**
   A centralized, U.S. F-IIR would go a long way towards reducing the threat of foreign involvement in the United States maritime sector, and support the national security posture. An accurate F-IIIR must include ownership and control details for: Ports, vessels, critical infrastructure, supply chain (and supply lines), and a range of intangible activities e.g., financing, digitally-connected systems, software/firmware and other cybersecurity risks. This will be particularly necessary for frontline critical infrastructure, such as the ship-to-shore cranes operating in U.S. ports.

Specific partnerships can also be created to combat foreign influence or control. For example, Class Societies like the American Bureau of Shipping (ABS) can contribute to the F-IIR as they complete inspections for vessel classifications. This will increase the standards of vessels in rotation, and could lead to a decrease in the number of mission-critical vessels controlled by foreign interests.

8. **Risk: Reduced collaboration between defense and the private sector**
   **Solution: The Maritime National Training Center (MNTC)**
   The Army's NTC has been highly successful. The U.S. should build a maritime equivalent. The programs attached to the MNTC would force a percentage of actively patrolling vessels into a short hiatus for close-in wargaming and simulations; in concert with other DOD forces, but more particularly to sharpen naval readiness, alongside commercial partners. The MNTC would be specifically designated as the place to learn about creative adversarial tactics, and the best ways to coordinate naval and commercial fleet activities in contested environments. The MNTC would utilize a range of digital systems - including advanced data analytics augmented by Natural Language Processing and machine-learning - to improve simulations and assist naval and commercial entities navigate through potential scenarios that may occur in the future.

9. **Risk: Domestic economy and double-counting**
   **Solution: Maritime Asset Database / Maritime Resource Map (MAD/MRP)**
   Recording all available maritime assets, especially those in dual-use roles, into a secure Maritime Asset Database (containing details about the asset), alongside

an interactive Maritime Resource Map (showing asset location) is an important first step. Solving the Double-Counting Conundrum requires a quick and simple answer to the questions "What assets do we have right now?" and "Where are they?". This needs to be completed during peacetime, prior to conflict arising. Mapping this accurately will be the best first step to minimizing domestic economic losses in the event of military escalation, and will allow the domestic industrial base to continue to function at an optimal level during a period of conflict.

10. **Risk: Capacity in the domestic maritime industrial base**
    **Solution: U.S. Maritime Dual-Use Strategy (MD-US)**
    Being intentional about dual-use activities - including recruitment of personnel, and asset procurement, construction, and repair - through the formation of a Dual-Use Strategy, will lead to an increase in understanding about the possibilities, and clarity around what roles, infrastructure and support is required to enable dual-use construction at U.S. shipyards. This would require an intentional integration process for the workforce, so there was a clear understanding of what longer-term goals would be achieved - e.g., a thriving U.S. maritime sector - and to reduce any tension or inefficiencies as each commercial or naval team was managed and deployed. New designs for shipbuilding yards should also be considered, alongside the supporting infrastructure required to accelerate dual-use builds.

11. **Risk: Cybersecurity and related emerging threats**
    **Solution: MTS-ISAC and sharing threat data**

Cybersecurity can no longer be considered an 'optional extra' and must be directly integrated into every facet of maritime operations, training and simulated warfare. Groups like the Maritime Transportation System Information Sharing and Analysis Center (MTS-ISAC) are entirely necessary, but have risen to prominence incidentally rather than intentionally, and require additional support. MTS-ISAC is well positioned to monitor cybersecurity threats and report on trends as they receive input from ports, terminal operators, vessel operators, the cruise industry, and the energy and government sectors. It is imperative that feedback from MTS-ISAC, and other carefully selected companies and skilled practitioners is integrated into the U.S. National Security, and U.S. maritime strategies.

The work of MTS-ISAC and other cybersecurity groups would be greatly enhanced by the collection and analysis of accurate data from industry participants, government departments and frontline transportation officials. Some work is already underway to encourage supply chain data sharing - for example the Department of Transportation's Freight Logistics Optimization Works (FLOW) initiative - however more can be done, especially with digital threat detection, critical infrastructure monitoring, and risk mitigation.

A Maritime Cybersecurity Escalation & Support smartphone app, with an associated national Support Hotline could accrue relevant information from a variety of sources, and also dispense advice in the event of a cyberattack or data breach. This service would be staffed by appropriately trained Government agents, or a rotating pool of industry participants. Reported events could be aggregated and analyzed to detect common or recurring threat events, with regular statistics published for transparency, and to maintain the integrity of the advice being collated for participants.

12. **Risk: Threats dispersed over a large geographic area**
    **Solution: Distant Water Fleet Overwatch (DWFO)**
    Distant Water Fleets (DWF) operating in Areas Beyond National Jurisdiction (ABNJ) need to be constantly monitored to detect illegal activity and to assist with the protection of Freedom of Navigation. Over 60% of the world's oceans are ABNJ, so the best way to increase the efficiency and effectiveness of surface-based enforcement is through space-based satellite technologies. Low Earth Orbit (LEO) satellites equipped with highly detailed image capture and sensor detection capabilities are well suited to this task.

    The DWFO will utilize a network of commercial LEO satellites to constantly monitor the oceans to detect infringements or illegal activity. The DWFO will also collaboratively partner with values-aligned companies, who will contribute expertise and assets to protect the ocean from Illegal, Unregulated and Unreported (IUU) fishing, and assist the USN and USCG in protecting Freedom of Navigation of the sea.

13. **Risk: Asymmetric Warfare**
    **Solution: Maritime Asymmetric Warfare Division (MAWD)**
    Task Force 59 in Bahrain (6th Fleet, and with expanded operations into the 4th Fleet) and USV Division One in San Diego are performing admirably, but the role of developing responses to asymmetric threats needs to be expanded across the entire Navy. The MAWD program would allow the U.S. Navy (along with NAVSEA and

TRANSCOM) to seek out aspiring startups and innovative private-sector technology providers that can boost the capabilities of deployed naval assets. This would include the creation of drones, autonomous ships and support vessels, and newly devised sensors attached to communication conduits that can manage low-cost, high volume swarms. These partnerships will more rapidly propel the USN Fleet blend toward the stated goal of being "up to 40 percent unmanned, by the middle of the century".

14. **Risk: Diminished U.S. naval presence on the world's oceans**
    **Solution: The Strategic International Maritime Alliance (SIMA)**
    The U.S. cannot be solely responsible for protecting the open ocean i.e., the 60% that exist in Areas Beyond National Jurisdiction (ABNJ). Being the maritime equivalent of 'World Police' carries an extremely high cost for the U.S. economy, and exerts pressure on the military assets and deployed personnel who perform this task. To assist with this critical role, the United States must forge partnerships with values-aligned international partners and Flag States that can contribute to upholding the rule of law, and maintaining Freedom of Navigation of the seas. Coordinating a coalition through the Strategic International Maritime Alliance (SIMA) will demonstrate global U.S. leadership, and encourage international cooperation through the impartation and completion of a range of shared responsibilities.

    The Strategic International Maritime Alliance would have the resources to enact solutions and solve complex problems. It would be specifically set up to cross-pollinate military and commercial resources, for the purpose of encouraging maritime excellence, enforcing the rule of law, protecting Freedom of Navigation, and reducing shipping's impact on the environment. Each nation involved in the SIMA will directly benefit from the protections afforded by the U.S. Navy and U.S. Coast Guard, and would offer up time and resources in return - Performing patrol duties, offering vessel repair or supply services, participating in surveillance, intelligence, and data gathering, and offering commercial cargo handling or port preferences to enhance supply chain security.

An example of a suitable Flag State partner for SIMA is Australia. The United States and Australia have a long history of working closely together on commercial and maritime endeavors. Both countries have long and proud maritime history's and are well aligned economically, philosophically and socially. Australia is also well situated geostrategically in the Pacific. Australia's maritime Flag is administered by the highly-proficient Australian Maritime Safety Authority (AMSA). AMSA has an exemplary track record of enforcing maritime rules, and maintaining law and order in domestic and regional waters. There is already established precedent for high-level collaboration on military operations, as evidenced by the AUKUS Trilateral Security Pact; which already includes maritime (primarily subsea) technology sharing and enforcement components.

Specific examples with Australia might include: The establishment of a U.S.-AU Green Trade Lane to expedite cargo between the two countries; combining the Royal Australian Navy (RAN) and AMSA's local expertise with U.S. naval assets to tackle regional IUU activities and DWF incursions; the development of

LEO-layer surveillance technologies to increase surface fleet efficiency; and the trade-facilitated development of each countries maritime sector, including collaborative builds for military or commercial vessels. Note: There is already precedent for collaborative shipbuilding activities, as evidenced by the presence of Australia's Austal, based in Mobile, Alabama, who already works closely with the U.S. Navy.

*This page is intentionally left blank.*

# ECONOMIC SECURITY

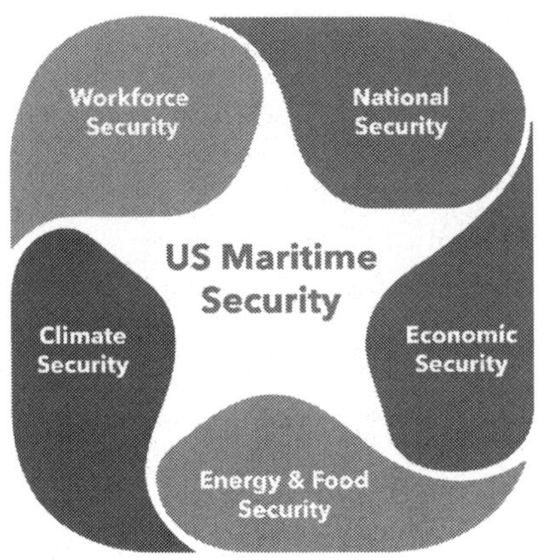


**Economic Security**

- *Dollar-denominated trade*
- *Investment nodes*
- *Critical infrastructure*
- *Blue Economy*
- *Inflation*

# II. ECONOMIC SECURITY

*We have come to a clear realization of the fact that true individual freedom cannot exist without economic security and independence. For unless there is security here at home, there cannot be lasting peace in the world.*

- President Franklin Delano Roosevelt, State of the Union (January 1944)

*We must retool our nation to prepare for the challenge we already face to maintain our position in the global economy. And this much is certain: America will not have national security without economic security.*

- U.S. Secretary of State, John Kerry

## Economic Security Context

Economic Security and shipping are inextricably linked. According to The United Nations Conference on Trade and Development (UNCTAD), global trade reached a record USD $32 trillion in 2022, with trade in goods around USD $25 trillion; an increase of about 12% from the previous year. Around 90% of all produced or consumed goods have spent some time at sea, including the commodities, machinery, agricultural products, vehicles, clothing, food, energy products, military equipment and medical supplies, required to sustain modern life.

As the world economy grows, so does the volume of freight transported by ships. Around 11 billion tons were transported by ship in 2022; a significant increase from the 0.1 billion metric tons in 1980. 11 billion tons equates to 1.4 tons for every person on the planet. An expansion of seaborne trade naturally leads to an increase in the movement of cargo, the majority of which is carried in the humble shipping container. A rotating stock of around 50 million containers carried over USD $14 trillion dollars' worth of goods all over the world in 2022. The most common container types are Twenty-foot Equivalent Units (TEU) and Forty-foot Equivalent Units (FEUs). Refrigerated units (reefers) are often used to transport food, wine, chemicals and temperature-sensitive produce.

The leading container-handling ports worldwide are all located in Asia-Pacific. 6 of the top 10 busiest container ports in the world are in China. The Port of Shanghai is the busiest in the world; about 47 million TEUs were processed across 2022. By comparison, the largest container port in the United States, the Port of Los Angeles handled one quarter of that volume, or around 10.7 million TEUs during the same period. The Port of LA is the only U.S. port in the top 10, and was ranked 9th in the world by volume; it is likely to slip out of the top 10 in 2024. In Europe, the Port of Rotterdam in the Netherlands (11th overall) is the largest container port on that continent, and handled over 8.3 million containers in 2022.

Growth in world trade has led to a dramatic expansion of the global container, commodity and bulk carrier fleet. Over 50,000 merchant ships are currently involved in international commercial trades. At the start of 2022, the world commercial fleet had a total carrying capacity of 2.2 billion deadweight tonnage (dwt), up 63 million dwt on the previous year. The total deadweight tonnage of all international trading vessels has increased by around 1.5 billion dwt since 1980. The top five ship-owning countries account for over 50% of world fleet deadweight tonnage.

In gross tonnage (gt), Greece used to have a commanding lead, however an August 2023 report from Clarkson's showed that China's commercial fleet now has the highest gross tonnage in the world; 249.2 million gross tons, edging out Greece's 249 million. Half of the world's tonnage is owned by Asian companies. European owners account for 39% and owners from Northern America for 6% of total tonnage. African, Latin American and Caribbean countries had a share of just over 1% each; Oceania just below 1%.

The companies involved in the global container trade have become increasingly concentrated: Over the last 25 years, the top 20 carriers have nearly doubled their market share from 48% to 90%, with the five largest carriers now controlling over 63% of global capacity. Including pending newbuilds the privately-owned Mediterranean Shipping Company (MSC) is currently the largest container ship operator globally, with a total capacity of over five million TEUs across 788 vessels, and around 18.6% of global container capacity. MSC is followed by Denmark's APM-Maersk (4.1 million TEUs, 678 vessels, and

14.8% market share), France's CMA-CGM (3.5 million TEUs, 619 vessels and 12.6%), China's COSCO (3 million TEUs, 485 ships, and 10.9%), and Germany's Hapag-Lloyd (1.9 million TEUs, 262 vessels and 6.9% market share).

Global shipbuilding is, and has been for some time, heavily concentrated in China, the Republic of Korea and Japan. These three economies accounted for 94% of shipbuilding in gross tonnage. The value of the shipbuilding market is estimated at USD $146 billion (2023), and is expected to reach USD $184 billion over the next five years. In the container market, newbuilds will add 2.34 million TEUs of capacity in 2023 and 2.83 million TEUs in 2024. In a related domain, 20 cruise ships were completed in 2022, with another 7 debuted after being built in 2021; the largest suppliers of cruise ships are based in Italy, Germany, and South Korea.

An increase in shipbuilding at one end, leads to an increase for ship recycling at the other. 443 ocean-going commercial ships and floating offshore units were sold to the scrap yards in 2022. 292 of these vessels were sold to yards in Bangladesh, Pakistan and India; three nations that jointly account for around 80% of all global ship recycling activities.

Part VII 'The High Seas', Article 92 of UNCLOS states: "Ships shall sail under the flag of one State only and, save in exceptional cases expressly provided for in international treaties or in this Convention, shall be subject to its exclusive jurisdiction on the high seas." Many commercial ships are registered under a flag that does not match the nationality of the vessel owner or operators. These maritime flags are commonly referred to as 'Flag States'. Many Flag States are also referred to as a 'Flags of Convenience' (FOC) due to the tax or regulation relief the Flag administrators may offer to owners and operators. For example, at the beginning of 2022, 49% of all ships owned by Japanese entities were registered in Panama,

25% of ships owned by Greek entities were registered in Liberia, and another 23% in the Marshall Islands.

Nearly half of the worlds tonnage is registered in just three Flag States: Panama has the most ships (8,500 vessels of all types, and 350 million dwt); Liberia has less ships (around 5,300) but recently surpassed Panama in total tonnage (around 352.2 million dwt); and, the Marshall Islands has more ships than Liberia at 5,700, but less tonnage at 290 million dwt. Panama's registry has remained almost unchanged over the last decade; the Marshall Islands and Liberia have caught up, with Liberia showing explosive growth over the last five years in particular.

## Economic Security and U.S. Shipping

The United States has the world's largest economy ($26.85 trillion, 2023 estimate) by nominal Gross Domestic Product (GDP), and the seventh-highest per capita GDP, at around $80,000 per person. Impressively, with just over 4% of the world's population, the U.S. economy accounts for over 25% (one quarter) of the total global economy. Excluding China, the U.S. economy has the same GDP as the next 10 economies *combined.*

The United States has successfully employed a range of mechanisms to secure U.S. economic interests across a variety of different domains, and across the world. For example, the U.S. has maintained a consistently visible presence in capital markets and is a world leader in banking and finance. By contrast, participation and investment in the commercial maritime sector has largely been absent, and if it has been present, has noticeably declined over the last 50 years. U.S. Economic Security is negatively impacted by the absence of investment and control over maritime assets, ships, personnel and infrastructure. Foreign countries and companies directly profit from an array of domestic maritime activities, diverting billions of dollars away from the U.S. economy every year.

The following facts illustrate the dwindling state of the U.S. commercial maritime industry:

- As previously conveyed, only *Zero Point Four* percent (0.4%), or 180 of the 50,000+ commercial, ocean-going vessels registered across the world fly the U.S. Flag, and 98% of all traded or consumed goods move into and out of the U.S. on vessels wholly controlled by other countries.

- Confirming the allure of Flags of Convenience for favorable tax, regulation, and other reasons, around 800 American-owned ships are flagged in other nations; about 4 times as many as in the current U.S.-Flag fleet.

- Over the last 25 years, the top 20 commercial carriers (steamship lines) have nearly doubled their market share from 48% to 89.4%. The top 10 carriers control 84.2%, and the five largest carriers now control over 63% of global capacity. There is only one U.S. commercial shipping company in the top 30: Matson, ranked 28th, that supplies just 0.2% of global capacity.

- Three global alliances, involving the top nine largest companies, control around 40% of total trade by volume: 2M, Ocean Alliance, and THE Alliance. None of the companies in any of these alliances are American. Note: MSC and Maersk recently announced they will discontinue the 2M alliance, by 2025; a development that industry veteran Lars Jensen describes as a move to focus on logistics vs engaging in continuous price wars.

- USD $3.35 trillion worth of imports and $3 trillion worth exports were moved into and out of the United States in 2022. Around $1.8 trillion worth of goods and cargo was moved by ship. The U.S. relies on shipping lines from other countries for this task: Maersk based in Denmark; CMA-CGM from France; MSC - Switzerland; COSCO - China; ONE - Japan; Hapag-Lloyd - Germany; Evergreen - Taiwan; HMM - South Korea; ZIM - Israel. None of these companies are American.

- Just 16 companies - eight shipping companies, three factory groups and five box lessors - control 80% of the world's shipping, container construction and leasing.

The top three builders are all based in China and produce 83% of all new shipping containers. The top five container leasing companies - primarily based in Bermuda, China and Japan - control 82% of the world's capacity. None of these companies are American either.

- U.S. shipbuilding has been on the decline for decades, in direct contrast to countries like China, the Republic of Korea and Japan. Adjunct Professor at the U.S. Merchant Marine Academy and former U.S. Merchant Mariner Dr Sal Mercogliano estimates that "the U.S. only builds about 0.05% of the world's commercial ships".

- 9 out of the top 10 busiest container ports in the world are in Asian countries; 6 of the top 10 are located in China. The largest U.S. Port (the Port of Los Angeles) is the only port outside of Asia, and was ranked 9th in 2022.

The vulnerabilities revealed by each of these concerning statistics, brings into focus a philosophy that is central to the Principle of Economic Security.

### *Economic Security is National Security*

The COVID-19 pandemic clearly illustrated the heavy reliance all nations have on supply-chain transportation and ship carrying capacity. This included emergency PPE and other critical medical equipment, but eventually extended into other areas as well; basic food supplies, fast-moving consumer goods, automotive components and microchips were all in short supply across the course of the pandemic. Relying on other nations to provide capacity represents a significant economic risk, especially during periods of financial volatility, or geopolitical conflict. These economic risks, if left unchecked, and if not structurally resolved over time, threaten social stability and then have an effect on National Security.

Economic Security *is* National Security: The interplay between these two forms of Security was addressed by Mahan in 'The Influence of Sea Power Upon History: 1660–1783' when he stated "Naval power must be built on maritime commerce". Mahan, and others since then argued that the presence of supportive and complementary commercial maritime activities (Economic Security) directly supports the operation of the Navy (National Security). This also means that the danger posed by maritime-facilitated economic threats must be regarded in the same manner, and calculated to have a similar degree of impact as a military threat; and resourced and responded to accordingly. It also means the opportunities presented in one area, can be capitalized upon to fund, support and promote the work that occurs in the other. This is most powerfully shown in a global context, by exercising balance in the application of hard and soft projection.

The interaction between Economic Security and National Security is tangibly evident in the maritime strategies of other nations, but largely absent in strategies employed by the United States. For example, there has been visible convergence over the last decade of China's military and commercial maritime activities. PLAN ships and merchant ships are commonly built side-by-side (dual-use), demonstrating that central planners understand the need for the two industries to work closely together. China's interpretation of the interplay between these two Principles has been understood for some time. The foundations established by Mahan were formally codified in 1997, in Deng Xiaoping's 16-Character Policy: *jun-min jiehe* (combine the military and civil), *ping-zhan jiehe* (combine peace and war), *jun-pin youxian* (give priority to military products), and *yi min yan jun* (let the civil support the military).

## Economic Security Maritime Risks and Vulnerabilities

A weak U.S. commercial maritime industry poses significant risks to international economic stability and U.S. Economic Security:

A. **International monetary volatility** - *Issues affecting the U.S. Dollar, and the potential risks associated with economic sanctions*

B. **Influencing the influencers** - *The influence of the shipping industry on the United States and how the U.S. might be overlooked in key strategic maritime decisions*

C. **Underinvestment encourages foreign involvement** - *Vulnerabilities introduced by foreign influence that impact U.S. Economic Security, the local economy and domestic production*

D. **Missed Blue Economy opportunities** - *How stifled innovation, misdirected taxes, and a lack of leadership leads to missed opportunities across the maritime sector*

E. **Shipping and the cost of living** - *How volatility in transportation costs affect the cost of living, inflation and other economic variables*

# A. International Monetary Volatility

## I. Threats to U.S.-Dollar denominated international trade

The activities of the shipping industry represent a significant proportion of activity inside the international monetary system. As measured by average dollar value, global merchandise exports and imports amounted to $25.26 trillion. Around 90% of all foreign exchange transactions involve U.S. dollars (USD). Around half of all global trade and three quarters of Asia-Pacific trade are denominated in U.S. dollars. This means that commercial trading partners, and the intermediaries involved in these transactions, like vessel owners and shipping companies, have a very high degree of influence over the currency that could be used for global trade transactions.

Without a strong U.S. owned commercial fleet, there is a risk that a significant portion of global trade may rapidly shift to be non-U.S. dollar denominated. With China's growing dominance in international shipping, there is a credible threat that Chinese merchants could demand that international trade be denominated in Renminbi (RMB). A large number of highly dependent partnerships and trade between nations would be affected, with many merchants having no choice but to comply. Adding to this credible threat, both China and Saudi Arabia have announced explicit monetary policy intentions in recent years to reduce their dependence on U.S. dollar denominated trade; in part, in response to the U.S. dollar being used as a policy lever for sanctions.

An abrupt and coordinated shift could have a significant impact on international monetary stability and the U.S. economy. The rapid decoupling of international trade from the USD would lead to a large oversupply of U.S. dollars, the unraveling of the international dollar market, and a rapid fall in the dollar's value.

With a scramble to create a more balanced portfolio of reserve currencies from other major currencies away from the U.S. Dollar and lower levels of international cooperation (e.g., the European Central Bank may see an opportunity to also strengthen demand for Euros), this could lead to the U.S. Federal Reserve intervening in unprecedented and disruptive ways. Such an intervention could strain the U.S. domestic economy and almost all U.S. citizens, risking U.S. domestic and international Economic Security. Large monetary shifts have happened in the past before in 1931 with the British pound shift away from the Gold Standard, as well as 1971 with the ending of the U.S. Dollar convertibility to gold by President Nixon. Both events led to a decade of international economic instability and stagflation (rising inflation with low economic and job growth).

## II. Economic Sanctions

For several decades, the U.S. has leveraged the power of the U.S. dollar when imposing economic sanctions against hostile nations. For example, after Russia invaded Ukraine, the U.S. and its allies froze nearly half of Russia's $640 billion foreign exchange reserves. Similar approaches have been used in the past to target U.S. dollars held by countries like Afghanistan, Iran and Venezuela.

However, a change is underway. While the U.S. economy has grown quickly over time, the global economy has grown even quicker. The U.S. share of total world economic output has fallen from 40% in 1960 to a little over 25% in 2022. The U.S. share of total world trade has dropped from 14% to 11% in the same period. And this happened, despite a rising GDP and even though the U.S. is the birthplace of some of the world's largest companies. With shrinking influence over the world's economic output, there is a risk that a more dominant alternate currency may displace the USD as the preferred currency for handling sanctions.

If global trade decoupled from the USD, and there was a commensurate rise in RMB-denominated trade, a significant risk exists that economic sanctions may be imposed by China or other countries, on the United States. This could cripple the U.S. economy financially and impact the functionality of trade across global supply chains. For example, vessels owned or operated from certain nations may not be permitted to trade with the United States, or run the risk of fines or penalties if they did. Such an outcome would also remove the effectiveness of any sanctions the U.S. has imposed on other nations, for example those leveled against the shadow tanker fleets transporting Russian and Iranian oil.

## B. Shipping as a Critical Node in Global Trade ('Influencing the Influencers')

### I. The shipping industry

A range of significant, globally-impacting decisions are regularly made by a relatively small number of highly influential shipping industry operators, carriers, companies and Flag States. Disproportionate levels of influence exercised by certain participants, can dictate what ports are developed; the types of marine fuels that are used; what regulatory standards might be considered; and the levels of emission, workforce, or financial disclosures that might (or might not) occur.

Recent commentary has questioned the approach of local municipalities using public money - via grants, tax breaks, or spending - to expand ports, wharfs, storage areas and cranes. This has been observed on multiple occasions in the United

States. For example, four ports - Los Angeles, Long Beach, New Jersey, and Georgia - have been allocated billions of dollars to expand port infrastructure, which some have claimed is spent "purely to meet the business priorities of international shipping lines". A commonly cited example is the construction work and dredging that needs to be completed to accommodate larger vessels such as Ultra-Large Container Vessels (ULCV). These ships tend to produce higher profit margins for operators by lowering per-slot costs, and a significant amount of work is required to build the infrastructure to support them. The deficiencies in these investment decisions became apparent during the height of the COVID-19 pandemic, where a greater volume of more flexible vessels would have been infinitely more useful to cope with disruptions in demand and supply.

This example is reminiscent of the Airbus A380 airplane. Following similar logic as large container ships ('bigger vessels, equals more slots and lower costs'), the A380 was comparatively taller, wider and longer than other equivalent aircraft. The A380 was designed to accommodate around 615 (two-class) passengers, and up to 853 passengers in a single-class configuration. By contrast, the packhorse of modern aviation, the 747, usually seats around 467 (two-class) and a maximum of 660 passengers in a single-class configuration. An increase in the physical dimensions of the aircraft, and a marked increase in passenger count, forced airports to upgrade to accommodate the A380, at a cost of tens of billions of taxpayer dollars around the world. This included changes to runway lengths, raising terminal heights, passenger loading infrastructure such as tunnels, gates and stairs, along with a range of peripheral support vehicles and equipment. For a variety of reasons, including comparably worse running costs at scale, the A380 ceased production after just 12 short years in commercial service. There is a possibility that 'Ultra Large' (20,000+ TEU) container ships may suffer the same fate.

Poor decisions will continue to be made if there is a lack of understanding among government administrators about the Economic (and National) Security imperatives that must be followed in proposals made by maritime industry participants. If well-informed, the United States will lead other countries in building ports that are smaller, more agile, with a lower carbon footprint, and specifically designed to process cargo efficiently for a flexible array of mid-sized vessels. Regardless of whether they are 'smart', or manually operated, these ports should be purposefully built to cater for what the U.S. economy will need over the next 50 years. Changing the size and role of U.S. ports will lead to an increase in the total number required, which will benefit exporters, importers, consumers and U.S. maritime labor. And, by increasing available options, other positive Economic Security outcomes will also eventuate, including decreased transportation costs, and improved infrastructure efficiency.

## II. Poorly resourced Government oversight

Strong industry influence could be countered by firm government oversight, however the two agencies tasked with establishing and enforcing regulatory guidelines - MARAD and the Federal Maritime Commission (FMC) - are both massively under-resourced, and underfunded. MARAD is part of the Department of Transport (DOT) and has a broad mandate covering "ships and shipping, port and vessel operations, national security, environment, and safety". MARAD employs around 880 people and has a budget of $1.4 billion (FY23). The FMC is "the independent federal agency responsible for regulating the U.S. international ocean transportation system for the benefit of U.S. exporters, importers, and the U.S. consumer." The FMC employs around 110 staff and has a budget of $44 million (FY23).

The FMC and MARAD oversee the operations of the entire U.S. maritime sector; a sector that is complicated and increasingly consolidated, and processes around $2 trillion dollars' worth of imports and exports into and out of the United States every year as well as over 11 million shipping containers (one in five of the global total). By contrast, the airlines and air cargo providers of the U.S. aviation industry - overseen by the Federal Aviation Authority (FAA) - processes around $1 trillion dollars of U.S. imports and exports every year and over 800 million passengers. The FMC and MARAD have just under 1,000 staff, and a budget of a little over $1.4 billion. The FAA has 45,000 staff, and a budget of $18.6 billion.

### III. Reduced U.S. influence in large international, strategic trade initiatives

Ports, shipping lanes, new vessel types, and streamlined supply chains for food and energy are all being created across the world without any meaningful, coordinated U.S. involvement for the first time in decades. This is detrimental to U.S. economic interests and introduces a range of short, medium and long-term risks to U.S. Economic Security. China's Belt and Road Initiative (BRI) involves 155 signatory countries, and includes transshipment hubs for fishing, and new port infrastructure investments that anticipate increased trade through the Arctic.

The BRI and related developments are setting in place the infrastructure highways that will be used in global supply chains across the next half century. Some are in the U.S.' backyard, such as transshipment centers in the Caribbean, while a significant proportion of these will run through nations that are not sympathetic to U.S. interests. The new Asia-Europe shipping lanes via the Arctic are estimated to reduce ship transit times and decrease operational costs by around 40%, but pass close to Alaska. These Arctic routes will be extremely attractive to cost-conscious carriers, and also highly dependent on port infrastructure and icebreakers from Russia.

Without a strong U.S. merchant fleet to influence the formation of global trade routes, new routes could be established that make U.S. transported cargoes and exports less competitive. For example, if U.S. ships were reluctant to navigate an Arctic route due to potential interference from Chinese or Russian vessels, then alternate, longer routes would need to be used instead. These longer routes extend transit times, and introduce delays that drive up the costs; an unfavorable condition that has a present-day precedent, with vessels that are forced to 'take the long way round' (through the Drake Passage at the bottom of South America) if they are unable to transit through the Panama Canal.

While the BRI has cost China over $1 trillion dollars thus far, it has, at the very least, demonstrated an intentional plan of expansion and investment in multiple regions across the world. To that end, China's BRI has similar aims as the 1948 Marshall Plan - which cost the United States around $13.3 billion ($173 billion in today's dollars) - but is significantly more ambitious in size and scale. For example, port infrastructure being built in BRI signatory countries will service 75% of the world's population, a group that produces around half the world's GDP.

## C. Underinvestment Encourages Foreign Involvement

### I. Asset ownership and control

Underinvestment by U.S. companies and the U.S. government in the commercial maritime sector has left the United States heavily reliant on foreign providers, owners and operators, in many areas of the shipping value chain. The following numbers starkly illustrate the diminutive U.S. share in each category, as a percentage of global totals:

- **Shipbuilding** - U.S.-built commercial trading vessels: 0.05%
- **Registrations** - U.S. ships in international commercial trade: 0.4%
- **Cargo** - U.S.-Flag vessels share of global carrying capacity: <0.5%
- **Tonnage** - U.S. share of the global commercial trading fleet: 0.57%
- **Seafarers** - Credentialed, suitable & available U.S. mariners: 0.62%
- **Exports & Imports** - U.S. cargoes carried by U.S.-flagged ships: <2%

These statistics are alarming, and even more so when considering the reciprocal numbers e.g, 99.5% of all ships the United States is currently using to carry international containerized cargo are foreign-flagged, and, over 98% of mariners involved in the movement of U.S. international cargo, are from other countries. The figure for U.S. port ownership was difficult to ascertain, but estimated to be around 20% 15 years ago, and is likely to be less than that now.

These statistics also present multiple Economic Security risks to U.S. companies, to the U.S. economy, and to U.S. producers and consumers. How might this play out in reality? The following three changes in behavior and practice by non-U.S. participants would detrimentally affect, and noticeably disrupt the entire U.S. economy:

i. Firstly, a foreign entity could decide to cease offering a particular service, due to a change in commercial interests, or because of a realignment favoring another entity that is an adversary of the United States. Ceasing a necessary service would disrupt the movement of U.S. cargoes, and cause economic strain on the parties dependent on that service. This can be observed in a semi-permanent feature of global supply chains, when carriers 'blank sail' container ships.

'Blank sailing' removes a vessel from a trade lane or a series of port calls, due to operational changes, or to adjust to market conditions. Blank sailings can also be used in a coordinated fashion across multiple carriers in an attempt to maintain higher freight rates during periods of reduced demand. Blank sailings benefit carriers, but can be extremely disruptive to shippers. For example, while commercial ocean carriers enjoyed bumper profits over the last three years, increasingly unreliable schedules, including blank sailings and rolled cargo, cost shippers between $5-10 billion dollars. Shipping veteran John McCown from Blue Water Capital, explained this in a recent interview, stating that "Shipping lines went into the Pandemic barely breaking even" but after COVID-19 hit they immediately took vessels off the water which helped to create the strongest "supply and demand dynamic ever".

ii. Secondly, a foreign entity may suddenly decide to increase service prices, which would severely harm U.S. suppliers, exporters and the U.S. economy. A rapid escalation of rates affects (transportation-related) sunk costs, and therefore the competitiveness of U.S. goods when compared to other suppliers. This very scenario occurred during the height of the COVID-19 pandemic, when ocean shipping rates skyrocketed across most trade lanes: The cost to ship a 40-foot container from China to the U.S. West Coast peaked at $20,600 in September 2021, whereas the same container can now be moved for around $1,400; an initial 1300% increase, that reverted to a 93% decrease. Without any control over the ships involved, the United States, along with other nations, became very unwilling participants in the most dramatic escalation in freight rates the world had ever seen.

iii. Finally, and more dramatically, a foreign provider may decide to deliberately disrupt or sabotage a port or shipping service, which would have a catastrophic flow-on effect to critical services and a wide range of sectors in the U.S. economy. This may occur out of protest, be motivated by financial or political reasons, or to support specific foreign military objectives. A template for how this might occur in the future was witnessed at the height of the pandemic: Foreign companies controlled (and still control) the majority of U.S. domestic terminals *and* the ships delivering the cargo to those terminals. If any of those companies had malicious intent, they could have 'weaponized trade' to cripple the U.S. economy.

## II. Economic influence, abroad

Of all the world's Flag States, the United States is the most concerned about (and is most affected by) the stability and health of the global economy. To maintain stability and influence requires the purposeful application of resources, which includes spending on key maritime and port infrastructure in developing (and geostrategically-positioned) nations. The United States has invested heavily in many countries overseas, supplying military oversight and intervention, and through the provision of aid and infrastructure support services. For example, over the last 10 years, the U.S. has committed between $6 and $10 billion in economic support to key countries across Africa. While this is admirable, a recent China Africa Research Initiative (CARI) report detailed that "from 2010 to 2020, Chinese firms and financial institutions committed over $159 billion in financing and investment to African countries during the same period".

Prioritizing spending for foreign infrastructure projects is complicated. Making sure the money is applied in the right areas, even more so. Balance is essential, as is intentionality; investments need to be made that will clearly achieve specific aims. To extend geostrategic influence, the U.S. has a long history of investing in military infrastructure in regions all across the world. Investments in large-scale maritime projects are not as common, however that may be changing.

In November 2023, the U.S. International Development Finance Corp (DFC) committed $553 million to build a deepwater port terminal in Colombo, Sri Lanka. This was the largest investment the DFC has made in Asia, and one of their largest infrastructure investments of all time. Additionally, the U.S. recently announced a $125 million investment in the Elefsis shipyard near Piraeus, Greece to provide alternate options for the region that were not tied to China. To extend influence across global trade lanes, and to further assure U.S. Economic Security abroad, the DFC and other strategically-aligned groups must carefully replicate these decisions elsewhere.

## III. Risky business practices

Even in the absence of hostile intentions directed at the United States, excessive foreign influence over critical assets and infrastructure unnecessarily exposes the U.S. to risky and opaque business practices. This is made more complicated if these practices originate in jurisdictions where the U.S. does not have effective oversight, or legal or trade agreements in place. Examples of these practices may include taking on excessive debt, engaging the services of exploited labor, using lax cybersecurity practices, collaborating with trading partners with higher counterparty risk, or operating with lower safety standards.

A nefarious practice that has garnered a significant amount of recent attention is 'modern slavery'; a set of specific legal concepts including debt bondage, forced marriage, forced labor, slavery (and slavery-like practices), and human trafficking. Exploited parties cannot easily leave these situations due the threat of violence, or the presence of coercion, deception, and/or an abuse of power. Such practices have become widespread in the industrial fisheries sector, especially across large parts of Asia and for Distant Water Fishing Fleets. On the maritime side, during the COVID-19 pandemic, poor business practices meant that over half a million seafarers spent a prolonged period of time stuck on their vessels beyond the end of their contracts throughout 2020 and 2021.

The United States can take proactive steps to eradicate such practices longer term. This can occur through advocacy, active industry engagement and, where necessary, hard and soft power projection. However, like many other areas explored throughout this book, exercising visible leadership is difficult when the United States does not have many mariners serving on international ships, and there is a diminished number of U.S.-flagged commercial ships traversing the ocean.

## D. Missed Blue Economy Opportunities

To maintain Economic Security longer-term, the U.S. must assess and pursue activities that build domestic maritime capacity, while capturing emerging opportunities in new and evolving sectors.

### I. The Blue Economy

According to the World Bank, the Blue Economy includes all of the employment, ecosystem and cultural services provided by the ocean; this includes fisheries and aquaculture, ocean energy and non-living resource extraction, and non-marine-based activities, like coastal tourism, shipbuilding and port activities. If the global 'Blue Economy' were a country, it would be the world's seventh-largest economy; generating revenues of between $3-$6 trillion, and comparable to Japan, Germany, India, or the United Kingdom.

The U.S. has access to some of the world's most advanced technologies that could readily be applied to these fast-growing sectors, yet does not provide leadership in many Blue Economy initiatives. This means the U.S. is rapidly being left behind on the world stage and also ceding billions of dollars to other countries by not pursuing profitable Blue Economy opportunities. These include projects, technologies and solutions involving coastal and offshore aquaculture; maritime waste processing and disposal; bioprospecting; ocean-based energy solutions such as tidal and offshore windpower; and, new types of efficient vessel propulsion systems and fuels.

In addition, the U.S. has a sophisticated international financial system. This system could find innovative new finance solutions for the Blue Economy, using new financial technologies to ensure provenance tracking of seafood, new fintech trade finance products (such as electronic Bills of Lading and derivative financial products), maritime insurance for short sea shipping and safer, more verified vessels, crew and cargo. Competitor infrastructure programs like China's Belt and Road Initiative, are supported by tailored financial products from the newly formed Asia Infrastructure Investment Bank (AIIB) and the New Development Bank (NDB). Even multilateral groups like the Asian Development Bank are developing Blue Economy Financing solutions ('Blue Finance'). The U.S. is falling behind in offering such innovative new Blue Finance products to build the sustainable Blue Economy.

## II. Global Commercial Carriers

As illustrated from the first pages of this book, global supply chains are heavily dependent on maritime transportation to move products across the world. The U.S. does not have a significant commercial fleet, and therefore cannot supply marine transportation services to participants, including its own, involved in global trade. Without an available fleet, the United States is unable to generate profit from trading opportunities that take place across the world, every single day. The attempt to expand the U.S. commercial fleet must be navigated carefully. Industry veteran Jon Monroe sums up this sentiment: "I would say this is possibly the toughest industry in the world to be a part of and make a profit. It has to be one of the most, if not the most, capital intensive industries in the world."

The carriers that transport shipping containers around the globe have historically faced cycles of pronounced boom and bust. A profitable boom period after the Global Financial Crisis in 2008/9, was followed by many years of losses. The volatility induced by the COVID-19 pandemic caused another shipping boom, which was far greater than anything the world had ever witnessed before. Consumer demand fell, then skyrocketed in certain product categories. Suppliers - retailers, producers and manufacturers - also experienced wild oscillations; over-ordering was followed by stockouts, which was followed by the accumulation of excessive inventories. Volatility in demand and supply required more goods to be shipped of course, which was highly profitable for most ocean carriers.

The United States does not have a commercial container carrier in the global top 10. The United States does not have a commercial container carrier in the global top 20. The largest U.S. commercial container carrier is Matson: Matson has 28 ships, supplies just 0.2% of global container carrying capacity (65,000 TEU) and is the highest ranked (and only) U.S. carrier in the global top 30, in 28th place. By contrast, Denmark's Maersk accounts for around 15% of global container capacity, and is ranked 2nd overall on vessel count (678) and total carrying capacity (4,119,154 TEU).

Unlike privately-owned, and first ranked Mediterranean Shipping Company (MSC), Maersk publicly discloses their financial and operational numbers which makes it possible to compare financial data between Maersk and Matson, during the shipping boom from 2020 to 2022.

- Maersk generated revenues of $39.7B in 2020, $61.78B in 2021, and $81.5B in 2022, for a total of $184B in revenue and a healthy profit (EBITDA) of $62.9 billion, over that three year period

- Matson generated $2.4B (2020), $3.9B (2021), and $4.3B (2022), for a total of $10.6B in revenue, and $2.4 billion in profit across the same timeframe.

Now, imagine if the U.S.-owned Matson was the size of Maersk: Firstly, during a period of heightened global disruption, Matson would have been able to stabilize local trade flows, by drawing on existing capacity to process U.S. imports and exports. Preferential treatment could have been extended to U.S. exporters in particular, who suffered greatly during the pandemic due to a lack of available export containers.

And secondly, if operating at the size and scale of Maersk (during 2020-2022), Matson would have been in control of over $180 billion in revenue and $62.9 billion in profit, while providing gainful employment to thousands of U.S. workers. To put that in perspective: If the full corporate rate had been paid, Matson's tax contribution would have almost single-handedly funded President Biden's $17 billion-dollar Bipartisan Infrastructure Law; "the largest federal investment in U.S. history" which has been designed to "improve the country's ports and waterways."

### III. Anemic domestic innovation

Government organizations involved in regulating and resourcing shipping activities have not proactively supported the U.S. domestic maritime sector, and are reluctant to initiate the reforms desperately required to fix structural issues. The combination of these and other related factors has resulted in an anemic domestic maritime industry that does not enhance U.S. domestic productivity, and decreases international competitiveness. This can be observed with U.S. exporters who suffer great financial losses whenever shipping capacity is unavailable; recent delays that left U.S. almonds in storage for over a year, resulted in a degradation loss of $2 billion to the U.S. almond industry.

Opportunistic, incumbent carriers, a lack of innovative thinking, and excessive foreign influence has meant that many solutions where the U.S. could lead have been quashed.

Examples include: Building modular micro-containers for more flexible shipping; the creation of a Green Marine Highways; establishing an Inland Waterway Authority to increase the competitiveness of domestic waterways for shipping; pioneering autonomous navigation technologies; developing floating crane infrastructure; and, exploring low carbon fuels technologies. These technologies are often proposed and opposed, when vested interests determine that individual profits are more important than collective economic gains for the U.S. economy.

U.S. domestic supply chains are another area that suffers from a chronic lack of investment and innovation. The U.S. needs logistics networks that are fast, low cost, and highly interoperable across all modes of transportation. Inefficiencies can cause ripple effects both up and down the supply chain, that lead to overordering, disruption in supply, and price volatility. While this is widely understood, a range of structural deficiencies - minimal data sharing, excess use of paperwork, few digitally enabled processes, and aging infrastructure that has not been improved for years - have existed inside U.S. supply chains for decades.

Because of these practices, domestic supply chains suffer from decreased efficiency and degraded security. Supply chain efficiency is important. Supply chain security is essential; required from point of origin, through to final destination, and in a continuous, repeatable fashion. Securing U.S. supply chains must also move beyond purely geographic concerns as is commonly debated with nearshoring and offshoring. Comprehensive supply chain security must be carefully considered and intentionally pursued, which has been the central mantra of the emerging ‘sure-shoring’ movement; a movement that has gained significant momentum over the past three years.

This is in sharp contrast to the power of other companies in the private sector. U.S. e-commerce firms like Amazon have completely re-imagined the shopping and shipping experience, and are now rolling out new fleets of electric vehicles across a global warehouse and logistics distribution business. This is creating trillions of dollars of new value pools. Similarly, U.S.-based carriers like FedEx and UPS are global leaders in freight logistics. With technology companies like Microsoft, Alphabet, Amazon, Apple all pioneering new approaches to their global supply chains and energy practices, the U.S. should be exploring how to create national public-private partnerships to leverage such expertise in creating a more efficient national logistics system.

## IV. Misaligned taxes

Other profitable initiatives like Short-Sea Shipping are unable to gain traction due to the uncompetitive nature of how maritime taxes are charged and spent. The Harbor Maintenance Tax (HMT) levies a 0.125% tax on cargo value and was originally designed to offset the costs of deep draught dredging operations. Since 2003, collected HMT produced a 'surplus' of $6.4 billion, and currently generates over $500 million a year for the U.S. Treasury. Much of the expended revenue is not re-invested to modernize U.S. port infrastructure or operations, but is used instead to equalize the federal deficit.

To make this worse, the way HMT is applied discourages the use of domestic waterborne transportation. Cargo entering the U.S. by ship is subject to HMT. If that cargo is transported by rail or truck to another destination within the U.S., it is not subject to any additional HMT. However, if that same cargo is then transported on another commercial vessel, such as a transfer to a vessel as part of a "marine highway," it is taxed HMT a second time, as soon as it arrives at that second U.S.

port. This 'double taxation' creates a significant penalty if a shipper opts to use (more efficient, less carbon-intensive) waterborne transportation to move cargo around inland locations. By inflating costs in this manner, the Harbor Maintenance Tax essentially kills the potential to develop a vibrant Short-Sea Shipping industry in the United States.

## V. Illicit trade

Shipping sadly plays a central role in facilitating the movement of illicit trade around the world and into the United States. The trade of illicit, illegal, or counterfeit goods significantly harms innovation, the U.S. economy, U.S. economic competitiveness and a range of domestic industries.

While estimates vary, the global amount of counterfeit goods sold each year comes in at somewhere between $1.7 trillion to $4.5 trillion. At around 60% to 80% for some product categories, American shoppers tend to purchase the highest share of counterfeit goods. Wine, as one category of many, was reported to have a counterfeit rate as high as 20%, or 1 in every 5 bottles. Over 39,000 U.S. wholesale jobs and 280,000 jobs in retail have been lost because of the introduction of counterfeit products into the U.S. marketplace. This equates to over $13.6 billion in wages and other benefits that could have been allocated to U.S. workers, and a subsequent reduction in tax collected by the government.

Smuggling includes the illegal movement of goods, guns, drugs, and people. Containerized transportation is commonly used for these activities, as demonstrated with the drug seizure involving the MSC Gayane in 2019. Cocaine bricks were discovered in the ship's hold that weighed around 20 tons and had an estimated street value of USD$1.3 billion; making this the largest drug seizure in the history of the U.S. Customs and

Border Protection agency. In a similarly impacting fashion, human trafficking yields $150 billion in illegal annual profits to the cartels and insidious individuals engaged in this loathsome trade. Around a 1/3 of these profits come from forced labor, while the other two thirds are made from commercial sexual exploitation, typically involving women and children. Smuggling is economically corrosive to both the originating and receiving destinations, causes chaotic social upheaval and intense misery for victims, and victims' families.

While the U.S. Navy and U.S. Coast Guard are actively involved in interdiction, more can be done - especially with supply chains entering the United States - to eradicate illegal and illicit goods, and reduce the impact of these products on the U.S. domestic market. Noting that the most effective way to minimize the frequency of these incidents occurring would be to increase the number of U.S.-flagged ships that are involved in international trade.

## E. Shipping and the Cost of Living

Between 2010–2020, U.S. inflation averaged 2.9%, but spiked to 5.2% during 2021; and reached its highest level in 40 years, in March 2022. Consensus is mixed about the factors that contributed to inflationary pressures and an increase in prices over this time, however the most feasible conclusion is that over the course of the pandemic, price increases can be attributed to an increase in shipping costs; partially, but not entirely. Other factors responsible for a rise in domestic prices included extreme demand volatility, the impact of government fiscal stimulus, and supply-side shocks that massively disrupted the operations and purchasing patterns of retailers, manufacturers, importers and exporters.

What *was* observed during this time was a higher proportion of shipping costs being passed through to purchasers; which in turn, was passed on to consumers. This was especially true for goods transported by sea (a high percentage of all goods) and for low-cost items that had disproportionately higher shipping costs; a commonly cited example was a standard couch, that is relatively cheap, but bulky, in volume to ship. Recent research has revealed there was a greater degree of pass-through in certain categories like food, machines, electronics, and spare parts. This suggests that perishable and intermediate goods are more likely to have higher pass-through values compared with other types of consumer goods.

Higher transportation costs impact consumers and the domestic economy in different ways. One immediate impact was the perception from consumers that they were now paying much higher prices for goods than they had before. This was not strictly (or mathematically) true for most purchases, but led to a general feeling that shipping was the primary reason behind the price rises; a notion seized upon by opportunistic retailers who disproportionately increased their prices and subsequently made sizable profits. Flow-on price increases - where each link in the supply chain adds a little extra to cover their own rising costs - did occur, which often meant much higher prices at the checkout; a cycle that continued until consumer sentiment changed, and demand receded across 2022.

The greatest impact during this time was not effectuated by a rise in shipping costs, as much as it was caused by extremes in *volatility*. Unnatural spikes in demand for certain goods - due to a reduction in COVID-restricted consumer service spending - influenced retailers to over-order, which burdened already stretched supply chains, and created a vicious cycle of boom and bust. This boom and bust cycle was clearly observable during 2023, in the rapidly cooling ocean freight-rate market that dropped considerably over the year; to below pre-COVID levels, in some trade lanes.

What was needed was structural policy reforms that could increase the degree of control over various instruments - in this case, ships, ports and other modes of distribution - that contributed to the volatility. Consider what might have happened if 10, 25, or even 50% of all U.S. commercial trade was able to be carried by U.S.-flagged ships during the pandemic? Extra tonnage would have been available to preferentially move U.S. cargo, and it would have been easier to clear backlogs at larger gateways, by redirecting compliant vessels to underutilized ports. Those same U.S.-flagged carriers could have also shared in the 'Great Maritime Gold Rush' and earned a noticeable share of the $360 billion windfall profit that commercial carriers generated over the course of the pandemic.

## Economic Security Maritime Solutions and Opportunities

The following solutions and opportunities are matched to the maritime risks and vulnerabilities explored throughout this Principle:

1. **Risk: Poor understanding of the role of shipping in the economy**
   **Solution: National Maritime Awareness Campaigns**
   Shipping is central to the functioning of the U.S. economy and should not be marginalized or omitted from public discourse. The Department of Transportation (DOT), MARAD and other associated agencies can play a strategic role in explaining how ships, shipping and maritime activities positively impact the domestic economy and U.S. consumers. This might also take the form of advertisements, statements, or campaigns that are specifically designed to raise the level of understanding about what these agencies and departments do, and how each department directly affects U.S. economic growth. For example, whenever a public announcement is made about how one of these agencies is allocating funding and resources, a small percentage of the assigned budget should be used to create a simple and purposeful awareness campaign that explains what this investment means for the U.S. maritime sector and the wider U.S. economy.

2. **Risk: "Economic Security is National Security" largely misunderstood**
   **Solution: National & Economic Security Plan - Maritime (NESP-M)**
   The NESP-M would bring much-needed attention to how these two traditionally siloed areas have

converged. Creating an NESP-M would be a joint exercise between institutions, agencies and departments involved in National Security on one side, and the economic planners (politicians, governors, academics, captains of industry and commercial entities such as the National Industrial Transportation League) on the other. Industry case studies along with simulations involving commercial and naval maritime operators would be run, to ascertain where risks could appear and where opportunities might exist. The creation of an NESP-M would be completed in collaboration with participants in the newly created Maritime National Training Center (MNTC) proposed in the Principle of National Security.

3. **Risk: International fiscal and currency flows and sanctions**
   **Solution: Expand financial offerings for commercial trade**
   Trade finance can be complicated to negotiate and arrange for commercial trading partners, particularly if they are separated by geography and also have legal or language barriers. Requirements for Know Your Customer (KYC), Anti-Money Laundering (AML), and Countering Financing of Terrorism (CTF) add necessary, but onerous layers to these transactions. U.S. financial institutions and corporations can pioneer payments processing for global trade, by using digital delivery channels, secured by modern methods of validation that have been implemented successfully in the banking sector e.g., smartphone-hosted multi-factor and multi-modal biometric authentication.

   Provisioning new services would also involve the provision of lending and financing facilities that could be more readily integrated into electronic Bills of Lading (eBLs). eBLs are currently being trialed between different industry participants and countries, and there is a verbal commitment by the world's largest container carriers to have eBL's integrated into the shipping industry by 2030. The risks associated with using U.S. Dollars (USD) for global trade would be mitigated, if the United States supplied highly-secure payment conduits to process transactions, and offered a range of financial services alongside friction-reducing initiatives like eBL's.

4. **Risk: Shipping industry influence and government oversight MIA**
   **Solution: Expand MARAD and the Federal Maritime Commission (FMC)**
   MARAD and the FMC require more funding and more people to complete all of the complicated tasks related to managing, regulating and enforcing regulations within the U.S. maritime sector. While staff size does not always equate to real results, an increase in headcount would mean that new, innovative, and intentional actions could be pursued by a team with the necessary resources and support to perform inspections, assessments, and enforcement actions, in the U.S. and abroad. This would balance out the influence of the commercial shipping industry and subsequently have a noticeable effect on global maritime affairs.

   In conjunction with focused investment and an expansion of the U.S. maritime sector in general, a proportional target should be set to increase the size of both agencies. Suppose the FMC and MARAD expanded to 10,000 people by 2035: While this sounds extreme, 10,000 staff would only be one quarter the size of the current staff pool at the Federal Aviation Authority. Furthermore, if the current FMC budget - $44 million for 110 staff, or $400,000 per staff member

- was used to calculate the staff spend of the FMC and MARAD with 10,000 team members, an annual budget of only $4 billion would be required. While this equates to a 4x increase on the current combined budget of both agencies, $4 billion is still 4.2x lower than the current annual budget of the FAA.

5. **Risk: Minimal U.S. representation during some strategic international discussions**
   **Solution: Greater U.S. influence at IMO & global conferences**
   The diminished presence of U.S.-flagged ships and U.S.-owned commercial assets engaged in international trade, could reduce the influence the United States can exercise over global maritime affairs; including critical issues like setting acceptable international trade routes, or drafting the rules that govern the environmental impact of shipping activities. This occurs at the IMO as conventions are implemented when an agreed national Flag tonnage threshold is reached; which effectively gives Panama, Liberia and the Marshall Islands veto power over IMO conventions as their combined tonnage outweighs the rest of the world. This reduction in influence will be even more pronounced, if the role, size and deployment routine of the U.S. Navy changes significantly over the coming decade.

   U.S. envoys, delegates and agency spokespeople (along with a new cohort of business leaders and entrepreneurs) must continue to be well represented at the International Maritime Organization (IMO) and maritime industry forums, to minimize the chance the U.S. will be relegated from leader to participant in the global commercial maritime domain. Representation at the IMO must include continuing on Council, promoting the critical work of the U.S. Coast Guard; the

USCG provides a large proportion of expertise for the IMO's Maritime Safety Committee as well as the growing body of technical expertise.

Advocacy at the IMO and presenting at events like the annual TransPacific Maritime (TPM) conference in Long Beach, California, CMA Shipping Conference, and Posidonia Conference in Greece, will provide tangible evidence that U.S. administrators and government departments are actively promoting the U.S. maritime sector, and are willing to engage with a wider group of international stakeholders. Increased visibility and advocacy will allow U.S. Maritime Administrators to hear the conversations taking place within the industry, and be an active voice in the collective decision-making that follows.

6. **Risk: Underinvestment, vested-interests and foreign influence**
   **Solution: The U.S. Economic Security Program (ESP)**
   An equivalent program to the Maritime Security Program (MSP) and the Tanker Security Program (TSP) with a focus on Economic Security must be explored. The priority of the U.S. Economic Security Program will be to increase the amount of U.S.-controlled, ocean-going tonnage, engaged in international trade. This may be achieved by rapidly flagging-in purposefully-selected foreign-built tonnage into the U.S. Flag fleet, or, as some have suggested, by creating a 2nd U.S. Register (second U.S. maritime Flag). Second registries implemented by other nations have had mixed results. Incentives for rapidly flagging-in foreign-built ships should include favorable taxation or insurance conditions, or other benefits that go beyond cargo preferences to offset the price differential of operating a

U.S.-flagged ship vs a cheaper foreign-flagged equivalent.

An intentional expansion of U.S. influence in the international commercial maritime sector must be pursued, regardless of which option is selected. One specific pathway would be to set realistic targets to acquire or solidify access to U.S.-controlled ships through the ESP within a specified timeframe. For example, 2% of the world's commercial fleet by 2030, 5% by 2038 and 10% by 2050. A bold growth strategy should be declared, and purposefully pursued. Expand from 0.4%, to 2% in 7 years (4% in ten years). 1,000 ships for the Economic Security Program is a justifiable initial target for the U.S. to begin to have a competitive international fleet.

**Why 1000 vessels?** There were about 80,000 foreign vessel port calls into U.S. ports last year involved in $1.8 trillion of traded goods and commodities. Assuming that involved about 6,000 distinct ships, then increasing the U.S. flag fleet to 1,000 ships making regular U.S. port calls could be about 17% of the port calls. Although that would not be enough capacity to support the entire U.S. economy, it's reasonable to assume that no more than half of the normal foreign flag fleet would abandon the U.S. trade in favor of a strategic competitor, therefore the import/export trade might only be reduced by 33% instead of 50%.

Other useful numerical comparisons are:

- There were about 800 US international commercial ships in 1982 (year of UN Convention on Law of the Sea). The U.S. negotiators of UNCLOS would likely have assumed that the U.S. would maintain around 800 commercial ships to assist the USN and USCG to monitor compliance and benefit from the convention.

- The pre-World War 1 and pre-World War 2 U.S. flag international fleets made up about 10% of the world fleet. That's a lot higher percentage than today's 1,000 of 50,000 would be, but today's globalization is likely ten times more extensive, so 2% percent may be comparable.
- Other maritime nations, China, Russia, Korea, Norway, UK, France, maintain a rough ratio of 1:1 nationally owned foreign flag ships vs. nationally flagged ships. Since there are about 1,000 U.S. nationally owned foreign flag ships, 1,000 U.S. flagged international ships would align with other country's fleet ratios.
- U.S. international commercial aircraft make up about 10% of all international commercial aircraft. Far less cargo is flown internationally, so again the impact of globalization on shipping may make two percent somewhat comparable. Since both modes go hand in hand supporting the economy it only makes sense that they share equal importance in our national strategies.

If the United States-controlled fleet reached 10% of the world's commercial, ocean-going ships by 2050, the U.S. merchant marine would be comparable in size to China's; with a similar global presence, and would have reaped significant economic rewards for the U.S. economy and U.S. citizens along the way.

The U.S. ESP must secure the maritime assets required to assure U.S. Economic Security for the *coming* century, and not be built around the activities of the one that has passed. To that end, the U.S. must build or acquire a fit-for-purpose commercial fleet blend that accommodates the evolving nature of globalized trade, the growing need for decarbonized transport, the anticipated sealift needs of DoD, and the efficiency gains that have come from modern, digitized processes.

7. **Risk: Overexposure to risky business practices**
   **Solution: Global Maritime Risk Index (GMRI)**
   A global index applied to the international commercial fleet would analyze the business practices of ship operators, service providers and Flag States, and supply metrics about the likelihood that these entities might engage in risky business practices. Similar statistics have been generated by a range of private companies, and have proved useful to commercial operators as decisions are made about third parties involved in transactions and trade. The GMRI provides an effective 'safety net' and improves the effectiveness of U.S. government administrators - overseeing tariffs and taxes - as well as law enforcement agencies involved in detecting supply chain threats including sanctions violations.

8. **Risk: Missed opportunities in the Blue Economy**
   **Solution: Effective communication of profitable maritime investments**
   To capture a wide range of Blue Economy opportunities, partnerships must be established with Wall Street and the U.S. investment community, so that increased funding can flow more quickly into the maritime sector. Collaborative value creation can be achieved by adopting a similar approach as the Department of Transportations' ARPA-I (Infrastructure) model, where shared responsibility and investment is split between the public and private

sectors. Education about the centrality of shipping, and clear articulation of investment returns for patiently invested capital in long-term projects must be factored into these discussions.

Blue Economy opportunities that might be attractive to investors in the United States include:

- Improving the percentages of plastic waste recycling, repurposing, reduction and removal from the marine environment, to encourage growth in the circular economy activities
- Using seaweed and other marine life such as algae to produce new materials to replace certain types of plastics and alternate types of biofuel.
- Investigating the potential of large-scale 3D-printing (metal and composites) for rapid part replacement, or to construct subsea assets and ocean-going vessels
- Developing more efficient components - e.g., reducing the amount of rare-earth metals - used in sustainable power generation technologies like offshore wind, floating solar farms and tidal turbines
- Creating a 'blue bond market' centered around the funding of sustainable Blue Economy projects. A model for this emerged recently when Morgan Stanley oversaw a $3.5 billion bond issuance for the Export-Import Bank of Korea; this included a tranche of $1 billion that would be allocated to sustainable marine transportation initiatives

Alongside these initiatives, a variety of other reward schemes can be formulated that would generate more opportunities for funding and investment. For example, U.S. ship-owners could be offered financial incentives to encourage direct investment in U.S. shipbuilding companies. This would de-risk the investments, and allow all participants to receive an appreciable return for expended effort, time and capital.

9. **Risk: Illicit trade and global supply chain security Solution: Intelligent Containerized Trade**
   Supply chain security is a niche discipline that generally only receives attention when something goes wrong. A growing number of commercial entities – most recently Hapag Lloyd, Ocean Network Express (ONE) and Maersk – are turning to intelligent containers to improve cargo and supply chain security, transparency and visibility. Some of this activity is consumer-led. For example there has been an increased desire to 'see' where globally shipped goods are to reduce delays, or to prevent product loss, damage or theft. Another factor that validates the need for intelligent containers is the increase in the shipment of electric vehicles and other consumer products that contain lithium ion batteries that are prone to catching fire in transit. Seals can reduce the incidents of theft of these high-value goods, and sensors can detect thermal runaway events with stored batteries before they escalate out of control.

   The U.S. could be a world leader in intelligent containerization through the development of modern electronic seals – that would replace the basic, single-use equivalents – and integrating sensors into containers, while encouraging data standards and interoperability between supply chain participants. This would help the U.S. CBP and USCG perform a greater number of data-augmented and risk-assessed container inspections; due to large volumes, and a lack of available personnel, less than 2% of all containers are inspected as they enter the United States.

Intelligent containers, when connected to more advanced forms of communications such as LEO-hosted communication satellites, can also track containers involved in intermodal delivery for diplomatic cargo, or those used by the DOD. These modern tracking and security solutions would have been very useful in the early 90's, prior to, and during the conflict in Iraq. Military cargo being shipped from the U.S. to Kuwait was only tracked using basic Radio Frequency ID (RFID) Tags, which did not prevent theft, or actively report tampering. This led to approximately $1.2 billion dollars' worth of military cargo being lost between origin and destination.

10. **Risk: Anemic innovation in the U.S. maritime sector**
    **Solution: U.S. Maritime Economic Innovation Fund (MEIF)**
    Due to the complex nature of maritime operations, it can be very challenging for maritime technology startups to scale up innovations beyond initial seed grants. Federal involvement - through funding, or the creation of innovation hubs - will help the U.S. build the next generation of products and services, and grow the next cohort of industry leaders, in a similar fashion to the private space sector. A Maritime Economic Innovation Fund (MEIF) would pool co-invested capital from Government and industry, and invest it into newly developed innovative maritime technologies, processes and assets.

    The solutions being funded through the MEIF would be directly aligned with the key imperatives of the U.S. maritime and Economic Security agendas. Funded technologies would be rapidly commercialized, with profits – derived from sales, licensing or IP - split between invested parties, and where possible, re-invested into the scheme to keep it sustainable over time. New strategically-aligned technologies might include:

- Developing new methods of propulsion, including redesigning of propellers and hulls, to reduce drag coefficients and improve fuel efficiency.
- Material science innovations to improve surface durability, and reduce the amount of toxic additives in marine paint, to improve environmental outcomes and decrease ongoing maintenance costs.
- Improving the range and decreasing the cost of marine communications and connectivity – with a focus on expanding LEO-layer coverage and performance – will allow for additional technologies to be tried and tested in previously unreachable areas of the world.
- Deploying transformational technologies and systems – e.g., using augmented reality and voice-controlled systems to enhance safety or when performing inspections – will increase operational efficiencies, allow for rapid onboarding of recruits and improve the transfer of knowledge.
- Developing Artificial Intelligence (Deep Machine Learning), Natural Language Processing, and 'big data' analytics tools to radically transform how trade data is handled. This will also generate new revenue streams for government departments and government agencies.
- The roll-out of intelligent containers will enhance the work of Customs and Border Protection

(CBP) and other enforcement agencies, reduce sanctions and tariff violations, and enhance overall global supply chain security, visibility, and transparency.
- The construction of semi and fully-autonomous vessels – feeder, barge or for short sea distribution – will drive sustainability outcomes and improve delivery efficiencies.

These and a plethora of similar solutions are being researched and constructed by allies and foreign competitors across the world. For example, Singapore, Israel, and various European countries have successfully created maritime startup innovation hubs to encourage the development of new maritime technologies. The United States can learn from these endeavors as the MEIF is rolled out into the U.S. maritime sector.

11. **Risk: Misaligned taxes and inefficient maintenance of inland and coastal waterways**
    **Solution: U.S. Inland and Coastwise Waterways Authority (ICWA)**
    The United States is highly dependent on 'Green Marine Highways' that connect ports and waterways across CONUS as well as outlying U.S. territories. Maintenance of these Marine Highways relies on a complex set of relationships between state, county and city public officials, and also the Army Corps of Engineers and the private sector. More domestic waterway planning managers are needed, but many positions have been left vacant. This has decreased the quality of signage, led to delays with dredging operations, and affects infrastructure maintenance schedules. Longer-term costs associated with maintaining waterways (due to reactive vs proactive

maintenance) also increases, as does the likelihood of accidents or mishaps, while overall efficiency decreases across the Marine Highway network.

Many regions of the world, like the EU, UK and India have a holistic Inland Waterways Authority that ensures all critical waterway infrastructure is modern, well maintained and properly managed. The U.S. ICWA would work in conjunction with the Short-Sea Shipping Coalition (described in a subsequent solution) and the Army Corps of Engineers (ACOE) to perform a range of necessary tasks to enhance Marine Highway functionality, and ensure that these crucial conduits of domestic supply are running at optimal levels. The ICWA would co-administer the allocation of funding from the Harbor Maintenance Tax (HMT) with the ACOE to ensure that unfair penalties are avoided by those using the inland waterway system, and that key improvements and upgrades are properly funded.

12. **Risk: Shipping, inflation and the cost of living**
    **Solution: Maritime Risk Register (MRR) & Economic Impact Barometer (EIB)**
    A Maritime Risk Register would aim to quantify what economic impact would be felt by all concerned parties, in the event of various probable and realistic disruption scenarios. A pertinent example from recent events: MRR data would quantify the impact of an escalated labor dispute that shuts down key West Coast ports and terminals. The initial purpose of an MRR – accompanied by a visual Economic Impact Barometer – would be to inform key stakeholders about how each of these events affects them, but would then move to prompt responsive action i.e. guide what to do in the event a disruption occurred. MRR and EIB data would be directly disclosed to key maritime stakeholders, and

then aggregated and distributed to the public. Trends would reveal the effect of different events on different sectors of the economy, and also provide information that would improve the general level of understanding about the impact of maritime issues on the U.S. economy as a whole.

13. **Risk: Underutilization of one of the most efficient forms of transportation**
**Solution: The Short-Sea Shipping Coalition (SSSC)**
For the last three decades Short-Sea Shipping (SSS) has been described as the most important development that has ever been developed for U.S. transportation. To highlight this importance, Short-Sea Shipping was recently renamed to "America's Marine Highways" and given priority status by the U.S. Department of Transportation (DOT), and has since received widespread bipartisan support.

As has been briefly mentioned, and will be reiterated across the Principles that follow, the inland waterway system in the United States is an untapped resource that could be used to drive increased transportation efficiency and massively reduce emissions. The United States has some of the best river systems, inland waterways, and favorable coastlines in the world, and yet has not implemented a major Marine Highway Plan, or spent a noticeable amount of money on related initiatives. MARAD's 2023 budget included $10 million for U.S. Marine Highways, which is in contrast to the billions that most large countries in Europe and Asia have successfully invested in Short-Sea Shipping over the last decade.

Two examples: The People's Republic of China is currently investing billions of dollars to purchase and build Chinese-owned and operated ports in Africa - over 100 seaports have been built since the early 2000's - many of which will supply SSS services. Secondly, the European Union uses Short-Sea Shipping to transport billions of dollars of goods every year - SSS accounts for over 60% of all seaborn cargo moved between member countries - which will increase even further over the coming years. For example, there are plans to shift around 30% of all truck hauls to alternate modes, which will predominantly move to various forms of shipping.

The following reasons demonstrate why Short-Sea Shipping plays an important role in increasing U.S. domestic productivity, reduces the impact of transportation on the environment, and helps to assure U.S. Economic Security:

- Short-Sea Shipping stimulates the national economy by providing a more cost-effective alternative for American businesses by utilizing existing ports and infrastructure. This shifts the reliance from larger regional super-ports, such as LA/LB, Houston/Galveston, Savannah and NY/NJ to a range of smaller, more geographically distributed alternatives.

- Environment, Fuel Consumption & Cost - In round numbers, waterborne transportation, including those using short-sea shipping routes:

    - Burns 3 times less fuel and emits 3 times less pollution than Trains (per ton-mile)

   - Burns 10 times less fuel and emits 10 times less pollution than Trucks.

   - Burns 100 times less fuel and emits 100 times less pollution than Planes.

- Without roads, bridges, crossings, or much signage required, SSS has less administrative overhead when compared to most other modes of transportation.

- SSS helps remove trucks from highly congested roads especially at vehicular choke points - where many cars and trucks move through narrow roads - or where physical features or regulations prevent expansion. This can decrease the amount of accidents that occur, and reduces the wear and tear on roads and other expensive infrastructure.

- SSS is much less susceptible to terrorist attacks and acts of war, as maritime vessels usually traverse through remote and less accessible locations.

- Short-Sea Shipping can provide the U.S. Merchant Marine with trained personnel and vessels. A ready supply of such personnel and vessels has been a critical factor in every conflict that has ever been fought.

- SSS can also play a role in transparently monitoring and enforcing emissions limitations which will assist to provide a level playing field for U.S. carriers.

To fully benefit from these and a range of other advantages, a U.S. Short-Sea Shipping Coalition (SSSC) should be created so that additional resources and funding is committed to SSS activities. The SSS Coalition will seek to actively collaborate with local, state, and federal stakeholders with the ultimate goal of creating SSS solutions that improve domestic efficiency and create new opportunities for partnership and investment.

*This page is intentionally left blank.*

# ENERGY AND FOOD SECURITY

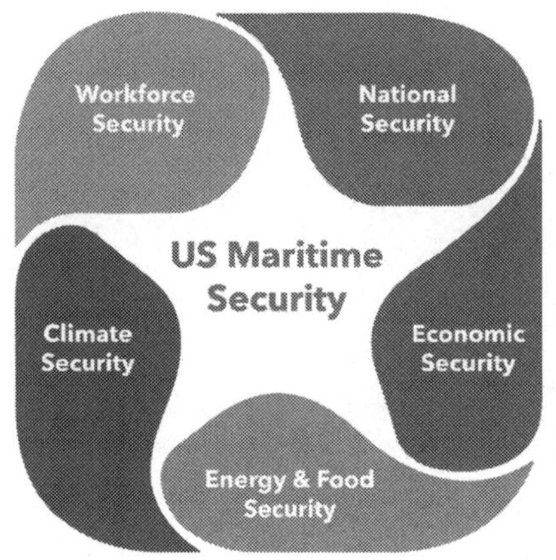


**Energy & Food Security**

- *Future national energy mix*
- *Energy and Food Ships*
- *Future maritime fuels*
- *Ownership*
- *Sanctions*

# III. ENERGY AND FOOD SECURITY

*One of the most serious long-term challenges facing our country is dependence on oil -- especially oil from foreign lands. It's a serious challenge. And members of Congress up here understand the challenge and so do I. Because this dependence harms us economically through high and volatile prices at the gas pump; dependence creates pollution and contributes to greenhouse gas emissions. It threatens our national security by making us vulnerable to hostile regimes in unstable regions of the world. It makes us vulnerable to terrorists who might attack oil infrastructure.*

- President George W. Bush, signing the Energy Independence and Security Act (2007)

*Food security is essential to the foundation of a broader peace and prosperity.*

- President Joe Biden, U.S.-Africa Leaders Summit (December 15, 2022)

## Energy and Food Security Context

As observed throughout various Industrial Revolutions, the nature of energy generation and distribution, and food production and consumption have markedly changed over time. From the days of steam power to the nuclear power plants of today, access to available, varied, affordable, and sustainable energy has been one of humanity's highest priorities. Food production has similarly changed in scope and scale, from the small-scale agrarian pursuits of yesteryear, to the large-scale crops and factory megafarms of today. This pursuit is justifiable: Access to abundant energy - to power machinery, run vehicles, generate light and heat - and being able to source adequate supplies of food - to improve health, increase productivity and sustain population growth - has often been the deciding factor between insecurity and security, lack and excess, or poverty and prosperity.

## Energy Security

A seismic shift is currently underway in the energy sector. Worldwide consumption of liquid fossil fuels is forecast to move beyond 100 million barrels per day in early 2024. If a world-wide commitment to transition to carbon-neutral fuels holds, this rate of daily fossil fuel consumption must migrate to a variety of different energy sources. As the world pursues decarbonization, a range of alternate fuel and energy types have emerged as potential candidates to displace the entrenched grip of traditional fossil fuels; for example Liquefied Natural Gas (LNG), Hydrogen, Ammonia, Methanol, Electrification, Nuclear and Biofuels.

Each of these forms of energy have differing systems for generation, control and regulation, and will need new techniques for supply and distribution. All of them, and especially those produced offshore, require some form of marine transportation; either for the movement of machinery and cargo, or to relocate fuel to bunkers and containment systems for storage.

How to improve global Energy Security is up for furious debate. While there is a widespread desire to transition to renewable and sustainable production and distribution, the process to do so is slow, and the mechanisms available to encourage adoption are often disconnected from economic and social realities. And while there is a plethora of research available about how to improve energy efficiency and reduce emissions, there has also been massive differences of opinion on which actions to pursue first.

This is made decidedly more complicated if conflicting information is disseminated by vested interests. A recent example has stemmed from advances in detection technology that proved methane slip is far worse in LNG-fueled marine engines than previously thought. This has caused a stir among supporters and activists alike. When confusion reigns, paralysis and indecision ensues; the latter being the worst state of all, as it means many years can go by without any significant shift in policies or practice, which leaves the world in the same place it was before (and with more emissions, pollution and mess).

Energy Security is of great importance to the maritime sector. Shipping is responsible for the movement of a large amount of energy: By weight, 40% of all maritime trade consists either of fossil fuels on their way to be burned, or of products derived directly from fossil fuels, for example coal, oil, gas and petrochemicals. While shipping is the most efficient form of transportation per ton mile, shipping is also one of the largest polluters. Recent changes in regulation, shifts in consumer sentiment, and improvements in visibility across supply chains, has placed increased pressure on the shipping industry to be more energy efficient. While increased visibility has been welcomed by some, it also introduces new cost pressures that impact profitability which eventually affects consumers.

Shipping faces the delicate task of balancing economic progress, and the need to be environmentally responsible and sustainable; and must do so within a domain that is disproportionately more complicated when compared to other sectors. To add to this complexity, ships that transport energy are opportunistically targeted by pirates in various regions of the world (e.g., off the West Coast of Africa) and have come under fire during the recent conflict in the Red Sea. These events endanger the crews transporting the energy products, and also affect the Energy Security of the recipients (nations, economies and communities) relying on these products to be safely delivered.

## Food Security

The World Bank definition of Food Security was drafted in 1996, and has remained largely unchanged for the last 27 years: "when all people, at all times, have physical and economic access to sufficient safe and nutritious food that meets their dietary needs and food preferences for an active and healthy life." This definition is underpinned by a set of four specific characteristics:

I. **Availability:** Food is readily available, in sufficient quantities. Supplied food is of an appropriate quality, and has been supplied through domestic production, or via imports (which may include food aid). Availability and the transportation of food (including minimizing spoilage in transit) are closely linked.

II. **Access:** Resources are available for individuals to acquire appropriate foods to maintain a nutritious diet. Resources may include 'entitlements' or various forms of commodity bundles over which a person can command, control or direct, according to the legal, political, economic and social arrangements of the community in which they live. This may include traditional rights such as access to common resources like land and water.

III. **Utilization:** Adequate diet, clean water, sanitation and health care are made available so that a state of nutritional well-being is possible. This meets physiological needs, and highlights the importance of non-food inputs in Food Security

IV. **Stability:** Stability includes elements of access and availability and is a key factor in determining how Food Security is measured. A population, household or individual must have access to adequate food at all times. The risk of losing access to food as a consequence of an economic or climatic crisis, or because of cyclical events (e.g. seasonal food insecurity) should be minimized or, preferably entirely eliminated.

These four characteristics paint a comprehensive picture of what Food Security (and, conversely, insecurity) looks like, for many people across the world. According to the Food and Agriculture Association (FAO), about 29.6% of the global population – around 2.4 billion people – were moderately or severely food insecure in 2022; 391 million more than 2019. These numbers are likely to grow over time, as populations are displaced or affected by conflict or wars, and as key food supply regions (including the ocean) are impacted by mismanagement, misuse or suffer from the effects of climate change.

# Energy & Food Security and U.S. Shipping

## A. Energy Security and U.S. Shipping - Historical maritime exploration

The United States has a long history of maritime energy exploration, production and distribution, ever since the earliest days of settlement.

### *Whale Oil*

Blue-water whaling began in 1712 when U.S. whalers near Nantucket discovered that sperm whales were a rich supply of highly valued whale oil. By 1774, two years before the start of the American Revolution, the colonial deep water whaling fleet numbered 360 vessels, hailing from 15 ports in New England and New York. An estimated 900 vessels were engaged in whaling worldwide by the late 1840s; over 700 of them were presumed to be American. One of America's biggest years of production was in 1845, when 525,000 barrels of whale and sperm oil were produced; and used for lighting, heating, cooking and lubricating a range of machines, from watches to chronometers.

### *Crude Oil*

Pennsylvania crude oil production began in 1859, with oil being shipped in 42 gallon barrels. By the mid-1860s, U.S. shipyards assembled early oil tanker prototypes with independent, or partly-hulled tanks to increase capacity and improve safety. These efforts resulted in the construction of the wooden sailing ship Atlantic, a 45 meter long brigantine delivered in 1865, and the 794-ton iron ship The Charles, in 1869. Both ships incorporated a set of separated tanks designed to store crude and refined oils. By 1880, the United States was responsible for 85 percent of the world's crude oil production and refining, and kerosene was the fourth largest U.S. export.

The U.S. is currently the largest producer and consumer of oil; which includes crude oil, and all other petroleum liquids, and biofuels. The Energy Information Administration (EIA) estimates the U.S. consumed an average of 20 million barrels of petroleum per day (bbl/d) in 2022, for a total of about 7.3 billion barrels across the year. This accounted for around 20% of the world's total. When combined with other metrics, it is clearly evident to see how the U.S. economy is 'powered by oil': 4% of the world's total population, combined with the 'work' of 20% of the world's oil, assists in the creation of 25% of the world's GDP.

The U.S. is also the world's largest oil producer, at around 20.2 million bbl/d, or 21% of the global total. While most U.S. crude oil is consumed domestically, exports have steadily increased in volume since 2016. Estimates by the EIA for 2022 place U.S. oil exports at 9.52 million bbl/d and imports at 8.33 million bbl/d; making the United States an annual net petroleum exporter (1.19 million bbl/d).

The U.S. has a commanding control over oil production, but plays a negligible role in distribution: Around 100% of all oil being moved into or out of the United States is transported on foreign-flagged tankers.

### *Offshore Oil*

Offshore oil and gas production began in 1947. Kerr-McGee Oil Industries drilled the first productive well beyond the sight of land, in shallow water about 10.5 miles off the coast of Louisiana. The first purpose-built semi-submersible floating drill rig, ODECO Ocean Driller, was built in New Orleans in 1963. From 1980 to 1999, about 7.4 billion barrels of oil were extracted from U.S. federal waters; or, the same amount in 19 years that the United States currently consumes annually. In 2020 offshore oil production in U.S. waters reached 641 million barrels, or 15% of total U.S. oil production. Deepwater (that is, greater than 1,000 feet) oil production began in 1985, and currently accounts for 93 percent of all U.S. offshore oil production. Drillships employ a range of technologies including dynamic positioning and routinely drill on new U.S. deep water leases.

The U.S. controls the method of extraction, but not the assets that do it: Most of the 95 drill ships in the world, even the ones working on U.S. leases, use foreign crews, and none of them are registered in the United States.

***Liquified Natural Gas (LNG)***

Natural gas has been a plentiful source of energy in the U.S. since the early 1800s. Methane Pioneer became the first liquefied natural gas carrier after its conversion in Mobile, Alabama, in 1959. The Pioneer's first shipment was delivered to Canvey Island in England. In the 1970s, U.S. government maritime policy encouraged U.S. shipyards to build LNG carriers; a total of 16 were built. Of these 16 U.S.-built ships, none are in operation. U.S. imports and exports of LNG remained relatively low through the 1990s despite growth in demand for power generation. Then from 2000 to 2004 LNG imports tripled. The development of fracking for U.S. natural gas in the 2000s caused domestic gas to be considerably cheaper than export prices.

About 11 percent of U.S. natural gas production is now exported as LNG. In 2022, total annual U.S. LNG exports, to over 46 countries, was 6.90 trillion cubic feet (Tcf), the highest on record. This continued into the first half of 2023, where the U.S. exported more LNG than any other country, surpassing traditionally dominant suppliers, Australia and Qatar. U.S. exports peaked to an all-time record of 8.01 million metric tons in April, 2023. China and Japan are among the world's largest LNG importers; an anticipated 13% increase in demand from Asian countries will encourage additional U.S. exports across 2024. Rising geopolitical tensions have seen global LNG exports being severely disrupted by the missile and rocket attacks occurring off the coast of Yemen. Late January 2024, saw the first instance (in modern history) where forced diversions around the Cape of Good Hope meant there were no LNG carriers transiting through the Red Sea.

The U.S. leads in LNG production, but is entirely dependent on other countries for transportation: The global LNG-carrying fleet currently consists of around 600 vessels. There are about 50 on order. None are registered in the United States.

### B. Food Security and U.S. Shipping - Domestic and international

The United States places a great emphasis on food security for its citizens and as a means to secure peace and stability around the world.

#### *Domestic Food Security*

The United States is a food production powerhouse. 2 million farms, covering around 900 million acres (1,400,000 square miles) produce the bulk of U.S. food consumed domestically and exported overseas. Agriculture, food, and related industries contribute over 5% of U.S. GDP - around $1.3 trillion - and employ roughly 10.5% of the population. When combined with imports, the U.S. food system is capable of supplying over 500,000 metric tons of food daily, or 3.8 pounds (1.7 kilos) per U.S. citizen, per day.

The U.S. exports around $200 billion worth of agricultural products abroad every year, just over 20% over what is produced, and leads the world in the export of: Rice - 1.3M tons, 2x more than Brazil in 2nd, and three times that of India in third; corn - 51M tons, nearly double the volume of Argentina (#2) and Brazil (#3); cottonseed - 312,000 tons, and ranks highly for exports of maize, soybeans, milk, wheat, sugar beet, sugar cane, potatoes, and chicken.

With such a high level of domestic production, and billions of dollars of food being exported every year, it would appear safe to assume that the United States is relatively immune from domestic food insecurity. However a recent study by the U.S. Department of Agriculture (USDA) found a total of 87.5% of U.S. households, and 82.7% of U.S. households with children, were reported as being 'food secure' during 2022. 17 million U.S. households (12.8%) struggled to get enough food in 2022, which was up from 10.2% (13.5 million households) in 2021. 5.1 percent (6.8 million) of U.S. households experienced 'very low' food security at some point during 2022.

Efficient transportation is essential to domestic Food Security. The U.S. food supply chain uses a complex web of interconnected infrastructure and assets to move supplies around the country. While not the fastest, the U.S. inland river system - or 'Green Marine Highways' - is the most efficient per ton-mile, with thousands of barges and vessels shifting a large proportion of U.S. corn and soybeans, as well as fertilizer, grain, fruits, vegetables, oils, and seeds around the country on a daily basis. Due to its high efficiency and low costs, U.S. inland waterways save between $7 - $9 billion annually compared to other modes of transport, employ around 250,000 people - on farms and in related industries - and contribute over $27 billion to U.S. GDP.

While domestic production is impressive, each mode involved in transporting food and food products suffer from common issues such as diminished government oversight, a lack of advocacy, or aging and broken infrastructure. Of the four primary modes of transportation - barge/ship, truck, train and plane - the assets and facilities used in the U.S. inland waterway system are the most underutilized, and most likely to be overlooked for upgrades or investment.

### *International Food Security*

The United States plays an integral role in securing access to food, across the world. This is critically important for the 870 million people in a range of countries who are undernourished, or lack access to consistent and safe supplies of food. The U.S. improves global Food Security through military intervention, economic stimulus, and aid programs delivered through United States Agency for International Development (USAID) and other agencies.

One of the very first shipments of international food aid provided by the U.S. occurred in 1812 under President James Madison, when $50,000 of wheat flour was sent to Venezuela following a devastating earthquake. Since that time, the United States has consistently led the world by supporting international food security programs; and in particular over the last century. After WWI, the American Relief Administration supplied millions of Europeans with food under the administration of Herbert Hoover. After WWII, a significant amount of food again went to Europe as part of the Marshall Plan. And, in 1954 President Eisenhower signed the Food for Peace Act, the first permanent U.S. food aid program that has positively impacted over 4 billion people with aid over its more than 60-year history. USAID continues this work to this day, supplying produce for the Food for Peace program to around 60 million people, in nearly 60 countries every year.

Admirably, the U.S. is the largest individual donor country of international food assistance, and spends over USD$4 billion every year to assist food-insecure countries. In 2022, USAID delivered nearly 1.8 million metric tons of food all across the world. Cargo preference laws dictate that 50% of all food aid cargoes must be moved on U.S.-flagged vessels, which means shipments through USAID and the USDA also supports the U.S. merchant fleet, and U.S. merchant mariners.

The U.S. Navy and U.S. Coast Guard consistently patrol the world's oceans, which increases the general level of protections afforded to container ships, bulk carriers and other food transportation vessels; whether U.S. or foreign-flagged. The necessity of a strong naval presence to assure safe passage of food has been recently highlighted in the Ukraine-Russia war, with the disruptions that have occurred in major agricultural supply areas around the Black Sea. As with energy, food supply disruptions have occurred due to Houthi attacks on container and bulk transport ships transiting the Red Sea. These attacks threaten the Food Security of countries in the region and disrupt supply for any market that is dependent on the Red Sea and Suez Canal transit corridors.

## Energy and Food Security Maritime Risks and Vulnerabilities

Food Security and Energy Security have been identified by the U.S. Cybersecurity and Infrastructure Security Agency (CISA) as two of the 16 critical infrastructure sectors where it is important to have strong U.S. oversight and world leadership. The U.S. Government, State and local communities are yet to conduct a full analysis of the vulnerabilities to Food and Energy Security from having such a high degree of foreign influence over the maritime supply chain.

The following five concerns have a direct impact on Energy and Food Security in the United States and subsequently, across the world:

A. **U.S. Energy generation: Heavily reliant on fossil fuels** - *Assessing the current state of fossil fuel usage, including how this affects the transportation of energy and generation of electricity*

B. **Energy & Food Transportation: Shortage of U.S. ships** - *How the shortage of U.S. tankers, bulk carriers, and container ships impacts national and international Energy & Food Security*

C. **Energy Security: The Future Fuels of Shipping** - *An exploration of low-carbon energy in shipping: Liquefied Natural Gas (LNG), Hydrogen, Ammonia, Methanol, Electrification, Nuclear and Biofuels.*

D. **Food Security: Securing the supply** - *Domestic and international concerns that relate to food production, distribution, and the protection of food-growing regions (including the ocean)*

E. **Energy & Food Security: Compliance and enforcement** - *The operation of shadow fleets and sanction violators, and secure distribution and strategic levers in global maritime affairs*

## A. U.S. Energy Generation: Heavily Reliant on Fossil Fuels

According to the EIA, fossil fuels accounted for about 81% of total U.S. primary energy production in 2022. The rest is generated using low-carbon sources including nuclear energy and renewables. Electricity is a secondary energy source that is generated from primary energy sources. The grid used 37% of the country's primary energy including those from non-fossil fuel sources. The transition away from fossil fuels, along with the decarbonization of energy generation will be an enormous undertaking, especially when projected future energy demand and the scale of required solutions are taken into consideration.

### *Natural Gas*

Around 80% of the natural gas produced in the United States is consumed in the domestic market; approximately 30% is used by industry, 20% is consumed by households, and 30% is used for electricity generation. Over half (around 1,900) of the 3,400 power plants currently in operation in the United States are gas-powered. Electricity generation from natural gas plants accounted for around 40% of total domestic generation in 2022.

Although the U.S. is a major exporter of natural gas, the U.S. domestic market relies on imports during winter months, which is delivered through a network of aging gas pipelines. In 2022, about 99% of total annual natural gas imports were from Canada and nearly all of that supply was delivered by pipeline.

Infrastructure spending has been lacking: Most pipelines are over 50 years old, and no major gas refineries have been built in the last 50 years, which increases the likelihood of network disruption or failure. This was witnessed when pipelines cracked during recent freezes in Texas, and also featured during the Colonial Pipeline cyberattack in 2021.

If critical gas infrastructure is damaged, destroyed or disrupted, the United States would be heavily reliant on foreign ships to move the required emergency gas imports to U.S. power stations. Furthermore, key regions of the U.S. remain highly dependent on gas transported by ship, as there are no gas pipelines connected to them; specifically Alaska, Hawaii, and Puerto Rico. Natural gas (LNG) is currently provided to these regions by foreign vessels from overseas sources.

### *Oil*

The United States is also a net exporter of oil, however two different product types exist: light crude oil and heavy crude oil. Light crude oil is primarily used to create fuels; gasoline, diesel and aviation fuels. Heavy crude oil is a common feedstock for plastics, petrochemicals, and road surfacing. In 2022, the U.S. exported 9.6 million barrels a day to 180 countries and 4 U.S. territories, generating over $200 billion for the U.S. economy. U.S. exports are predominantly light oil, which is suitable for new refineries in other countries, but is not compatible with domestic refineries.

As previously stated, the U.S. has not built any new refineries with significant downstream capacity for over 50 years, which means that domestic power infrastructure remains reliant on heavier oil. This includes the 1,084 oil-fired power plants that currently generate around 1% of the nation's electricity. In order to cater for these and other needs, the U.S. imports on average, 8.3 million barrels of oil and refined petroleum products per day. Most of these imports arrive on foreign-flagged tankers, with 12% being shipped from countries in the Persian Gulf, a region prone to instability and geopolitical tension.

### *Coal*

Coal usage for power generation peaked in the United States in 2011. At that time, output from coal-fired capacity was 317.6 gigawatts (GW), and generated 44% of all power being produced in the United States. There are 210 coal-fired power plants in operation in the U.S. today. These plants only produce 20% of the sector's electricity. Just under half (around 80.6 GW) of the remaining plants are set to close by the end of 2030. By 2026, total generation from coal-fired plants will equal 159GW, which is half of the 2011 peak.

Historically, coal has played an important role in steelmaking, for powering steam trains, and for heating homes and businesses. Around 2 percent of the U.S. workforce - some 800,000 workers - were employed in coal mining industries in the 1920's. Coal expanded beyond historical uses in the 1950's and transitioned to being primarily used for generating electricity. Demand for coal increased, as the domestic economy and demands from industry grew. Due to a variety of factors, coal consumption started falling rapidly in 2008, which was brought about by sliding prices for wind, solar and natural gas. This decline has continued ever since, and with the exception of power-generation that continued until 2011, coal has seen decreased use in most sectors of the economy for the last 15 years.

The story of coal should serve as a reminder that it *is* possible to transition away from a seemingly dominant fossil fuel, to cleaner and more efficient equivalents in a short period of time.

### *Nuclear Energy*

Nuclear energy has played an important role in reducing the reliance of the U.S. energy grid on fossil fuels.

The United States has a significant degree of expertise with nuclear energy. The first commercial electricity-generating nuclear-powered plant reached its full design power in 1957, and was located in (the aptly named) Shippingport, Pennsylvania. At present, total U.S. nuclear capacity sits at around 91.5GW, generated by 93 reactors spread across 30 different states, and accounts for just under 20% of total domestic supply.

Nuclear fuel is incredibly energy-dense, is not reliant on external sources for generation (as is wind and solar), and does not release carbon dioxide into the atmosphere. This makes nuclear energy the only viable candidate able to reliably decarbonize energy generation at scale. Emissions-free operations are of significant benefit, especially in the face of rising global temperatures and a changing climate: It has been estimated that nuclear power has reduced global CO2 emissions by over 60 gigatons over the past 50 years, which is around two years' of global energy-related emissions.

### *Renewables*

Renewables have also played a role in reducing the U.S. energy grid's fossil fuel dependence.

The United States is a large, resource-rich country with abundant renewable energy resources. Renewable energy sources - hydropower, wind and solar - account for around 20 percent of utility-scale U.S. electricity generation. Hydropower generated 262 terawatt-hours (TWh), or around 6.2% of total U.S. electricity generation in 2022. In the same year, wind turbines generated around 10.2%, and utility-scale solar generated 145.6 TWh, or around 3.4% of the total supply. Renewable energy sources of generation - and their associated benefits of comparatively low maintenance and low-carbon emissions - has skyrocketed in recent years, and is now the fastest-growing energy source in the United States. One renewable energy growth area that is particularly relevant to the maritime domain is offshore wind farms.

The U.S. offshore wind energy industry began off Rhode Island in December 2016, 28 years after the first commercial wind farm began operating off the coast of Denmark. The industry has grown slowly over this time, but received a recent boost when the Biden Administration set a goal of having 30 gigawatts (GW) of offshore wind farms installed by 2030, and 15 GW from floating wind generators by 2035. The offshore wind industry has been dominated by European companies, but floating offshore wind systems could provide an opportunity for U.S. designers and shipyards to gain momentum. Only 0.1 GW of floating offshore wind generation has been deployed globally, which means there is ample opportunity for the U.S. to take a pioneering position.

The Biden administration's proposal, dubbed 'Floating Offshore Wind Shot' is designed to fund R&D and drive the cost of floating offshore wind down to $45/MWh by 2035. Winners in the first U.S. floating offshore wind lease sale off the West Coast were publicly announced on December 7, 2022. The five companies' bids exceeded $757 million. Proposed wind farms are expected to produce 4.6 GW, which will require significant support from the maritime sector during construction and commissioning, and across the maintenance lifecycle of installed systems.

## B. Energy & Food Transportation: Shortage of U.S. ships

While shipping is critical to the stability and security of the U.S. economy, the U.S. will find it continually difficult to lead from behind: Without ownership or control of a noticeable amount of commercial shipping tonnage, there is a risk the U.S. will not be able to direct the conversation on the decarbonized energy blend required in the future. This has already occurred to some extent; current conversations about planned maritime fuels are almost solely led by vested interests, industry players, and commercial stakeholders, very few of whom are based in the United States. A lack of tankers and bulk carriers to transport energy and food has a direct impact on domestic production, redirects earnings from exports to foreign entities, and affects strategic exports to allies.

But, there is still hope: The United States has been pioneers in the past, and with a focused strategy that includes intentional investment in the maritime sector, can take the lead again.

### I. Oil and liquid bulk tankers

The U.S. has some of the world's largest oil companies who own and charter non-U.S. flagged tankers from all over the world. Despite this, and even though the U.S. has large export and import volumes of oil and other bulk liquid products, the U.S.-flagged commercial fleet comprises a few dozen (smaller) tankers that are mostly involved in domestic trade. As observed with other forms of ocean transportation, foreign tankers and foreign crews are vulnerable to hostile actions; non-U.S. providers may decide to restrict access to protect their own commercial interests; or, other nations may recall ships and shipping assets during a time of conflict. Any of these scenarios would have a cascading effect that impacts Energy & Food Security, Economic Security, or National Security; and in times of war, all three, at the same time.

## II. LNG tankers

Multiple records were set in 2022, and broken in 2023 for the LNG production, LNG sales and therefore LNG shipments. The United States does not have *any* LNG tankers in the U.S.-Flag fleet. This means the United States is entirely dependent on foreign-flagged vessels and crews to move the voluminous amounts of LNG that is being shipped into and out of the country. The fact that there are no LNG carriers under the direct control of the United States should be immediately alarming. The fact the United States must source tankers from other countries to transport its own LNG is a rather bewildering scenario, too; especially as U.S. energy companies like Exxon and Chevron are some of the largest transporters of energy products in the world. LNG tankers are incredibly specialized vessels that require complex engineering to operate and maintain. This makes it unlikely that the U.S. will be able to build any domestically in the short term, so will remain dependent on foreign-built vessels for many years to come.

## III. Bulk carriers

There are around 12,700 dry bulk ships in the world. The United States has direct access to 4. The U.S. is projected to export 66 million tons of grain in the 2023/24 season. The overwhelming majority (over 99%) of this grain will be shipped on foreign-flagged vessels. The U.S. has a similar problem with bulk transport as it does with oil and LNG: Founded in 1865, and based in Wilmington, Delaware, Cargill is the largest dry bulk agriculture company in the world, and largest privately held

U.S. company in terms of revenue. Cargill operates over 500 ships that handle and move over 200 million tons of commodities per year. Most of these ships, with few exceptions for mostly domestic trade, are foreign-flagged.

Fertilizer is essential to agricultural production and is commonly shipped in bulk bags, or in the holds of bulk carriers. 329.1 million tons of the three most common ingredients used in fertilizer - ammonia, phosphoric acid and potassium chloride - were produced across 2022/23. Worldwide usage is expected to be 192.5 million tons. The United States imports and exports around 49 million tons of fertilizer each year. There are no U.S.-flagged ships dedicated to the fertilizer trade.

## IV. Refrigerated transportation (cold chain)

Around 50,000 ships are engaged in commercial trade across the world. Around a tenth (6,000) of them are container ships, of various shapes and sizes. A large proportion of these ships are capable of carrying refrigerated shipping containers, commonly called reefers. Reefers are robust and versatile. Most reefers have diesel generators on board that can keep refrigeration equipment powered even if the container is in transit. When a reefer is at a port, or moving on a vessel, it is usually plugged into an electrical outlet, called a reefer plug.

Due to their ability to maintain temperature, keep food fresh and reduce spoilage, reefers are essential for the movement of many different types of edible produce, all across the world; this includes meat, fruit, vegetables, seafood, cheese and dairy products. The world-wide reefer trade was 137.5 million tons in 2022, and is increasing 3% year-on-year. Between 2010 and 2020, three major shipping gateways moved a significant amount of refrigerated exports: Around 40% of all containers shipped out of the Port of Oakland in that decade were reefers.

At the Port of Los Angeles, it was around 30%. And at the Port of Long Beach, 25%.

The U.S.-flagged ocean-going container-ship fleet is very small, and the amount of available reefer plugs on these vessels, even smaller still. If the U.S. container fleet has the same ratio of reefer plugs (10-15% of a vessel's total TEU's) as the world's top three carriers, then U.S.-flagged ships have around 22,000 reefer plugs in total. The three largest shipping lines MSC, Maersk, and CMA-CGM have a combined total of around 1.5 million reefer plugs.

## C. Energy Security: The Future Fuels of Shipping

### Context: Fuels and the global shipping industry

Large trading ships that move across the ocean are almost exclusively powered by fossil fuels. These ships are, essentially 'large oil-fired power stations in the middle of the ocean, attached to a transportation device'. Most of the fuel being used on these ships is some of the worst sludge that is left over at the end of the oil refining process. This has led some commentators to state that the global shipping industry as essentially "a half a trillion-dollar subsidy for large oil companies". The move away from fossil fuels, to 'transition' or new types of low-carbon fuels is essential, if the world is to improve ocean sustainability and meet climate targets.

## The Future Fuels of Shipping

There are seven alternative fuel types and energy systems available to the shipping industry: Liquefied Natural Gas (LNG), Hydrogen, Ammonia, Methanol, Electrification, Nuclear and Biofuels.

### I. Liquified Natural Gas (LNG) fuel

Natural gas liquifies at cryogenic temperatures (–162°C) which creates Liquified Natural Gas. LNG is around 600 times less voluminous in a liquid state, compared to a gaseous state which assists during storage and transportation, however the very low temperatures of LNG adds a range of complications to these processes. For example, LNG must be stored in insulated tanks so it remains in a liquid state. Heat ingress from the surrounding environment can increase the temperature inside the tank which causes the liquid to evaporate, and generates boil-off gas (BOG). These factors can increase the risks associated with the handling of LNG including discharges, fire and explosions.

As a fuel, LNG is inexpensive and clean-burning, producing 40% less Carbon Dioxide (CO2) than coal, and 30% less than oil. LNG produces less toxic substances like Nitrogen Oxides (NOx), Sulfur Oxides (SOx) and Particulate Matter too, which means LNG will meet existing and imminent shipping emissions requirements. This makes LNG an acceptable 'transitional fuel' and is being used the world over to try and decarbonize transport, electricity grids and economies.

A number of challenges remain for expanding the use of LNG in the maritime sector. These include: A lack of available LNG refueling points; the relatively high costs for retrofitting existing ships, and increased construction costs for new vessels; planned global fuel capacity, which is not distributed evenly across the world; and issues associated with uncontrolled methane emissions (methane slip). On the latter, methane leaks, from containers or pressure vessels, can occur anywhere along the LNG supply chain.

Methane slip occurs when uncombusted fuel escapes from an engine, and has tarnished the reputation of LNG as an environmentally-friendly fuel. A report compiled for the IMO by the International Council on Clean Transport (ICCT) explains why using LNG to powers ships can be highly problematic: "Methane, which traps 86 times more heat in the atmosphere than the same amount of CO2 over a 20-year time period, represents a small but rapidly growing share of greenhouse gas emissions from shipping. The 150% growth in methane emissions from 2012 to 2018 was largely due to a surge in the number of ships fueled by liquefied natural gas".

Even though such data exists, there has been a marked increase in newbuild orders for LNG-powered ships, particularly over the last 10 years. According to Clarksons Research, there are around 936 commercial vessels (including passenger ships) in service at present, which includes a number of "LNG-capable" ships designed to burn either fuel oil or LNG. Around 870 LNG-capable ships are on order. 413 ships in service are "LNG-ready," which means they could be converted to future LNG-fuel use. 95 LNG-ready ships on order. Comparative build costs are noticeable; LNG dual-fuel newbuild container ships are around 20-25% more expensive than their conventionally fueled counterparts. These numbers represent a noticeable investment in LNG as a fuel; investments that may stall if the impact of methane slip are not properly addressed and resolved.

While not investing in new refineries, or LNG-carrying ships, the United States is making some investments into domestic LNG infrastructure and novel LNG-powered vessels: U.S.-Flag shipowners Harvey Gulf, Tote, and Crowley pioneered U.S.

LNG (fueling and powering) operations in 2015. The first North American LNG bunkering facility was established in Port Fourchon, LA and Jacksonville FL in 2016. Crowley's 'Commitment Class' ships were some of the first liquefied natural gas (LNG)-powered, combination container and Roll-On/Roll-Off (ConRo) ships that had ever been built in the world. And, West Coast operators, Pasha and Matson, have followed on with newly-built ConRo ships that will be fueled with LNG in California.

## II. Hydrogen fuel

Hydrogen is the most abundant element in the universe, however, pure hydrogen (H2) is relatively uncommon. Hydrogen is commonly found in water (H2O) and other organic compounds, like methane (CH4). Hydrogen gas can be used for synthesizing chemicals and refining crude oil, and has been proposed as an acceptable fuel for various types of transportation including commercial vehicles. Unlike most other fuels, hydrogen does not produce CO2 when burned: when combusted it yields water. While that is positive, burning hydrogen can also produce a significant amount of NOx emissions.

There are challenges with the use and storage of hydrogen, because of its very low density and the requirement to store it at either high pressure or very low temperatures. Transporting hydrogen in volume is possible if it is liquified, however liquid hydrogen must be maintained at a temperature of -253 degrees Celsius; 100 degrees colder than LNG. Hydrogen is also extremely flammable and has a larger ignition range than other traditional fuels.

Around 90% of all hydrogen is derived from the fossil fuel methane, through 'Steam methane reforming' (SMR) that produces hydrogen from natural gas. SMR is a very carbon intensive process: Current global production of hydrogen emits 830 million metric tons of CO2 every year, to produce around 74 million tons of gas. 830 million metric tons is nearly double the entire CO2 emissions of Australia. Low-carbon hydrogen produced through electrolysis releases virtually no carbon emissions, and will need to feature prominently if hydrogen is to be considered as a decarbonized transportation fuel.

An advantage of using hydrogen in shipping is that a global hydrogen market already exists. Worldwide industrial use accounts for around 70 million metric tons of hydrogen, and approximately 10 million metric tons are produced in the United States. The hydrogen market is expected to grow as private firms and countries expand production capacity in expectation of rising demand for less CO2 intensive fuels. 'Blue' hydrogen (from Natural Gas, with carbon capture) and 'Green' hydrogen (that uses renewable energy for electrolysis) provide a pathway for the shipping industry to significantly reduce GHG emissions. Some hydrogen fuel cell technologies allow ships to produce their own hydrogen from seawater and so can operate without emitting greenhouse gasses or fine particulates.

The United States funds a significant amount of energy research via the Department of Energy (DOE). President Biden's Bipartisan Infrastructure Law includes $65 billion in clean energy investments for the DOE. For example, $7 billion has been allocated to the establishment of a 'Regional Clean Hydrogen Hubs Program'. Seven hubs will be created in regions with strong maritime presence - in California, the Gulf of Mexico, the Mid-Atlantic and the Pacific Northwest - and are projected to produce more than three million metric tons of clean hydrogen per year.

## III. Ammonia fuel

Ammonia is one nitrogen atom bonded to three hydrogen atoms. In 1919, German scientist Fritz Haber found a reaction that split the chemical bonds in nitrogen (N2) and combined the atoms with hydrogen, to make ammonia. The reaction requires a lot of pressure - up to 250 atmospheres - and high temperatures, between 4-500 degrees Celsius (°C). German chemist Carl Bosch would industrialize this process, which allowed for ammonia to be produced at scale.

The energy-intensive Haber-Bosch process most commonly uses fossil-fuel derived hydrogen (from methane), and subsequently accounts for over 1.4% of global carbon dioxide emissions and consumes an estimated 2% of the world's total energy production. Burning ammonia releases NOx and Nitrous Oxide; both of which are strong global warming pollutants.

The world currently produces around 175 million tons of ammonia per year (over $60 billion worth), which is mostly used as fertilizer. The most common interactions people have with ammonia is when they use cleaning chemicals that smell foul and produce toxic gasses. However, ammonia is also very energy dense by volume - nearly double that of liquid hydrogen - and stable under heat and light. Ammonia liquefies at -33°C at normal atmospheric pressure or at room temperature (around 20°C) at eight bar pressure. These characteristics make it easier to ship and distribute than hydrogen and LNG.

The use of ammonia as a shipping fuel has raised concerns, and new safety guidelines have been developed by the IMO, which are expected to be implemented in 2024. If ammonia was adapted for use on large ships, several new safety measures would have to be introduced due to its explosive potential; this was dramatically illustrated when a stockpile of ammonia nitrate exploded at the Port of Beirut in August, 2020. Several trials are underway, for example, in April 2023 the Global Centre for Maritime Decarbonisation (GCMD) successfully completed a safety study for an ammonia bunkering pilot in the port of Singapore, paving the way for a trial by the end of the year.

Another large-scale ammonia project is in Saudi Arabia's Neom. Neom is a new urban area planned by the Kingdom of Saudi Arabia to be built in its northwestern Tabuk Province. The site is north of the Red Sea, east of Egypt across the Gulf of Aqaba and south of Jordan. Neom's green energy megaplant will use ~4 GW renewable power from onshore solar, wind and storage to produce up to 1.2 million tons of green ammonia annually; or, around 600 tons of green hydrogen daily.

One of the regions inside the *Neom* precinct is *Oxagon* (originally 'Neom Industrial City'), a floating industrial complex in the shape of an octagon. *Oxagon* covers around 200–250 square kilometers (77–97 sq mi) and is being designed to become "a new focal point for global trade flows" that will provide shipping capacity for ammonia and hydrogen, and service new shipping routes throughout the Red Sea.

## IV. Methanol fuel

Methanol is an organic chemical that is a light, volatile, colorless, and flammable. It is produced industrially by hydrogenating carbon monoxide (CO); a reduction reaction that saturates the CO with hydrogen atoms. Methanol has a distinctive alcoholic odor, similar to ethanol, and is a liquid fuel under ambient conditions. This makes it easy to transport, store, and bunker. This also means it can be handled in a similar way to diesel, and can use the same, well-proven safety procedures. Comparatively, methanol has around half the energy density of diesel, so twice as much is needed to generate the same power from an internal combustion engine. When compared to ammonia and hydrogen, methanol has a higher volumetric energy content, which makes it a better choice for longer voyages, as it reduces the need for frequent bunkering.

Methanol also has a lower viscosity (flows easier) compared to conventional marine fuels like Heavy Fuel Oil (HFO) and diesel, which means that particular attention is required to ensure proper combustion, and to prevent leaks in seals and pipes. Proper care with storage and transportation must be observed to minimize the risks of explosion or fire. If proper combustion is achieved, SOx and Particulate Matter emissions can be reduced by 95 per cent, and NOx by up to 80 per cent when compared to conventional fuels.

Global annual methanol production currently exceeds 100 million tons, and is most commonly used in the chemical industry. Methanol fuel accounts for around 1/10th of this total, and is mostly used as a blend into gasoline; most modern vehicles can safely mix up to 15% methanol (M15) without causing damage to the engine. Global demand for methanol has grown over the last few years and it is currently available at more than 125 of the world's largest ports.

Adoption has increased for ships as well: Dual-fuel engine technology is already available, and most current dual-fuel engines can already handle green (renewable-derived) methanol, which offers a clear pathway to decarbonization without the need for expensive hardware changes in the future.

Recent examples of methanol use in shipping: Stena Line, one of the largest ferry operators in Europe, has operated the methanol-powered ferry, Stena Germanica, since 2015 between ports in Sweden and Germany. New tanks and fuel systems were added to convert the ferry from conventional fuels. Compared to when it was operating on traditional marine diesel, this methanol conversion has reduced the ferry's carbon emissions by up to 25%, NOx by 80%, and SOx by 99%.

Maersk has championed methanol as the most viable replacement for traditional marine fuels. Maersk ordered the first methanol vessel in 2021 and announced a range of initiatives (for transportation and bunkered) that would allow methanol to be used around the world. The industry quickly responded; shortly after this announcement, over 100 methanol-powered newbuilds were on order. Maersk took delivery of the methanol-powered vessel, Laura Maersk, in July 2023 and now has 25 methanol vessels on order for delivery between 2024 and 2027, including six that were ordered in June 2023.

The United States is well positioned to produce 'green' methanol due to a significant base of 'gray' (natural-gas derived) methanol infrastructure, the wide adoption of renewable energy, and an abundance of non-food biomass and excess $CO_2$ for green methanol production.

## V. Battery-powered electric ship propulsion

Integrating batteries into marine propulsion involves replacing traditional fossil fuel–powered propulsion systems with electrically-powered equivalents. Vessels using electricity to drive propulsion have significantly reduced emissions that comply with current and proposed (and increasingly strict) environmental regulations. New technologies also bring other advantages like increased efficiency, reduced noise and vibration, improved maneuverability (due to more predictable weight distribution), and lower maintenance costs (due to less moving parts).

Many ships have been partly electrified for years: Diesel-electric transmission systems are currently in use on up to 80%

of all ships. In this arrangement, diesel generators generate electricity, which then drives an electric engine that moves the ship's propeller. This has many advantages: Firstly, it reduces fuel load by between 5 and 20 percent. Secondly, electrical machines are less prone to faults, and have less wear and tear, which translates into reduced energy loss and higher efficiency.

Operation of electric power-driven ships requires shore-side infrastructure; to supply power to the vessel and charge onboard batteries. Shore power, also known as cold ironing or Alternative Maritime Power (AMP), involves connecting ships to onshore electrical grids while they are docked. This allows ships to turn off their engines and rely on shore-based electricity for power, reducing air pollution and noise emissions in port areas. Interconnectivity, interoperability, and are key challenges to address for shore-side electricity connection.

Demand is growing quickly: The global market for electric ships is projected to expand from around $4 billion in 2023 to over $12.8 billion by 2030. However, current energy densities of battery systems are low, which restricts electrified ships to short-distance routes, or in services that do not require a high degree of autonomy; like smaller ferries and coastal vessels. To maintain emission reductions, ocean-going ships traversing longer routes would have to use hybrid systems that draw power from renewables or low-carbon energy sources. Tesla's March 2023 Investor Day presentation hinted at a future that could include battery-powered long-range ships. This is an exciting prospect, but will only come to pass with significant improvements in battery energy density, and complementary advances in fluid dynamic ship design.

China, Germany, Sweden and Norway have been the pioneers in various forms of electric shipping. For example, the pioneering *MV Yara Birkeland* is a battery-powered, autonomous container ship with 120 TEU container carrying-capacity, that moves chemicals and fertilizer between two ports in Norway. The Birkeland uses two azimuth pods (highly rotational primary thrusters) and two tunnel thrusters (for low-speed lateral movement). The Birkelands batteries are rated at 6.7 MWh. It has an optimal sailing speed of 6 knots (11 km/h) and a maximum speed of 10 knots (19 km/h).

China has begun trials on a range of new larger-scale electric vessels. COSCO Shipping Development, (the financing arm COSCO Shipping), recently announced the launch of a 700 TEU electric container ship that will service a 1,000-km stretch of the Yangtze River. The vessel is 10,000 dwt and is powered by 36 portable container-sized batteries. Two 900 kW engines provide propulsion. The vessel cannot complete the journey on one charge, and will have to replace its batteries at ports along the way. This is made possible by the 30 ports available on the Yangtze's 2,700km of navigable waterways. COSCO is also the founder of the China Electric Ship Innovation Alliance; top national authorities, and over 80 companies have joined the Alliance.

The White House set a target of 80% renewable energy generation by 2030 and 100% carbon-free electricity by 2035. The DOE has posed a strategic and purposeful approach to decarbonizing all forms of transportation and has given serious consideration to electrifying shipping. The EPA is actively working with stakeholders to reduce the emissions around Ports, which will include rolling out shore-side infrastructure that can be used to power ships and recharge batteries.

## VI. Nuclear ship propulsion

Nuclear energy has been considered a viable method to provide power to marine propulsion systems for nearly three quarters of a century. Nuclear reactors vary in size and capacity, but generally operate in a similar fashion: Water is heated by the reactions of nuclear fuel, which creates steam. That steam is used to drive a turbine, and the turbine turns a propeller via a gearbox or electrical motor. Once the steam has completed this work, it is condensed back down into water, and the cycle begins again. This is a self-contained process, which means nuclear reactors only generate very small amounts of emissions. Some submarines may split water to create oxygen and release the remaining hydrogen into the sea, however this is a benign process that causes minimal impact to the surrounding environment.

Due to complexity and secrecy, most nuclear propulsion systems are only installed in larger military vessels such as submarines and aircraft carriers. Only a small number of commercial ships have been built with nuclear reactors onboard, including, in recent times, Russian ice-breakers that operate in Arctic regions. Nuclear fuels are extremely energy dense, which equates to lower maintenance over a much longer lifecycle before fuel replacement is required; for example, the U.S. aircraft carrier Gerald R. Ford will operate without refueling for 20 years. While there are many benefits of nuclear power there are significant risks to consider as well. These concerns cover a broad spectrum: From extreme (terrorism), to economically disruptive (commercial theft of IP) and alarming (environment fallout in the event of an accident or disaster).

The U.S. Navy has over 70 years' experience with nuclear propulsion, ever since Admiral Hyman G. Rickover fired up the first test reactor plant at the Naval Reactors Facility in Idaho, in 1953. This test was soon followed by the first nuclear-powered vessel (submarine USS Nautilus) that was put to sea, just two years later, in 1955. The United States built the first nuclear-powered merchant ship in the world, in the late 1950s. Named after the SS Savannah, the first steamship to cross the Atlantic, the NS Savannah was designed and built for a total cost of $46.9

million, which included $28.3 million for the nuclear reactor and fuel core. The reactor was designed to commercial standards using low-enriched uranium, yielded about 22,000 horsepower (16 MW) and could propel the Savannah to a maximum speed of 24 kn (44 km/h). The NS Savannah was launched on July 21, 1959, remained in active service until 1972, and, after a protracted period of negotiation, is set to be completely decommissioned by 2031.

As will be described in later sections, the United States can take this knowledge and expertise, and apply it to new forms of maritime propulsion that will transform (and decarbonize) the global commercial maritime sector.

## VII. Biofuels

Biofuels are fossil fuel replacements made by processing organic material. Biofuels can typically be handled like fossil fuels and require very little modification of internal combustion engines. The two most common types of biofuel are ethanol (generally sourced from starch-based crops) and bio-diesel (from vegetable or cooking oils, or animal fats); biofuels derived from these sources include fatty acid methyl ester (FAME) and hydrotreated vegetable oil (HVO). While a unique solution, biofuels also pose unique problems for both Energy and Food Security. A major concern for biofuel production is that it could displace necessary food production and take up valuable land. For example, an area twice the size of Switzerland would need to be farmed just to meet the needs of Sustainable Aviation Fuel alone. Furthermore, the European Union currently uses land about the same size as Ireland for biofuel production; land that could feed around 120 million people, and absorb twice as much CO2 as is currently being saved by using biofuels.

Offshore algae production offers an alternative for biofuel production. Given its production location, this also makes it a viable source of fuel to replace diesel on ships. It's possible that in the foreseeable future, major shipping lanes will have large algae farms operating around offshore wind turbines to produce biodiesel at scale, which is then directly supplied to ships. This would be an intelligent way to solve multiple issues at the same time; production is more sustainable, and transportation and storage would occur in very close proximity to where the fuel is distributed for consumption.

The U.S. has to be clear on the international supply chain of low-carbon energy, to ensure national and international Energy Security and Food Security risks are managed effectively. National Security is also involved: If a significant portion of new, low-carbon energy takes place offshore (e.g., via offshore wind farms, or algae plants that produce biofuels), then a revised strategy for these production areas must also be formulated, to safeguard operations and protect stored energy stockpiles.

## D. Food Security: Securing Supply

A strong maritime sector is crucial for domestic and international Food Security. Without a noticeable presence, and with reduced influence in commercial shipping, the U.S. remains vulnerable.

### Domestic concerns

U.S. Food Security, like Energy Security, is essential to modern living. Very few Americans are subsistence farmers, and most are accustomed to choosing from a wide variety of food without being concerned how it is grown or sourced. Additionally, as with energy, the U.S. is a major exporter. Hence agricultural exports are a significant element of the national economy.

**i. U.S. shipping:** According to the USDA the U.S. is projected to import $195 billion of food and export about $181 billion in FY23. The movement of food represents a significant portion of overall U.S. international seaborne trade. As has been articulated in several previous examples, the U.S. relies on foreign-flagged ships, and foreign mariners to move this food; this endangers Food Security, and will affect the U.S. economy if a conflict occurred that removed foreign-controlled food-shipment assets like commercial bulk carriers, liquid bulk tankers and container ships.

**ii. Climate change:** U.S. domestic food production is increasingly vulnerable to climate pressures and extreme weather events. The impact of recent droughts in the Mississippi region is estimated at upwards of $20 billion (and counting), with the latest figures showing that costs to move cargo on the River has increased by 5x over the last year. This highlights the critical nature of the U.S. inland waterway system to move goods around the country, and has a protracted impact on U.S. manufacturing, suppliers, importers and exporters (and consumers). In the event of extreme weather conditions, there is no U.S. maritime agricultural fleet to ship food from international markets to the U.S. to act as an insurance for the U.S. food supply chain; the U.S. would be entirely reliant on external assistance to cover any shortfalls.

**iii. Cybersecurity threats:** Significant cyber-risks in U.S. ports and in the shipping industry represent a significant threat to U.S. food security. U.S. food production infrastructure has been, and is likely to continue being targeted by hostile actors. Recent examples:

- The large international meat supplier JBS S.A. suffered a ransomware attack on May 30, 2021, which disrupted the company's operations in the United States, Canada, and Australia. The impact to the world's meat supply was extreme as JBS is responsible for one-fifth of all meat production globally; it is the world's largest producer of beef, chicken, and pork (by sales). Production had to be shut down in many U.S. meat processing facilities which impacted supply to consumers. The attack also temporarily disrupted the U.S. Department of Agriculture's ability to offer wholesale beef and pork prices, and only ended when the company paid an $11 million Bitcoin ransom to the Russian-based criminal group, *REvil.*

- An Iowa grain cooperative that was targeted by Russian-linked attackers, via a ransomware attack in May 2021. The attack impacted 40% of grain producers that were using the same software, and directly impacted 60 elevator locations across north-central and western Iowa. The cooperative will be increasingly susceptible to a range of similar attacks in the future; over 50% of their operations utilize computerized and automated processes. The ransom demand was never disclosed, but may have cost the company $5.9 million in ransom payments.

- Dole PLC is a multibillion-dollar company that sources produce from dozens of countries all around the world. Dole has four processing plants in the U.S. and employs more than 3,000 people. Dole suffered a ransomware attack in February 2023, which impacted production, and affected the supply of multiple products to U.S. consumers. Upon detecting the attack, Dole took steps to contain it, including employing the services of leading third-party cybersecurity experts and also notifying law enforcement. The attack cost the company around $10.5 million in disruptions and lost sales.

**iv. Market consolidation:** There has been a marked degree of consolidation in the U.S. food market over the last 30 years. This has led to a small number of large companies controlling the majority market share for most grocery items that are commonly bought by U.S. citizens. The size and influence of these companies allows them to dictate what 2 million U.S. farmers grow and how much they are paid; and to a large extent, how much groceries cost and even what consumers eat. A recent study by the Guardian found that consolidation in the U.S. market has allowed around four firms to control 50% of the market for around 80% of all groceries.

**v. Aging infrastructure:** The waterways of the Missouri, Ohio and Mississippi Rivers are critical to U.S. food exports. The infrastructure along these waterways is aging, and in need of repair and/or overhaul. Locks 52 and 53 on the Ohio river were recently replaced with modern equivalents, but had not received much attention since their construction in 1929. More maintenance work needs to be completed across the inland waterway system. If sections of these waterways fail, it will present a serious bottleneck, slowing down innumerable supply chains nationwide, including that of grain. If they were to fail entirely, then commodity transport, domestic consumption and export supply chains would be completely disrupted.

**vi. Missed opportunities:** The U.S. does not have a strong aquaculture presence, despite seafood being the fastest growing source of sustainable protein, and with many leading technologies originating from the U.S. Similarly, the U.S. remains a laggard in offshore algae production, where it has some of the biggest opportunities in various coastal waters (e.g., around Alaska). The U.S. has the readily-available locations, expertise and a willing market of consumers to take a leading role in aquaculture and algae production, which would positively improve U.S. Food and Energy Security, boost exports to other countries, and create new forms of domestic employment.

## International Concerns

**i. Food aid:** In FY 2022, USAID provided more than $2.6 billion of in-kind Food Assistance through two support programs, totaling 1.8 million metric tons (MT) of food to support around 60 million people. Food aid shipped by USAID and USDA accounts for less than 1% of the overall agricultural export volume. 50% of food aid must be shipped on U.S.-Flag vessels, with an equivalent amount carried by foreign flag ships. The overwhelming majority of food aid is shipped on dry bulk ships. As previously mentioned, there are only 4 U.S.-flagged dry bulk ships (210,902 DWT) available for shipping bulk food products. The very limited number of U.S. flag ships capable of shipping food in bulk, is unlikely to assure the continued effectiveness of the U.S. international food aid program.

U.S. food exports and food aid have been a useful element of global soft power. Many countries are dependent on imported food. If the U.S. is not able to deliver what they need, or ensure a U.S.-friendly source of food is available, they are likely to find another global power who can provide it. For example, the U.S. exported $38.2 billion worth of grain in FY23, or around 66 million metric tons. Even while being distracted by the ongoing conflict with Ukraine, Russia is projected to export 65 million tons. Top Russian wheat exports are sent to a mix of countries that aren't always aligned with the U.S. geopolitical agenda, including Turkey, Egypt, Iran, Saudi Arabia, Sudan, and Algeria.

**ii. Food Spoilage:** Food spoilage is a major factor that impacts Food Security. Spoilage rates during transportation are affected by a variety of factors, but are staggering at a global level: Between 7-15% globally, and as high as 50% in developing nations. If an average of 14% of food is wasted from production to plate, then 1.3 billion metric tons are lost annually, at a cost of $1 trillion; this is expected to rise to $1.5 trillion over the next decade.

Recent estimates for specific food categories, from research industry analysts Food Engineering calculated wastage rates for a variety of food groups:

- Fruits and vegetables: Up to 45% is wasted, which is equivalent to 3.7 trillion apples
- Roots and tubers: Around 45% is wasted, the equivalent of 1 billion bags of potatoes
- Fish and seafood: Up to 35%, or around 3 billion Atlantic salmon
- Meat wastage - Around 20% of the total, which is equivalent to 75 million cows

Transportation, and shipping in particular, plays a critical role in these statistics. A recent study in the

Journal *Science* found that the maritime industry was responsible for moving around 59% of the food that is transported across the world; 30.97% travels by road, 9.9% by rail, and a diminutive 0.16% travels by air. This means that the maritime industry, primarily through large dry bulk carriers, and in dry and refrigerated containers, moves the majority of the worlds' food, and is therefore responsible for transporting that food in a safe, secure, and sustainable manner.

**iii. Fishing and Seafood:** The U.S. is the largest single-country market for fish and fish products, the third largest wild seafood producer, and the fifth largest exporter of fish and fish products. Illegal, unregulated, unreported (IUU) fishing affects about 20 percent of the global fish yields, which cost about USD$23 billion a year. This includes the removal of an estimated 90% of large predatory fish such as sharks, cod and tuna.

The U.S. has a small international fishing fleet, and remains ineffective in influencing global fisheries policies around the world (e.g., via the UN-Food and Agriculture Organization backed Regional Fisheries Management Organizations, or RFMOs). This has led to significant overfishing and depletion of strategic fish stocks around the world, and has increased regional instability as fishing communities look for alternative livelihoods e.g., as witnessed with the transition in Somalia and West Africa / Niger Delta from tuna fishing to piracy.

This is just the impact on fish and other marine wildlife due to commercial fishing. Other human detrimental effects are: oil spills, toxic wastewater runoff, proliferation of invasive species, microplastics, acidification, noise pollution, dredging, and subsea strip mining. These activities are stark reminders that humans are largely unable to steward this incredible asset, nor act in a way that ensures it can be enjoyed for many generations to come. An alarming array of readily-available figures and data describes the damage that is regularly inflicted upon the ocean. As mentioned in the first chapter, nearly half of the planet (3.3 billion people) rely on some form of food from the sea for a proportion of the protein they eat and will subsequently experience Food Security challenges, if the world's oceans continue to be misused.

**iv. Modern conflicts:** Food supply and disruption can resolve or worsen international relations. Famine leads to anarchy, and forces mass migration. The war in Ukraine has disrupted critical food supply chains, endangering the lives of many, especially in developing nations in the Middle East and Africa. Ukrainian monthly grain exports fell by 87 per cent in the second quarter of 2022 as compared with the same period in 2021. Ukraine is one of the world's largest suppliers of sunflower oil, barley, maize and wheat.

Since the naval blockades began in February 2022, an estimated 20 million tons of grain was trapped at port, unable to be exported. In July 2022, a deal was temporarily negotiated that allowed for over 33 million tons of backlogged grain to be exported via select corridors in the Black Sea. Since then, a number of attacks - most notably on the grain export terminals in Odessa - have disrupted the passage of food, which has once again, affected the Food Security of millions of people. Similarly, and as already mentioned, continued attacks in the Red Sea will affect the global distribution of food and (refrigerated and dry) produce that is used in the food production process. This will, in turn, affect local and commercial food processing timetables, and therefore reduce the types and volumes of food that can be produced.

## V. Energy & Food Security: Compliance and Trade

### I. Shadows and sanctions

Somewhere between 450 and 1,000 tankers (above 10,000 deadweight tons) are currently thought to be involved in moving sanctioned oil to, or from Iran, North Korea, Russia and Syria. New research from Lloyd's List has calculated around 10% of this fleet is directly controlled by China. The movement of these tankers around the world endangers the energy mix for all users. While a primary concern is how the sale of sanctioned products funds Russian, Iranian or other sanctioned state aggression, another serious concern is how covert transportation and distribution impacts calculations about the available supply of both energy (and to a lesser extent, food).

This aging substandard fleet often operates under negligent Flag States, which presents major risks to the U.S., its allies and to global shipping lanes. Serious risks arise because of vessel deterioration, crew mismanagement, accident, collision or spillage, as was dramatically illustrated in May 2023 when the aging Gabon-registered Aframax oil tanker '*Pablo*' exploded off the coast of Malaysia. Such events can seriously disrupt energy supply, but also have a negative impact on the environment. The existence and prolific activity of the shadow fleet illustrate why Flags of Convenience – that generally lack any enforcement mechanisms outside of class society pressure, bans or a sternly worded rebuke – are not the most effective mechanism for moderating the safe movement of cargo and commodities around the world.

Technology can play a role in reducing the impact of substandard ships and shadow fleet vessels. It is common for the vessels of sanction-avoiding countries to disable (or spoof) AIS, to evade detection while they trade these products across the ocean. There is a range of more sophisticated and appropriate technologies available to assure the oceans are safeguarded that could be rolled out, but requires strong U.S. leadership in order to do so.

## II. Secure distribution

U.S. Energy and Food Security remains vulnerable in international choke points around the world where non- U.S. vessels are commonly used. Among other complications, this limits options for U.S. influence and intervention. Regardless of the options that are chosen, the future fuel mix will require fuel to be transported via ship, internationally. This also applies to food, as production and food growing regions evolve over the coming century.

**Energy Security:** International shipping requires the availability of different fuel types, spread out around the globe for consumption by commercial vessels. Ensuring the commercial fleet fuel supply and protecting that supply is an essential part of keeping the U.S. economy competitive. U.S. suppliers are heavily involved in the ship bunkering industry, but foreign control of commercial ports and terminals far exceeds U.S. control. Additionally foreign subsidies could limit the competitiveness of U.S. companies, especially considering the extraordinary need for capital investments during the transition to lower-carbon fuels.

Regardless of the future fuel blend, energy transportation will continue to take place through international chokepoints like the Straits of Hormuz, Malacca Straits, Red Sea, or through the Panama and Suez Canals. The Strait of Hormuz is responsible for the passage of about a fifth of the world's supply of seaborne crude oil and oil products, and is prone to military attacks and piracy. This was witnessed in April 2023, when the Iranian military seized a Marshall-Islands flagged, Turkish owned, oil tanker bound for Chevron's oil refineries in Houston, Texas. The U.S. imports around 12% of its oil from states in the Persian Gulf, so while disruptions in the region may not dramatically affect U.S. energy security, they would have a material impact on the earnings of U.S. energy companies who generate over $500 billion dollars in revenue every year; around 3% of the Fortune 100 total.

At the same time, U.S. energy companies use oil and gas tankers to transfer energy from one location to another, and pass through other geopolitical hotspots. For example, Chevron's Kazakhstan oil fields export by ship via the Black Sea which has been affected by the Ukraine-Russia conflict. The U.S. Navy is unwilling to enter the Black Sea to protect these vessels as they are not U.S.-flagged. The economic risk is significant; any one of these vessels could have as much as $200 million of energy (oil or gas) onboard.

The situation in the Black Sea – and the ongoing conflict in the Red Sea - is similar to the 'caught in the cross-fire' era in the Persian Gulf during the tanker wars of the 1980's. However, at that time the U.S. was able to reflag and crew Kuwaiti tankers that were protected by the U.S. Navy to maintain critical energy supplies for the rest of the world.

**Food Security:** The control of chokepoints and the formation of new global trade routes also impacts the secure and safe distribution of food. The U.S. is the largest user of the Panama

Canal, with U.S. exports and imports accounting for around 73% of the Panama Canal's total traffic. Forty percent of all U.S. container traffic travels through the canal every year; around $270 billion in cargo. Recent droughts have changed the capacity-handling potential of the Canal, which dramatically impacts U.S. agricultural exports. If the Panama Canal is unavailable, U.S. commodities are diverted through the Suez Canal to reach Asian and other international markets, which adds significant time (and ton-miles) to the journey.

New transport routes that cross through an ice-free Arctic will affect the distribution of food across the world. China has sent multiple container ships through the Arctic over the last year, and in mid-August 2023, sent the Capesize bulk carrier '*Gingo*', one of the largest vessels to attempt an Arctic transit. Russian ports and refueling depots are being built across the Arctic and are complemented by a large fleet of Russian icebreakers. Without icebreakers or supporting infrastructure, the U.S. will remain uncompetitive and vulnerable in the trade routes that cross through Arctic regions, which in turn, will affect the global distribution of food and other commodities.

## III. Strategic levers

Exports of U.S. energy products (oil and gas) generate significant revenues for the United States, but can also be used as strategic policy levers. A recent example of how this can be applied was observed with the Russian military strikes in Ukraine that left millions of Ukrainians without power, heat and running water, just as cold weather set in. Western nations joined Kyiv in accusing Moscow of trying to "weaponize winter". Over one third of U.S. gas is exported directly to Europe, which reduces the reliance European countries have on Russian gas. This removes revenues from the Russian economy, which may be used to purchase arms, or fund regional aggression.

The U.S. is one of the largest exporters of refined oil and a strategic oil-trading partner to over 150 countries all over the world. Establishing active partnerships through trade represents an important, strategic lever that builds trust, stabilizes global energy markets, and helps to further beneficial geopolitical outcomes. Even though these levers are powerful forms of global influence and control, they are entirely reliant on the direct involvement of foreign-owned, flagged and crewed vessels to enact them. While it's feasible to assume such crews might support the United States when called upon, there are a number of scenarios where no amount of money would compel supportive action; another example where 'buying your way out' may not be an option.

As previously presented, food distribution can be used as an effective form of soft power projection. While it is unpalatable to hold any country to ransom through food aid programs, there is precedent by certain countries to use food and agricultural products as a mechanism to sway international opinions or to achieve geostrategic goals. This may have been the motivation behind a recent announcement by Russia to give 25,000-50,000 tons of "free" grain to six countries: Somalia, Burkina Faso, Eritrea, Zimbabwe, Central African Republic and Mali. While this act of generosity received a positive response, it must be viewed in the context of Russian aggression in the Black Sea region, which is responsible for disrupting the export of many millions of tons of food to developing countries all over the world.

## Energy and Food Security Solutions and Opportunities

The following solutions and opportunities are matched to the risks and vulnerabilities explored throughout this Principle:

1. **Risk: Incorrect fleet blend to support U.S. Food and Energy Security**
   **Solution: The Flag-In Security Program (FISP)**
   The Flag-In Security Program is designed to streamline the flag-in process and incentivize internationally operating, U.S.-owned energy and food companies to transition operations away from Flags of Convenience and instead use U.S.-flagged vessels. Reflagging into the U.S. registry has been streamlined for MSP and TSP ships, but not regular commercial ships. The FISP will use modern techniques and technologies for assessment and review, and offer requisite incentives - like tax breaks, or insurance benefits - to encourage participation. Specific thresholds would be established to acquire the right blend of vessels over the next 5 years, for example: 50 LNG carriers, 100 oil tankers, 100 container ships and 100 dry bulk ships for the transportation of food.

   While those numbers represent a marked increase in the current U.S.-Flag fleet, they are relatively small compared to global totals. Among other imperatives, the Flag-In Security Program would ensure that U.S.-flagged ships are available in the event of a national emergency and to maintain freedom of trade around the world. The FISP would also need to review SOLAS certification requirements for new flagged-in vessels, and also make provisions for a streamlined (structured, and carefully administered) 'Flag-Out' process, should commercial operators need to remove tonnage from the U.S.-Flag fleet.

The FISP should particularly focus on flagging-in modern LNG tankers. Fifty U.S. LNG carriers are needed to manage an export load of 11.2 Billion Cubic Feet/day (bcf/d): One LNG tanker takes 2 Bcf, so 5.5 tankers per day equals 50 vessels in total, assuming 10 day transits and 24 day round trips. The acquisition of these LNG ships is advantageous for multiple reasons but would primarily allow ultimate control over the distribution of the U.S. LNG energy stockpile. Such vessels may also participate in Military Sealift or other DOD activities, which would give both commercial and military groups access to a readily-available low-carbon transition energy fuel.

2. **Risk: Distribution of transition and new maritime fuels**
   **Solution: Global Maritime Energy Security Map (GMESM)**
   An outworking of the U.S. MESS would be the creation of a GMESM; an interactive map that takes input from multiple sources, to accurately display the locations of globally available maritime energy stockpiles. The Map would be hosted in the U.S. on secure servers, with limited access extended to a select group of vetted operators. The GMESM would contain data gleaned from Open-Source Intelligence (OSINT), from the movement of ships across the world (using AIS and other marine tracking resources), and also information from commercial announcements or press releases; for example, the recent public disclosure form Maersk about their proposed sources of eMethanol.

3. **Risk: Securing the correct maritime future fuels blend**
   **Solution: Establish MESS and MERC**
   A clearer strategy, set of objectives and profitable outcomes for maritime energy supply must be communicated to an engaged group of government, commercial, research and academic partners. This includes investigating what energy blend will be required in the future, and sourcing the commercial and industry partners who will be able to supply the appropriate blend to the U.S. maritime sector.

   The focus of the U.S. Maritime Energy Security Strategy (MESS) will be to map out the available and proposed energy needs of the maritime sector, and then perform a detailed analysis on how those energy requirements will be secured: In terms of supply, storage, transportation and transmission/distribution. This Strategy will be formulated in close collaboration with a diverse array of stakeholders: military, commercial, government agency and government departments. Particular scrutiny will be given to the future energy blend and on vessels that are powered by renewable-derived fuels, electrification and nuclear.

   The Maritime Energy Research Coalition (MERC) would be driven by the Department of Energy, Environmental Protection Agency and the DOD, and be guided by industry participants, university researchers and the input of the DOT and MARAD. Energy-sector professionals and serving or ex-Merchant Mariners, would also provide input from their experience and domain knowledge. Note: MARAD is currently pursuing an unfunded task to create a Center for Maritime Innovation (CMI) that may seek to address the issue of Energy Security in the Maritime sector. The

American Bureau of Shipping has created a coalition for the CMI, but its scope is limited to new marine technologies rather than the overall needs of the U.S. maritime sector.

4. **Risk: Food spoilage across domestic and international supply chains**
   **Solution: U.S. Food Transportation Spoilage Scheme (FTSS)**
   Food spoilage occurs when food is damaged or destroyed during or after transportation is a major problem in both domestic and international supply chains. There are primary and secondary effects of spoilage on the economy, on consumers, and on U.S. Food Security: Obviously, spoilage directly impacts the availability of food. Less obvious, are the impact that food spoilage has on adjacent sectors and U.S. agricultural productivity. For example, farms and food manufacturers adjust their output according to demand. However, the food spoilage components within those demands figures are largely unknown, which distorts statistics about actual food consumption, and can lead to massive oscillations in supply.

   The Food Transportation Spoilage Scheme (FTSS) seeks to map out where spoilage occurs, with a particular focus on the maritime and cold-chain transportation links that are responsible for the transportation of food. Once problem areas are identified, the scheme would actively work with a variety of public and private partners to reduce the risks of future spoilage, by deploying novel technologies, or by implementing new processes and procedures.

   Domestically, the FTSS would include an analysis on the inland waterway system and coastwise trade, to ascertain if any regions, zones or practices existed that abnormally contributed to spoilage statistics; a review of the domestic maritime cold-chain would also form part of the dataset included in the FTSS. Similarly, international maritime supply chains would be inspected, to find any patterns or trends that may increase food spoilage as food moves across the world. Data would be collated from a variety of sources, and would greatly benefit from an increased presence of U.S.-flagged ships, who could readily participate in the scheme.

Data from the FTSS and support from FTSS partners would be made available to farms, food producers and manufacturers to reduce supply chain dysfunctionality, to minimize overproduction, and therefore improve U.S. agricultural productivity.

5. **Risk: Lack of investment in maritime infrastructure**
   **Solution: Maritime Capital Investment Fund (MCIF)**
   The MCIF would be a government Capital Investment Fund to support U.S. maritime projects during the decarbonized energy transition, and to support the secure distribution of U.S. food and food products. The U.S. Treasury would manage the fund much like it manages the post-COVID Capital Project Fund which provides \$10 billion to states, territories and local governments to assist with the response to the public health emergency.

   A MCIF would provide money for shipyard improvements, large-scale energy technologies, port infrastructure, and fuel and food storage (particularly cold chain) projects. Expertise, industrial strength, engineering resources, and collaborative business partnerships would be included in funding arrangements, to advance the energy transition for the U.S. maritime sector, and to tackle the complicated problems associated with food wastage during transportation. One specific area of investment would be to fund research into improving the efficiency of reefer containers; to reduce spoilage in transit, while reducing emissions from generators and attached power systems.

6. **Risk: Misalignment between Government initiatives and the private sector**
**Solution: Annual Government and commercial alignment audits**
Given a long history of success in the maritime domain, the U.S. should be a world leader in the application and integration of all forms of maritime energy production - including wind, solar, hydropower, tidal and other renewables - and the sustainable harvesting of fish, seafood, and aquacultural products. However, complications arise when such targets are derived from, and applied in the - sometimes reticent, and often purely profit-motivated - commercial sector.

As such, the plans from the Whitehouse, DOE, EPA, USDA and other departments should be annually audited to ensure they are directly aligned with commercial imperatives. Reciprocally, commercial operators should proactively supply government representatives with the array of opportunities that are being presented in the commercial maritime sector, so that mutually-beneficial decisions can be made.

7. **Risk: Food and Energy shipment protection Solution: Fund USCG expansion in regional hotspots**
The United States Coast Guard has a long and proud history of being deployed in areas across the world, to provide oversight and protection for maritime activities. The USCG has a great depth of expertise in a range of activities, including interdiction and interception, boarding hostile vessels, and performing maritime search and rescue. The role of the USCG should be expanded to include regular patrols to be conducted in various maritime chokepoints and critical trade lanes including the Suez Canal, Panama Canal, and Strait of Hormuz. This is underway to some extent already, as witnessed by the USCG cutter that transited the Strait of Hormuz - along with the USN and an Unmanned Surface Vessel - in June 2023.

   Regular USCG patrols in these areas would mirror similar efforts being undertaken in the IndoPacific, such as through Operation Southern Shield that was launched in October 2023. USCG patrols would reduce the demands on the U.S. Navy, and change the perception of U.S. involvement in those regions from a primarily military focus, to instead being associated with protecting Economic, Food and Energy Security. These patrols would also perform the critical role of protecting any newly acquired or built U.S.-flagged commercial ships that transit through these regions, or the commercial ships of any other Flag State that may one day be using U.S.-supplied nuclear propulsion technology.

8. **Risk: Lax standards of practice for commodity shipping**
   **Solution: Energy and Food Security Maritime Risk Register (EFS-MRR)**
   The EFS-MRR would be specifically designed to provide U.S. exporters and importers access to a ratified list of shipping providers and include details about the risks involved with using those companies to move food, produce, commodities or energy. Cooperative monitoring, with requisite methods of enforcement would mitigate major risks to the United States economy, and U.S. exporters and importers. Data presented in the EFS-MRR would include the physical state of vessels involved in distribution; the status, and past treatment of the crew; a log of previous accidents, collisions or spillages a ship has been involved in; and, details on a ships administrative management record and beneficial ownership structure.

9. **Risk: Cybersecurity threats affecting Energy and Food Security**
   **Solution: APT Threat-Modelling Program (APT-TMP)**
   Advanced Persistent Threats (APTs) are typically stealthy attackers - often nation state or state-sponsored - who gain unauthorized access to a system or network and remain undetected for an extended period. APTs are notorious for disrupting critical infrastructure, as they commonly plan attack activities around remaining hidden until they can extract necessary information, manipulate assets for their own purposes, or cause maximum possible damage. This type of attack is difficult to detect and can cause a serious amount of disruption if not attended to in the correct manner.

The APT-TMP would conduct threat-modeling and assessment at a national level, with a specific focus on shipping and maritime assets involved in energy and food distribution. This would occur in collaboration with the Marine Transportation System Information Sharing and Analysis Center (MTS-ISAC), industry professionals, and participants who are already engaged in using the Maritime Cybersecurity Escalation & Support app and Hotline. The APT-TMP would target systems, providers, or regions where disruptions would have a severe impact on the U.S. economy, or U.S. consumers; e.g., geographic areas where there is a high concentration of suppliers that use the same digital systems, or sections of the supply chain that provide food or energy to government institutions or military installations.

10. **Risk: Missed opportunities with U.S. Navy technologies and expertise**
    **Solution: U.S. Navy Technology Commercialization Accelerator (USN-TCA)**
    The deep experience of the U.S. Navy is evident, particularly with operating a diverse fleet, refueling and resupply in remote locations, and also with hull and propeller design, and advanced propulsion systems e.g., nuclear reactors. Additionally the deep experience of the U.S. Navy could be utilized to globally lead the discovery and proliferation of alternate maritime fuel types: Hydrogen, methanol, ammonia, and biofuels.

    The U.S. Navy Technology Commercialization Accelerator would seek to identify U.S. Navy technologies (and operating procedures) that have a viable path to commercialization, and then work with industry collaborators to accelerate developing and integrating those solutions into the commercial maritime sector. This might include the introduction of CONSOL equipment on U.S.-flagged commercial tankers to enhance their dual-use capabilities; introducing new methods to distill or transfer biofuels as commercial vessels deliver food and energy products around the world; or, processes or procedures that relate to sustaining and feeding a ship's crew as they participate in long voyages.

Due to National Security implications, technologies being developed through the USN-CTA must be carefully vetted, to minimize the chance of revealing sensitive information about methods or approaches that are used by the U.S. Navy to increase force posture or Fleet reliability.

11. **Risk: Lack of U.S. leadership in the clean energy shipping revolution**
    **Solution: Produce scalable Small Modular Reactors for commercial ships**
    The United States can become a noticeable leader in the commercial maritime sector, by providing the propulsion systems that power the ships involved in international trade. Other countries may supply the hulls and superstructure but the United States is in a unique position to 'completely control the engine room'.

    As has been communicated throughout this Principle, the U.S. has a clear advantage, and deep experience in the use and deployment of nuclear reactors. Some commentators dismiss nuclear power due to the perceived risks involved, however it's important to remember that the U.S. Navy has operated nuclear submarines for 70 years (and aircraft carriers for over 60 years) without an incident that can be directly attributed to the nuclear reactor; in some of the most trying, subsea, surface and conflict scenarios that could ever be imagined.

The U.S. also has commercial precedent with the integration of a nuclear reactor into a commercial ship with the NS Savannah. Although some may argue that a sole example that failed to operate profitably is not entirely convincing, it's worth keeping in mind that the Savannah was built over 60 years ago in an era that did not have many of the concerns that are present today: The geostrategic risk of the U.S. being under-represented in the commercial maritime domain did not exist in the 60's, as the U.S. commercial fleet carried nearly three quarters of the world's total seaborne cargo. Climate change and the risks associated with excessive CO2 emissions and other forms of particulate pollution were not considered priorities back then, either.

The emerging Advanced Nuclear Reactor Industry has been heavily supported by major investors and DOE, including the Maritime Nuclear Application Group from the Department of Energy's National Reactor Innovation Center. R&D funding is focused on Small Modular Reactors (SMR) which would be manufactured at a different scale and with a much smaller containment perimeter than historic reactors. SMR's use new methods of uranium enrichment, including reuse of spent uranium fuel, and are expected to be certified and on line by 2030. The U.S. DOE and SMR industry are looking at deployment on ships, not just for propulsion, but also for mobile electricity generation. The U.S. Department of Energy's 2022 budget included USD $1.85 billion for the Office of Nuclear Energy, including USD $1 billion for nuclear reactor R&D and testing.

The economics of SMRs for an equivalent amount of power would be game-changing due to the avoidance of commodity fuels. Even with a CAPEX of USD $500 million for the SMR, a typical container ship would have a lifecycle cost less than half when compared to a diesel or LNG fueled ship. The SMR industry plans to sell the power or lease the reactor to the ship owner; the only increased capital cost would be extra steel for the reactor compartment, however, that would easily be recovered by operating at a higher speed that is made possible by the onboard reactor, with no extra fuel cost.

The advantages of installing nuclear reactors on ships extends even further. Not only can they augment a traditional ship's diesel-electric system to create hybrid propulsion, they can also provide power to port-side electrical systems. This means bulk electrical power can be supplied on short notice, close to (or directly) where it is needed. Unlike the complicated processes required to build land-based power plants, ships are built in shipyards where permitting and community agreements are simplified, unlike the agreements that are typically present in communities where power is consumed. Seaports are often located near these heavily populated areas, too. This means that a ship's SMR could be used to produce renewable fuels (such as hydrogen) locally, which would reduce the need for massive distribution pipelines, or the ships themselves could be used as a mobile, modular power plant.

The potential for nuclear energy to transform and decarbonize shipping presents a range of exciting, environmentally beneficial, and profitable options, however a range of challenges exist: Advanced reactors for the commercial maritime industry must be tested and certified for use at sea separately from naval reactors;

this would involve input from the Nuclear Regulatory Commission. Acceptable routes and operation areas must be validated. Merchant mariners and nuclear engineers must be cross trained. Trading countries that are reluctant to accept nuclear-powered ships must be assured that these ships will not destroy local maritime environments; this can take nuanced diplomacy, and many years to negotiate.

Furthermore, new nuclear-powered ships must be built and the reactors prefabricated and installed in a U.S. shipyard (regardless of the ultimate owner), which will require new labor, expertise and production procedures. SMR manufacturers must generate a sufficient customer base for the suppliers to be cost effective and for the OEMs to maintain a mature, highly reliable operation of each reactor anywhere in the world. And finally, the potential for accidents or mishaps must be factored in, which requires the construction and deployment of specialized support vessels and equipment, and new training and safety procedures for mariners and crew.

The most controlled way of rolling out commercial nuclear propulsion, would be to preferentially install SMR's on commercial vessels flying the U.S. Flag. This would protect the technologies and Intellectual Property involved by putting the systems under the direct supervision of U.S. merchant mariners, and protection of the U.S. Navy and Coast Guard. This would set an historically momentous precedent: Unlike the safe passage that has been assured to other nations for decades, for the first time in the modern era, the USN and USCG would be directly engaged in the protection of *U.S.-flagged commercial ships* on the open ocean. The conflict in the Red Sea has provided a modern-day, real-life opportunity to assess what is required to protect

U.S.-Flagged trading vessels that carry sensitive cargo e.g., those operating under the Maritime Security Program. Lessons must be gleaned from this conflict to inform the response required to security scenarios that may occur during and after the roll-out of SMR's on commercial ships.

Installing nuclear-powered propulsion into commercial vessels would give U.S. commercial vessels noticeable advantages over fossil-fuel powered rivals; with operating costs, ship speed, and emission-levels. Higher average speeds, and reducing the need for 'slow steaming' will decrease average transit times and, in turn, increase crew and asset utilization. Nuclear-powered vessels may only need to be refueled every 10-20 years, which means a massive reduction in fuel usage and therefore running costs; fuel can equate to 50-60% of a carrier's total daily operating spend.

The United States is in a unique position to pioneer the integration of nuclear propulsion into the global commercial maritime sector. Doing so, would decarbonize the industry, decrease running costs for operators, and also establish the U.S. as an undeniable contributor to international commercial maritime affairs.

# CLIMATE SECURITY

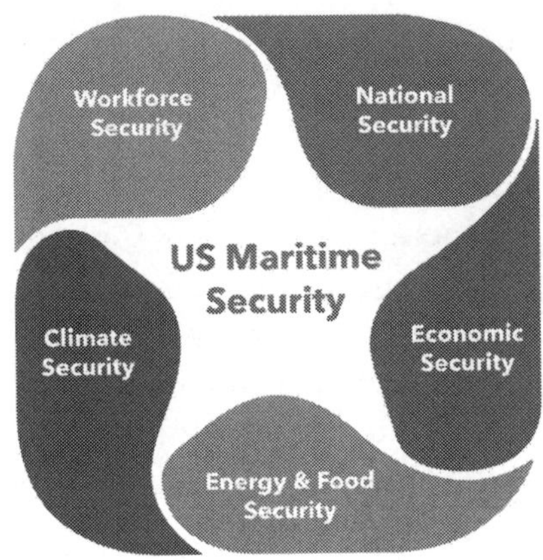


**Climate Security**

- *A changing ocean*
- *Climate friendly vessels*
- *National security risks from climate*
- *New business models*
- *Blue Economy institutions*

# IV. CLIMATE SECURITY

*No water, no life. No blue, no green.*

- Dr. Sylvia Earle, U.S. Marine Biologist, Oceanographer, Explorer

*The sea, the great unifier, is man's only hope.*

- Jacques Yves Cousteau, Oceanographer, Explorer

## Climate Security Context

Our ocean is changing faster than at any point in modern human history. The biology, chemistry and physics of the ocean will alter more in this generation than during any prior generation, largely due to human activity. This will radically impact U.S. and international security, and force a major adaptation in the years to come both for the U.S. and around the world as the world passes irreversible planetary tipping points. The maritime industry has a critical role to play to adapt to new climate realities, transition to greener fuels and business practices. This should be seen as an opportunity for the U.S. to take a global leadership role in the multi-trillion dollar Sustainable Blue Economy sector, which the U.S. is currently falling behind in.

Although the title for this chapter is labeled as 'Climate Security,' the content refers to the broader environmental impact on the planet that is taking place and will impact U.S. security. This means the impact of collapsing biodiversity (e.g., disappearing marine life and fish stocks in the worlds' oceans), acidification and deoxygenation of the ocean (40% fall in ocean-bound phytoplankton that generates 50% of the planet's oxygen), rising sea levels, extreme weather events, land-originating plastic pollution, overuse of nitrogen fertilizers than end up in the ocean and global water systems, maritime sound pollution, among others. All of these challenges have solutions, for which the U.S. can help the world transition into a sustainable green and blue industrial revolution through the power of policy, innovation and new business practices.
The climate crisis is also now one of the major drivers of social, political, economic, and technological mega-trends.

For example:

- A younger generation expresses stronger values for climate issues across different parts of the country and world, compared with older generations, who are more dismissive of climate and environmental concerns.
- Climate is emerging as a dividing issue to distinguish between political parties and leaders. This has led to the rise of major environmental policy initiatives (e.g., G20 and Central Bank-driven TCFD or Taskforce on Climate Disclosures).
- More activist shareholders and consumers forcing businesses to shift environmental disclosures and business practices, such as the rise of ESG indicators to drive new, greener business practices.
- Major investments in climate-focused technological solutions for the planet, such as electric vehicles, battery technologies, alternative fuels, offshore windfarms and aquaculture farms to shift business models (e.g., pursuing circular economy solutions).

Yet the urgency for action is clear. Science is showing that increasing temperatures, volatility in weather patterns, and the loss of key species have been particularly noticeable in the ocean:

- The world is getting hotter. The oceans absorb most of that heat; over 90% of it. The hottest year on record for the ocean was in 2018. And then 2019. And then 2020. And then every year since. All of the top six hottest levels recorded in the ocean have occurred in the last six years. The last 10 years were the ocean's warmest decade since at least the 1800s, and the next 10, predicted to be even warmer still.

- Warm oceans means weather volatility, at scale. More violent storms, more frequent storms, more destructive storms, taller and more frequent rogue waves. Larger cyclones, typhoons and hurricanes (all those words mean essentially the same thing). Longer droughts, wildfires, and more unpredictable winters, but a tendency towards more hotter hots, and less colder colds. Climate change is also exacerbating more extreme and unpredictable long term weather patterns caused by El Niño and La Niña effects.

- Warm oceans also means rising sea levels. Melting polar ice caps and salt water expansion could lead to sea level rises of 3.5 mm per year (or around 12 inches by 2050), but could be significantly greater if tidal surges are taken into account. This is significant enough to fully cover several low lying countries such as Kiribati, causing more international instability as these islanders are forced to seek new homes as climate refugees.

- Oceans also change when they absorb carbon dioxide (CO2). The oceans absorb about 30% of the CO2 that is emitted, the rest ends up in the atmosphere. Humans are really proficient at generating CO2 by doing things like burning fossil fuels. 36.8 billion tons were generated from global energy-related emissions in 2022. This pushed the current global average concentration of CO2 in the atmosphere to 421 parts per million (ppm). 350 parts per million was the safe level of CO2 in the atmosphere at the start of the first industrial revolution, and 450 parts per million is the high risk level at which most scientists expect the world to hit an irreversible temperature tipping point toward 2C by the end of the century, leading to the extinction of 99% tropical coral reefs by then.

- Dissolving carbon dioxide in seawater creates carbonic acid. This acid breaks up into H+ (hydrogen ions), and another ion called bicarbonate. Increasing H+ leads to increased ocean acidity. It has been calculated, and can be accurately measured, that since the Industrial Revolution, the ocean's surface has become about 30% more acidic worldwide.

- Hot water tends to kill living things. Hot acidic water does a better job. Not everything though. Some things can adapt, migrate, or aren't as affected. Coral isn't that adaptable, and is reluctant to migrate. While corals only cover 0.2% of the seafloor, they support at least 25% of the marine species in the ocean. At least 14% of all corals have either died or been seriously bleached since 2019. 25% of all major reefs that were recently surveyed showed signs of 'severe' bleaching. At this rate, and if global temperatures continue to rise, 90% of all tropical coral reef ecosystems will be extinct by 2050.

- Some fish species can adapt to warmer, acidic water, but this also makes them generally less productive. That means a decline in fish stocks, over time. Lower fish stocks, means less fish to eat, which impacts around a half of the planet that relies on some form of fish protein in their diets. It also means a net migration of fish towards the Poles, and away from the hotter temperatures in tropical waters. This means less fish in many developing countries that tend to rely on fish as their main source of protein.

Climate change has, and will continue to impact every region, every country, every economy, every industry sector, every company and organization, every cultural group, and therefore every individual. Unless there is a concerted effort to address the effects of climate change, the following three outcomes are predicted, and are becoming increasingly predictable:

1. **Competition for limited resources:** Conflict, supply chain disruptions, the COVID-19 pandemic, and geopolitical instability have caused food insecurity to reach record levels across the world. Around 300 million people in 58 countries faced acute food insecurity during 2022. 50 million people entered 2023 on the brink of famine. Over 2 billion people still lack access to a clean, reliable source of drinkable water. Because of climate change, agricultural productivity has decreased 34 percent across Africa, where many countries already struggle with food insecurity. The growing world population is already competing for limited resources, which will only be exacerbated by extremes in weather and temperature.

2. **Mass displacement:** Over the next 25 years, climate change could force over 215 million people, in six affected areas of the world, to move within their own countries or regions. The World Bank estimates that as many as 86 million internal climate migrants could be forced to move within Sub-Saharan Africa; 49 million in East Asia and the Pacific; 40 million in South Asia; 19 million in North Africa; 17 million in Latin America; and, 5 million from Eastern Europe and Central Asia. Climate relocation is predicted to continue in various forms over the next 50 years at least, due to low crop productivity, water scarcity and rising sea levels. The forced movement of such a large number of people can incite existing tensions, or create new ones. This may lead to conflict, and in some extreme cases, war.

3. **Rise in insecurity and polarization:** Climate change can deepen inequality, and exacerbates social

grievances, especially within vulnerable communities. Insecurity can also fuel political polarization and extremism. According to the Global Peace Index (2022), for 11 out of the last 14 years, there has been a measurable increase in political instability, violent extremism, strained neighbor relations, and displacement within and across borders. This has a physical effect on the communities that experience them, and a psychological impact on the people that witness them; hyper-connectivity through the internet and social media brings awareness, and also despair.

These factors, and there are many more, illustrate why climate change, and impacts it has on Climate Security must be addressed through immediate, purposeful, and diligent, global cooperation. This isn't just a problem that will impact the select few. This is everyone's problem.

## Global Shipping

One of the greatest impacts on the planet, and therefore the climate, is caused by burning fuel to propel ships across the ocean. The fuels burnt by global shipping are some of the most toxic, heavy fuels in use. Burning these toxic fuels releases a range of greenhouse gasses (GHGs), notably carbon dioxide (CO2), carbon monoxide (CO), nitrogen oxides (NOx), sulfur oxides (SOx), and Particulate Matter (PM) including one of most impacting of all, black carbon. Marine Heavy Fuel Oil (HFO) is a commonly used fuel, and is approximately 86% carbon, which equates to about 3.15 tons of CO2 per tonne of fuel consumed.

The 50,000+ vessels engaged in global trade burn roughly 300 million metric tons of fossil fuels each year, which is over 1 billion tons of carbon dioxide emissions. That's around 3% of the global total, making shipping the sixth-largest emitter in the world - just after China, U.S., India, Russia and Japan - and with higher emissions than Germany and France *combined.*

Most ships burn fossil fuels to move, and a large proportion *carry* fossil fuels to trade and sell. As mentioned previously, around 40% of all maritime trade by weight, consists of fossil fuels on their way to be burned, or of products derived directly from fossil fuels. This means that a significant proportion of global shipping revenues comes from transporting fossil fuels, such as coal, oil, gas and LNG. Fossil fuels provide the energy for propulsion, and also generate significant revenues: Given the intertwined nature of this association, it is obvious to see why some participants might be reluctant to abandon fossil fuels, and move to less perceivably profitable alternatives.

Decarbonizing the shipping industry must become an international priority to address climate change. Global shipping emissions have been growing significantly year on year, and, unless unchecked, are expected to be 50% higher by 2050, which may tip the world beyond its carbon budget. While the world has to halve greenhouse gas emissions within a decade to avoid a runaway climate scenario, the shipping industry is on course to increase emissions by 14% over this time period. Reversing this course provides a unique opportunity for ships compared to the rest of the transportation sector which must decarbonize by shifting to electric charging or a low carbon fuel with a diesel-equivalent energy density. Large ships are able to burn lower density zero-carbon fuels with less impact on cargo capacity.

A critical meeting of the IMO in July 2023 produced the 'IMO Strategy on Reduction of GHG Emissions from Ships' that was designed to set targets against emission goals. The following agreements were reached after long and protracted discussions:

1. Global fleet emission reductions would be "at least 20 per cent" while "striving" for 30 per cent by 2030
2. Emissions would be reduced by "at least 70 per cent, striving for 80 per cent" by 2040
3. The final goal is "net-zero" to be achieved "close to 2050." Net-zero by "close to 2050" is very different to 'zero emissions by 2050'.

Responses from the global shipping community and industry observers were mixed. Some thought the wording in the Strategy was vague and was devoid of firm deadlines. Due to a past history of disagreement and member state demands, some were incredulous that *any* agreements had been decided. Others responded positively and were enthused by the fact that a clear direction had been determined and could now be collectively achieved. Additional discussions will be required, among a wide group of stakeholders to solidify these goals into practical and measurable outcomes. The strategy is planned for 2028.

When combined, all modes of transportation emit around 23% of the energy-related CO2 that contributes to global warming. Shipping is not entirely to blame. There are many other contributing factors, and many other parties involved, from a range of other sectors and industries. For example, the aviation industry contributes 2.5% of global GHG emissions, and affects the upper reaches of the atmosphere in a variety of complex ways. Compared to planes, and indeed most other forms of transport, large ships are incredibly efficient. As mentioned previously, one gallon (3.8 liters) of fuel can transport 10 tons of cargo 6 miles by truck, 1 mile in an airplane, and over 50 miles on a ship. Large ships emit less than 35-40 grams of $CO^2$ per ton-mile, the lowest of all transport types.

So why focus on shipping? Simply put, because irresponsibly managed ships can cause considerable harm to the land, sea *and* sky. Simultaneously. Ports, coastal infrastructure, dredging, strip mining, and ship anchors destroy critical marine habitats in the physical and subsea environments. Pollution, spills, acoustic noise, and 'scrubbed' engine emissions are regularly dumped into the sea. And dirty pollutants and other toxic emissions from burnt fossil fuels are continuously pumped into the sky.

The ability to inflict scaled damage on shared environments sets ships apart from other contributors: A large freight plane crash may sadly claim the lives of the crew, but would be contained in an area the size of a football field. What happens if an oil tanker hits a reef, as happened with the *MV Wakashio* off the coast of Mauritius in July 2020? The *Wakashio* incident occurred in one of the world's most important biodiversity hotspots in the world, amid calm waters and weather. A review found that the cause of the accident was likely caused by the ship's crew that had sailed too close to the reef in an attempt to obtain cell phone signal coverage. Regardless of why this occurred, the *Wakashio* ended up significantly impacting the livelihoods of thousands of people, killing thousands of fish, aquatic mammals and seabirds, and irreversibly damaging hundreds of kilometers of pristine coastline.

The responses that occur after such incidents also demonstrate the lack of priority that is often given to shipping: When a plane crashes, a team of highly-trained aircraft investigators immediately scour the crash site, then spend months meticulously recreating all aspects of the flight plan to ascertain why it happened and to ensure a similar accident does not happen again. In the case of the *Wakashio*? The IMO's response was heavily criticized; the immediate cleanup ended up being led by volunteers on the island at their own risk of exposure to the leaked fuel; over 100,000 people protested on the streets of the capital city in the weeks following the oil spill; three tug boat sailors died assisting in salvage operations; and the shipowner and Protection and Indemnity (P&I) club associated with the vessel were criticized for opaque disclosures.

Global greenhouse gas emissions have a pronounced impact on Climate Security. The biology, chemistry and physics of the ocean will alter more in this generation than during any prior generation, largely due to human activity. Atmospheric pollution is increasing global temperatures. Imminent (and irreversible) collapse of certain fish stocks and the possibility of large-scale marine extinction events has moved from probable to inevitable. Relying on commercial participants to take the lead to solve these complex problems is slow and cumbersome. Similarly, if collective goals are vague, and timeframes arbitrary, it will be difficult to bring about lasting or sustainable change. It is time to act with urgency. The crisis is severe.

Suffice to say, all of these issues will dramatically impact the United States and the international community, and force radical adaptation in the years to come. All four of the other Principles are affected by climate change: National, Economic, Energy & Food, and Workforce Security will all be heavily impacted, and require bold solutions to mitigate risks and capitalize on opportunities.

Some progress has been made, but much more can be done. And much more *must* be done.

## Climate Security and U.S. Shipping

The United States has emitted a quarter of all world GHGs to date, more than any other country. While China eclipses the U.S. in terms of total annual emissions, GHG emissions in the U.S. amount to over 15 tons per person; the highest of any country. If the world rises to U.S. standards of living, we would burn through four times our planetary resources. Radical new lifestyle choices are needed. In the U.S., about 25% of U.S. emissions are derived from electricity and power generation; 24% comes from industry; 13% from commercial and residential buildings and 11% from agriculture. The remaining 27% comes from the transportation sector, a sector that not only contributes a noticeable proportion of emissions, but is also highly susceptible to the effects of a changing climate.

Of all potential challenges, the environmental complexities facing the U.S. maritime sector, including its ports and waterways, are the most pressing. Many ports are grappling with the impacts of increased shipping activity, while rising sea levels and other climate-related challenges pose a significant threat to U.S. coastal infrastructure. U.S. commercial ships and shipping would also be affected, however, as has been discussed, the sector is largely non-existent at this present time.

If the United States is to expand into new areas of commercial maritime operation, resilient vessels, ports and critical infrastructure that can cope with a changing climate and extreme weather will be required. 'Resilience' is no longer just a practical (operationally transformational) concern. Due to climate change, it is now a critical (necessary and unavoidable) characteristic. But it's not just about coping in the present, the United States has to strategically build for the future.

What can be done? As one of the largest emitters of greenhouse gasses, the U.S. must take a leading role in minimizing the effects of economic progress on climate change. This is essential if global temperatures are to remain below a 1.5C degree threshold by the end of the century; a point that if reached, will lead to irreversible planetary tipping points that will increase global temperatures dramatically. The U.S. can pioneer global shipping industry reform while pursuing opportunities to adapt to a rapidly changing planet through novel shipping and Blue Economy strategies.

Irrespective of the trajectory of the energy transition or climate change, the United States must take proactive steps to pursue Blue Economy initiatives. These new opportunities will lead to a wide range of very rewarding outcomes. Rewarding, as in mutually beneficial, but also as in financially rewarding. If managed responsibly, sustainability can be profitable. A strategy, along with mechanisms to exert influence are essential. Unfortunately, the U.S. currently lacks a holistic strategy or credible institutions to become a leader in global shipping or the Blue Economy, and is being outpaced by strategic advances in China and Europe. Without a strategy, many profitable activities are being successfully completed and capitalized on by allies and adversaries. And without a strong commercial maritime fleet, the U.S. is only able to influence the shipping industry from the sidelines.

Opportunities are abundant; few are fully understood, and even less are being actively pursued.

## Climate Security Maritime Risks and Vulnerabilities

The following five concerns have a direct impact on Climate Security and will also affect U.S. allies and partners across the world:

A. **The changing state of the ocean** - *The impact on shipping and the marine environment with changes in currents and ocean surface hazards*

B. **Climate change and maritime operations** - *How climate change will impact shipping operations, navigation, security and ship and port design*

C. **Climate Security and National Security** - *The climate crisis: One of the biggest threats to U.S. National Security over the next 20 years*

D. **New business models** - *The United States lack of innovative investment affects maritime innovation, and incites consumer and shareholder activism*

E. **Absence of U.S. Blue Economy Institutions** - *How slow-moving international regulations, and inconsistent U.S. environmental leadership affects Climate Security*

## A. The changing state of the ocean

From the perspective of an individual, it seems impossible that any actions performed by a single person could create a chain of events that might detrimentally affect the entire world. The world is so large, and oceans so grand; they appear indifferent and impervious to the actions of human beings. However, this has never really been the case. A lot of individual humans have, through action and inaction, caused significant impact on the planet's atmosphere and oceans, which is only now being recognized and measured. Climate change proves that small actions can have big consequences, especially as it relates to the ocean.

### I. Changing ocean currents

As mentioned in 'Pre-Eminence', ocean currents are essential to the survival of marine ecosystems, and can assist (and hamper) the movement of ships across large bodies of water. Currents also move water and heat around the world, which means they are crucial for maintaining global temperatures. Currents are also susceptible to changes in global temperatures. Currents operating at scale in the ocean are largely invisible, but their effect is felt in many different ways; from influencing wind speed, to rain fall, and the intensity and frequency of storms.

Changing ocean and atmospheric conditions impacts U.S. security in many ways.

For example, discussions have recently taken place about the potential slowdown of a system of ocean currents in the Atlantic, called the Atlantic meridional overturning circulation, or AMOC. The AMOC is characterized by the northward flow of warm, salty, upper layer water in the Atlantic, and a flow of colder and deeper waters in a southward direction. The AMOC transports around one quarter of the global atmospheric-ocean heat into the Northern Hemisphere and is responsible for the relative warmth of many regions and countries throughout Europe.

If climate-change led to the slowing down of the AMOC, it would lower average temperatures and precipitation rates across the European continent. This would dramatically reduce the region's agricultural output, and may have a substantial effect on extreme weather events. Predicted outcomes include an increase in 'superstorms' and major flooding, changes in rainfall in the tropics, Alaska or Antarctica, more frequent and intense El Niño events, and a dramatic decline in plankton biomass. This could lead to an eventual slowdown of the Gulf Stream, which is responsible for the stable climate of much of Europe. A climate-change initiated shutdown of the AMOC, followed by the Gulf Stream would cause devastation at a global scale.

A small change - calculated to be one degree Celsius - in average global temperatures, and a subsequent rise in ocean temperatures could initiate these crippling scenarios. This is one example, and there are many other catastrophic outcomes, illustrates why it is critical that proactive steps are taken to reduce emissions, and therefore minimize the chance these events will occur.

## II. Algal blooms and garbage patches

Sargassum is a leafy brown seaweed that floats on the open ocean. It is covered in cherry-sized air pockets, and unlike many other marine plants, reproduces on the water's surface. A vast bloom of brown Sargassum algae has grown in the Atlantic Ocean, and now extends all the way from West Africa to the

Gulf of Mexico; an astonishing 5,500 miles (8,850 kilometers) in length, estimated to weigh around 11 million tons. Positively, the bloom has its own ecosystem, and provides food and habitat for fish, sea turtles and marine birds. But it has also grown massively in size: Sargassum absorbs sunlight, which means an increase in ocean temperatures in the waters surrounding the mat. It also poses a disposal problem when it drifts ashore and rots. When Sargassum rots, it releases hydrogen sulfide gas, which is unpleasant for humans, and toxic to birds and aquatic life.

Changes in wind patterns, sea currents, rainfall and drought affect the size of the bloom. Warming waters also contribute to seaweed growth, as does runoff from the Amazon and Orinoco rivers that are often rich in nitrogen from fertilizers used in local farming. After extensive study, it has become evident that the 'Great Sargassum Patch' acts as a heat synthesizer and a disruptor of surficial currents. Further warming of ocean temperatures must be avoided, particularly in a region that is already prone to severe weather events including hurricanes. It is possible that the Sargassum Patch may even be disrupting the Gulf Stream.

A growing patch of garbage and debris poses similar problems in the Pacific, but with the compounding issues associated with plastics and micro-plastic pollution. The Great Pacific Garbage Patch (GPGP) is located in the central North Pacific Ocean. It is an ocean gyre (large circular ocean current) of marine debris, and covers around 1.6 million square kilometers (620,000 square miles). This is an area twice the size of Texas, half the size of India, or three times the size of France. It is estimated to contain somewhere between 45,000–129,000 metric tons of plastic and other waste, which is mostly small and fragmented microplastics that are likely to be swallowed by birds and fish. The Pacific gyre is estimated to contain approximately six pounds (2.7 kilos) of plastic for every pound (half kilo) of plankton.

Pioneering activity by The Ocean Cleanup, a nonprofit environmental engineering organization based in the Netherlands, has provided more detail about the GPGP in recent years than was ever known before. For example, extractions from the patch - collected through a novel netting system - brought up onto support vessels reveals that most of the large waste in the GPGP is discarded fishing gear. This is obvious to witness when viewing the retrieval videos The Ocean Cleanup regularly posts to online forums; large amounts of netting, floats, drums and other fishing equipment make up most of the garbage that is weighed and sorted. This reinforces the need for more regulation and oversight of the fishing industry, which is a noticeable contributor to marine waste.

Algal blooms and garbage patches illustrate how small activities can have a large impact on the ocean. Excess fertilizer runoff in the Amazon, leads to algal blooms that can stretch across the Caribbean, wash up on the beaches of Florida and may alter the Gulf Stream. And a broken fishing net, lazily thrown overboard by a fisherman operating off the coast of Hawaii, ends up contributing to a growing rubbish pile that endangers marine life, and the long-term future of the very industry they work in.

## B. Climate Change and Maritime Operations

The global shipping industry needs to adjust to this new climate reality. The scale of runaway climate change events and the changing nature of the ocean will affect every participant in the commercial maritime sector. These events will also influence how ships are designed and operated, change the way ships are protected, and impact the productivity and profitability of maritime assets including ports:

## I. Ship design

A changing climate will impact how ships are designed. Vessels will need safety adjustments to cope with higher safety thresholds when navigating extreme weather. An increase in ocean ferocity and wave activity will impact decisions around the structural integrity of a ship's hull, as well as the vessel's length, width, and materials used during construction. The Irish Navy has responded to this threat by changing the construction of its ocean-going vessels, stating that climate change has made the Atlantic rougher and more unpredictable. Climate change may also make it more difficult for the crew to operate outside in exposed areas in certain parts of the world, for example, in the tropics. This will force a rethink of how crews move and operate on deck, and what actions can (and need to be) performed outside.

Changes in swells, tides and currents may require more propulsive capacity to be added to certain vessels that navigate through altered ocean regions. This will impact fuel loads, and therefore affect fuel storage. Ships will require new safety standards, containment and storage systems, and updated operating procedures if future fuels types - e.g., nuclear energy or battery power - are used. The processes involved in rescue, recovery and combatting onboard fires, along with the requisite systems that assist with these processes will also need to change with the introduction of these new fuel types.

Ships engaged in the container and commodity trades will have to contend with changing sea levels, which will alter the ships profile at seaports against docking and mooring infrastructure, and when loading and unloading supplies. This may require a redesign of existing systems, or the deployment of revised equivalents. Higher ambient temperatures will impact the carriage of shipping containers (and reefers) which may require a rethink of how containers are carried above deck. When moving across the ocean, the effect of increased wind shear, and the presence of rogue waves will alter how containers are stored, lashed, and is likely to impact maximum possible stack heights.

Higher ocean temperatures will also increase the amount of biofouling that grows on the surface of a ship's hull. Biofouling - microorganisms, plants, algae, or small animals - can increase drag, which leads to a loss of speed at constant power, or increases the need for power increases to maintain constant speeds. Both of these scenarios lead to increased emissions. According to a study by class society Det Norske Veritas (DNV), the accumulated costs of hull fouling could be as high as $30 billion across the global fleet, and also result in millions of additional tons of CO2 being released annually. New hull designs, new types of ocean-friendly hull coatings and novel cleaning technologies will need to be incorporated into future designs. Australian companies have shown a high degree of initiative in the development of novel technologies to transform maritime and adjacent domains: Sydney-based *MicroTau* has developed 'shark skin' technology that reduces surface drag on plane wings and ship hulls, while *Hullbot's* autonomous rovers are able to scrub hulls clean, which reduces the need to apply toxic, marine-ecosystem-destroying, biocidal paints.

Finally, emission systems for all ships - and particularly fossil-fuel burning ships - will need modification to adhere to new emission standards and to reduce the amount of particulate matter that is ejected into the atmosphere. Specific attention should be given to the reduction of black carbon, especially for those ships navigating newer arctic trade routes; black carbon emissions are responsible for around 20% of shipping's climate impact over a 20-year period, and also has a pronounced impact on polar regions as it accelerates the melting rate of snow. Shipbuilders and shipowners should be encouraged to install these redesigned components regardless of the level of regulation being imposed by the IMO and other bodies, as a way to proactively participate in reducing shipping's impact on the environment.

## II. Operation and navigation

The changing nature of the world's oceans will affect where and how mariners sail. Changes in seasonal variability will affect what routes can be taken, and whether or not certain ocean regions are available for shipping at different times of year. While newer Arctic routes offer a reduction in sailing times from Asia to Europe, they also introduce a range of new risks that have not been entirely mapped out by the IMO and other international agencies that oversee global shipping. New regulations should be enacted (and quickly) to ensure that ships that traverse these regions are safe, compliant, and do not adversely affect the pristine regions around the North Pole.

Extreme weather, including higher winds, more damaging waves, and a higher frequency of hurricanes, will change how mariners navigate across the ocean. Rogue waves are likely to increase in frequency as oceans warm, and current change. Rogue waves can reach a height of 30 meters, and are currently estimated to be 1 in 10,000. A rogue wave may have been responsible for the damage to the containership ONE Apus, which lost around 1900 containers ($200 million worth) in late 2020 when it attempted to navigate through a storm cell. It is suspected that the Apus was hit by a rogue wave that might have been 16 meters high. If rogue waves are detected with higher frequencies in certain areas, it may make those areas unnavigable by smaller or less capable vessels. Similarly, more frequent occurrences of violent storms at seas may change entire trade lanes, and restrict parts of the oceans to certain vessels that are designed to handle these conditions.

Due to escalating volatility, there will be increased reliance on predicting and mapping weather patterns for ships in the future. This will mean the deployment of new types of technology to allow ship Captains to sail with greater confidence, and with less concern for the welfare of the vessel under their command. This could involve vision (Augmented-Reality and AI-assisted image processing) systems on the bridge, or satellite sensor and communications systems to assist with weather detection, route-planning and navigation. The installation of new systems will lead to procedural changes in how ships operate, including the priority given to monitoring changing environmental conditions. This will be important in busy waterways such as the Singapore Strait, or in narrower passages like the Suez Canal; a repeat of Evergreen's *Ever Given* 6-day blockage of the Suez Canal would be incredibly disruptive to shipping operations and global supply chains that are increasingly based on precision and just-in-time logistics.

## III. Protecting shipping

The frequency of piracy events may increase if climate change brings about a pronounced decrease in the availability of fish. This has happened in the past, in particular around island nations and developing states that rely heavily on fishing for nutrition and trade. Piracy has generally been on the decline in shipping over the last decade, however there still is a pronounced amount of activity occurring in the Gulf of Guinea, around Somalia (the Horn of Africa), the Red Sea and Gulf of Aden, the Straits of Malacca and the Singapore Straits. For example, piracy in the Somali Sea and surrounds peaked during

2011 with 45 vessels hijacked, 176 boarded, 113 fired upon, and over 1,200 people held hostage.

Modern day pirates travel in fast boats (skiffs) and are sometimes armed with light weapons; such as hand guns, or Kalashnikovs. They usually attempt to steal cargo from containers or storage compartments onboard the vessel, or siphon off commodities to a waiting tender using a ship-to-ship transfer. They can sometimes attempt to abduct the crew. While it hasn't been common, and would be logistically difficult, desperation may force 'climate pirates' to attempt to rob larger tankers or container ships. This would lead to a sizable pay-off: Large tankers can haul upwards of $200 million worth of oil, and large container ships can carry hundreds of millions of dollars in cargo.

If instances of piracy increase, ship operators passing through certain regions will need to increase security personnel deployed on transiting ships; commonly referred to as Private Maritime Security Companies. Ships might also need to have detection, defense systems or physical barriers installed to repel boarders. Insurance will be affected for these ship operators, as would the costs associated with managing the crew who may need to be trained on new procedures. All of these changes can dramatically increase base operating costs, which may end up being prohibitively expensive. If sea routes are closed because costs are too high, and there is a lack of naval escorts to mitigate risks, then entire regions may end up without a reliable supply of fuel, food, or other essential items commonly delivered by ship.

## IV. Productivity and profitability

The productivity and profitability of ships and shipping assets are also impacted by climate change. Productivity and profitability are usually intertwined: For example, if round-trip efficiency is low, due a lack of available routes caused by changes in weather patterns, then profitability will be adversely affected. How prolonged droughts impact shipping productivity and profitability can be observed in three different regions that are heavily dependent on shipping - The Panama Canal, the Mississippi River, and the river Rhine:

- **Panama Canal:** The Panama Canal - an artificial waterway connecting the Atlantic and the Pacific Ocean - has been a major thoroughfare for international trade for over 100 years. Over 14,000 transits were completed through the canal in 2022, by ships carrying more than 291 million long tons of cargo. The Canal handles around 5% of all seaborne trade annually, and generates around 6% of Panama's total GDP. The top three destinations for cargo through the Canal are the United States, China and Japan; ships moving to or from the United States account for nearly three quarters of the Canal's total traffic.

  The Panama Canal uses a unique system of locks for vessel movement that draws water from surrounding lakes. A prolonged drought, caused by changing weather patterns, and a 30% reduction in rainfall in the region has reduced the amount of water available to fill the locks. 38 ships can typically transit the Canal per day. This has been cut to 31 in November 2023. Reducing the number of daily trips through the canal causes delays and queues to form at either end. These delays impact ship operators who are paying day rates for the ship and crew, or may miss scheduled port calls and risk commercial penalties. One ship operator paid $400,000 - almost double the standard rate - to jump ahead in the queue in August, 2023. This was dwarfed by a record $3.89 million that Japanese energy company

Eneos paid to queue jump, in November 2023, just three months later.

- **Mississippi Region**: The Mississippi is a critical part of the U.S. inland waterways system. Transportation of produce and goods along the river is usually handled by barges and tows; tows are non-powered barges that have been lashed together. Barges are an incredibly efficient form of transport: A single barge can carry the equivalent of 16 rail cars or 70 semi-trucks. When tied together, a single tow of barges can move the equivalent load of 1,000 semi-trucks; using around 4.5x less fuel. Barges carry the majority of produce - around 175 million tons per year - that has been sourced from the productive growing regions within the Mississippi basin. For example, around 60 percent of all exported U.S. grain is sent down the Mississippi by barge to the Gulf Coast.

  In November 2023, the entire path along the Mississippi River was in 'moderate drought' to 'exceptional drought' according to the University of Nebraska-Lincoln's Drought Monitor. A lack of available water affects the system of locks and dams that operate on the river; if water gets too low, barges can get stuck in the silty mud on rivers bottom. The costs to move cargo on the River has increased by around 5x over the last year. The total impact of the drought has been estimated at upwards of $20 billion (and counting). As with the Panama Canal, these costs are immediately imposed on transportation providers, but are eventually passed onto consumers in the form of higher food and commodity prices.

- **Rhine River:** The Rhine is Germany's most important waterway. Around 85% of all freight that travels on the inland waterway system was carried completely or partly on the river Rhine. Oil, chemicals and grains are commonly shipped on the river using small vessels and barges. As with the barges of the Mississippi, the barges on the Rhine are incredibly efficient. One barge (about 135m long, and with a 3m draft) can carry 2,700 tons of cargo; the equivalent of 110 trucks.

Shipping volumes on the Rhine have been consistent for the past two decades, but started to drop off in 2021; a decline that has continued ever since. This has been caused by an historic drought that has affected most of Europe, and also a reduction in the Alpine and glacial water that feeds the river. Calculating the economic impact of disruptions caused by the drought is complex, however it has been calculated that if the water level drops and 25% of all river traffic is disrupted, that Germany's total industrial output drops by around 1%.

These three examples are a small subset of larger numbers that can be applied to global shipping. A recent report by nonprofit research institute RTI International for the Environmental Defense Fund estimates that the shipping industry could lose $10 billion a year from extreme weather conditions between now and 2050. This equates to a $250 billion loss to the industry if no meaningful action is taken. This cost would be realized by shipowners, ship operators, shipping lines, ports and terminal operators, and other supply chain participants. This will affect consumers through delays and disruptions to supply, but will also be passed on to consumers in the form of higher food and commodity prices.

## V. Ports and critical infrastructure

For obvious reasons, ports and naval bases are often built close to the ocean, or on the edges of connected inland rivers and waterways. Around 90% of U.S. maritime infrastructure, including ports and naval bases exist in low-lying coastal regions. According to the National Oceanic and Atmospheric Administration (NOAA) "one third of 55 coastal sites in the U.S. will see 100-year storm surges become 10-year or more frequent events by 2050". This means ports and naval bases will be increasingly susceptible to a range of climate-related risks including sea level rise, extreme weather conditions and being damaged by hurricanes and storms.

Disruptions increase down time, and cost a lot of money. The Port of Houston, located in the Gulf of Mexico is the largest U.S. port for foreign tonnage (220.5 million short tons in 2022), the 5th ranked U.S. port for TEUs, and handles around 73% of all container moves in the Gulf Coast. Houston accounts for 75% of U.S. waterborne exports of plastic resins, moved over $70 billion worth of petroleum products across 2022, and has shifted more than 42.4 million short tons of cargo since the start 2023. The Port also handles a lot of domestic trade; some 200,000 barges call though Houston every year.

A recent report from Oxford University identified The Port of Houston to be the most at-risk port in the world, due to the potential damage from cyclones, heavy winds, pluvial (rainfall-induced) and fluvial (river-channel) flooding. The Gulf of Mexico regularly experiences frequent extreme weather. In 2017, Hurricane Harvey cost the State of Texas between $125 - $190 billion in damages, and disrupted the Port of Houston's operations for around 10 days; assuming the port's annual trading volume (around $240 billion) was spread evenly across the year, a 10 day outage would have affected $6.6 billion in cargo.

Maritime ports and naval bases will need to be redesigned to cope with climate change. This will mean the creation of new flood mitigation, wind protection, and rainfall management systems. Ship-to-shore cranes, gantries, container stacks and other infrastructure exposed to extreme winds and storm forces will likely need to be redesigned. Rising sea levels, and more forceful currents will affect the loading and unloading of ships, which may mean piers and mooring hardware (bollards, ropes, and other equipment) require modifications. Extremes in temperature will affect outdoor storage facilities, especially for refrigerated and dry produce containers. Similarly, naval bases will need to carefully think through the security and safety implications of storing and handling armaments, weaponry and military vehicles.

## C. Climate Security and National Security

Apart from directly affecting the economy - through reduced productivity, degraded agricultural efficiency, and increased transportation costs - the United States will have to contend with how climate change affects military operations and serving personnel; domestically and abroad.

According to the DOD, the climate crisis is a critical national security issue, and represents one of the biggest threats to National Security the U.S. will face between now and 2040. In an address to cadets in August 2023, at the Sustainable Infrastructure, Resilience and Climate Consortium, Deputy Defense Secretary Kathleen Hicks said "A question I hear often is, 'Why does the Department of Defense care about climate change?’ The answer is simple, although the solution is not. Climate change is a national security issue, and for the national security community, that declaration is not controversial - it's fact". These statements should have been very familiar to the audience; as mentioned in chapter three, the effects of climate change on National Security have been documented in military circles since 1990, and in regular Intelligence briefings since 2008.

Hicks' went on to directly correlate Climate Security and National Security by citing statistics about how much time the National Guard, and other military personnel had expended to assist with hurricane relief, and to fight increasingly ferocious forest fires. More time providing aid, and putting out fires, equates to less time training and being ready for combat. Hicks went on to explain: "In recent budgets, we have been forced to absorb billions of dollars in recovery costs from extreme weather events… $1 billion for rebuilding Offutt Air Force Base, Nebraska after historic floods… $3 billion to rebuild Camp Lejeune, North Carolina after Hurricane Florence… $5 billion to rebuild Tyndall Air Force Base, Florida after Hurricane Michael." Climate-related threats to military and commercial maritime infrastructure are very real: As stated previously, 90% of U.S. ports and Naval bases are in low-lying coastal regions, are at risk from sea level rise, extreme weather conditions and damaging storm surges.

Every department involved in National Security - Army, Navy, Air Force, U.S. Coast Guard, National Guard, the Department of Homeland Security (DHS), and the Transportation Security Administration (TSA), along with support services and intelligence agencies will be impacted by climate change. Each department will need to adjust existing management, deployment, and operational strategies to adapt to extremes in weather and temperature. This will impact the individual warfighter directly exposed to the elements, as well as the deployment regime of a Carrier Strike Group patrolling in foreign waters.

Equipment choices, training regimes, clothing and personal supplies, the administration of rations, and movement of certain types of cargo will all be directly impacted. Infrastructure deployed into areas that are more prone to extreme weather events will need to be redesigned and reinforced. Armament production, storage and handling procedures will need to be reviewed. Refinement, realignment or replacement will need to take place across the entire military apparatus to adapt to these new, prevailing conditions. These changes will be expensive, and take time, effort and resources to complete.

U.S. military operations will be impacted the world over. This will force unpredictable operational changes on the U.S. Navy and U.S. Coast Guard as they patrol the world's oceans. For example there will be an increase in incursions into sovereign waters and security incidents involving nations that are suffering from climate-related food shortages. Distant Water Fleets will increase their presence across the world; deploying new and more aggressive techniques to harvest dwindling reserves of fish. Foreign navies may become more aggressive as they assert ownership rights over scarce marine resource areas. And there may be increased incidents of piracy involving container ships and commodity vessels that traverse the ocean. Most of these incidents will be driven out of desperation, and a desire to secure food or fuel for citizens suffering the effects of climate-instigated shortages.

Changes in operational tempo, and an increase in rates of interception and interdiction will push already stretched naval resources to the limit. If these events occur in a more accelerated fashion than is currently predicted, it will lead to a range of completely unsustainable outcomes for the U.S. Navy and Coast Guard; detrimentally impacting personnel and assets, and leading to a significant rise in operating costs. The work of the USN and USCG in international waters will be further complicated by the presence of vessels flying Flags of Convenience. There will be little appetite to engage any ship in those locations that does not have U.S. citizens on board, and has little, or no, direct connection to U.S. national interests. An increase in frequency of these scenarios may lead to regional conflicts, and potentially to widespread anarchy on the open ocean.

The DOD has been discussing the impact of climate-change for decades. The potential for U.S. military operations to be seriously affected is evident. All indicators show that time is running out: The United States must prepare for these Climate Security scenarios now, before they inevitably come to pass.

## D. New, Greener Business Models

### I. Innovative investments needed

There are many risks associated with climate change that affect Climate Security, but there is also a growing number of opportunities that can be capitalized upon. If a new strategic approach is formulated and followed, the United States will be able to lead, and also financially benefit from, a range of exciting and profitable sustainability initiatives:

i. The shipping industry has not historically invested in technology and innovation. In the early 2000's, venture capital investment in the maritime sector was close to non-existent. By 2019, it had spiked to over $1 billion dollars, driven largely by investments in a small number of technology companies; companies that, as of today, are hemorrhaging money, firing staff and closing down without having made much difference to the industry. The predominance of this misplaced money led to hyper-growth in one niche area of the shipping value chain - software - but did very little to change any of the fundamental problems that are now being heavily regulated.

Investing $1 billion dollars into technology and innovation in the maritime sector sounds significant, however it's worth keeping in mind that the top commercial carriers generated around $360 billion in profit between 2020 and 2022. $1 billion is 0.27% of $360 billion. Closer collaboration is required: The right investments, by the right investors, into the most impactful areas will ensure that capital is intelligently deployed, and that real solutions are actually created. Solutions must be prioritized that noticeably reduce structural inefficiencies and emissions, and improve Climate Security outcomes for providers and industry participants.

ii. According to IMO estimates, it will require between $1-$1.4 trillion in cumulative investments across the shipping industry, to reach the IMO's target of reducing absolute emissions by at least 50% by 2050; that is, around $50 to 70 billion annually between 2030 and 2050. To meet the goal of fully decarbonizing the industry, cumulative investment would need to be $1.4 - 1.9 trillion between 2030 and 2050.

A price tag of $2 trillion to decarbonize the sector may seem rather large. However, that spend is spread out over 30 years and pales in comparison to total global energy subsidies: The International Monetary Fund (IMF) compiled data across 170 countries and found that explicit subsidies (undercharging for supply costs) amounted to $1.3 trillion in 2022 alone. Implicit subsidies (undercharging for environmental costs and forgone consumption taxes, after accounting for pre-existing fuel taxes and carbon pricing) came in at a colossal $5.7 trillion. If the true cost of damage to the environment - as calculated by revised scientific research - was factored in, implicit subsidies would top $10 trillion.

When presented with these numbers it becomes not only feasible but hard to ignore that investing in decarbonizing shipping represents a huge investment opportunity that will also create jobs in a new, sustainable and entirely necessary sector. The United States has a great depth of experience in financial markets, so could be involved in supplying the necessary capital to fund the projects that will assist in meeting the IMO's objectives. The U.S. has ingenuity and know-how too, so can also participate in building and commercializing the products, technologies, and innovations that are required to meet these ambitious goals.

iii. As mentioned in the Principle of Economic Security, if the global 'Blue Economy' were a country, it would be the world's seventh-largest economy and generate revenues of between \$3-\$6 trillion. The U.S. is falling behind in global leadership on Blue Economy initiatives, despite having some of the world's best technical universities that could lead on smart maritime clean technologies (e.g., MIT, Princeton, Stanford, Berkeley). This poses two problems: Firstly, many millions of dollars that could be made by U.S. companies and institutions are ceded to other countries. And, secondly, it reduces the U.S.' ability to influence the creation of solutions that will derive the most value from Blue Economy participants, and most effectively reverse environmental damage.

The United States also has access to some of the most innovative companies in the world: Tesla is a world leader in vehicle autonomy and electrification; Amazon, in robots and global distribution; SpaceX in unique fuels and propulsion systems; Microsoft in compute power and software; and Apple's material design and innovations in scaled manufacturing, have defined new production methodologies and spawned entirely new industries. Any one of these world-leading companies could provide engineers, expertise and investment in the U.S. maritime sector, and cross-pollinate established technologies and ideas that could drive innovative change in U.S. Blue Economy initiatives.

iv. Seven alternative fuel types and energy systems have been proposed that could power vessels in the future: Liquefied Natural Gas (LNG), Hydrogen, Ammonia, Methanol, Electrification, Nuclear and Biofuels. Each of these have pros and cons, with additional environmental consequences beyond just climate emissions. However, there is currently not enough focused U.S. investment on any of these seven fuel types to drive meaningful change, and a current lack of investment in R&D or strategic integration to hit critical mass. It has been increasingly left up to industry (and market forces) to discover and fight through adoption, production and deployment; to mixed results. While some subsidies have been made available to certain sectors, there has not been a concerted or focused effort to push for mass adoption of any of them.

Stronger environmental standards are required, as is more definitive leadership from U.S. government departments and military decision-makers about what fuels will be used in combat and commercial scenarios. The United States can take a pioneering role in these endeavors by establishing domestic and global partnerships to advance research and development, and the deployment of these future fuels into the global shipping industry. The U.S. has a long and profitable history of energy exploration, production and supply; it is time for this ingenuity and focus to be applied in the maritime domain.

v. Port-side infrastructure investments will also assist to improve Climate Security and reduce shipping emissions. A 'quick win' solution would be to invest in, and rapidly deploy shore connection, shore-to-ship power (SSP) or alternative maritime power (AMP) facilities; sometimes called 'cold ironing' systems. Such facilities should exist at every port in the U.S. and across the world and could rapidly assist in decarbonizing shipping, particularly if cleaner, renewable sources of power were used for shore-side energy generation. Shore-based power also assists to reduce noise pollution, decreases engine usage and maintenance costs (thereby increasing asset lifespan).

Shore-based power can significantly improve air quality by reducing emissions. Recent estimates have calculated a 30% reduction in CO2 emissions and more than 95% of NOx and particulates. The California Air Resources Board (CARB) "...estimates a 55% decrease in cancer risk by 2031 due to air quality improvements by using shore power instead of auxiliary engines at berth". A decrease in cancer risks, and improvements in air quality would provide estimated health benefits of $2.32 billion at a cost of $2.23 billion. Recent calculations place capital costs of installing cold ironing technology for a medium-sized port at around $8.1 million. Such an installation would save 108 tons of NOx, 2.7 tons of particulate matter and 4,767 tons of CO2 emissions every year. Even further reductions would be realized if shore-based power systems used low-carbon fuels, or wind, solar or hydropower.

The United States can take a leading position to invest, fund and resource a range of Blue Economy and sustainability initiatives. This would demonstrate global leadership, and encourage the development and commercialization of new technologies that can be used to reduce global emissions, and the impact of shipping on the environment.

## II. Stakeholder activism

Consumers are more informed, educated, and able to more rapidly share information, and are subsequently demanding more from brands, organizations and industries than ever before. Mainstream and social media are awash with stories about climate change, environmental devastation, rising temperatures, heatwaves and record droughts. Repeated coverage of the same events – with little change between occurrences - has left many fatigued and angry. This has led to a rise in stakeholder and shareholder activism.

A recent report from leading shareholder data provider Proxy Preview calculated that a record 540 proposals had been filed by shareholders since the start of 2023, demanding companies address environmental, social and corporate governance issues. Resolutions that focused on climate change accounted for about 25% of the total; an increase of about 12% from the same point in 2022. The results of these findings led report publisher Andrew Behar to observe: "The extractive economy is winding down; a new economy based on justice and sustainability is emerging. Leading corporations understand that now we are finding solutions, not hiding from big systemic risks like climate change and racial injustice. Companies will outperform if they embrace innovative ideas in these shareholder resolutions."

A number of companies are now grappling with this new reality, and have responded by restructuring operations, supply chains, sourcing, and production, to adapt to volatile weather and food, water and component shortages. Companies are also attempting to cope with the refined demands of more informed and vocal stakeholders:

- Multinational oil and gas major Shell, suffered a shareholder revolt against its energy transition strategy during its 2023 Annual General Meeting. For the second year in a row, Shells' annual meeting was disrupted by climate activists. 20% of shareholders voted against Shell's transition strategy and rejected the report on the progress that had been made in the past 12 months. While the silent majority approved the company's plans, a significant amount of concern was expressed about how strategy and practice should change in the coming years.

- After receiving vocal feedback about the company's investment portfolio during meetings in 2023, global insurance giant Chubb Ltd will now be limiting its underwriting and investing in coal and oil sands. Chubb will also require clients in the oil and gas industry to prove measurable cuts in methane emissions, and will direct funding and resources to new sustainability and clean-energy initiatives. While some shareholders believed the stated goals were not aggressive enough, a legitimate concern was expressed by administrators that pursuing certain objectives may not lead to meaningful change, as "it would be difficult to accurately measure emissions targets".

- The world's largest asset manager Blackrock Inc. with over $9.42 trillion dollars currently under management, announced a change in investment direction in 2020. Blackrock proposed that supporting sustainability and climate-risk mitigation would become central to their core investment strategy. This caused a significant ripple effect among the global investment community, and led other asset managers and firms to also alter investment priorities. While the pace of investment in sustainable activities has slowed in recent years, a significant announcement was made in November 2023: In conjunction with the government, Blackrock launched a $2 billion fund specifically aimed at making New Zealand the first country in the world to be 100 percent powered by renewable electricity.

The actions of activists are viewed as extreme by some, however must be viewed in a broader context: Every human is a stakeholder and holds shares in the future of the planet, and therefore has a duty to ensure the best decisions are made about expended effort and investment. Decisions that meet the needs of, and directly benefit the collective, and not just a select few.

## Stakeholder Activism and Shipping

The supply chain crisis during the COVID-19 pandemic highlighted the important role played by shipping, particularly in containerized trades. Up until that point in time, the shipping industry had operated in the background and been largely ignored by the general public. With an increase in interest, came an increase in scrutiny. This led to an escalation in the number of opinion pieces, headlines and reports about the shipping industry, and subsequently, investigations into the effect of shipping emissions on the environment.

Fed by changing consumer sentiment, reports started to correlate the use of container ships by large retailers, importers, and Beneficial Cargo Owners - a BCO is the party that ultimately owns the product being shipped - with the emissions generated for each voyage. While similar reports had been available before, more recent versions have included emotive infographics, and highly visual statistical representations, which has made the underlying data more understandable by a wider audience. These reports are illuminating, and feed into different forms of stakeholder activism that can evolve into brand-shaming and the targeting of brand executives, partners and key investors. One example of many:

*Ship It Zero* is a "climate and public health campaign to move the world's largest retail companies to 100% zero-emission ocean shipping". In 2019, Ship It Zero released the 'Shady Ships' report, to explain the impact that containerized imports from major retailers had on the environment. Data was collected on product import volumes, and correlated with the number of containers used; deduction then allowed for CO2 calculations to be completed for each retailer. Major retailers included Amazon, Walmart, Target and IKEA.

Shady Ships found that the maritime imports of 15 large retail companies were responsible for the release of 12.7 million metric tons of CO2, and 7.3x more cancer-causing SOx pollution than all vehicles in the United States combined; some 2 billion cars and trucks. Total climate pollution equaled about as much as the energy use of 1.5 million U.S. homes. Walmart's container imports were estimated to produce 3.7 million metric tons of CO2; as much as a coal-fired power plant would emit across an entire year. Target's container imports produced 2.2 million metric tons of CO2; the entire CO2 output of 20 of the world's smallest countries (that also happen to be the most vulnerable to climate change).

The release of this report led to protests outside various IKEA outlets demanding the retailer shift to renewable fuel sources, and reduce its dependency on 'dirty ships'. The report, and the protests garnered a lot of media attention. The retailers took action: IKEA responded three months later by announcing, alongside Amazon, to move their products off fossil-fuel-powered cargo ships by 2040. Given the staggering import volumes of Amazon and IKEA, and the current lack of available zero-carbon ships and low-carbon fuels, zero-emission shipping by 2040 is a rather ambitious target.

Fueled by more readily available information, from these and a range of other reports, the actions (or inaction) of the shipping industry to climate change has prompted other forms of protest as well: Greenpeace boarded a Shell-contracted heavy-lift vessel *White Marlin* at sea, north of the Canary Islands carrying banners saying 'Stop Drilling. Start Paying' in February, 2023; a similar protest against deep-sea battery mineral mining company then named *DeepGreen* (since renamed to *The Metals Company*) occurred in the Pacific Ocean in 2021. Loud protests by activist groups such as Extinction Rebellion were held outside the IMO headquarters as emissions targets were debated in June, 2023. In the same month, cruise ship *Zuiderdam* was temporarily prevented from leaving the Port of Rotterdam by protesters carrying banners reading 'You're not welcome here like this'; a reference to the cruise liner industry's reluctance to adopt net-zero targets, and in the case of the port at Rotterdam, increase the use of shore-side (cold-ironing) electrical power to reduce emissions.

Activism by stakeholders and activities has an obvious effect on the conduct of targeted companies. Positively, this has prompted the formation of various alliances that aim to reduce the impact of their activities on the environment:

1. Initiated by the Aspen Institute in 2021, Cargo Owners for Zero Emission Vessels (CoZEV), brings together several large international companies that have a vested interest in shipping and climate solutions. CoZEV has set a goal of zero-carbon ocean freight transport by 2040.

2. Several members of CoZEV have since created ZEMBA, the Zero Emission Maritime Buyers Alliance. In September 2023, over 20 ZEMBA members announced a Request for Proposal for Zero Emission shipping services. The proposal requests ocean shipping services powered by zero-emission fuels for the transport of 600,000 twenty-foot containers (TEUs)

over a three year period. Amazon is a founding ZEMBA member. IKEA joined ZEMBA in March 2023.

3. Launched in 2019, *The Getting to Zero Coalition*, is an alliance of over 160 companies with the ambition to accelerate maritime shipping decarbonization. The group aims to encourage the development and deployment of commercially viable deep-sea zero-emission vessels by 2030, and has a strategy for full decarbonization by 2050.

4. ZESTAs (Zero Emission Ship Technology Association) is a global group committed to the rapid and large-scale uptake of technologies leading to absolute zero emissions by 2043.

## E. Absence of Critical U.S. Blue Economy Institutions

### I. No holistic U.S. Blue Economy Strategy

The U.S. is more ocean than it is land (55% ocean, 45% land) and has the largest territorial waters than any other nation (3.4 million square nautical miles of ocean in its Exclusive Economic Zone). The next two decades will see some of the biggest advancements along U.S. coastal waters and waterways. This includes the development of offshore windfarms, aquaculture, algae farming, short-sea shipping as well as the electrification of waterway transportation.

However, despite the U.S. having the largest EEZ in the world, it is not organized to effectively govern this area. Governing across the ocean is very different from how land-based Ministries are organized. To govern across these ocean territories requires coordinating across multiple agencies and Departments. For example, introducing new regulations may need to gain approval from officials sitting in NOAA, Department of Commerce, Department of State, Department of Defense, U.S. Navy, U.S. Coast Guard, Treasury, Environmental Protection Agency, U.S. Fish and Wildlife Service, Department of Energy, Department of Transportation, MARAD, Homeland Security, U.S. Customs and Border Protection, Department of Agriculture, among others. And this does not include the approvals required in State waters (rather than Federal waters).

For years, the U.S. has suffered from a lack of coherent vision, strategy and institutions for a Sustainable Blue Economy. Basic alignment on which sectors to pursue and regulations to put in place has been lacking. As a result, the U.S. has lost its competitive edge in the Blue Economy to countries in Scandinavia, across Europe and China, all of whom are developing new standards that the U.S. would need to respond to, rather than drive forward.

This has meant that the U.S. continues to use outdated computing systems to capture critical statistics that are used to govern fisheries. It also means that the U.S. is not driving innovation in short sea shipping, green and autonomous waterways, autonomous pelagic fisheries technologies or even the use of dynamic marine protected areas that can move with species at different times of the year.

The U.S. needs a radical re-think of its Blue Economy Strategy involving all major public sector stakeholders. An annual summit, with all key stakeholders presenting and aligning their Blue Economy Strategies and networked with key investment funds and a broader community (e.g., of scientists, NGOs, companies and the public) will start to move the U.S. toward best practices for developing Blue Economy Plans. New Blue

Economy Institutions will then be needed to support the rapid execution of such plans, particularly in driving sustainability in U.S. Maritime and building up the new offshore sectors in the Sustainable Blue Economy.

The U.S. has started to see this shift in other domains too. For example, in 2001, after the first private space flight, NASA had to redefine its role from operator of spacecraft to commissioner of services. This also led to other divisions of the U.S. being built up to oversee critical space assets, such as the U.S. Space Force. A re-think and consolidation of critical Blue Economy institutions is needed as well, including the capabilities such new institutions will need.

## II. Domestic maritime policy

In 1989 the Exxon Valdez ran aground in Alaska and spilled 10.8 million U.S. gallons (260,000 bbl, or 37,000 tons) of crude oil into the sea. It was the largest at the time, and became the second largest oil spill in U.S. waters behind Deepwater Horizon in 2010. The oil spill affected 1,300 miles (2,100 km) of coastline; 200 miles (320 km) were heavily or moderately oiled. 100,000 and 250,000 seabirds; at least 2,800 sea otters; 300 harbor seals; 247 bald eagles; 22 orcas; and, an unknown number of salmon and herring all perished as a result of the spill.

During the previous decade, major oil spills from tankers had been occurring in South Africa, Nova Scotia, Tobago and France; where the Amoco Cadez spilled over 7 times as much oil as the Exxon Valdez. All eyes focused on the U.S. when the Exxon Valdez oil came ashore on its own pristine shoreline. Finally, ignoring the influence of major oil companies, the U.S. Congress acted unanimously in passing the Oil Pollution Act of 1990 (OPA90). The Act included requirements for double bottom hulls, tanker escorts, spill response equipment and many other provisions that could no longer be ignored by the International Maritime Organization. Within only a few years, every tanker in the world had to meet the IMO's revised MARPOL standards which mirrors large parts of the Oil Pollution Act of 1990.

From tragedy to transformation: The United States has led in the past, and can lead the global shipping industry again.

## III. International maritime policy

The shipping industry, similar to aviation, faces the challenge of regulating a global industry with thousands of players. Regulations are discussed and adopted at the International Maritime Organization (IMO - a specialist United Nations agency) by 175 member states but implemented and enforced by a nation's port state control and by Flag State Administrations. While aspirational, it would be advantageous for IMO to accelerate its environmental timeline. For example, the IMO began discussing noxious exhaust gasses in 1973, at the first ever International Convention for the Prevention of Pollution from Ships (MARPOL) convention. The IMO adopted Annex VI, which established limits on NOx and SOx emission in 1997; 24 years later. The limits went into force 8 years later. A 3.5% sulfur cap was set for 2012, and a 0.5% cap for 2020. 1973 to 2020: 47 long years, from when the first serious problems were identified.

The recently established Marine Environment Protection Committee (MEPC) emissions reduction targets (July 2023) are designed to encourage the shipping industry to switch from conventional fuels to zero, or near zero emission fuels by 2050.

What factors contribute to the IMO's ability to make rapid decisions and take bold and meaningful action?

When the IMO was established in 1958 only 13% of ships were flagged under open registries. Today, around 75% of all vessels are registered in open registries, with just three registries (Panama, Liberia and the Marshall Islands) accounting for over 50% of the global total. Some registries have a poor track record of following regulatory standards, or enforcing maritime rules. A large majority offer offshore services such as anonymous company registration, and favorable handling of taxation; which is why many open registry states are referred to tax havens or secrecy jurisdictions.

Financial contributions to the IMO are based on merchant fleet tonnage. Member States with greater tonnages are expected to contribute more, with the assumption that those States have a greater shipping presence. There is little transparency about the exact formula for contributions, and even less transparency about the influence that certain Member States with higher tonnages may have on the decision-making process. This style of representation can also disadvantage less-developed Member States, who may not have the state-sponsored support or administrative capacity to be properly represented at IMO meetings.

Without proper representation, there is a possibility that certain Member States with higher tonnages may unduly influence proceedings, and further hamper the progress that is required to set, and achieve, more ambitious climate goals. With an unbalanced mechanism to determine participation; a lack of transparency during the decision-making process; the potential for vested interests to influence outcomes; and, when combined with external administrative structures that deliberately obscure ownership and reduce accountability, the IMO is in danger of compromising its credibility.

## Climate Security Maritime Solutions and Opportunities

The following solutions and opportunities are matched to the maritime risks and vulnerabilities explored throughout this Principle:

1. **Risk: Lack of U.S. coordination with maritime climate risk initiatives**
   **Solution: Develop a holistic national Blue Economy Strategy supported with new Blue Economy Institutions and a National Maritime Climate Strategy (NMCS)**
   The National Maritime Climate Strategy will map out requirements and proposed solutions for major climate problems, and ensure that stakeholders are aligned with national climate objectives. This will include adjustments to mission, purpose, and project scope of each individual project so that collective outcomes are achieved more quickly and effectively. The NMCS will seek to quantify the most pressing climate-related issues in the U.S. maritime industry - from shipping emissions, to risks impacting port infrastructure - and then work with stakeholders and decision-makers to source (or build) creative solutions to meet those challenges.

   The NMCS will coordinate the activities of government departments - including DOT, MARAD, EPA and the ACOE - as well as commercial companies, infrastructure managers, researchers, industry associations and well-respected organizations like the North American Marine Environment Protection Association (NAMEPA) that are working on maritime climate change initiatives. Additional input should be sought from relevant departments in prominent U.S.

colleges - MIT, Stanford, Harvard, Berkeley, Caltech - so that advanced research, analytics and computational intelligence can be applied to each area of concern. Coordinating these activities will reduce administrative overheads, and allow for the redirection of funds and resources to the areas of greatest need. Increased collaboration between stakeholders will improve project outcomes, lead to increased job creation and the development of innovative technologies, while providing new avenues for scientific research and academic partnerships.

2. **Risk: Global fleet emissions are not accurately measured**
   **Solution: Global Maritime Emissions Map (GMEM)**
   Contrary to the view that "it is impossible to accurately track shipping emissions", detailed research, analysis and commentary from world-leading economists and maritime industry analysts confirm that is entirely feasible, and could be done without expending as much effort as has been described in the past. Modern technologies - including hardware sensors that could be attached to exhaust stacks, and LEO-based satellite detectors that can monitor plumes - are all available today. Tracking fuel usage per vessel is also relatively simple; they all refuel somewhere, which means that consumption can be tracked at those locations.

   The Global Maritime Emissions Map (GMEM) maps out the emission tracks of ships as they cross the ocean, and provides accurate data on which ship types, routes, and activities produce the most pollution. This would not just apply to CO2, but also NOx, SOx, methane, Particulate Matter, black carbon and nuclear radioactivity. One way this can be visualized is to analyze the repeated (AIS) track of vessels across the ocean, and then overlay discovered data about vessel type, loads, weather, and routing decisions. The Map would start with emissions and then incorporate information on discharges, pollution and other forms of environmental damage. The ultimate goal of the GMEM is to definitely quantify, and visually display the impact the shipping industry has on our shared marine environments.

3. **Risk: Port emissions from power-generating assets Solution: Expand the Clean Ports Program**
   The Department of Transportation (DOT) and Environmental Protection Agency (EPA) have committed $3 billion through the Clean Ports Program, to fund zero-emission port equipment and technology, and to help ports develop action plans to reduce air pollutants. This initiative should be expanded, so that it can be positioned to be a world-leading template for other ports across the globe. As mentioned previously, the implementation of cold-ironing facilities at all major U.S. ports will assist to decarbonize shipping and also reduce emissions in and around ports.

   At the One Ocean Summit in 2022, 21 major ports around the world signed a shore power declaration stating they would use 'best efforts' to deploy "shore-side electricity by 2028 where possible". The phrases 'best efforts' and 'where possible' are not entirely convincing. An expansion of the Clean Ports Program would ensure that firm targets for cold-ironing are set, and that appropriate sources of low-carbon and renewable energy are available to complement grid power if and where required.

A revised Program should also seek to work more closely with the U.S. Navy - who have successfully used cold-ironing for decades - and global cruise-ship operators who have committed to being 'shore-power ready' by 2025; only 2% of the world's cruise ports have shore-side power systems at present. New Clean Port Program outcomes would be aligned with the objectives of the Port Infrastructure Development Program (PIDP) that was awarded $684.31 million in FY 2022 to improve domestic port infrastructure.

4. **Risk: Incentivize the use of electric vessels and electric power**
   **Solution: Maritime Electrification Incentive Scheme (MEIS)**
   The Maritime Electrification Incentive Scheme (MEIS) will exist alongside the revised Clean Ports Program. A similar concept has been implemented in the EU and China. The MEIS would provide financial incentives and funding for the roll-out of shore-power systems, and would also encourage the installation of reciprocal power systems and hardware on vessels. The experiences of the automotive sector - e.g., as Tesla rolled out its 'SuperCharger' network, and as the automotive industry negotiated plug standardization - can be used to accelerate decisions around key port infrastructure and the hardware being used on ships.

   The MEIS will also draw integration and roll-out timeframe inspiration from other countries around the world. For example, the EU regulation 2014/94/EU requires European ports to provide shore power by 2025. China-flagged vessels built on or after January 1, 2020, including coastal container ships, cruise ships and ferries, passenger ships over 3,000 metric tons, and dry bulk carriers over 50,000 metric tons must be equipped with shore power systems.

5. **Risk: Sea level rise and extreme weather disrupting U.S. ports**
   **Solution: OctoPorts - Offshore, climate-secure cargo processing facilities**
   The OctoPort concept was publicly shared, for the first time, by one of the author's in 2022. An OctoPort is a large, eight-sided, off-shore, cargo and commodity processing facility that complements the role of a traditional port facility. Once constructed in a U.S. shipyard, OctoPorts are floated out into position and anchored to the seafloor in a similar fashion as an oil and gas platform. Modeling wave and weather patterns will determine the best final location; this might be close to a coastline, or situated in protected waterways a few miles offshore.

   OctoPorts are designed with numerous beneficial features, including:

   - An entirely climate-secure design: rising sea level, tsunami, flood and hurricane-proof
   - Suction (or magnetic) mooring systems to improve vessel berthing times
   - A fully automated and roboticized design to improve handling capacity and accuracy
   - A load-to-center design that improves cargo-handling throughput and efficiency
   - A conveyor system via twin tunnels to shuttle cargo and commodities to the mainland, *or* a rotation of semi-autonomous electric barges that can tranship from the OctoPort to land
   - Exemplary entertainment and shift-change facilities for crew and ship personnel

- Connectivity via tunnel for the transmission of power, water, and waste processing

Apart from the Climate and Economic Security benefits, one other benefit of an OctoPort is the way it enhances National Security. A traditional port, attached to expensive static real-estate may never recover from a terrorist attack or airstrike, whereas an OctoPort can easily be replaced by a rapidly-constructed equivalent. OctoPorts may also be supplied to other nations, built in the U.S. then installed in sovereign waters overseas and administered by U.S. operators. This would immediately improve port capacity in the nominated country, and given the OctoPorts ability for dual-use operations, would also perform a secondary role as an object of soft power projection.

6. **Risk: International shipping lanes require emission controls and security**
**Solution: Navy Green Shipping Corridors (NGSC)**
Green Shipping Corridors have been proposed for some time - including with more detail and 22 signatory nations at COP26 in 2021 - however have struggled in implementation. Some encouraging signs occurred across 2023, including the announcement in September of the formation of a Green Shipping Corridor across the Transpacific between the Port of Shanghai and the Port of Los Angeles and Long Beach. The plan was developed with support from 'C40 Cities' - a global network of "nearly 100 mayors of the world's leading cities that are united in action to confront the climate crisis." Partner carriers will deploy reduced or zero lifecycle carbon capable ships on the corridor by 2025. The aim by 2030 is to test the feasibility of deploying "… the world's first zero lifecycle carbon emission

container ship." Carrier partners include CMA CGM, COSCO Shipping Lines Co., Ltd., Maersk, and ONE.

The enhanced version of a Green Shipping Corridor is a Navy Green Shipping Corridor (NGSC). A NGSG carries all of the advantages of a standard Green Shipping Corridor, but also implements oversight and protection from the U.S. Navy and Coast Guard. Users of the NGSC would pay for these protections via a transparently administered levy, which would be offset by reduced risks across the length of the voyage, along with other cargo and port preferences at each end of the NGSC that reduce overall operating costs .

NGSC participants would use enhanced container and cargo security mechanisms at destination and origin, which would reduce security risks, and the need for frequent inspections; a more modern and secure equivalent of the CTPAT program. The NGSC would also serve as a template for the future state of shipping that will include more U.S.-Flag (and eventually, other, select Flag Stage) vessels carrying nuclear-reactors.

The NGSC would be the first ever large-scale maritime program combining commercial and naval operations, with trade and climate change-related objectives.

7. **Risk: Lack of transparency about retailer and BCO shipping emissions**
   **Solution: Mandatory Emission Disclosure Scheme (MEDS)**
   Beneficial Cargo Owners (BCOs) and retailers often seek to transport goods using the lowest possible cost, and generally avoid disclosing shipping emissions. This can lead to 'just above the bar' compliance. Vocal consumers are changing the behaviors of these larger

suppliers, and putting increased pressure on retailers to be more responsible about transportation choices.

The Mandatory Emission Disclosure Scheme (MEDS) will involve the collation and public disclosure of all transportation-related emissions of products from every U.S. retailer and BCO. This will include all GHGs and Particulate Matter, including black carbon. Metrics and statistics will be made available to consumers, who will be able to make purchasing decisions based on the carbon footprint of the item they are purchasing. Similar, small-scale, industry-lead initiatives - e.g., AllBirds creative labeling of jeans in 2020 - have been attempted in the past. MEDS will differ as it will be nationally mandated, and be enforced across every market segment and vertical.

MEDS will source data from shipping and transportation manifests and Customs and Border Protection (CBP) import data. Modern technologies such as digital sensors and detection systems and satellite-based tracking will increase transparency along supply chains; supplied through partnership agreements with commercial suppliers. These new forms of accountability means that disclosed figures can be checked against external sources. The Scheme will be designed to run at low cost, and operated in a similar fashion to the Task Force on Climate-Related Financial Disclosures (TCFD). MEDS will supply the accountability required to ensure such retailers procure shipping from the most responsible and ethical transporters. This will, by default, benefit U.S.-Flag merchant fleets that will be operating at higher levels of safety and sustainability than most other Flag States.

8. **Risk: Lack of standards for new-builds and overhauls**
**Solution: Green Shipping Certification Program (GSCP)**
Environmental and sustainability standards are required for new vessels that will be built over the coming decade, and also for vessels that are overhauled to comply with new standards. Class Societies - such as the American Bureau of Shipping - should be encouraged to incorporate new sustainability standards into the certification process. These 'green' standards will project ship performance over time (to gather emissions and other waste calculations) and also assess the ships total environment footprint; for build and disposal. The latter will include the materials used during construction, and therefore what can be recycled at end-of-life.

Collected assessment figures will give a Total Cost of Impact score that will be incorporated into the Green Shipping Certification. The GSCP will use this information to inform administrators of parallel programs - e.g., Green Shipping Corridors - and to identify foreign-built vessels that might be suitable for the Economic Security or Flag-In Security Program. These standards will prompt immediate action but will also take a realistic approach as some changes - especially for overhauled vessels - will need to be completed over time. The goal of the Green Shipping Certification Program (GSCP) is to ensure that all vessels have a plan to address the most serious environmental and sustainability problems within their fleet and can demonstrate measurable progress in reducing the impact of their vessels and operations over defined periods of time.

9. **Risk: The global shipping industry will not meet climate targets**
**Solution: Advanced Research Projects Agency - Maritime (ARPA-M)**
Consider the practical implications of the IMO's most recent mandates on emission reductions. If enacted in the timeframes stipulated, these mandates will mean that the world's *entire* commercial maritime fleet must fundamentally change over the next 30 years. This represents a huge opportunity for the United States to leapfrog past other countries, and build the ships and shipping infrastructure for the century that is to come.

This will include:

- The design and construction of new, fit-for-purpose ships that are purposefully built to be faster, sleeker, more agile, and generate less emissions
- Invention of new construction standards that are more efficient, technology-driven, and incorporate new materials that are less carbon intensive
- Incorporation of new types of propulsion systems that are electrified, run on nuclear-power, or are fueled by low-carbon alternatives.
- Creation of new materials for hulls and superstructures that have reduced drag, to decrease fuel and energy consumption
- Development of new procedures and processes for ship management, operations, and safety to assist crews adapt to changing conditions
- Evolutions on traditional port infrastructure and port handling technologies to increase resilience and allow for enhance adaptability in the face of extremes in weather and temperature

The best mechanism to accelerate the creation of new technologies, manufacturing processes and production facilities will be to establish an entirely new, Public-Private Partnership (PPP) innovation incubator, the Advanced Research Projects Agency - Maritime (ARPA-M). ARPA-Energy, ARPA-Climate, ARPA-Health and ARPA-Infrastructure have been created to address major challenges in these respective fields. Given the essential nature of shipping to National, Economic, Energy & Food, Climate and Workforce Security, it is time that maritime had its own Agency. ARPA-M draws inspiration from the U.S. military's Defense Advanced Research Projects Agency (DARPA). With some of the technological breakthroughs needed in maritime, there is a need to address these challenges in a way that only public funds can achieve. DARPA was one of the early catalytic funders of autonomous road vehicles, as well as UAVs. ARPA-M can pioneer the rapid development of autonomous ships, AUV and UUVs.

DARPA's mission is simple: To make pivotal investments in breakthrough technologies for national security.

The mission of ARPA-M is simple: To make pivotal investments in breakthrough technologies for maritime supremacy.

ARPA-M will advance deep technology research and develop unique systems, innovations and solutions for the maritime domain. ARPA-M will accelerate the commercialization of new technologies, build new partnerships domestically and abroad, stimulate the private sector to invest in the maritime sector, and strengthen U.S. competitive advantage. ARPA-M will aim to be entirely funded by commercializing the novel products produced inside the organization; that is, to be self-funded, and commercially sustainable.

Public-Private Partnerships are foundational to the success of ARPA-M. ARPA-M will pursue cross-agency collaboration with any group involved in maritime: The U.S. Navy, U.S. Coast Guard, U.S. Marine Corps, Department of Defense, Department of Homeland Security, Department of Commerce, Department of Transportation, Department of Energy, Nuclear Regulatory Commission, the Environmental Protection Agency and NOAA, among others. Collaborative research will also be completed with the world's best technical universities: MIT, Princeton, Stanford, Berkeley, Caltech, Georgia Tech, Carnegie Mellon, and UCLA.

National Security will be a component of ARPA-M's work. ARPA-M will partner with DARPA to develop force-posture-aligned solutions, and systems and infrastructure to pioneer dual-use capabilities for ships, shipyards and personnel. This will include shipyard design; mechanized and roboticized construction equipment; hull and surface friction-reduction additives; weather detection and routing systems; new and novel maritime communications solutions (include satellite connectivity and sensor arrays); techniques to accelerate the cross-development of commercial mariners and naval crews; and, the integration of protection and fire suppression solutions for future fuel systems.

Energy Security is also a key component of ARPA-M's work, so close collaboration will be needed with the DOE's ARPA-E (Energy). ARPA-E carries a similar mandate "to radically improve U.S. economic prosperity, national security, and environmental well-being", and does that by advancing "high-potential, high-impact energy technologies". Combining ARPA-E and ARPA-M will lead to the establishment of partnerships with renewable energy companies supplying wind, solar, biomass and nuclear expertise in the commercial sector. Cross-pollinating knowledge from these domains into maritime will yield an array of new solutions and products that have not been envisaged before.

Industry partners will be identified and purposefully pursued. Thankfully, the United States has direct access to, and can learn from the best: Tesla can inform the development of autonomous vehicles, electrification and manufacturing at scale. Amazon can bring expertise about robotics, storage and transportation systems, and how to build global networks for distribution. SpaceX can offer experience with alternate fuel types, high-tensile and robust material coatings, and novel systems of propulsion. Microsoft can share compute power and the insights of software integration into disparate hardware environments. And, Apple's product knowledge and scaled manufacturing innovations will be transformational to the ARPA-M program.

A long list of technologies and advancements will be pursued through ARPA-M:

- Develop a rapid build, scale-up and deployment strategy for OctoPorts
- Create hardware for the use and storage of electrified and nuclear propulsion
- Build novel electrification infrastructure for the U.S. Inland Waterway network

- Establish new digital standards for maritime cybersecurity and data sharing
- Integrate rust-resistant materials on ships and create new frictionless coatings for hulls
- Integrating AI into maritime: Large Language Models and Natural Language Processing to assist with large datasets and complex problems like weather routing

One specific solution that is particularly exciting is the potential to use large-scale manufacturing and 3D-printing techniques to make ship and submersible components. This is the concept of a 'GigaShipyard', which would rapidly accelerate U.S. shipbuilding efforts, and allow for U.S.-built commercial vessels to sail the oceans once again.

Drawing inspiration from a pioneering U.S. entrepreneur is appropriate. Elon Musk founded *SpaceX* in March 2002. *SpaceX* is now a world-leader in rocket construction and the provision of space launch services. *SpaceX* launched the satellite communications network Starlink that has more than 2 million active customers, across 7 continents and 60 countries. He has similarly disrupted other sectors such as electric vehicles through *Tesla*, transportation through *Hyperloop*, Urban infrastructure through the *Boring Company*, Computer-Brain interfaces through *Neuralink*, among other companies he has founded or has run. This shows the power of getting to first principles to challenge the status quo, building powerful public-private partnership and unleashing the power of entrepreneurial capital.

Through ARPA-M, backed by world-leading Public-Private Partnerships and using new technologies and techniques, the United States has the potential to be the world's greatest superpower of *maritime* innovation.

# WORKFORCE SECURITY

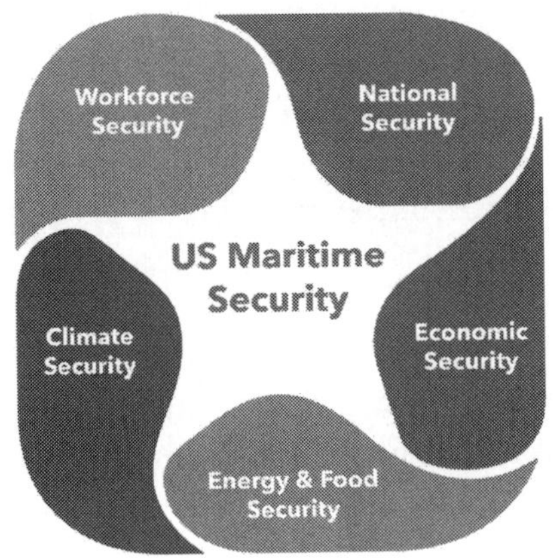


**Workforce Security**

- *Shortage of mariners*
- *Overhaul training institutes*
- *Revamp talent pipeline*
- *Unions*
- *Foreign influence*

# V. WORKFORCE SECURITY

*According to the latest ICS/BIMCO study, we will be 96,000 seafarers short by 2026 [internationally]. A huge challenge. That's a lot of certified officers we're going to be short of; that's something we need to embrace.*

- Guy Platten, International Chamber of Shipping (ICS)

*The U.S. Merchant Marine is in every war plan that I review, I guarantee you, because you're going to be the fourth arm of defense.*

- U.S. Secretary of Defense, James Mattis (2018)

## Workforce Security Context

Every country on earth relies heavily on the input and output of accessible, capable and productive people. A collection of people applying their skills for the advancement of a country or cause, is called a workforce. The availability of such a workforce is often taken for granted during discussions on advancement and economic progress. This can be observed when government planners identify a geographic region for industrial development, or during debates on the future of a certain industry. The prevailing narrative runs along the lines of "Build it, and they will come". For a variety of reasons, that sentiment doesn't work anywhere near as well as it used to.

Globalization has shrunk the world down to the length of a plane flight. In parallel, increased accessibility to information, and extreme workforce fluidity has opened up a litany of new opportunities across a range of market segments. A wide variety of choices are readily available, especially for the affluent, educated and well-connected. These opportunities can be permanent, or, in some cases, may just alter a daily or weekly commute. One relevant example is the rising number of Fly-In Fly-Out (FIFO) workers that live outside of the State or county (and sometimes country) in which they work, and commute by plane. This is common practice in the mining regions of Australia and Canada, and also for many mariners working in the global shipping industry.

In developed countries, demographic shifts and technological change have brought many benefits, but also introduced unpredictable variables: A rapidly retiring Boomer generation (born between 1946 to 1964) collided with declining birth rates, altering workforce stratification. The internet created and displaced more jobs than any other invention in human history. While choice abounds, the modern workforce faces the constant threats of outsourcing, downsizing, economic volatility, and evolving technologies. A recent report by the Institute for the Future (IFTF), found that around 85% of jobs that will exist in 2030 haven't been invented yet, presenting opportunities, but also unpredictability for particular job types and sectors.

The less-developed world has experienced structurally positive changes: A sobering 8.5% of the world still lives in extreme poverty, however over 2 billion people have moved out of that category in just the last 30 years; the result of industrialization, technological change, and for agriculture, more ready access to fertilizers. Around 86% of people now have some form of basic education, up from 17% just 100 years ago. And, while still disturbingly high, the global under-5 mortality rate has dropped by 59% since 1990. These statistics are cold comfort to the 2 billion people who lack access to clean water, and the hundreds of millions that face extreme climate change-related threats, and rely on subsistence farming, or the ocean for food.

The shipping industry is truly global and sources the bulk of its workforce from developing countries. Simultaneously, many developing nations are unable to source workers from within their own borders. Some things have been built, but the workers have not come. In developed countries, job satisfaction and job security are heavily intertwined: Workers want to do meaningful work and contribute to a greater cause; build or receive knowledge; expect fairness and equity; seek positive health and education outcomes; be given the chance for recreation and leisure activities, and are selective about the culture or context where work is conducted. For many in the developing world, job security simply means having the same job tomorrow that was completed today; not getting injured, and being paid consistently are bonuses. All of this is to say that the definition of Workforce Security is entirely dependent on perspective, which must be kept in mind as the rest of these topics are explored.

Workforce Security is the most readily overlooked, yet the most salient of all Principles: National Security is fundamentally about protecting *people*. Economic Security can only be assured by the productive output of *people*. Energy and Food Security is entirely dependent on meeting the needs of *people*. And without *people*, climate change, and therefore Climate Security is irrelevant.

If people are our greatest asset, Workforce Security is extraordinarily important.

## The workforce of the global shipping industry

There are currently 1,892,720 seafarers in global shipping, of which 857,540 are officers and 1,035,180 are ratings (ratings are everyone else on a ship that is not an officer). These seafarers serve, work and inevitably live for long periods of time on the 50,000+ ships, registered in over 120 countries that make up the international fleet.
The top three crewing countries that supply officers and ratings are:

- The Philippines: 498,000 seafarers, and the leading supplier of ratings
- China: 400,000 - 800,000 seafarers, and the leading supplier of officers
- India: Currently around 250,000 and growing rapidly

The Russian Federation - 198,123 seafarers - and Ukraine - 76,442 - round out the top five, and account for around 14.5% of the total, however total numbers have been impacted by the ongoing conflict in the region. Another contender is Indonesia. Indonesia has a sizable domestic fleet, and noticeable Flag fleet, however similar to China, official totals are hard to verify. Figures released in 2022 stated that Indonesia had over 1.2

million seafarers, however did not specify how many were engaged in domestic and river trades across the archipelago's 17,000 islands.

The maritime industry is dominated by men. According to a 2021 BIMCO study, only 1.2 percent (24,059) of seafarers are women.

## I. Crewing Costs

The number of crew on a vessel is dictated by safety regulations and depends on a variety of factors such as vessel type, size and the nature of the duties required onboard. For example, a deep-sea seismic ship needs more specialized (and expensive) mariners than a standard dry bulk carrier. Due to improvements in electromechanical and hydraulic systems, the average number of crew required per vessel has decreased over time, even as ships have grown markedly in size; an Ultra Large Container Vessel (ULCV) carrying 20,000 containers, and exceeding 240,000 dwt only needs around 20 mariners to function, around half as many as was required on much smaller vessels 30 years ago. While crewing minimums are well defined by regulations, safe minimums can be entirely different. Enforcing safe minimums is important, especially because large ships can cause a serious amount of damage to the environment in the event of an accident; as was dramatically demonstrated when the MV X-Press Pearl caught fire and sank off the coast of Colombo in 2021.

In 2017, Clarksons Research reported that the total operating expenses (OpEx) of the world's international commercial fleet exceeded $100 billion for the first time. Crewing costs were the largest component, accounting for around 43% of the total, and were expected to increase by around $2 billion every year. With such high costs associated with crewing, it is understandable that ship operators would seek out the most cost-effective crews, and try, wherever possible, to minimize the total number of crew on the payroll. This also explains why training, upskilling and attending to the psychological welfare of the crew are sometimes relegated down the list of priorities.

## II. Pay

The working conditions and wages for seafarers are administered through the United Nations' International Labour Organization (ILO). Specific details are set out in the Maritime Labour Convention (MLC), which was first established in 2006. Often described as a 'Bill of Rights' for seafarers, the MLC is the fourth pillar of international maritime law, alongside Safety of Lives at Sea (SOLAS); STCW (International Convention on Standards of Training, Certification and Watchkeeping for Seafarers); and MARPOL (International Convention for the Prevention of Pollution from Ships). The ILO meets annually, and the recommended minimum wages for seafarers are discussed every two years in the Joint Maritime Committee. As of August 2023, the MLC has been ratified by 104 countries. While the USCG enforces compliance for U.S.-Flag ships in international trade - including the issuance of an MLC certificate by a recognized Class Society - the United States is yet to ratify the MLC.

The MLC aims to protect all seafarers and create a 'level-playing field' for ship owners. It covers the minimum requirements for seafarers to work on a ship; conditions of employment; hours of work and rest; wages; leave; repatriation; accommodation; recreational facilities; food and catering; occupational safety and health protection; medical care; welfare and social security protection. Reaction to the MLC from the seafaring community has been mixed. Some believe it covers all seafaring activities adequately, and others point out that it fails to address key issues such as requirements for nutritious food, and the minimum size for cabins on cargo ships.

When disparities exist between the MLC and real-world experience, or when disputes arise, a representative union may advocate on behalf of the seafarer. The International Transport Workers Federation (ITF) is one of the leading advocates for seafarers in the world. It is a global union with 19.7 million members, from 700 affiliated trade unions across 150 countries. In September 2023, the ITF secured a base pay-level increase of 6% - to be administered over two years - that will benefit around 250,000 seafarers serving on over 10,000 vessels. This increase will improve on the previous ILO minimum monthly basic wage for an able seafarer, which in 2022 was: USD $658 as of 1 January 2023, USD $666 as of 1 January 2024, and USD $673 as of 1 January 2025.

Even though these rates are very low - $658 is less than $22 per day - and the global average sits around USD $18,000 ($50/day), ITF inspectors recover huge amounts of wages owed to seafarers every year; some $35 million in 2022 alone. Through Port State Control (PSC), the Australian Maritime Safety Authority (AMSA) regularly works alongside the ITF, and will ban ships from Australian waters that have been found to be violating the rights of the crew, or underpaying or withholding wages. A Liberian-Flagged coal-carrier bound for Japan was banned for one year, in August 2023. A Marshall Islands-Flagged container ship for 90 days, in October. As at September 2023, over $10 million in lost wages have been recovered from ships traveling in Australian waters, with the ITF estimating that it might climb to $20 million by the end of the year.

Sourcing definitive figures on seafarer pay is complicated. Shipping is a global enterprise, and pay rates vary according to country, region, and market segment. As can be expected in a free market, crewing companies and ship operators respond to market demand, and offer rates to attract the needed workforce for the vessels they manage. Some general observations are as follows:

- Higher-ranked officers from developing countries usually command the most pay e..g, from the United States and Europe.
- Due to the presence of cheaper labor from Asian countries (and a general lack of concern from FOCs), unlicensed crews from the United States and countries in the European Union are almost non-existent
- Wages are comparable for seafarers outside of the EU, and for Indian and Asian officers.
- Wage disparities are more pronounced in lower ranks. For example an Asian deck cadet working on an oil tanker might command $400/month, whereas a U.S. equivalent might earn twice as much.
- The offshore and Oil and Gas industries tend to pay better than other industries. The Master of a Seismic vessel might make $16-$18,000/month. A Master on an LNG or Chemical tanker might make between $12-$15,000/month. The Master of a container ship, between $8-$12,000/month.

Wages are a key component in job security, but are less important with other concerns relating to job satisfaction. If pay is high, but the working environment is unpalatable, then attrition will increase, and Workforce Security will decrease.

## III. Conditions and Treatment

Seafaring is an incredibly rewarding profession, but can also be very hard. Some jobs require a high degree of physicality, or mean constant exposure to dangerous or hazardous conditions.

Other roles require being at sea for many months at a time, with minimal contact with family or friends. Yet, every day, nearly 2 million seafarers across the world choose to participate in this noble and necessary profession; crossing the sea, while exercising, as Columbus intoned, “the courage to lose sight of the shore.”

The COVID-19 pandemic illuminated the plight of international seafarers like no other event in human history. Although critical to the function of global supply chains, and therefore the delivery of PPE and medical supplies, seafarers were not deemed “essential workers". Crew changes were either prohibited or severely restricted. An estimated 400,000 were stuck at sea for prolonged periods of time, with many forced to work beyond the length of their contracts; 6 months, 12 months, and 18 months or more. Due to deteriorating conditions and minimal contact with friends and family, mental health incidents, and suicidal ideation rates increased, along with incidents of Sexual Assault and Sexual Harassment (SASH). Many experienced reduced access to medical treatment and other essential services, and a large number struggled to gain timely access to vaccinations.

The headlines were dramatic and attention-grabbing, yet little was formally done to alleviate the strain that many seafarers were experiencing on a daily basis. Some countries launched awareness campaigns, and others attempted to directly support the seafarers inside their own territorial waters, however responses were generally driven by volunteers, in a sporadic and intermittent manner. Governments were indifferent or distracted by their own national problems. Many Flag States remained silent. The IMO - along with ICS, BIMCO and other shipowner groups - responded strongly, but lacked the necessary resources to directly enforce, or influence the implementation of any recommendations.

These incidents increased advocacy and support, but also highlighted the negligent way that seafarers were (and could be) treated. While real statistics are yet to emerge, it is highly likely that the negative experience of many seafarers during this period will detrimentally impact recruitment into the maritime sector. This means less people who are willing to join the profession, or fill necessary positions, and will put increased pressure on those inside the industry, further exacerbating the problem.

## IV. Seafarer Shortages

BIMCO and International Chamber of Shipping (ICS) data indicates that international shipping will be 96,000 seafarers short by 2026. When considering the experience of seafarers during the pandemic; increasing workforce fluidity and choice; disruptions caused by geopolitical unrest and war; and, the development of new technologies which require additional training, the shortage is likely to be much greater. There is already an acute shortage of officers: Drewry's latest Manning Annual Review and Forecast (June 2023) reported the shortage of ship officers was the most severe that had ever been observed, ever since they started tracking the market 17 years ago. The widening availability gap is set to reach a deficit of around 9% of the global pool of officers by the end of 2023, a significant increase on the 5% shortfall of the year before.

These shortages will impact the industry's short-term productivity, and may also endanger the industry's longer-term decarbonization ambitions as well. A study released in late 2022 by DNV (commissioned by the Maritime Just Transition Task Force) revealed that 800,000 seafarers will require upskilling by the mid-2030's if the industry is to meet planned decarbonization goals. This research sparked intense debate at Conference of the Parties 27 (COP27) in Egypt in November

2022, and prompted the release of a 10-point action plan by the Maritime Just Transition Task Force entitled 'Mapping a Maritime Just Transition for Seafarers'. The Action Plan, jointly prepared by members of the Maritime Just Transition Task Force Secretariat, ICS, the ITF, and the UN Global Compact, included recommendations to: Strengthen global training standards; ensure a health-and-safety-first approach; and, establish national advisory maritime skills councils.

These shortfalls significantly impact the efficiency and effectiveness of the international maritime sector. A coordinated effort is required, at all levels, to address the current shortages and upskill today's workforce, while seeking out and training the workforce of tomorrow.

## Workforce Security and U.S. Shipping

The United States has a long and proud maritime and seafaring tradition. Since the founding of the country, the American maritime industry, and U.S. mariners have played a critical role in protecting the national, economic, and homeland security of the United States. During peacetime, around 40,000 U.S.-Flag ships operate in U.S. coastwise and inland trades, and move approximately one billion tons of cargo per year between U.S. ports. This produces around $154 billion in annual economic output. The domestic U.S. maritime industry supports an estimated 650,000 jobs, resulting in over $41 billion in labor compensation. As has been thoroughly established, these domestic numbers are *very* different to those of the U.S.-flagged commercial fleet that is currently operating around the world.

A lack of U.S.-flagged vessels engaged in international commercial trade is detrimental to U.S. Economic Security. More disturbingly, the diminished number of U.S.-Flag ships poses a grave threat to U.S. National Security. This is because the U.S. merchant fleet is constantly practicing one other important role: To assist the U.S. military during times of war. This seems obvious given that 90% of all U.S. military cargo moves via ship, however what is commonly overlooked is that *people* are required to operate those vessels. The ships themselves are of secondary concern: New vessels can be built (albeit, with current domestic capacity constraints, very slowly), or bought, or acquired from allies overseas. A primary concern is a distinct lack of *people.* And more specifically, U.S. merchant mariners.

During peacetime, the U.S. military moves cargo around the world to supply overseas bases, and assist with humanitarian efforts. These ships are nearly entirely operated by U.S. merchant mariners. If the U.S. engages in a pre-planned conflict, the requisite cargo must be sourced and delivered to where it is needed in preparation for the battles that follow. U.S. merchant mariners perform these tasks and are generally required from the earliest days of planning. If the U.S. is suddenly engaged in a surprise conflict, and has to quickly assemble forces and deploy overseas, U.S. merchant mariners will be desperately needed; in great numbers, and with enough reserves to ensure rotations are possible, or if losses are encountered.

As will be explored in further detail, U.S. merchant mariners are a key component of U.S. maritime strategy; essential in peace-time, and indispensable during war. The sentiment by Former Secretary of Defense, Jim Mattis on the first page of this Principle was echoed by Deputy Defense Secretary Kathleen H. Hicks in the graduation address at the U.S. Merchant Marine Academy, in June 2023: "Again and again throughout history, America's Merchant Mariners have delivered. Today, Merchant Mariners remain an indispensable component of our national defense, because they continue to deliver."

The United States needs a reliable and sustainable supply of merchant mariners for effective and sustainable commercial and naval operations. Due to a near non-existent U.S.-flagged ocean-going fleet; a lack of investment in maritime training; an inability to attract, equip and retain recruits; domestic policies and practices that hamper progress; and, a general lack of investment in the U.S. maritime sector, the United States does *not* have ready access to a reliable and sustainable supply of merchant mariners.

A new strategy must be employed to reverse this precipitous decline, which will require a complete rethink of national maritime priorities. A longer-term view is also required. It takes many years of training and sea time to be credentialed for unlimited service, and will take decades for a competent national maritime workforce to be built. Upskilling and certification processes will need to be revised, and simplified. Joining the U.S. merchant marine also needs better promotion as a valid and rewarding career path. All of these efforts must be coordinated between governments, labor organizations, educational institutions, and industry stakeholders.

Solving this problem will not only improve U.S. maritime Workforce Security, it makes it possible to achieve the goals and ambitions of all of the four other Principles; National, Economic, Energy & Food, and Climate Security.

# Workforce Security Maritime Risks and Vulnerabilities

A. **The critical shortage of U.S. mariners** - *A crisis during peacetime, and disastrous in times of war*

B. **Maritime training and education** - *The current pathways into the maritime industry and to pursue a career in shipping must be promoted and protected*

C. **An inclusive U.S. maritime workforce** - *The necessity and challenges of building a deep and sustainable recruitment, training, and retention talent pipeline*

D. **The influence of U.S. maritime Unions** - *The complex and necessary role that Unions have played, and can play, in transforming the U.S. maritime sector*

E. **Foreign influence and international partners** - *How a shortage of mariners affects the United States, and what the U.S. can learn from allies and the global community*

## A. The Critical Shortage of U.S. Mariners

### I. Peacetime

The United States has the fourth largest coastline in the world, is ideally placed between two major oceans, and has unfettered access to the world's largest trade routes. Despite these advantages, having the world's largest economy, and a long history of maritime endeavors, the United States has almost no global, commercial maritime presence. A shrinking U.S.

commercial, ocean-going - *Zero Point Four* percent - fleet, leads to a shrinking U.S. maritime workforce. This leads to a shrinking sector which reduces the chance of being able to perform diverse, scalable, or cutting-edge work. Without such work, it becomes difficult to entice people into the maritime industry. And, the downward spiral continues.

9 out of 10 U.S. mariners work are engaged in domestic activities, which means only 10% are involved in any form of international commercial work. Places to work are limited: Only 180 U.S.-flagged commercial ships employ mariners with unlimited credentials, which includes ships involved in domestic trades, the Maritime Security Program, and a few other large ships with unlimited capabilities. This small fleet restricts the total number of available billets for U.S. merchant mariners, and the potential for any meaningful degree of career advancement within the U.S. Flag fleet. Even though the total number of available commercial ships is shrinking, the U.S. maritime sector may be facing a shortfall in available mariners already. A Transportation Institute's Mariner Workforce Survey conducted in 2023 indicated that "as many as 13% of mariner positions in the U.S. maritime workforce may remain unfilled". Several factors were identified to explain this gap: Firstly, new vessels being introduced into the fleet are expected to amplify workforce demand, and will require an additional 1,300 mariners to operate effectively. Secondly, the offshore wind sector is growing at pace, and is projected to require a substantial workforce; potentially 4,000 mariners to support offshore wind operations. The offshore wind industry offers a unique opportunity for economic development and clean energy, and has been identified as one of the emerging clean-energy sectors that the U.S. might hold a definitive advantage in, when compared to other countries. A shortage of mariners to support the offshore wind energy sector could stifle growth, and affect the job creation in an industry that has considerable environmental benefits.

This commercial merchant mariner total does not include full time government employees with merchant mariner credentials who crew the combat logistics fleet. Civil-service mariners, 'civmars' account for 80% of Military Sealift Command's workforce, which is around 6,000 personnel. Some vessels such as submarine tenders and command ships, are led by a naval officer, but the rest of the crew are often U.S. merchant mariners. This means that U.S. merchant mariners work on the support vessels that provide ammunition, fuel, equipment and supplies to the U.S. Navy at sea. U.S. merchant mariners operate the afloat prepositioning ships (PM3 fleet) that deploy during the initial stages of an engagement; transporting Marine and Army brigades, and vehicles, fuel and materiel to the frontline.

An estimated 5,000 U.S. mariners are required for the commercial vessels that service domestic routes (including Hawaii, Puerto Rico, Guam and Alaska) in peacetime. However, the number of mariners required for normal commercial services are very different to the number of mariners who are qualified, experienced, and ready to assist the U.S. Navy. Not all merchant mariners are obligated to serve, however many are required to serve because of a contractual arrangement between their employers and MSC, or because of a Union they may have joined. The number of qualified, experienced, ready and obligated merchant mariners is difficult to ascertain; it's likely these numbers are less than the totals that are often quoted. Especially the 'ready' part. In the last definitive review (in 2017, six years ago) former MARAD Administrator Mark Buzby stated there were only "11,768 qualified unlimited tonnage / horsepower active mariners available to crew either commercial or Government reserve ships". A mariner with an unlimited credential is qualified to crew on a ship of unlimited tonnage with unlimited horsepower. Administrator Buzby also noted the distinct lack of "senior-level mariners with unlimited credentials who had sailed in the last 18 months". In 2019, just one year after these statements, only 682 mariners were available for a Sealift Turbo Activation trial. As described in The Principle of National Security, this activation resulted in only 60% of ships being considered ready, with less than 40% able to depart port. Administrator Buzby's conclusion to the mariner shortfall underpins the prevailing sentiment of this Principle: "We got it [mariners], but the industry felt it. This was only a ten-day call. But if this was going to be an open-ended call, one has to wonder if there would be the same turnout."

What is categorized as 'qualified, experienced, and ready' is also different to 'what is sustainable': Assuming the U.S. needs 250 logistics vessels to support the MSP, TSP, CSF and RRF, and the average ship requires 60 crew (2 rotational shifts, of 30 crew, every 6 months and accounting for training and leave), it would be preferable to have 15,000 U.S. fit-for-duty, unlimited tonnage, unlimited horsepower (and obligated) mariners available. In other words, 15,000 mariners is the bare minimum required to sustainably operate the current U.S.-Flag commercial fleet, while supporting the basic needs of the U.S. Navy. This means, in a best-case-scenario where all 11,768 were available, the United States has a deficit of 3,232 mariners; 75% more than the "shortfall of 1,839 mariners" that has been mentioned on several occasions over the last 6 years.

One final consideration is to calculate how many mariners might be needed for the fleet blend required in the future. This moves beyond meeting the needs of the current (small) number of ships, and instead considers the workforce that is required for the United States to hold a degree of influence over international trade.

The ship numbers from The Principle of National Security serves as a guide:

- 1,000 support ships (container ships, ROROs, bulk carriers)
- + 100 tankers (oil, LNG and liquid transport)
- + 20 specialty ships (ice-breakers, subsea inspection vessels, ship carriers)
- = 1,120 ships.

Assuming the majority of these ships are crewed by U.S. merchant mariners, and 60 crew are required per vessel - two teams of 30 in rotation, to account for specialized roles, sustainable operations, leave and training - then the United States needs 67,200 mariners for this future fleet.

This is 4.5x the 15,000 sustainable minimum. The final count will be higher still: 67,200 mariners does not include the rapid expansion of the offshore wind industry, or the potential deployment of commercial nuclear propulsion that also might require additional personnel.

- 15,000 merchant mariners ensure current U.S. maritime sustainability.
- 67,200 merchant mariners convey future U.S. maritime competitiveness.
- Only 11,768 suitably qualified U.S. mariners are available today.
- This means there is a shortfall of just over 55,000 mariners to convey future U.S. maritime competitiveness.

## II. Wartime

Maintaining an adequate number of qualified merchant mariners for an extended wartime scenario is nearly impossible without re-establishing emergency training centers and methods similar to those created for the U.S. Maritime Service in WW2. Losses due to enemy actions as well as necessarily not double-counting qualified merchant mariners who will still be crewing ships to support the home-front economy must be accounted for.

Outside of vocal industry champions, and academic analysts, the number of mariners that may be required in a contested conflict environment is also rarely spoken about. One of the reasons for this is that the U.S. has not been involved in a conflict involving long-range, contested, maritime supply chains for some time. A commonly cited example, Desert Storm, was labeled a 'triumph of logistics'. This is true if considering the rapid victory that followed allied advances, and the staggering volumes of materiel, fuel and equipment delivered to troops and bases inside the war zone. However, this sentiment doesn't carry when reflecting on the total length and breadth of the campaign. For example, Desert Storm ran to an allied-controlled timeline from the beginning which allowed time for sourcing the necessary logistics and supply chain support. Such a luxury may not be available in a modern conflict that escalates rapidly or unexpectedly. Secondly, and most pertinently: Maritime supply lines (from outside the war zone into staging areas) were never seriously threatened by enemy forces.

Multiple historical examples involving extensive maritime operations in contested environments happened during World War II. The majority of experience the U.S. has in contested logistics comes from this era. Sadly, the personnel involved, along with the skills required, and learnings gleaned have all but disappeared. Nearly a quarter of a million U.S. Merchant Mariners served in World II, and around 9,500 tragically lost their lives. The number of support ships that were sunk during WWII was around half of the total ships lost across the war. If that same ratio holds true today - and it may well, given the presence of modern satellites, drones and long-range missiles - then around 60 support ships would be sunk, which is about 2,000 merchant mariners.

While it is difficult (and a little distasteful) to calculate total losses, it is plausible to assume that after 5 ships were sunk, the number of commercials signing up to join the merchant marine would decrease markedly. The only sure preventative measure to maintain supply continuity for a campaign that lasts longer than 12 months would be to massively increase the starting size of the merchant marine to account for losses. An additional 16,500 merchant mariners to support the 15,000 mariners crewing the 250 wartime logistics ships would add in enough buffer to cover domestic operations and losses.

In summary, a worst-case scenario - prolonged conflict in heavily contested environments – would require around 31,500 in total to meet minimal needs for the United States. 31,500 mariners sounds significant, however this represents only one sixth of the currently available Russian mariners, one eighth of the available Indian mariners, and just 6% of the current number of available mariners from the Philippines.

In summary, to understand U.S. merchant maritime workforce numbers under various scenarios, especially given the 11,768 suitably qualified mariners available today, please see table below.

*Anticipated U.S. Merchant Maritime Workforce under various scenarios:*

| | "MINIMAL NEEDS" FLEET | "FUTURE COMPETITIVE" FLEET |
|---|---|---|
| WAR TIME | **500 U.S. ships**<br>**32K U.S. mariners (includes 5% buffer for casualties)**<br><br>Implies 250 additional ships required as backfill for domestic ships needed for war theater of operations.<br>Note: The disadvantage of this scenario is that 17K U.S. mariners have no U.S. vessels during peacetime. | **1120 U.S. ships**<br>**70K U.S. mariners (includes 5% buffer for casualties)**<br><br>Assumes 1120 ships similar to Peace Time / Future Competitive scenario with 250 ships for DoD in conflict zone, 250 ships required as backfill for domestic ships needed for war theater of operations and 620 ships in active international trade. |
| PEACE TIME | **250 U.S. ships**<br>**15K U.S. mariners**<br><br>Assumes 250 U.S. ships to meet minimal security needs. | **1120 ships**<br>**67K U.S. mariners**<br><br>Assumes the following U.S. commercial ships: 1000 support ships + 100 tankers + 20 specialty ships (ice-breakers, subsea cables, ship carriers) = 1120 ships. |

## B. Maritime Training and Education

*"The health of Merchant Mariner Readiness requires continued assessment to ensure an adequately trained supply to crew our surge fleet while minimizing impacts to commercial industry. The supply of contract mariners is sufficient to meet the initial sealift surge when government reserve ships are activated but will be challenged with the ability to sustain crewing requirements over an extended period. The post-COVID recovery has highlighted significant workforce concerns to maritime stakeholders to include recruiting and retention."* General Van Ovost, Commander USTRANSCOM, testimony before the House Armed Services Committee, March 28, 2023.

There are three primary pathways to pursue a maritime career or become a licensed officer in the US maritime industry:

I. "Climbing the hawsepipe"
II. Vocational and Technical Schools
III. Merchant Marine Academies

### I. Climbing the 'Hawsepipe'

A hawsepipe is a hole on the side of a ship that the ship's anchor passes through. The metaphor for this mode of career advancement is that 'climbing the hawse pipe' represents moving from lower ranked roles (where many unlicensed mariners start), to the ships' bridge where the officers (and captain) are located through hands-on experience. Someone who starts their career in this fashion, is called a 'hawsepiper'. Unlike formally studying at an academy or training institute, hawsepipers learn by working on ships, gradually gaining skills, studying and obtaining knowledge, and sea time, which will allow them to qualify for a license. Hawsepipers are generally regarded as being more practically equipped than graduates from maritime academies, but also face greater difficulties in career progression; especially with deep-sea or specialized offshore vessels that are difficult to obtain placement on, or require certain types of formal qualifications.

## II. Vocational and Technical Schools

There are a number of vocational and technical schools that offer a range of practical courses to new recruits, and to industry professionals who may be seeking out additional qualifications.

Some examples include:

- **Paul Hall Center for Maritime Training and Education -** Established in 1967, is located in Piney Point, Maryland. The Paul Hall Center is the largest training facility for deep-sea merchant seafarers and inland waterways mariners, offers a wide range of STCW-compliant courses, and has trained more than 100,000 mariners. The Paul Hall Center is affiliated with the Seafarers International Union (SIU). The SIU is a federation of 12 autonomous unions representing more than 80,000 merchant seafarers, fishers and inland navigation workers and was formally founded in 1938 but has a history that extends back to the International Seamen's Union (1892) and the Sailors' Union of the Pacific (1885).

- **STAR Center** - First opened in 1983 in Toledo, Ohio, and now in Dania, Florida, STAR Center is a division of the Safety & Education Plan of American Maritime Officers (AMO). AMO is the largest maritime labor organization for licensed merchant mariners in the United States, and was founded on the 12th of May, 1949. STAR Center courses meet USCG, STCW,

Society of International Gas Tanker and Terminal Operators (SIGTTO), Military Sealift Command and IMO Model requirements, and more U.S. Coast Guard approved courses than any other simulation training center.

- **Calhoon MEBA Engineering School (CMES) -** CMES serves the training needs of members belonging to the Marine Engineers' Beneficial Association (MEBA). CMES offers STCW and IMO compliant courses, as well as learning certificate programs endorsed by the Environmental Protection Agency (EPA), Military Sea-lift Command (MSC), American Welding Society (AWS), and Det Norske Veritas (DNV). CMES was founded in 1966, and is located in Easton, Maryland.

- **MITAGS -** MITAGS is a non-profit vocational training center in Linthicum, Maryland that offers around 168 different courses to mariners around the globe, and one of the few schools in the U.S. that offers all of the STCW courses necessary to progress from Ordinary Seafarer to Unlimited Master. MITAGS is the primary training facility for the Masters, Mates & Pilots Union, and issues around 6,000 certificates every year. The origins of MITAGS can be traced back to the Maritime Advancement, Training, Education, and Safety (MATES) Program, created in 1968 by major Steamship Lines and the International Organization of Masters, Mates and Pilots (IOMM&P).

Technical and vocational colleges are highly regarded, and produce a majority of the graduates that make up the U.S. domestic maritime workforce. Due to the direct association between these schools and maritime unions and industry partners, most graduates secure jobs immediately after finishing formal qualifications.

## III. Merchant Marine Academies

Formal training for U.S. merchant marine officers is handled through the federal U.S. Merchant Marine Academy (USMMA) at Kings Point, and through 6 State Maritime Academies (SMA); California State University Maritime Academy (Cal Maritime), Vallejo, California; Great Lakes Maritime Academy, Traverse City, Michigan; Maine Maritime Academy (MMA), Castine, Maine; Massachusetts Maritime Academy (MMA), Buzzards Bay, Massachusetts; SUNY Maritime College, Throggs Neck, New York; Texas A&M Maritime Academy - Galveston, Texas.

The USMMA and SMAs set a minimum 3, and usually 4-5 year course that results in the issuance of a degree; e.g., in Shipping and Logistics, or Maritime and Naval Studies. If a cadet wishes to become a member of the U.S. Merchant Marine, additional study will allow them to obtain a U.S. Coast Guard (USCG) Merchant Mariner Credentials (MMC) upon graduation. The MMC is a required document for all crew members aboard U.S. ships with over 100 registered gross tons, or all vessels required to operate with a licensed Master, regardless of size.

Graduates of the USMMA are appointed to the Navy Reserve, and have a five year obligation to serve as merchant marine officers aboard a U.S.-Flag ship; apply for active-duty service in one of the branches of the U.S. Armed Forces; or, serve in the National Oceanic and Atmospheric Administration (NOAA) Corps, or the U.S. Public Health Service (USPHS) Corps. Alternate options are available that require special permission from MARAD, including serving on a U.S.-Flag ship in an unlicensed capacity, in a shoreside role, or as an officer on a foreign-flagged vessel. The minimum military service obligation for newly commissioned uniformed services officers (active or reserve component) from the USMMA is 8 years. Unlike the USMMA, students from the SMAs are not automatically appointed as members of the Navy Reserve, and are not guaranteed commissions as military officers. The USMMA is free to attend, but includes a mandatory service component. The SMAs charge tuition, room and board, plus a fee for the required sea time for recruits to earn a license.

Around 70% of the nation's unlimited tonnage / horsepower merchant marine officers - i.e., who can operate a vessel of any size or power, in any region - are graduates of State Maritime Academies, and around 80% of all Sealift Officers are from the USMMA. This highlights the important role these academies play in training U.S. Merchant Marine officers, and supporting the personnel needs of Military Sealift.

## Summary: U.S. Maritime Training and Education

The United States has a long and proud history of training maritime professionals however the emphasis in recent times has been on increasing the skills of the domestic workforce. The number of 'hawsepiper' mariners has decreased over time, and Vocational and Technical Schools face increasingly complex challenges in attracting candidates. USMMA and SMAs are unable to supply the numbers of U.S. mariners required to support commercial and naval operations. Only around 1,400 graduates are processed through these academies on an annual basis. With the exception of the Great Lakes Maritime Academy in Michigan, only a small percentage of those 1,400 graduates will actually go on to sail. If graduates do sail they face an uncertain career path due to a dwindling number of available U.S.-Flag vessels.

If the ocean-going U.S.-Flag fleet increases in ways previously described, the United States will need over 67,000 mariners in the next few decades. The shortfall of availability of U.S. mariners is acute, and will continue to be unless new strategies are pursued. To cope with increasing demand, all three of these pathways of education and training need to be promoted and expanded.

## C. An Inclusive U.S. Maritime Workforce

Investing in the U.S. maritime workforce can make a significant impact on many historically underrepresented communities. Most of the ports in the U.S. are located in cities with a higher representation of people of color. Many of these port areas have historically suffered from environmental pollution, health challenges and growing deprivation as workforce numbers have reduced in U.S. maritime. However, new investments in the Blue Economy and U.S. Maritime could open up new career paths for historically underrepresented communities (e.g., installation and maintenance of offshore windfarms, aquaculture, greener port and shipping operations). Greater investment into socio-economic groups with a higher propensity to spend locally, such as port communities, can create a significant local multiplier effect to rejuvenate many of America's most deprived cities (e.g., around the Ports of Oakland, Long Beach). 21% of the population in Long Beach City live below the poverty line, double that of the U.S. average of 13%. The Port of Oakland is the second largest job generator, indirectly employing almost 100,000 in local jobs and generating almost $170 billion a year. Employing more mariners from such communities in higher paying jobs will create a significant economic dividend, greater than the direct investment alone.

On gender, there have been notable female trailblazers in U.S. maritime, such as Dr Sylvia Earle as the first female Chief Scientist of NOAA (National Oceanic and Atmospheric Administration) in 1990, Diana Josephson as the first female NOAA Administrator in 1993, and more recently, Admiral Linda Fagan who was appointed as the first female Commandant of the U.S. Coast Guard, Rear Admiral Ann Phillips as the first female Administrator of MARAD and Admiral Joanna Nunan as the first female Superintendent of the U.S. Merchant Marine Academy, all three of whom were appointed in 2022. Within the LGBT community, Secretary of Transportation Pete Buttigieg became the first openly gay Cabinet Secretary when confirmed on February 2, 2021, with responsibility for maritime affairs. This shows that the U.S. maritime sector has the potential to create a future workforce where anyone from all communities can thrive, and reflects the changing tides in maritime.

Such change would not have been possible without leadership from those outside of formal Government structures. For example, influential voices such as Alaina Basciano at American Maritime Officers Union who was also a Master in the Merchant Marines, Ally Cedeno who founded Women Offshore dedicated to reducing the gender gap on the water following a career dynamically positioning drill rigs in the Gulf of Mexico, and the Organization of Black Maritime Graduates, a non-profit organization founded in 1994 by Captain Robert Cook, Captain Howard Wyche and four other SUNY Maritime College graduates to increase the educational possibilities for minority students and cadets at Maritime Colleges.

More broadly, if the U.S. can catalyze a move toward more sustainable maritime fuels (such as methanol) through a strong U.S. commercial fleet, then this will create tens of thousands of agricultural, biofuel manufacturing and refining jobs, all of which require an appropriately skilled U.S. workforce, again in many historically deprived communities. All of this needs a holistic strategy and workforce planning.

The MARAD framework of 'Attract, Equip, Retain' is used to frame the discussion about how to increase the number of people involved in the U.S. maritime industry from all walks of life.

## I. Attract

Encouraging anyone to consider a career in the maritime sector can be complicated. Despite being the dominant form of transportation that supplies nearly all consumed and consumer products, most people would struggle to identify a connection between shipping and daily life. Headlines during the height of the COVID pandemic were dominated with stories about shipping, however there is little evidence that this additional attention has translated into a substantial increase in the amount of people who want to join the shipping industry.

The U.S. maritime sector will need to be conscious of the following as it attempts to 'Attract' more people:

- Collaboration will be required as recruitment activities increase. Coordination will ensure that schools, academies, or industry participants are not competing for the same pool of candidates. Industry partnerships need to be forged, and input will also be required from the academic community. Assistance and funding from the Government is likely to be required.

- The pre-employment pipeline needs additional attention in particular. Shipping must be regarded as a 'valid pathway to a rewarding career', from a young age. Work is already underway on this pipeline, through the twenty

K-12 Maritime Academies that are dotted around the country, however more focused effort is required. Organizations such as MPSEC (Maritime Primary and Secondary Education Coalition) are currently working to fill the void.

- Messaging, tone and language must be aligned with the intended audience that is desired for the industry. Money, in and of itself, is not as great a motivator as it once was. Younger workers are now interested in working in a job that instills a sense of purpose, or contributes to a greater cause. Ships do both, and regularly carry essential food items, life-saving medications and a range of other products necessary to support human life; facts that must feature in recruitment advertising.

- Appropriate channels to communicate the requisite messages - e.g., social media and online forums - will need to be established and maintained by motivated people. The U.S. shipping industry does not have coordinated representation in many online publications, or a pronounced online presence. gCaptain is one of only a few outlets dedicated to analyzing and promoting the maritime industry; the exception, rather than the rule.

- The activities of the shipping industry are commonly misunderstood, so public education and awareness campaigns will be required. These campaigns will need to dispel the myths about shipping, and also promote the benefits of being involved in the sector. This has been made difficult by recent reports about seafarer welfare, and negative stories about the environmental impact of shipping; both of which, erode the perception in a younger generations mind, that shipping represents a desirable, and ethically responsible career.

- Workplace benefits and conditions will be top-of-mind for most candidates: Connectivity is taken as a 'given' in most professions; even if workers are operating remotely or in rural areas. Connectivity has been all but assured across the world due to recent enhancements to global satellite networks. A reduction in costs has accompanied this expansion as evidenced by the comparatively low monthly prices associated with SpaceX's LEO-layer Starlink network. Internet connectivity should be accompanied with the provision of education services to allow mariners on ocean-going vessels to study, attend tuition courses, and perform research while at sea. Ships engaged in global trade should be regarded as 'Floating Universities'.

- There is a distinct need to attract talent at all levels of operations: From the lowliest deck hand, all the way through to senior administrators. This will become quickly apparent if MARAD is expanded in the manner previously described i.e., to 10,000 personnel over the next decade from the current base of around 800 employees. As stated, this increase is dramatic, but still significantly less than the FAA's 40,000 employees and NAVSEA's 80,000.

- The nation cannot build its next generation of mariners by excluding one segment of society. Recruiting and retaining skilled women mariners is fundamental to building a critical workforce already lagging in supply. As per the previously quoted 2021 BIMCO / ICS report, the global maritime industry is dominated by men, with women constituting barely 1.2 percent (around 24,000) of the total. The United States has a higher proportion of credentialed women mariners (around 7%) but more needs to be done to encourage further participation. This requires a purposeful strategy, with practical goals, to raise the profile of the shipping industry, and to convey that ships can be a safe and meaningful place to work.

Words are not enough: Attracting more women to the industry must be accompanied with structural reform. Far from being considered fellow shipmates, many women have been subjected to range of Sexual Assault and Sexual Harassment (SASH) and abusive incidents over many years. Some work has been started: The National Defense Authorization Act (FY23) now includes a new law requiring commercial ship owners, operators, masters, and employers to report complaints and incidents of sexual harassment, and sexual assault that violate any law or company policy to the U.S. Coast Guard. Congress increased the potential civil penalties for failing to report such incidents from $5,000 to $50,000 per violation. Much more still needs to be achieved.

If the United States maritime industry acts in a coordinated and collaborative fashion, it will be able to outcompete other sectors and attract the mariners to meet present-day needs and fulfill future demand.

## II. Equip

Once engaged with the maritime sector, mariners will need appropriate training for their current roles, and also be given opportunities to upskill for the tasks they may need to complete in the future. Considerations that relate to properly equipping mariners are as follows:

- A fit-for-purpose workforce is essential. Due to a lack of U.S.-flagged, ocean-going commercial ships, there is a distinct lack of opportunities on deep-sea vessels for U.S. mariners undergoing training. For example, if the U.S. does not own any LNG tankers, the chance of having experienced captains for an expanding LNG fleet is comparatively low. If the U.S. does not have many deep-sea vessels, then the chance of having highly-skilled U.S. mariners who can captain, operate, or maintain these vessels is also low. That is to say, that building, or acquiring, new ships must be accompanied with an increase in the available training capacity that corresponds to these new ship types.

- Education standards and passing ranks must be reviewed to ensure uniformity across all schools, academies and institutions. A recent example, highlighted by The Consortium of State Maritime Academies (CSMA) in April 2023, explains why such a review is necessary: Maritime students embarking on a four-year degree must be able to complete the 'Chart Plot module'; one of seven within the Third Mate exam. Cadets have historically been able to pass this module at an acceptable rate, and will go on to serve the U.S. Merchant Marine with a high level of competency. New exams were introduced in 2021, and passing rates plummeted. Results from five SMA's showed passing rates as low as 0% - at Maine Maritime Academy - and just under 20% at California State University Maritime Academy. Feedback from cadets included observations about vague wording and a change in structure that made questions more difficult to answer. CSMA officials also highlighted that the necessity of this module may need to be reviewed, as many graduates will never sail with paper-based charts, and because newer ships have been fitted with Electronic Chart Display and Information System (ECDIS).

- Interoperability with naval operations and promoting 'dual-use' skills must be encouraged. This can happen at all education and training levels; from pre-employment maritime academies through to adult vocational schools. Intentional training must occur with U.S.-Flag operators to increase the general level of understanding about naval operations that may need to be performed by commercial vessels as they support U.S. Navy activities. The use of CONSOL equipment, and associated procedures for naval replenishment must be integrated into these training efforts. This will be assisted by the expansion of the specialist Tactical Advisor (TACAD) program across a growing U.S.-Flag fleet. The integration of dual-use training will require an ethos and cultural change that may take decades to occur, but will result in a more engaged workforce that has the capability to effectively assist with any emerging or potential National Security threats.

- Equipping U.S. mariners on new equipment and new ships will improve training outcomes. This is especially important when considering the future state of the U.S. maritime sector. MARAD has been working with local shipbuilders on the design and construction of five National Security Multi-mission Vessels (NSMVs). An NSMV has the capacity to train up to 600 cadets at sea, or accommodate 1,000 people if used for humanitarian aid or disaster relief. NSMVs are outfitted with numerous training spaces including eight classrooms, a full training bridge, lab spaces, a helicopter pad and an auditorium. Empire State VII, the new training ship for SUNY Maritime College was delivered in September 2023. The next training vessel, NSMV II, destined for the Massachusetts Maritime Academy will be completed in 2024. The keel laying for NSMV III (Maine Maritime Academy) and steel cutting for NSMV IV (Texas A&M Maritime Academy) have already been completed. And the final ship, NSMV V (California Maritime Academy) will begin construction shortly, with the intention of all vessels being delivered by 2026.

- MARAD's 'Centers of Excellence' (COE) program received $30 million under the FY 2023 National Defense Authorization Act. The COE program supports 27 training institutes and vocational schools across 16 different States. This expands MARAD's training and educational mission beyond traditional blue-water mariners to now include a wider range of professions and positions, both afloat and ashore. MARAD should ensure the institutes and vocational schools in the COE program are aligned to the objectives of a national agenda, including the requirements of Sealift and the U.S. Navy. This will ensure that graduates are equipped with cross-domain and dual-use skills, and directed towards designated skill areas that promote the growth and expansion of the U.S.-Flag Fleet.

- Strategic Sealift Officers (SSO) embody the concept of a dual-use mariner, and are a key component of the command structure inside Military Sealift Command. Any commercial vessel used by MSC is crewed by merchant mariners, and led by an SSO. All SSOs hold unlimited-tonnage deck or engineering merchant marine licenses, and must be proficient in a wide range of skills, including the application of a chronometer, barometer and sextant to map a course across the open ocean. During peacetime, these SSO's serve onboard commercial ships, and are obligated to serve the nation in times of war. Around 80% of all SSO's are graduates from the USMMA. There are approximately 2,000 SSOs currently available to MSC, however more will be required as the U.S.-Flag and Sealift-capable fleet expands, and with the increased convergence of U.S. naval and commercial operations.

Equipping mariners with the requisite skills for the tasks at hand, while providing valid ways to obtain cross-domain expertise, greatly improves job satisfaction, and is an effective way to add depth to the U.S. naval and commercial fleets.

## III. Retain

Workforce retention is an important factor in every market segment. If workers are not given adequate opportunities, or adequate pay, or aren't offered rewarding or interesting work, they may choose to move on to other positions, or potentially other professions. The U.S. commercial maritime industry has been in a state of decline for some time, which has a cumulative impact on morale and retention.

- A review of factors that increase or decrease retention rates (and reciprocally, attrition rates) in the U.S. Merchant Marine must be completed at every level, from the earliest graduate through to the most long-serving member of the workforce. This should attempt to ascertain at what point mariners are exiting the workforce, and why. These reviews are conducted by other services regularly, for instance the U.S. Marine Corps reached approximately 97.2% of its retention goal for the past nine years, and exceeded 100% for the first time in July 2022. Even though stated goals have been met, the Marine Corps are still adapting their methods to increase retention to ensure they will always have the right amount of warriors, trained and ready for combat.

- The complex and intertwined nature of the commercial and naval domains has likely fueled the lack of government oversight and interest in the U.S. maritime sector. As previously discussed, MARAD is understaffed and under-resourced for the tasks that it has been assigned, which makes the current state of Sealift and other essential naval support services somewhat predictable. If it is difficult to successfully meet the mandate to attract and retain a suitably trained maritime workforce, it will be near impossible to also employ an active strategy to encourage workforce retention. MARAD must share this role with the Academies, and other vocational training centers, or otherwise the U.S. merchant marine runs the risk of losing key personnel to other expanding sectors.

- Retention is also affected by a lack of Blue Economy opportunities and available billets to gain experience on deep-sea or specialized offshore vessels. The expansion of the floating wind industry will assist with this, however much more work needs to be done to attract, equip, and especially retain the right blend of mariners across the entire U.S. commercial and naval fleets.

- Three areas that have not been historically well catered for in the maritime domain are: Work-life balance, providing diverse and culturally-aware workplaces, and job satisfaction. Work-life balance is an important factor during all stages of career ascendency, and has become a key differentiator for a younger generation of workers. Diverse and culturally-aware workplaces assist with retention of those people who may otherwise have felt ostracized by a homogenous majority.

Diversity of age and thought, also brings great benefit to the industry, and will lead to out-of-the-box thinking, and new innovations that may not have been historically considered. Job satisfaction, including the ability to choose a career that is flexible and rewarding, and to work in environments that are safe, is another important consideration for many workers, including women, and those entering the maritime sector for the first time.

## D. The Influence of U.S. Maritime Unions

With a history stretching back all the way to 1875 with the formation of The Marine Engineers' Beneficial Association (MEBA), Unions have played an important role in the U.S. maritime sector. Unions have had a long history of advocating on behalf of members, and have been vocal supporters of building the U.S. maritime industry and protecting U.S. maritime workers. Unions represent mariners on U.S.-flag fleet ships, or who work in domestic maritime industries (on ships, ports and waterways) to ensure they are fairly paid, have access to necessary pension and health benefits, and are able to complete their jobs safely. Unions assist to equip the U.S. maritime workforce through Vocational and Technical schools, as well as on-the-job training in a diverse array of workplaces all across the country. A zeal to protect jobs, and to ensure Union members are well represented and well paid, has often led to conflict with companies, employers, administrators, and sometimes the general public.

A number of topics pertinent to all five Principles, have garnered attention in recent times:

1. Staunch Union endorsement of the Merchant Marine Act of 1920 (often referred to as 'The Jones Act') has led to a firmly established position on the importance of

protecting domestic maritime transportation, and the operations of the U.S.-Flag fleet. Some have described this position as unyielding, and have labeled the Act, and Union activity along with it, as a significant contributor to the downfall of the U.S. maritime industry. Observations about the Merchant Marine Act are discussed in a later chapter, suffice to say the claim that the Act and the Unions are solely to blame for the downfall of the U.S. maritime sector is a maligned oversimplification of an incredibly multi-layered problem.

2. One common theme that arises during Union actions is the importance of protecting the rights of U.S. maritime workers. This is a noble endeavor and should be encouraged, if those actions are based on the ambition to secure current *and* future jobs. That is, the jobs that receive a pay rise in the immediate, as well as the jobs that come after them in the years that follow. If actions are taken that only benefit current Union membership, then an issue is likely to arise with the ability to attract and retain an appropriate workforce (union-affiliated or not) over time. Among other reasons, this reduction in longer-term workforce availability occurs if the requested wage rise is not commercially sustainable by the industries or companies that have been asked to bear the cost of it. In this way, any actions that supplant free market dynamics by unnaturally increasing wage costs, can reduce the competitiveness of the companies supplying services. If this frequently occurs, a company - and in the case of a port, an entire geographic region - can miss out on previously profitable activities due to higher associated costs; customers will take their money and business elsewhere. And, if this occurs over a protracted period of time, those companies will fail,

which will remove the chance for longer-term employment for Union (and also non-Union) members.

3. Common themes have been present in various port disputes overseas - for example the industrial disputes with Patrick Stevedores in Australia in the late 90's - and have been more recently witnessed during the contract negotiations between the International Longshore and Warehouse Union (ILWU) and employer group Pacific Maritime Association (PMA) across 2022 and 2023. In this example, the ILWU was successful in securing a deal for 22,000 dockworkers that amounted to a 32% pay rise, and a one-time "hero bonus" of $70 million for those who worked through the turbulence of the pandemic. The PMA released figures that claimed the average full-time earnings of an ILWU longshoremen was currently around $200,000 per year, which meant the average wage would increase to about $260,000 per year by 2029; and this didn't include Union clerks and foremen, who would often earn more. While there was some dispute about just how many people would receive those larger amounts, some commentators in the public sphere had already deemed the numbers to be excessive, which led to furious debate and analysis over the months that followed.

There will always be a tension between determining the appropriate pay for work completed, while considering how to maintain the competitiveness of U.S. maritime assets and the U.S. maritime sector. A mistake that can sometimes be made by labor advocates, is to forget that short-term victories can be very detrimental longer-term. For example, pay can be secured for one generation, and, because of closures caused by reduced competitiveness, rob the next generation of employment. Or, as has happened on a few occasions, labor demands are made to secure local jobs for local citizens, only to find that an asset (and in the case of the present discussion, a port) is then bought by a foreign entity who slowly exerts adverse control over the domestic workforce, over time. Union representatives must keep this external threat in mind; that is, if demanded financial compensation is not matched to productivity and output, a scenario may arise that cedes an entire industry, region or asset to foreign interests. To that end, conflict between U.S. companies and U.S. labor is not the most productive endeavor. As these conflicts slowly play out, foreign companies and foreign ports are becoming increasingly efficient, and reaping the economic benefits for their role in supporting gross national productivity and output.

To add to this perspective: Labor disputes in major trading gateways are never just localized, and affect the entire U.S. economy. West Coast ports move about 50% of all U.S. imports, accounting for about 12.5% of U.S. GDP. A stoppage at the Port of LA/LB is estimated to result in $2 billion *per day* in economic losses. Inefficiencies at ports are also a factor: The 2022 World Bank and S&P Container Port Performance Index (CPPI) "is based on available empirical objective data pertaining exclusively to time expended in a vessel stay in a port and should be interpreted as an indicative measure of container port performance". U.S. ports feature heavily in the lower numbers. Of the 348 ports in the CPPI, the Port of Houston ranks 335th; Port of Los Angeles (336); Port of Oakland (343); Long Beach (346); and, at the bottom of the list, the U.S. East Coast Port of Savannah in the 348th spot.

4. Debates about port and labor efficiency often include strong opinions about the use of automated assets.

Autonomous container trucks, remotely operated ship-to-shore (STS) cranes and automated straddle cranes have introduced a range of efficiency gains in many ports all over the world. China's Tianjin Port is the largest port in Northern China, and ranked around 7th in the world by volume. Inside Tianjin's port boundary is a 'smart terminal' that operates with just 200 workers, compared to around 800 required at a conventional terminal. Automation has noticeably improved container and ship handling times, reducing berthing times by 7%, and ship load / unload times by up to 80%.

Due to continuous operations and other advantages, highly-automated ports can handle more throughput and are generally more efficient and less costly to run. Examples in China, Japan, the Netherlands, Australia, and other countries confirm that increased automation can bring considerable productivity gains, and therefore increased profitability. U.S. ports have been slow to adopt automation technologies, predominantly due to the threat of worker displacement and Union resistance. The United States must balance the labor risks associated with automation, with the structural threats that supply chain inefficiencies impose on the broader U.S. economy.

U.S. labor Unions can lead this transition by embracing a revised version of the future where their members are still hard at work, just on a variety of new and different tasks; and for multiple generations to come. A wise perspective was heard recently that encapsulates how this transition can occur: "You won't lose your job. You might lose your *old* job." If completed collaboratively, incredibly productive (and profitable) outcomes will eventuate for all parties involved. Partnering to build a solution is key, as is a deep understanding about how decisions with automation will impact productivity, and also the workforce. The need for a mutually-beneficial partnership was echoed in the sentiment of former ILWU president James Spinosa in an interview in late 2022: "Union dock workers would go along with mechanization, as long as mechanization took them along."

5. Despite the essential role of U.S.-Flag ships for coastal supply chains, critical sealift capacity, and the movement of overseas aid and military shipments, the current U.S. approach for having enough mariners depends largely on the negotiations between unions and commercial ship owners. Commercial ship operations inherently seek to have just enough employees to comply with commercial standards and crewing regulations, as extra crew means extra expenses. Unions similarly prefer having just enough members. An oversupply of mariners would drive wages down. The solution to this impasse is to increase the amount of opportunities available to U.S. merchant mariners; in the United States, and, where possible, overseas. China has employed this to great effect, and has around 150,000 mariners serving on foreign-flagged vessels. As previously described, this not only increases China's Economic Security by allowing them to influence the movement of traded goods across the world, it also extends China's geostrategic reach as well. More U.S.-flagged ships, or more U.S.-controlled ships operating in the international commercial, maritime sector, will achieve this outcome. It is entirely possible to expand the U.S. fleet, and map out a pathway to profitability that would also increase the benefits experienced by U.S. mariners, and subsequently the Unions that represent them.

Unions play a key role in influencing how the U.S. maritime sector will evolve over time. With judicious oversight, and a forward-postured approach, Unions, along with their members and other aligned stakeholders can implement effective strategies that will usher in a new era of U.S. maritime prosperity and productivity.

## E. Foreign Influence and U.S. Shipping

As detailed in various sections throughout this book, there is an over reliance on non-U.S. mariners in the U.S. maritime sector, and as outlined below, there is additional impact caused by the presence of the 'War Workforce'.

### I. Domestic considerations

The U.S. is heavily dependent on foreign mariners to handle import and export cargo, and the majority of international commercial activities. The U.S. is a major importer and exporter, and accounts for a large percentage of global trade. There are around 50,000 vessels involved in global trade. If 10,000 ships are involved in moving U.S. imports and exports; and, each of those ships have a crew of 50 in rotation (i.e., two teams of 25, slightly less than the U.S.-Flag fleet average, and accounting for leave and training); then, a minimum of 500,000 foreign mariners are required to move U.S. goods into and out of the country.

If the U.S. has 15,000 mariners available to handle imports and exports, U.S. mariners represent just 3% of those 500,000 personnel. This means the U.S. is dependent on foreign mariners to fill 97% of the positions required to sustain the vast majority of U.S. commercial trading activity. This is an unnaturally weighted dependence, and would be a cause for alarm in most other scenarios and for most other sectors. The risk this poses to U.S. Economic Security is more obvious, but as has been explored throughout this book, there are also significant risks that exist for National, Food and Energy, Climate and Workforce Security, too. A brief summary follows of previously conveyed sentiment, about the challenges facing the U.S. that relate to this dependency:

- Non-U.S. crews may be required by their home countries to cease provision of services to U.S. routes and companies; because of trade sanctions, or an escalation in tension or to advance a military agenda

- Non-U.S. crews might resist or refuse to serve in risky situations on behalf of the U.S. Government. For example, carrying cargo or commercial cargo into a theater of war such as the Black Sea between Russia and Ukraine

- Non-U.S. crews could sabotage, steal, counterfeit, damage or contaminate U.S. cargoes that are moving around the world on ships under their control

- Non-U.S. crews might use their vessel as a weapon to ram other ships, disrupt naval operations, damage critical infrastructure (e.g., running into the side of the Panama Canal) or by disrupting strategic chokepoints (e.g., by deliberately grounding a vessel in the Suez Canal).

Defense logistics are also highly reliant on foreign workers. A U.S. Army logistics review conducted in 1991 after Desert Storm, found that 37% of all cargo was carried on chartered commercial ships, 22% on foreign-flag vessels, and just 15% on U.S.-Flag ships. A similarly prolonged or complicated campaign in a distant country will inevitably lead to the establishment of long maritime supply lines, and therefore the creation of open market contracts involving non-U.S. companies. This will mean a sharp uptake in non-U.S. labor to support the war effort; labor that may be entirely unwilling to be compliant or perform requested duties.

It is during times of heightened tension and conflict that compliant, skilled, and mission-aligned mariners are needed the most. And it is during those times the U.S. would face a serious shortfall. The same is true for ports, support ships, and any other asset required to move and manage the commercial and naval fleets involved in combat operations. This will be, yet another scenario where the U.S. will not be able to 'buy its way out of the problem'.

## II. The War Workforce

The shortfall in available mariners is made even more acute when analyzing the numbers associated with the countries that have aligned with Russia in the recent conflict in Ukraine. This provides insights into the impact of what might happen to the available maritime workforce if a future conflict involves similar countries.

The following show the numbers of mariners associated with countries that have either aligned with Russian interests during the war, or have remained neutral and therefore may not lend mariners to any U.S. initiatives. Note: A very conservative estimate has been included for China.

1. Directly-aligned: Russia, Cuba, Nicaragua, Venezuela - 215,000
2. Indirectly-aligned: Syria, Iran - 18,000
3. China - 300,000
4. India - 250,000

   **Total: 783,000**

This means that around 40% of the total available global mariner workforce (from 1,892,720 total) is directly or indirectly influenced by the actions of Russian foreign policy and aggression. As can be obviously deduced, if around half of the world's total seafarers are removed from the available pool, it becomes *extremely* unlikely the U.S. could obtain the necessary workforce to move defense equipment and materiel across the world; especially if a conflict involved one of the other countries in that list.

## Workforce Security Maritime Solutions and Opportunities

The United States can reduce Workforce Security risk by pursuing the following solutions and opportunities. The context of the below solutions assumes that a longer-term plan is also being considered to constantly increase the size of the U.S. flag fleet. New tonnage through initiatives like the Flag-In Security Program (FISP) and Economic Security Program (ESP) are key mechanisms to solve for a number of these challenges. The FISP and ESP will bring in a greater amount of new tonnage, and therefore increase opportunities for U.S. mariners, which will lead to an expansion of the U.S. maritime workforce.

The following solutions and opportunities are matched to the maritime risks and vulnerabilities explored throughout this Principle:

1. **Risk: Poor public understanding of the role of shipping in the economy**
   **Solution: 'No Shipping, No Shopping' Campaign**
   Awareness is key. Drawing inspiration from passionate industry advocates Captain James Foong, Gordon Foot, Jillian Carson-Jackson, The Seafarers Charity and other vocal advocates, a U.S.-led global awareness campaign will highlight the importance of shipping to the general public, consumers, producers and suppliers, while also supporting the work of seafarers. This will be paired with the vital work of other groups, such as NAMEPA, that communicate the value proposition of the maritime industry to port communities and students. This compassion-led campaign would partner with industry advocate groups, and charities, and use any proceeds from advertising partnerships or donors to fund seafarer welfare initiatives.

2. **Risk: Numbers of available mariners unknown**
   **Solution: Qualified Available Mariner Audit (QAMA)**
   Numbers from MARAD and other official sources are often difficult to ascertain, and may not be entirely clear for the administrators and officials involved in either. A national Qualified Available Mariner Audit will allow these numbers to be better understood, and so they can be used to calculate shortfalls that may exist for crewing the RRF and other needed auxiliary services ships. The QAMA will draw information from official sources (including the USCG, USMMA, SMAs and COEs), and other affiliate partners so that accurate figures can be documented. The final compiled list will be disclosed to relevant internal working groups, and guide subsequent discussions about the status of the U.S. Merchant Marine, and what can be done about recruitment and retention. This work must include the involvement of the Unions so that details can be obtained about their established pipeline to attract, equip, and retain the necessary mariners to fill available commercial positions.

3. **Risk: Lack of qualified officers, SSO's and mariners for Sealift**
   **Solution: Expand USMMA and State Maritime Academies**
   The USMMA and SMA's enrollment and class sizes should increase to expand the available pool of mariners; for commercial activities, dual-use operations, and to maintain high levels of support for the U.S. Navy. Where possible, the State Maritime Academies should work with the USMMA to attract and train students who are willing to commit to obligated service as well. Current trends might be useful to motivate new recruits into a career in maritime or to

attend the USMMA or an SMA. For example designing course material that will allow students to participate in plans to build new ships; design autonomous systems; participate in efforts to decarbonize the industry; develop system to support future fuels; deploy real time data sharing capabilities; implement sensor-enabled condition-based maintenance; or, be involved in large-scale projects that assist build the nation.

4. **Risk: Attracting the needed mariners to the U.S. merchant marine**
   **Solution: Appropriate Parity with U.S. Military Personnel**
   Since merchant mariners are critical to national security and perform duty overseas in support of national objectives, they should receive certain benefits granted to U.S. military personnel. These should include federal and state tax breaks when they work in hazardous duty areas designated by the Department of Defense that allow military personnel to exclude wages from federal and state taxation. Additionally, merchant mariners who are lawful permanent residents and have served the U.S. merchant marine for one year should be eligible for naturalization similar to a U.S. military person with the same status.

5. **Risk: Lack of command opportunities**
   **Solution: U.S. Merchant Marine Advanced Leadership Program (MM-ALP)**
   There is no defined career path 'from the deckplate to headquarters' for mariners serving in Military Sealift Command. This brings ambiguity to career positions, and stifles the chance of progressing beyond being a Port Captain or advising an area commander. Under the MM-ALP, Junior MSC mariners (2nd Mates or

engineers) would be given the option to spend time ashore in MSC area commands, to communicate the particular needs of merchant mariners to naval personnel.

In a similar fashion, Senior Masters and Chief Engineers could spend time in collaboration with naval officials about the operations of MSC. These activities will naturally lead to an expansion of dual-use capabilities and potentially to the invention of new methods and innovations, too. Furthermore, Merchant Mariners engaged in the MM-ALP who are involved in unlimited tonnage, deep sea careers should receive government benefits similar to armed forces members or at least career civil servants. This would also allow career paths that seamlessly transition back and forth between the merchant marine and military, or civil service positions.

6. **Risk: Reduced U.S. mariner competitiveness Solution: U.S. Mariner Benefits and Insurance Scheme (MBIS)**
   International fleets are reluctant to employ U.S. mariners because of a higher liability risk and therefore the potential for increased costs. Rather than asking U.S. commercial interests to take on this risk, one pathway would be for the U.S. Government (under MARAD) to agree with the main trade unions about how to cover the liability. This would mean commercial operators could employ U.S. mariners on similar commercial terms as crews from other countries, with stronger liability coverage provided by the U.S. Government. There are similar programs for other critical workforce groups for example the United Services Automobile Association that support veterans, and government-sponsored enterprise Fannie Mae. Group liability would be handled in tranches, or applied across the entire U.S.

Merchant Marine. For example, to cover 50,000 U.S. merchant mariners with liability coverage of $100,000, would require an insurance bond of $5 billion.

Alongside insurance benefits, the MBIS will encourage the passage of legislation that gives mariners tax forgiveness for participating in a range of international sailing activities. This would be similar to the 'Foreign-Earned Income Exclusion' rules that apply to U.S. expat tax collection. Other benefits may include group-negotiated discounts for a range of helpful services, such as financial support programs, or professional training resources.

7. **Risk: Lack of available support personnel and serving mariners**
**Solution: Expand the 'Military to Mariner' Program**
There are 200,000 military veterans who retire each year from every major service (Navy, Army, Air Force, Coast Guard). 42% are officer rank, 52% are enlisted, and most will have skills that are highly relevant to maritime. Around 60% of retirees seek non-military work upon retirement, and a significant proportion might choose to join the U.S. Merchant Marine if there is a potential for career advancement and a recognition of prior military service and certification.

The work of MARADs Military to Mariner Program should be expanded and resourced to attract more ex-military members. An acknowledgement of previous military service and qualifications will be a component of this expansion: Transparent accounting would be completed for days served, and bridging courses would be offered to convert prior experience to the merchant marine equivalent e.g., STCW-approved firefighting, first aid, navigation and so on. Additional funding and further coordination with industry and veterans affairs groups will assist to expand this program so it can effectively attract, recruit and retain military veterans.

8. **Risk: Unknown numbers with mariners in conflict scenarios**
   **Solution: Advanced Maritime Contested Logistics Simulations (AMCLS)**
   AMCLS is an academic collaboration to obtain realistic calculations and to perform accurate simulations about the effect on the workforce of contested (logistics and geographic) domains. This involves using AI and computational intelligence to calculate various scenarios, including how many personnel are needed during a period of sustained conflict. These numbers will then be used to adjust the numbers required for training and deployment, and also directly inform talent acquisition and recruitment schedules. Training data and computational capacity may be obtained through a COE partner, Vocational Training school, or from leading U.S. universities.

9. **Risk: Lack of participation from industry**
   **Solution: Develop industry-sponsored Scholarship Programs**
   Industry-sponsored Scholarships will provide another avenue for students to be supported as they attend a Vocational School, COE or academy. Finding the right industry partners will make this more effective; not only does it provide needed funding to offset the students' costs, but it also aligns the student with a potential future employer. Given that shipping is a truly global activity, partners should be sourced from every single industry vertical. For example, Nike is a major shipper of products all around the world, and could nominate to sponsor a student through a maritime training program.

That student might consider working in Nike's shipping and logistics department to gain further experience during the term of their study, before finishing off their education and either returning to that placement position, or pursuing a different employment pathway.

10. **Risk: Reduced incentive to continue in the merchant marine**
**Solution: Maritime Incentives & Rewards Program (MIRP)**
This is a mature idea in the aviation sector - SkyMiles or AAdvantage - and has also been successfully deployed by major companies to support workers and increase staff morale. The MIRP offers a range of incentives to students and cadets for completing certain tasks, or being involved in certain activities. Implementing a reward system would positively impact job satisfaction and assist students to maintain a healthier work-life balance. This would not always be monetary, and could include time off for personal events; incentives to study and upskill (locally or abroad); access to discounted health care or insurance; unique travel experiences, or the ability to bring family members along on certain voyages.

## A Tribute to the United States Merchant Marine

The U.S. Merchant Marine's sacrifice, dedication and tenacity in securing U.S. victories has largely faded into the pages of history. During World War II, 243,000 U.S. Merchant Mariners served, and around 9,497 (3.9%) tragically lost their lives; the highest ratio of any service, at around 1 in 26. More than 1,800 U.S. Naval Armed Guard personnel were killed or declared Missing In Action while manning guns on merchant ships.

Merchant mariners faced bombings, kamikaze attacks, sabotage attempts, and torpedoes, and suffered through ice, wind and storms to deliver supplies to millions of troops. Their ships carried mostly fuel, ammunition and other supplies for the frontline, which made them frequent targets of enemy forces. In total, the Merchant Marine delivered nearly 270 billion long tons of cargo, or an average of 17 million pounds of cargo every hour. Over 1,554 merchant ships were sunk.

The U.S. Merchant Marine made an undeniable contribution to the Allied war effort. Yet, even though they faced the same dangers as U.S. Navy sailors, were not considered veterans when the war finished, and had to patiently wait over 40 years to receive veteran status (and access to benefits). In May 2020, Congress passed the Merchant Mariners of World War II Congressional Gold Medal Act to finally recognize the contribution of the U.S. Merchant Marine. This acknowledgement, for numerous acts of sacrifice and valor, took 80 years to be realized; another example of merchant mariners being frequently observed, but barely recognized.

This treatment largely continues to this day.

In the modern era, if merchant mariners serve in the same regions, and face the same dangers as U.S. Navy sailors, they are still not treated in the same way. As Captain John Konrad explains: “They do not get veterans benefits, special privileges, government healthcare or retirement pay. They have no special right to carry weapons on land or enter most military bases without special permission. They are commercials.” This treatment does not honor the sacrifice the U.S. Merchant Marine made during previous times of war, nor the sacrifices that serving members continue to make today.

The humbling example of the U.S. Merchant Marine evokes emotion and also provokes the thought that one of the most honoring responses to the past is to learn from it. This was echoed in the address by U.S. Merchant Mariner Dave Yoho, 94, of Vienna, Virginia during the Gold Medal presentation:

"And, so, when you're with others, say to them of what we did; urge them to read about us and find out about us. Greet us today if you can [and] then say to those, 'We gave up our yesterdays for your better tomorrow.'"

The U.S. Merchant Marine: Full Ahead to Victory!

*This page is intentionally left blank.*

# CHAPTER 4 | PARTNERSHIPS

*Coming together is the beginning. Keeping together is progress. Working together is success.*

- Henry Ford, American Industrialist and Business Magnate

*Our own land and our own flag cannot be replaced by any other land, or any other flag. But you can join with other nations... to accomplish something good for the world that you cannot accomplish alone.*

- Eleanor Roosevelt, First Lady of the United States (1933-1945), Diplomat and Activist

The United States has two unique mechanisms to influence global maritime affairs:

1. Firstly, the world's oceans have been purposefully secured through the operations of the United States Navy, assisted in various strategic settings by the U.S. Coast Guard. Protecting Freedom of Navigation (FON) and international shipping lanes encourages global trade, deters a range of potential threats, and fosters a healthy perception of the United States in the international community. While primarily hard projection, the activities of U.S. naval forces represent a clear demonstration of both intent *and* practical resolve; a potent reminder of capability, capacity and the willingness of U.S. operators to apply oversight in every corner of the globe.

2. Secondly, the United States maintains a commanding global position via a network of collaborators and allies. The wide-ranging benefits derived from collaboration must not be underestimated, nor should the highly attractive nature of the economic and political systems that underpin U.S. activities; namely capitalism and democracy. Building and sustaining a range of healthy partnerships is the most effective, geo-strategically advantageous, and economical way to solve a range of complicated problems, including: Securing elongated naval supply lines; improving mission-aligned asset utilization; extending geographic presence, and, increasing Fleet lethality and resilience.

The ocean is the exemplar of a universal and shared resource, and the United States cannot act alone to protect it. Concerted and bold action is required, at an international level, to better manage and preserve marine environments and wildlife. This action must be purposeful, intentional and similarly universal and shared; the combined efforts of many individuals - a 'Coalition of the Willing' - who recognize the importance of the world's oceans, and who actively work to minimize the harm from anything that operates in, moves upon and benefits from them.

## The International Maritime Organization (IMO)

One such coalition that exists at the international level is the United Nations International Maritime Organization (IMO). The 175 Members, and three associated Member States of the IMO have been tasked with coordinating, administering and overseeing ocean safety and security, and to implement global environmental standards. While progress has been made in the past, and the representative governance structure underpinning the IMO is sound, the organization, in its current form, is in danger of losing its way. The IMO needs to be decisive, formidable, and courageous, and avoid becoming insular, ineffective and dominated by vested interests.

To regain its standing, the IMO needs to be reformed around universally-shared values, fit for the modern era, and characterized by the urgent need to protect our planet. The direct result of this reformation should be, among other measurable developments, the implementation of noticeably stronger environmental standards. These new standards must be paired with appropriate enforcement mechanisms implemented via Port States (countries) and Flag States, so those deliberately flaunting the rules can be held to account. These new, enforced, standards will greatly reduce the impact of maritime activities on coastal areas and island nations, while reducing pollution, controlling vessel emissions and restoring affected marine biodiversity.

As the only nation with a globally-engaged Navy, and direct access to the resources of the USCG and related agencies, the U.S. is uniquely positioned to assist the IMO with responsible adherence and enforcement. The world is seeking this out, as evidenced in the following statement delivered to the U.S. House of Representatives some 20 years ago: *"When the U.S. delegation speaks in the chamber of the IMO, everybody gets quiet and looks at the U.S. delegation. That means they are looking to the U.S. for leadership. So, I think the Congress needs to back up the U.S.' presence in this most important arena."*

Enforcing the IMO's mandates requires the U.S. (along with other countries) to demonstrate fearless leadership on an international scale. Strong leadership and close collaboration will yield potent outcomes, in particular with critical environmental and sustainability initiatives. For example, the U.S. could define universal, measurable decarbonization standards, and be a vocal and provocative protector of shared marine environments. The U.S. can also champion the reduction of pollution, and be a recognized authority on the application of new technologies. Words must be firm, purpose-driven and practical, and followed by actions that are courageous, decisive and tangible.

Unfortunately, the U.S. cannot exercise a great degree of influence in its current guise. With diminished control over its own commercial fleet, and only 0.4% of the world's vessels under its own Flag, the U.S. is, for the most part, a passive participant on the global maritime stage. Partnerships flourish when all elements of influence are balanced, thus a refined approach is required: The U.S. must first clarify how it will interact with the IMO, and then demonstrate strong leadership by intentionally rebuilding U.S. commercial maritime assets and infrastructure. This refined approach will improve the effectiveness of the IMO, and also encourage other partnerships to be more efficient, disciplined, and actively uphold universally-agreed values.

Beyond the IMO, ocean-based maritime activities require the involvement of global partners who center their activities around monitoring, interdiction and upholding a rules-based order. Nefarious activity occurs frequently in the 60% of the ocean in 'Areas Beyond National Jurisdiction' where surveillance and enforcement are limited. Countering the impact of these activities has led to the formation of various security-postured alliances such as Five Eyes (FVEY), AUKUS, the Quad and NATO.

## Five-Eyes (FVEY)

The Five Eyes coalition of the U.S., Canada, UK, Australia, and New Zealand is one of the strongest security partnerships in the world today. The origin of FVEY can be traced back to the espionage and intelligence-sharing activities that occurred during World War II and the Cold War. FVEY reach and capabilities have grown significantly since then, which has attracted a certain degree of attention and controversy. Organizations from member states are mostly in the intelligence community, for example the U.S. participants are: The Central Intelligence Agency (CIA), Defense Intelligence Agency (DIA), Federal Bureau of Investigation (FBI), National Geospatial-Intelligence Agency (NGA) and National Security Agency (NSA). Each organization gathers data from multiple sources, including defense intelligence, signals intelligence (SIGNIT), human intelligence (HUMINT) and geospatial intelligence (GEOINT).

To counter potential threats to member states and their allies, the FVEY Five Country Ministerial (FCM) established a globally-applicable strategy called the 'Border of the Future:

2030'. This strategy seeks to minimize the risks associated with cross-border movement of people and cargo, through collaboration, information-sharing, counter-terrorism activity and the application of advanced technologies. These initiatives - when applied in a maritime context to the movement of containerized goods - resulted in discussions about the need for more comprehensive supply chain security procedures, and the deployment of intelligent shipping containers.

The U.S. can build on the work of the FCM by revising the current practices of Customs Trade Partnership Against Terrorism (CTPAT). Created in the wake of the terrorist attacks on September 11th 2001, CTPAT seeks to protect and strengthen foreign trade and U.S. border security. A voluntary public-private sector partnership program administered by Customs Border Protection (CBP), CTPAT would benefit from more direct alignment with the FCM Border of Future: 2030 Strategy, in particular, the adoption of new technologies like smart seals, IOT and satellite sensors, data analytics, AI, and Augmented Reality. Trials could be run within Member States, and then expanded more broadly with aligned trading partners. These enhanced partnerships will reduce the threats posed by terrorism, trafficking and sanctions violations, while improving tariff compliance, and significantly increasing the security of domestic and global supply chains.

## AUKUS

Another partnership that has garnered recent attention is AUKUS. Announced in September 2021, AUKUS is a trilateral security pact between Australia, the United Kingdom and the United States. The primary focus of AUKUS is to extend joint military capabilities, which separates it from the intelligence-gathering mandate of the FVEY community. Sharing highly-secretive and closely-guarded nuclear submarine propulsion technology forms the cornerstone of the AUKUS pact. Co-developing and deploying other military capabilities - advanced cyber mechanisms, artificial intelligence and autonomy, quantum technologies, undersea capabilities, hypersonic and counter-hypersonic, electronic warfare, innovation and information sharing - also feature in the agreement. The intention to deepen maritime ties between the two nations was clearly on display during the July 2023 commissioning of the Independence-class littoral combat ship *USS Canberra*, in Sydney.

AUKUS highlights the increased focus the U.S. has on the Indo-Pacific, and will have a significant impact on trade and military operations between participants and the regions they represent. Extending nuclear submarine capabilities to Australia is geostrategically significant, especially considering the need for strong partnerships in the Pacific, maintaining Freedom of Navigation in critical trade lanes and the possibility of escalating tensions in the South China Sea. The U.S. should seek similar collaborative deployment opportunities with other allies; this refines the processes involved, and builds confidence the U.S. will intentionally share solutions and technologies that bolster regional, and by extension, global security.

## The Quad

The Quadrilateral Security Dialogue (QSD) commonly known as the 'Quad', is a strategic security forum established between Australia, India, Japan and the United States. Initiated in 2007 by Japanese Prime Minister Shinzo Abe, the Quad plays a strategic role in U.S. global security policy by aligning U.S. planning and strategy with three geostrategically situated partners. The members of the Quad have been instrumental in redefining the "Asia-Pacific" region as the "Indo-Pacific", a move designed to purposefully solidify India's connection to the Pacific Ocean. Quad members are committed to furthering a shared vision of a "free and open Indo-Pacific" which includes a "rules based order for the East and South China Seas." Joint military and naval exercises have been conducted over the years, alongside detailed economic and diplomatic discussions. Some view the formation of the Quad as a direct counter to the rise of Chinese regional influence: China recently described the Quad as 'Asian NATO' and 'exclusionary', declaring the building of "small cliques and stoking bloc confrontation" as "the real threat to a peaceful, stable and cooperative maritime order."

The global economic and military influence of the Quad is significant: these four nations have a combined GDP of USD $36.7 trillion, representing 34.7% of Gross World Product (the combined Gross National Income of all countries in the world); combined armed forces total 3.2 million active duty personnel; and invest over USD $1.03 trillion a year on Defense-related activities.

I. Australia has been a close U.S. ally since World War I. Australia willingly signed the Australia, New Zealand and United States Security Treaty (ANZUS) in 1951, and the Australia-U.S. Free Trade Agreement (AUSFTA) in 2004. The two nations also hold regular intelligence and strategy - Defense and Foreign Affairs - discussions through the Australia-U.S. Ministerial (AUSMIN) forum. Bilateral trade of goods and services are valued at around USD $77 billion (2022), and to put one example of intentional co-investment in perspective: The AUKUS nuclear submarine program is valued at USD $268-368 billion, with some estimates placing the final investment at more than $500 billion over the life of the program.

II. Ties between the United States and Japan have strengthened considerably since the Second World War. Japan is the 4th largest purchaser (USD $80.1 billion in 2022) of U.S. goods in the world, with bilateral trade in goods and services valued at $280 billion. The geo-strategic importance of military collaboration between these two partners is clearly evident: Japan hosts the largest number of U.S. troops outside the United States (approx. 55,000 as of 2022), and assists with the management of the U.S. 7th Fleet - the largest forward-deployed U.S. fleet, with 50-70 vessels - in Yokosuka, Central Honshu.

III. India is also an important trading partner of the United States, almost doubling bilateral goods and services volume from 2014 to 2022, to USD $191 billion. As a sign of strengthening naval ties between the two nations, Indian officials recently brokered a Master Ship Repair Agreement (MSRA) between the U.S. Navy and an Indian shipyard located in Kattupalli, Tamil Nadu.

## NATO

Signed into existence on 4th April 1949, The North Atlantic Treaty Organization (NATO) is an intergovernmental military alliance between 31 member states; 29 are European, and 2 - the U.S. and Canada - are North American. The U.S. was one of 12 founding members. Finland joined in 2023, and Sweden is anticipated to be the 32nd NATO Member over the coming year.

NATO is one of the most significant security partnerships that exists in the world, and plays a unique role in maintaining global stability. NATO relies on collective security: Each independent member state has committed to defend each other against attacks by third parties. The combined militaries of NATO members include around 3.5 million soldiers and personnel, and their combined military spending constitutes over half of the global total. Each member state has committed at least 2% of their GDP to fund NATO operations by 2024. The U.S. is the exception, due to the disproportionate size of the U.S. economy, and the outsized contribution the U.S. makes to NATO's military, missile, intelligence, surveillance and maritime capabilities.

Understanding the geostrategic positioning of NATO member states becomes immediately apparent if a world globe is viewed from the top down i.e., with member countries arranged around the Arctic in the center. Viewing the world from this angle not only highlights why the Arctic is now a highly contested domain, it also provides a visual representation of why Russia, and other aligned powers, are opposed to NATO activities - Member countries cover about half of the upper reaches of the northern hemisphere, veritably surrounding Russia who occupies the rest.

The war in Ukraine has reignited the need for NATO's existence, and highlighted why purposeful intentionality is required among values-aligned partners. Most NATO countries have been involved in military exercises since the conflict began, and also contributed to the war effort. The U.S. is a noticeable stand out, directing over $75 billion in assistance to Ukraine thus far, in the form of humanitarian and financial aid, weapons, training and equipment. This is around twice as much as the next highest contributor (European Union institutions) who have committed around $33 billion.

The U.S. contribution to Ukraine has been extensive: Infantry equipment including Stinger, TOW and Javelin missile systems, body armor, protective equipment and night-vision goggles; medical supplies, cold weather gear, generators and spare parts; artillery and mortars with ammunition; tanks and armored carriers, including Armored Personnel Carriers (APC) and Mine-Resistant Ambush Protected (MRAP) tactical vehicles; ground support vehicles like Humvees, trucks and logistics support vehicles; air defense systems; air-to-ground missiles; manned aircraft; explosive and surveillance drones; coastal defense systems; radar and communications system including jamming equipment, and commercial satellite imagery services.

The U.S. commitment to Ukraine is an embodiment of the U.S.' ongoing commitment to NATO. In any given year, the U.S. plays a pivotal role in protecting the interests of member countries, by supplying equipment, intelligence data, expertise, training and leadership. Member countries regularly work alongside the United States Navy in the critically important work of maintaining Freedom of Navigation of the seas; the USN easily supplies the most assets, time and resources to these endeavors of any NATO country.

NATO can be used as a great lever for good in the world, and while the U.S. is unwavering in its support of NATO, an optimization of the existing relationship may lead to a range of previously undiscovered, and mutually beneficial outcomes. Five bold initiatives, structured around the five previously communicated Principles are explored in the pages that follow:

I. National Security - NATO Support Fleet (NSF)
II. Economic Security - NATO Maritime Investment Accelerator (NMIA)
III. Energy Security - NATO Future Fuels Institute (NFFI)
IV. Climate Security - NATO Climate Technologies Lab (NCTL)
V. Workforce Security - NATO Merchant Marine Academy (NMMA)

## I. National Security - NATO Support Fleet (NSF)

Freedom of Navigation (*mare liberum*) directly impacts all nations engaged in international trade. If cargo and commodities move freely across the ocean, a plethora of profitable activities can be continuously pursued. These activities increase a nation's influence and prosperity, and directly contribute to the health and welfare of a nation's citizenry. When access is withdrawn, major economic disruptions can occur, that subsequently give rise to political and social instability, and eventually war.

Global cooperation is required if Freedom of Navigation is to prevail. The majority of the work involved in protecting *mare liberum* is completed by the United States Navy, supported by the U.S. Merchant Marine and U.S. Coast Guard. The act of protecting such freedoms is noble, but comes at a great cost to U.S. taxpayers, citizens, administrators and serving personnel. If a creative approach is taken, NATO can play an expanded part in maintaining a rules-based-order on the high seas, while bolstering U.S. commercial maritime interests at the same time. A mechanism to achieve these objectives is through the NATO Support Fleet (NSF).

The NATO Support Fleet gathers commercial vessels from Treaty countries into a replenishment and supply ready-reserve force. Modern, fit-for-purpose ships and appropriately trained crews, would commonly ply cargo and commodity trades, then be available to support NATO military operations if required. ‘Tyranny of distance’ is overcome by readily available, geostrategically positioned assets. This applies equally to naval support and resupply in wartime, as it does to mutually profitable commercial trade during times of peace.

Vessel enrolment, the coordination of fleet activities, documentation submissions, payments processing, the transfer of asset control, and status updates could all be handled through a secure, cloud-based platform. Auxiliary services like satellite communications, monitoring, ordering, or the distribution of training materials, could also be hosted online as well. On the U.S. side, the NSF would operate in a similar fashion as the Maritime Security Program, and be managed by MARAD in partnership with Military Sealift Command, TRANSCOM and U.S. Fleet Forces. European operations would work alongside the NATO Support and Procurement Agency (NSPA) in collaboration with Movement Coordination Centre Europe (MCCE).

The NATO Support Fleet provides numerous benefits to participating members:

1. New global standards will be set for asset and ownership transparency, and ensure registered vessels are maintained at a superior level. This increase in the general level of responsibility will be a catalyst to clean up the rest of the international fleet.
2. Newly formed cooperative agreements define what occurs in the event of conflict, moving asset engagement plans from incidental, to intentional. This structure gives increased certainty to vessel operators, and the chance to plan and de-risk activities around a range of scenarios.
3. Specific pathways would be developed for NATO merchant mariners in training and simulation exercises, and used as a template for other nations across the world.
4. Economic and efficiency incentives would be extended to all participating members. For example: On top of incentives for stand-by, NSF ships might receive preferential access to NATO-hosted ports.
5. Finally, specific insurance benefits, and financial and investment opportunities (e.g., positioning NSF assets

to be attractive to sovereign wealth funds) would be explored in the open market, for the benefit of all participating members.

A NATO Support Fleet would provide noticeable and reciprocal benefits to the United States:

1. First and foremost, the U.S. gains access to a geostrategically positioned commercial support Fleet. This is particularly important for any prolonged conflict - for example in the Pacific - that requires long-range replenishment and supply. Instead of relying only on U.S.-flagged vessels, the U.S. can call on a variety of allied-owned, securely vetted assets to assist with all aspects of maritime operations. Note: This feature is a strong complement to the Navy's planned adoption of Distributed Maritime Operations (DMO).
2. By using allies and known providers the NSF can meet surge and charter needs in a more controllable manner. The NSF fleet could be used preferentially for any international trade activities the U.S. was not able to complete using U.S.-flagged vessels. This extends the options available to U.S. logistics planners as they manage sensitive cargo movements across the world.
3. A carefully chosen NSF fleet blend will be directly aligned to Military Sealift requirements, which reduces risks and operating costs, while providing access to modern, mission-aligned tonnage.
4. The NSF reduces Flag of Convenience (FOC) dependency: Flag States control a significant number of the worlds' vessels, with around half of the world's merchant ships in open registries. This poses serious complications for NATO and other alliances, and directly impacts vessels and their associated mariners. Building the capability of the NSF will naturally lead to other positive initiatives - e.g., a 2nd U.S. Flag in

commercial trade, and the Economic Security Program (ESP) - by modernizing existing efforts around responsible and transparent shipping practices.
5. By providing billets and training opportunities on new (e.g., deep-sea) vessels, the NSF will assist to address the U.S. mariner skills shortage in a way that also bolsters national security.

In summary, the NSF represents a highly effective way for the U.S. to gain access to fit-for-purpose, strategically placed, tonnage (and personnel) in an agreeably short amount of time. The NSF also positively impacts U.S. commercial maritime operations, and increases Fleet sustainability, agility, and survivability, in peace-time operations or during times of war.

## II. Economic Security - NATO Maritime Investment Accelerator (NMIA)

Norway's Sovereign Wealth Fund (Norges Bank Investment Management) is the largest in the world, with over $1.2 trillion dollars under management. Built around the nation's formidable oil and gas reserves, the Fund has grown to such an extent that it now holds 1.5% of all shares within listed companies, globally; some 9,000 companies in 70 countries. The Fund recently announced it is seeking to become "the world's leading investor in terms of how Climate risk is managed" and has set an ambitious net zero emissions target, for all portfolio companies, by 2050.

The mere presence of Norway's SWF, with a climate-aligned mandate and mission, should be welcome news to the maritime community. Shipping is the 6th largest emitter in the world, and primed for a transition to new standards that lower emissions, decrease pollution, and reduce the impact on the environment. Sizeable investments will be required if the aspirational goals of the IMO and private industry leaders are to be fully realized. A proportion of investment capital will come from smaller financial institutions, however the larger Funds - including Sovereign Wealth, and Pension Funds - should also be pursued, with the express aim of deploying patient capital to accelerate decarbonization and reduce greenhouse gas emissions.

What greater legacy-defining opportunity exists, than to invest heavily into a critical segment, to assist it achieve net zero, while making a commercial return in the process? The maritime domain presents such a unique opportunity, and needs to capitalize on this in order to attract larger investments. One mechanism to achieve these aims is through the creation of the NATO Maritime Investment Accelerator (NMIA).

The NATO Maritime Investment Accelerator purposefully seeks to fund maritime startups who are:

1. Mission-aligned: Investments will be prioritized for those entities who demonstrate clear knowledge of the goals of NATO and the urgency required to reduce the environmental impact of maritime activities. Successful candidates must be able to create specific solutions that address the areas of greatest concern, and that enhance national, economic, energy, climate or workforce security.
2. Commercially viable: Have domain knowledge and build iteratively for Product Market Fit. Business models must be designed around sustainable profitability, producing solutions or services based on clearly assessable value creation for customers, industries and investors.
3. Future-focused: Ability to intelligently scale; talent pipeline management; materials acquisition; lifecycle management (of staff, product and related company activities) have all been factored into the planning and

execution process, to maintain business continuity well into the future.

Once suitable candidates have been identified, required documentation - business plans, product descriptions, governance structures and investment paperwork like information memorandums - will be circulated to all participating NMIA members. After a period of assessment by a suitably appointed Board, investments are made by each applicable member, with oversight, coaching and partnerships provided to successful applicants. Applicants will also receive access to the combined resources of NATO Member States, and be able to use suitably defined 'sandboxes' for experimentation and development.

Note: The Defense Innovation Accelerator for the North Atlantic (DIANA) challenge program, launched in June 2023, might be used to provide access to deep tech, defense and dual-use partners and innovators. It is unfortunate to note, at time of writing, that maritime interests are not represented to any large extent in the DIANA program. Of the 10 accelerator sites, 22 participating countries and 90 test centers, only two (2) sites - one in Spain, and one in Italy - are pursuing maritime activities.

## III. Energy & Food Security - NATO Future Fuels Institute (NFFI)

*"In addition, the war [in Ukraine] again elevated energy supply to a matter of national security, particularly in the EU. It has led to a renewed commitment to accelerate decarbonization which will have a lasting impact on coal and oil shipments."* - Niels Rasmussen, Chief Shipping Analyst, BIMCO

The conflict in Ukraine has highlighted the need to secure a consistent supply of energy to industries, businesses and citizens; it has also disrupted the supply of food, however this has been addressed in previous chapters.

The transportation of energy across large distances, or through hostile territories, has been particularly fraught; a pertinent example being the sabotage of Nord Stream pipelines NS1 and NS2 in the Baltic Sea, during September 2022. Disruption to the supply of energy leads to economic instability, a reduction in output and production capacity, an escalation in prices, and eventually, social unrest. As Niels Rasmussen states *"energy supply [has become] a matter of national security."*

Issues facing stationary energy pipelines and land-based infrastructure are compounded in the maritime domain. Maritime assets are dynamically positioned, and naval fleets may be fighting halfway around the world; energy supply lines are likely to require protection in contested environments. NATO must have access to both hydrocarbon and non-hydrocarbon equivalents, and in a timely manner. Storage, access and distribution must be considered, alongside the need for access to the correct (and sustainably available) energy blend. To that end, NATO must devise strategies to source and secure energy at rest, and in transit.

One way to enhance maritime Energy Security is through the formation of the NATO Future Fuels Institute. The NATO Future Fuels Institute (NFFI) seeks to develop and produce new fuel types that are profitably used by commercial operators and NATO member naval fleets. This includes:

1. Electrification / battery-powered: Including local waterway and long-range, ocean-going vessels.
2. Increase the production of green ammonia, methanol, and other fuels from renewable sources.

3. Advance the development of commercial nuclear vessels, in close collaboration with the U.S. Navy.
4. Enhance transition fuel efficiency e.g., with combustion catalysts, and reducing LNG methane slip
5. Innovate with complementary renewables: Wind, solar, hydro, and tidal power systems.

The Institute will build collaborative partnerships with ship management organizations, so that production and use are closely aligned. These partnerships will be built in a commercially sustainable, and mutually beneficial way. Secure storage of developed fuels, within actively patrolled regions, and in designated locations across the world, will ensure the correct energy blend is available to the NATO Support Fleet and NATO naval vessels at all times. Energy storage facilities would operate in a similar fashion to NATO's highly successful Multinational Ammunition Warehousing Initiative (MAWI). Secure distribution through a network of geostrategic providers, will extend the ability of NATO forces to persist within contested areas.

The NATO Future Fuels Institute will also work with all stakeholders to develop new standards to measure and reduce emissions from a range of maritime activities. This will include sensors and other hardware that can detect and prevent fuel spills and leaks, alongside energy usage reporting mechanisms to allow governments and other institutions to accurately calculate energy usage. Through the pioneering work of NFFI, NATO can lead the world in the creation and distribution of alternate and sustainable fuels, which will enhance NATO's Energy Security, and also greatly benefit the planet.

## IV. Climate Security - NATO Climate Technologies Lab (NCTL)

Global collaboration is required for the creation of unified, measurable decarbonization goals along with the introduction of tangibly impactful environmental standards. This is particularly true for maritime activities. In many areas, the desire for change is consumer led: Pressure is being applied to corporations, producers and brands by vocal individuals and concerned lobby groups. This is reflected in the rise of 'shareholder activism' that asks corporate decision-makers to carefully consider sustainability, Environmental, Social and Governance (ESG) targets and emission-reduction schemes. These non-financial factors are increasingly being applied by investors, to analyze material risks and also identify potential growth opportunities.

The U.S. and NATO can work alongside the IMO and industry partners to reduce pollution, promote efficient and sustainable shipping practices, and positively contribute to climate-related initiatives. Given the state of the planet, and the impact our collective actions have on the ocean, this work must be completed with urgency and purpose. One mechanism to achieve these aims is through the creation of the NATO Climate Technologies Lab (NCTL).

The NATO Climate Technologies Lab specifically focuses on the development and distribution of technologies that reduce the climate-impacting effects of maritime activities. The NCTL will work alongside the NATO Future Fuels Institute, NATO Innovation Hub and aligned partners to develop new forms of emission-reduced propulsive power, while exploring other initiatives designed to meet known climate goals:

1. Develop comprehensive testing and measurement mechanisms for ocean temperature and acidification, for

example through an open, calibrated network of buoys or autonomous vessels

2. Build out new capabilities that leverage the power of new Low-Earth Orbit satellite sensors to track pollution, illegal discharges, spills, leaks, algal blooms and unreported emissions

3. Work with NOAA, NASA, EUMETSTAT (the European Organization for the Exploitation of Meteorological Satellites) and industry partners on intelligent weather mapping and related navigation aids to assist with route planning, and therefore improve overall vessel efficiency.

4. Manage technologies to monitor newly devised 'green maritime corridors' between NATO member states: Designated trade lanes that incentivize shipowners to reduce the environmental impact of their vessels, in exchange for preferential port access and faster border processing.

These activities will be bolstered by the development of a suite of complementary technologies:

1. Augmented Reality (AR) overlays digital walkthroughs and procedures over real-world assets. This allows new methods, concepts and systems to be learned in a more rapid fashion.

2. Artificial Intelligence synthesizes captured data, and generates scalable, accurate simulations. Generative AI, along with Large-Language Models and Natural Language Processing assists with the creation of media and content including multilingual manuals for research and training.

3. IoT monitoring and reporting sensors are intentionally designed to be deployed en masse in a commercial capacity, and then used in NATO operations if required.

The NCTL is a one-of-a-kind, globally-accessible and mission-aligned, climate-focused incubator. Through a well-structured and highly iterative process, newly developed technologies will clearly demonstrate NATO's innovative and future-focused desire to solve critical environmental issues.

### V. Workforce Security - NATO Merchant Marine Academy (NMMA)

The global pipeline for mariners is shrinking. As mentioned in 'Workforce Security' the world is facing a stark mathematical shortfall of around 96,000 mariners by 2026. This has not been assisted by the extremely poor treatment of seafarers - in many instances, bordering on incarceration - over the peak years of COVID. Many maritime workers were stuck on board many months beyond the end of their contracts, and suffered reduced contact with family and the outside world. A lack of access to appropriate medical support and mental health services led to an increase in incidents of self-harm and suicide.

Compounding these pressing concerns is the nature of Flag State allegiances. This should be of particular concern NATO as certain Flag State (particularly Flag of Convenience) operators are aligned to nation states or regimes opposed to NATO's influence and activities. The disconnect between the Flag State operator, the vessel and crew, and what NATO requires, will become quickly apparent during a time of conflict; by then it will be too late to realign interests and regain control of the needed assets to achieve the objectives of any given NATO maritime mission.

NATO can solve these complex problems - and champion the cause of seafarers - through the creation of the NATO Merchant Marine Academy (NMMA). The NMMA program is designed to attract mariners from partner countries, who are then specifically trained in a way that is aligned to NATO's global interests. To increase mariner proficiency, and realize academic and research goals, the NMMA would partner with training institutions like the U.S. Merchant Marine Academy (USMMA), the World Maritime University in Malmo, Sweden, and the Maritime Academy and Training Center Aboa Mare, in Finland.

Through the pioneering work of the NMMA, the following benefits would be realized:

1. Seafarers would be given the chance to train across multiple vessel types - from commercial RORO, tanker or Ultra Large Container Vessel (ULCV), to a range of other NATO Support Fleet vessels - that may not be available in their own country.

2. NATO mariners would train with mariners from other member nations. This brings together a melting pot of cultural backgrounds that will galvanize a collaborative spirit and hone a range of unique skills

3. Diversity will naturally increase, as a wider range of candidates - of all ages, genders, and levels of expertise - come together to participate in training opportunities.

4. Cross-pollinated skill sharing will lead to the development of new processes, methods and technologies - e.g., with AR and VR, AI and IoT - that may never have existed before

5. Opportunities to travel and interact with new colleagues and vessel types will increase workforce satisfaction and retention. Increased workforce satisfaction will have a positive impact on mental health, likely lead to a reduction in incidents of Sexual Assault and Sexual Harassment (SASH) and encourage new applicants to consider a long-term career at sea.

A fully-functioning NMMA will bolster each member country's Merchant Marine capabilities and, by increasing training efficiency and decreasing costs, allow funds to be spent more effectively. This 'rising tide' lifts all boats, and will lead to more mariners with practical skills and International Convention on Standards of Training, Certification and Watchkeeping (STCW) certifications available to NATO and U.S. partners.

The United States will 'go far' if it 'goes together' with other values-aligned strategic collaborators. The importance of advancing these activities across multiple domains, through robust and proactive international partnerships, cannot be overstated. Strong international alliances will also facilitate a more rapid increase in domestic output and production, which will lead to a diverse array of new opportunities for U.S. workers, the invention of new technologies and sustainability solutions, and the re-establishment of the United States as an international maritime leader. Healthy partnerships directly contribute to global stability and prosperity, and will ultimately allow the U.S. to achieve Mahan's vision of maritime supremacy, by leading *"a transnational consortium, acting in defense of a multinational system of free trade"*.

*This page is intentionally left blank.*

# CHAPTER 5 | PROTECTIONISM & PRACTICALITIES

*Developing protectionism regarding trade and our reluctance to place fiscal policy on a more sustainable path are threatening what may well be our most valued policy asset: the increased flexibility of our economy, which has fostered our extraordinary resilience to shocks.*

- Alan Greenspan, Former Chair of U.S. Federal Reserve (2005)

## A. The Merchant Marine Act of 1920

The most significant piece of maritime legislation in the history of the United States was signed into law on June 5, 1920 by President Woodrow Wilson. The Merchant Marine Act of 1920 was penned against the turbulent backdrop of World War 1. The United States, along with allied nations, had lost many ships and lives at sea; a tragic example being the May 1915 sinking of the passenger liner RMS Lusitania off the coast of Ireland, killing 1,198 people, including 128 Americans. The U.S. merchant marine, responsible for sustaining the war effort, and carrying trading goods to markets overseas, endured noticeably heavy losses. By the end of the war, German U-boats had sunk 10 vessels off North Carolina alone, and 200 American ships in total. The frequency of these attacks on merchant vessels were regarded by many as the primary catalyst for the U.S. entering the War.

When introducing the Merchant Marine Act of 1920 to Congress, Senator Wesley Jones stated the intention of the Act was *"to lay the foundation of a policy that will build up and maintain an adequate American merchant marine in competition with the shipping of the world"*. These noble intentions continued in the legislation's preamble, through the explicit articulation of two strategic goals: The Act was necessary to the U.S. *"for national defense and for the proper growth of its foreign and domestic commerce."* This emphasis was particularly important in light of events at that time: U.S. reliance on foreign vessels for trade and national security posed an extreme and unmanageable risk to sovereign stability, especially during times of war.

To achieve the Act's intended outcomes, the United States would need access to *"a merchant marine of the best equipped and most suitable types of vessels sufficient to carry the greater portion of its commerce and serve as a naval or military auxiliary in time of war or national emergency"*. Furthermore, the vessels should *"ultimately to be owned and operated privately by citizens of the United States"*. Finally, to drive home the criticality of such an important piece of legislation, that preamble *"declared [it] be the policy of the United States to do whatever may be necessary to develop and encourage the maintenance of such a merchant marine"* and tasked the administrators upholding these provisions, and when writing laws or regulations to *"keep always in view this purpose and object as the primary end to be attained"*.

Subsequent updates to the Merchant Marine Act further strengthened these desired outcomes. A major revision occurred in 1936 - championed by Representative Schyler O. Bland, of Virginia - adding weight to provisions for ships to be U.S. owned, built and crewed. One stipulation for example, was that by 1938, 90% of all crews aboard U.S.-flagged vessels had to be U.S. citizens. In 1940, Congress expanded a part of the Act to include towing vessels. Stipulation in the 1936 revisions also led to the creation of the United States Maritime Commission, the early precursor to the U.S. Federal Maritime Commission (FMC), and U.S. Maritime Administration (MARAD).

The revisions to cargo preferences in 1954 required U.S.-Flag vessel participation in the carriage of United States Government impelled cargoes; 50% government-impelled cargoes (by volume) must be transported in privately owned U.S.-registered vessels, but "only to the extent that such vessels are reasonably available at fair and reasonable rates". In 1958, a previous exemption that excluded Alaska, was reversed to include Alaska that had recently become a State. In 1988, the Act was amended so that qualified vessels had to be used for the transport of certain waste materials from dredging and municipal activities. Revisions in 2006, included recodifying the Act into the U.S. Code.

To summarize, the Merchant Marine Act of 1920, and subsequent revisions, were proposed to expand the U.S. merchant marine, which in turn would:

1. Increase U.S. international competitiveness,
2. Improve national security and defense outcomes,
3. Encourage the growth of domestic and foreign trade,
4. Use the best equipped blend of vessels for commerce and military support, and,
5. Encourage U.S. private ownership and operation of vessels and associated crews

These sound beneficial and admirable, and could well feature on any nation's list of non-negotiable maritime priorities. And if intention matched reality, there should be noticeable improvements within those sectors that benefited from the Act's protections. This was strikingly apparent from the time the Act was written, through to the 1950's. Encouraged by the Merchant Marine Act's vision, and boosted by the widespread industrial productivity gains associated with World War II, the U.S. merchant marine flourished. Vessel construction speed and the number of serving personnel dramatically increased, assisted by innovations from pioneering experiments in manufacturing and supply chain automation. One pertinent statistic: The U.S. went from commanding 5% of the worlds' tonnage in the 1920's, to over 32% of a much larger global tonnage pool, only thirty years later.

The U.S. merchant marine's rise was as velocious as its fall. From 32% of global tonnage in 1950, to 5% in the 1980's, to half a percent today. From a bustling armada of vessels and serving personnel spread out across the world, to an anemic commercial fleet and shrinking workforce, mostly engaged in domestic trade. Such a precipitous decline over the last 70 years leads to the inevitable question: What happened? The Merchant Marine Act and other policies along the way were explicitly designed to boost maritime activity and output, so why had the opposite happened?

Fierce debate rages about the answers to these questions. Numerous books, articles and parody YouTube videos have been released, arguing for and against the intentions of the Merchant Marine Act, and what has occurred since it was originally written. Critics vocally oppose the Act's competition-eroding principles, pointing to, as one of many examples, the rules for cabotage in Section 27 (46 USC. 883). Section 27 expressly forbids the transportation of cargoes between U.S. ports unless the ship is managed by a U.S. company; owned by U.S. citizens; crewed by U.S. mariners; and built and registered in the United States. Such a provision is decried as unrealistic, abnormally protectionist and is the cause of increased shipping costs, for Americans living in Puerto Rico, Guam, Alaska and Hawaii.

Supporters say the Act protects a critical industry, and ensures the U.S. can build, use and maintain the correct blend of vessels for trade and military sealift activities. This in turn, reduces the reliance on foreign companies, mariners, and Flags of Convenience who are not always aligned with U.S. interests; which is of particular concern during times of war. Proponents also point out that U.S.-owned ships are subject to high American taxes, which benefits the local economy, and to stricter labor laws that guarantee worker safety. Adherence to environmental codes and consumer protection laws mean U.S. ships are less likely to pollute, or engage in illegal behavior, when compared to those registered elsewhere.

There is a veritable tsunami of other viewpoints, for and against. A detailed analysis will not be attempted here, and for one very strategic reason: It would be a complete waste of time.

An inordinate amount of energy has been futilely expended building overly elaborate arguments about why certain policies, or certain points of view, are undeniably correct or incorrect. Blame has been cast, plots uncovered, victims identified, and villains ousted. Corporations have enjoyed either glorification or vilification, depending on perceived motivation. Patriotic allegiances have been qualified or questioned. And, vested interests either excoriated for skewing the narrative for exclusive gain, or exonerated as champions of a righteous cause. The arguments have changed little over time. Many of the accusatory phrases, on both sides, are exactly the same. Confusion reigns and paralyzing indecision has followed.

The Merchant Marine Act of 1920 is not the problem. Arguing about the Merchant Marine Act is. If equal time was applied to pursuing productive outcomes, as has been dedicated to arguing why they have not eventuated, the U.S. would now be an undeniable leader in commercial maritime affairs. Arguments may deceive, but statistics don't lie: While the debates rage, the numbers - available merchant vessels, mariners, skills and capacity - continue to decline, and have done so for the last 70 years. A new approach is required. Squabbling about supposedly restrictive policies should be set aside, and all stakeholders should instead fixate on solving real problems that demonstrate measurable progress. These efforts must be overtly collaborative, perceivably transparent, intensely practical, and decidedly bold.

Where to start?

When considering this question, some commentators rush to declare the Merchant Marine Act devoid of value and call for its immediate repeal. This is not the right approach. Replacing the Act will not lead to desirable outcomes, and would likely make an already tenuous situation worse. Surviving the last 100+ years with little alteration, the Act has successfully fended off concerted attacks from a range of think-tanks, industry lobbyists, and high-profile government officials. And while debatable as to what degree, the Act has certainly played a role in protecting the commercial maritime activities still under U.S. control; the domestic market, for example, may well be even worse off if it wasn't for the protections the Act offers.

The Merchant Marine Act of 1920 does not need to be replaced. But it does need to be *refined.*

The Act requires adaptation to a modern context, while preserving the most profitable foundational principles contained within. Amendments must maintain national security protections, and encourage the development of a U.S.-controlled international commercial fleet. Attention must be given to increasing external trade volumes along with an expansion of internal maritime capacity. This will naturally lead to increased opportunities for U.S. mariners, and investment into the sector from U.S. capital markets. This clarified Act, while primarily domestic in focus, exists within a global context: Allies and trading partners may be evaluated for the supply of specialized components, materials or services, appropriately constrained within mechanisms that control undue foreign ownership and influence. Refining the Act is one way to tangibly elevate the activities of the maritime domain in public and political discourse, but what else can be done?

One additional, bold and purposeful step must be taken: The formulation, ratification, and implementation of a comprehensive, fit-for-purpose U.S. Maritime Strategy.

## B. The Need for a New U.S. Maritime Strategy

Before we begin: Former U.S. Navy surface warfare officer and the Chair of Maritime Strategy at the Naval War College, James R. Holmes reminds us that the U.S. has previously formulated *many* maritime strategies: "U.S. Navy and Marine Corps leaders published a '*Maritime Strategy*' in the pages of Proceedings in 1986, unveiled a post–Cold War successor titled '*A Cooperative Strategy for 21st Century Seapower*' in 2007, and refreshed the '*Cooperative Strategy*' in 2015. Most recently, Sea Service leaders issued a tri-service maritime strategy, '*Advantage at Sea*', in 2020, adding the Coast Guard to the mix for the first time. And that list overlooks 1990s' strategic directives bearing such titles as '*From the Sea*' and '*Forward... from the Sea'*."

As will be contended over the following pages, a newly devised U.S. Maritime Strategy must incorporate the key learnings from the past, purposefully consider the context of the present and also factor in how maritime endeavors will evolve and change in the future.

## I. A Holistic U.S. Maritime Strategy - Not Just a Naval Strategy

First, and foremost, this must (definitively) be a *Maritime* strategy, not just a Naval strategy. Beyond semantics, a maritime strategy includes defense and national security, but widens the scope to include geopolitical, geostrategic, economic, energy, climate and workforce considerations. A clear articulation of the unique and co-dependent relationship between the military and commercial sectors is critical. As Mahan and other commentators have written, diplomacy, trade, and a highly productive industrial base are crucial to facilitate, and fund naval activities; the former generates the prosperity that sustains the latter.

Near-peer competitors know the power of this 'virtuous cycle' very well, as evidenced by their intentional expansion of global fleets, assets and serving personnel. The U.S. can evolve its current approach in a similar fashion, by carefully balancing resources - people, time and money - between Defense activities and the U.S. commercial sector and U.S. Merchant Marine. Thus, a new U.S. Maritime Strategy should be viewed as a complement to existing Naval strategies, and not as a mechanism to bolster one, to the detriment of the other.

This Strategy will inform and coordinate the pursuits of a diverse array of stakeholders - private enterprise, Government agencies, global alliances and otherwise - and include provisions for the interactions that take place, and the opportunities that exist at an international level. In developing a holistic National Maritime Strategy, it should be clear that this strategy should not be constrained by any current vested interests or industry incumbents, but look toward a future competitive state of the country.

## II. Present-day Realities

Along with previously stated considerations, a comprehensive U.S. Maritime Strategy must take into account present day realities, including:

- Globalization's impact on manufacturing, production, consumption and wealth distribution
- The presence and influence of Flags of Convenience on vessel ownership and crew management
- How the ultra-concentration of vessel-building capacity, ownership and distribution within specific

geographic regions affects global commerce and the supply of critical materials

- The colossal scale and volumes present in international containerized and commodity trades
- How military operations have evolved due to longer-range weapons, autonomy, drones and AI
- Specific dependencies required by a resilient industrial base to sustain these military operations
- Reduced workforce participation, and unavailability of talent for the maritime (and naval) sectors
- The impact of extreme labor force mobility within and between sectors, and across the world
- Complications posed by a changing climate, volatile weather and temperature fluctuations
- The resources required for environmentally sustainable services, products and practices
- How internet connectivity via subsea cables - providing high-speed access to data across the globe - and satellites - that provide tracking, analysis and sensing - alter human interactions
- An acknowledgement that over-the-horizon and low-earth orbit technologies have fundamentally shifted the dynamics of global supply chain visibility and also warfare, and
- An understanding of the beleaguered position of the IMO and other international agencies, who are stymied when attempting to create effective policies, and do not possess direct mechanisms for enforcement.

These variables were of little concern to the authors of the original Merchant Marine Act of 1920, as most would not be discovered, invented, or debated for many years to come. It is also understandable why the writers of subsequent revisions may have overlooked similar factors: Fast-paced technological change, the convergence of military and commercial endeavors, and globalization's effect on the integration of previously tangential disciplines, have made the global maritime domain complicated to navigate, regulate and manage. This is exactly why a refined Merchant Marine Act along with an all-encompassing U.S. Maritime Strategy is entirely necessary: To move the United States beyond the insular protectionist practices of the past, to a commanding position that capitalizes on future opportunities.

## III. Practical Examples

To ground these aspirations in reality, a few practical examples, building on previous sentiment and structured around the five Principles are as follows:

1. **National Security -** A refined Merchant Marine Act, and newly drafted U.S. Maritime Strategy would provide a framework for national security decision-making. For example, a recent proposal to locally build a naval frigate at an initial cost of over $1 billion, would be assessed alongside the potential to project soft power using commercial vessels instead. Assuming a premium to international prices, around ten Ultra Large Container Vessels (ULCV) could be built in the United States for the same billion dollar price tag. A U.S. Maritime Strategy would clarify if the benefits of building ten ships outweighed the functionality and security provided by one. A refined Act, and U.S. Maritime Strategy would detail provisions and incentives to encourage U.S. shipbuilders to complete the most beneficial option; with either choice bolstering local capabilities, and reducing the dependency on foreign-built ships for national security-related activities.

2. **Economic Security -** The benefits of higher levels of U.S. involvement in international maritime trade should feature in the refined Merchant Marine Act and U.S. Maritime Strategy. There are incredible opportunities available to provide services to the U.S. export market, and to carry traded goods around the world. Those that say this is impossible - due to the increased costs of U.S. labor and shipbuilding - need only look at near-peer competitors who have successfully overcome these barriers and are regularly engaged in these endeavors. If prioritized at a national level and given the necessary support, the U.S. can build a flexible, modern and modular fleet of competitive vessels, and use the profitable activities of these ships to fund a range of other nation-building initiatives. A Blue Economy plan must also be provided for in the strategy.

3. **Energy & Food Security -** When the Merchant Marine Act was originally written, the primary sources for marine propulsion were wind, steam / steam turbines (using wood, coal and fuel oil), and from the early 20th century, diesel electric. It is telling that a predominance of text within the Act refers to 'steamship' lines, in reference to the most popular propulsive source of that time. A refined Act, and U.S. Maritime Strategy would provide detailed and structured guidance about an array of new fuel types, including LNG, low-sulfur fuel oils, battery-powered (electric), and nuclear.

   Commentary around the transportation and use of these fuels in a secure and sustainable manner - must be included in these regulatory frameworks, given the collective desire to reduce shipping's impact on the environment. An increase in efficient, U.S. built ships entering the international market, will also greatly improve international Food Security. Large, U.S.-owned, U.S.-crewed container ships and bulk carriers could deliver food aid and provide humanitarian support, while directly benefiting from the mission-aligned protection of the U.S. Navy and Coast Guard.

4. **Climate Security** - The concepts associated with environmental impact did not feature heavily in the wording of the Merchant Marine Act of 1920, or subsequent revisions. Commonly used terms such as ‘pollution’, ‘emissions’, ‘sustainability’ or the ‘environment’ do not appear at all. One amendment included provisions for the movement of hazardous cargo, however could not be construed as a comprehensive strategy to address broader issues like climate change, or the dangers posed by toxic greenhouse gasses. A refined Act, along with a boldly worded U.S. Maritime Strategy will outline the urgent action required to minimize the impact of maritime activities on shared marine areas, and provide a framework on how to balance the oft-competing needs of economic growth and environmental sustainability.

5. **Workforce Security** - Trade Unions and organized labor groups have become powerful voices in national politics, and in many major shipbuilding and port cities around the world. The rise and fall of industrial areas like Glasgow, the London Docklands, Meatpacking District of New York, and the Ports of San Francisco and Oakland, testify to the influence that organized labor can have on certain regions. In some instances, the voices of organized labor prevented the deployment of efficiency-deriving innovations, and the industry responded by moving to alternate locations. This was not just about seeking lowest cost; in many instances, it was determined by access to better technologies that

could augment the skills of workers and ensure continued employment over time. A refined Merchant Marine Act, and U.S. Maritime Strategy, will sensitively propose ways to rebuild the U.S. maritime sector, in a way that leads to job creation and increased opportunities for U.S. labor, and other participants working in complementary industries.

Describing the critical importance of the Act to Congress in 1920, Senator Wesley Jones declared: *"I want ships to fly the American flag on the Pacific"* and *"It is said this bill will drive foreign shipping from our ports. Granted. I want to do it."*. The diminutive number of U.S.-Flag ships on the Pacific, and the proliferation of foreign vessels calling at domestic ports clearly illustrates why a new approach is needed, and enacted in a purposeful and diligent fashion. A refined Merchant Marine Act, and comprehensive U.S. Maritime Strategy will ensure the most necessary and advantageous maritime activities are protected and pursued.

When this occurs, the United States will be able to fulfill, and then exceed the Act's original intentions:

1. To increase U.S. international competitiveness,
2. Improve national security and defense outcomes,
3. Encourage the growth of domestic and foreign trade,
4. Use the best equipped blend of vessels for commerce and military support, and,
5. Encourage U.S. private ownership and operation of vessels and associated crews

# CONCLUSION | From *Zero Point Four* to *Four Point Zero*

From ***Zero Point Four*** to ***Four Point Zero*** is a call to action. Today, the United States stands at the junction of two different pathways with two distinctly different futures:

- If the current status quo is maintained, inevitable decline, and shrinking U.S. influence over global maritime and international affairs will follow.

- The alternate pathway, that promotes the U.S. maritime sector, increases the tonnage and capability of U.S. commercial ships, and provides gainful opportunities for U.S. labor, is littered with incredibly profitable and impactful opportunities. Opportunities that will enhance and increase National, Economic, Food & Energy, Climate and Workforce Security across a variety of pathways.

The U.S. needs an all-encompassing national maritime strategy that should center on values, collaboration, systems thinking and good governance. The Fourth Industrial Revolution is upon us, and we have an unprecedented opportunity to lead through this revolution as we have in previous industrial revolutions.

- **National security** will require the right number and blend of oceangoing U.S. commercial fleet ships for long range military deterrence operations and to sustain a combat-ready presence if necessary. A strong U.S. commercial fleet is needed to leverage alliances and certain asymmetric technical capabilities to overcome an adversary's geographic and resupply advantages on the other side of the world.

- **Economic security** depends on U.S. commercial fleet ships to support the nation's global supply chain. A robust U.S. commercial fleet would also capture the maritime markets, ocean routes and investment dollars to help grow the economy, while displacing foreign control of imports and exports.

- **Energy and Food security**, essential to the heartland of the U.S., should be provided with an assured U.S. commercial fleet for domestic needs, commercial exports and strategic commodity distribution. New fuels and ocean routes provide a unique opportunity to leapfrog global competitors in these trades.

- **Climate security** requires U.S. leadership at home and in the global commons. Opportunities for the U.S. commercial fleet on the high seas, which make up seventy percent of the earth's surface, are endless. Americans thrive on solving generational challenges like climate change once they are equipped with the necessary platforms and national investment.

- **Workforce security** underpins every major industry. The U.S. commercial fleet is no exception. A bold new maritime strategy requires the best people in the U.S. to become mariners. They have done that in the past and will do it again - former merchant mariners have gone on to become Astronauts, U.S. Senators and Presidents.

Partnerships and practical pathways rooted in national values, the rule of law and a certain degree of compromise are the essential means to the necessary end state of the U.S. maritime strategy.

A collective hope is that a future edition of this book describes a proud, sizable U.S. international commercial fleet, fit for purpose and globally respected. This prompts the question: is it possible to move from *Zero Point Four*, to *Four Point Zero* in the decade that follows? Through purposeful action and the implementation of bold and intentional national maritime strategies, it is entirely feasible. And when considering the need to lead by example with pressing issues such as maintaining a rules-based international order and adapting to climate change, it is entirely necessary.

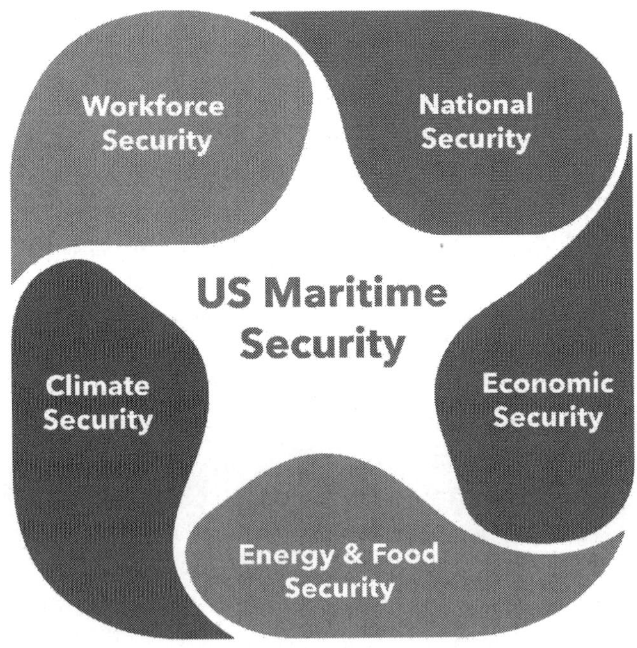

# A 57-POINT U.S. MARITIME NATIONAL ACTION PLAN

The following is a recap of the 57 key actions identified in the book at the end of each Principle needed to transform the U.S. Maritime Industry from *Zero Point Four* to *Four Point Zero* percent of global shipping. These steps could form the basis of a National Maritime and Blue Economy Strategy to guide decision-making across all key agencies that touch the ocean.

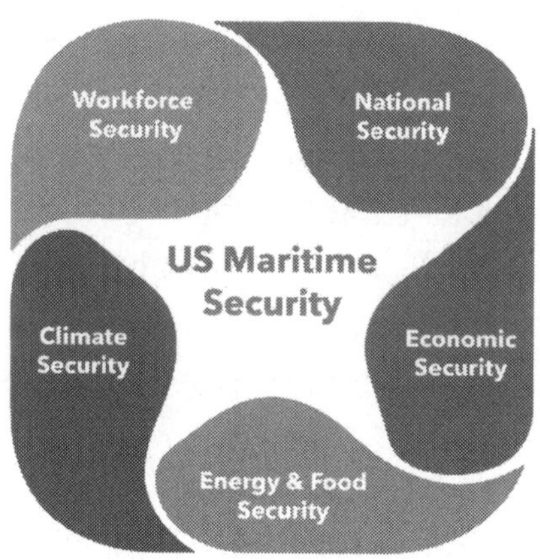


## NATIONAL SECURITY

1. **Risk: A lack of understanding about the U.S. Maritime Sector**
   **Solution: Maritime Awareness Campaigns & Partnerships**
   Launch public awareness campaigns in partnership with key industry, academic and public organizations to

increase general understanding about shipping, highlight the security risks of a weak U.S. maritime sector, and attract new recruits.

2. **Risk: Incomplete support fleet blend**
   **Solution: Dual-Use Capabilities Register (DUCR)**
   The Department of Defense should have stronger coordination and interoperability with the commercial sector. To do so requires a Dual-Use Capabilities Register that can set dual-use parameters, such as deck heights and weight limits for commercial ROROs.

3. **Risk: Lack of subsea vessels and equipment**
   **Solution: Subsea Support Fleet (SSF)**
   The U.S. requires expertise, vessels and equipment to repair internet cable and energy assets in deepwater environments. A Subsea Support Fleet would be a collection of commercial vessels, submersibles and unmanned vessels to perform such tasks.

4. **Risk: Lack of appropriate tankers**
   **Solution: Creatively reform the Tanker Security Program**
   The Tanker Security Program should be reformed to flag-in modern, allied-made foreign hulls using new incentives and benefits. This should be completed in collaboration with the commercial sector, so that the right blend of tankers is acquired for the right price.

5. **Risk: The Ready Reserve Force**
   **Solution: Redefine the role and management of the RRF**
   There needs to be a marked increase in fit-for-purpose ships and mariners. The RRF needs to be radically overhauled so vessels can be rotated out with the existing naval fleet, or employed in 'dual-use' roles with the commercial sector.

6. **Risk: Dysfunctional MSP and VISA**
   **Solution: Annual MSP/VISA Report Card**
   Greater transparency is needed of the MSP and VISA programs. A 'MSP and VISA Report Card' should be made available every year by MARAD, to increase accountability and transparency of both programs and include key performance metrics.

7. **Risk: Excessive dependencies on non-U.S. entities**
   **Solution: Foreign-Interest Impact Record (F-IIR)**
   A centralized, U.S. F-IIR system that includes details of ownership and control for critical maritime infrastructure such as ports, vessels, cranes, financing, digital systems, is required to reduce the threat of hostile foreign involvement in the U.S. maritime sector.

8. **Risk: Reduced collaboration between defense and the private sector**
   **Solution: The Maritime National Training Center (MNTC)**

The U.S. should build a maritime equivalent of the Army's NTC. The programs attached to the MNTC would force a percentage of actively patrolling vessels into a short hiatus for close-in wargaming and simulations with the private sector.

9. **Risk: Domestic economy and double-counting**
   **Solution: Maritime Asset Database / Maritime Resource Map (MAD/MRP)**
   The U.S. needs to record all available maritime assets into a secure Maritime Asset Database including those in dual-use roles which may need to be backfilled. This will quickly identify which assets are available immediately and what location they are in.

10. **Risk: Capacity in the domestic maritime industrial base**
    **Solution: U.S. Maritime Dual-Use Strategy (MD-US)**
    The creation of a Dual-Use Strategy (e.g., around recruitment, asset procurement, construction and repair), will help identify what infrastructure and support is required to enable dual-use construction at U.S. shipyards and better integration of the workforce.

11. **Risk: Cybersecurity and related emerging threats**
    **Solution: MTS-ISAC and sharing threat data**
    Greater sharing of data is needed to reduce rising cyber-security threats. Coordinating bodies like the Maritime Transportation System Information Sharing and Analysis Center (MTS-ISAC) could see their impact

transformed by collecting and sharing data from industry, Government bodies and frontline public officials.

12. **Risk: Threats dispersed over a large geographic area**
    **Solution: Distant Water Fleet Overwatch (DWFO)**
    Distant Water Fleets (DWF) operating in the High Seas need to be constantly monitored to detect illegal activity and to assist with the protection of Freedom of Navigation. New sensors in satellite technologies (such as Synthetic Aperture Radar) can be catalytic for a Distant Water Fleet Overwatch program in partnership with the Navy and Coast Guard.

13. **Risk: Asymmetric Warfare**
    **Solution: Maritime Asymmetric Warfare Division (MAWD)**
    The U.S. Navy needs to develop new responses to asymmetric threats. Current programs need to be radically scaled, and new strategic investment funds created into innovative private-sector technology providers that could assist the Navy toward its stated goal of being "up to 40 percent unmanned, by the middle of the century".

14. **Risk: Diminished U.S. naval presence on the world's oceans**
    **Solution: The Strategic International Maritime Alliance (SIMA)**

The High Seas consist of almost half of the planet and are ineffectively monitored or enforced. The U.S. could coordinate a coalition through a Strategic International Maritime Alliance (SMA) that could demonstrate U.S. leadership and encourage international cooperation through the impartation and completion of a range of shared responsibilities.

## ECONOMIC SECURITY

1. **Risk: Poor understanding of the role of shipping in the economy**
   **Solution: National Maritime Awareness Campaigns**
   Shipping is central to the functioning of the U.S. economy and should not be marginalized in public discourse. The Department of Transportation (DOT), MARAD and other associated agencies can play a strategic role by raising awareness of how ships and maritime activities positively impact the domestic economy and U.S. consumers.

2. **Risk: "Economic Security is National Security" largely misunderstood**
   **Solution: National & Economic Security Plan - Maritime (NESP-M)**
   Creation of an NESP-M that could regularly run joint exercises between institutions, agencies and departments involved in National Security on one side, and the economic planners (politicians, governors, academics, captains of industry and commercial entities

such as the National Industrial Transportation League) on the other.

3. **Risk: International fiscal and currency flows and sanctions**
   **Solution: Expand financial offerings for commercial trade**
   There are many financial technologies that could be pioneered in the U.S. that could reduce the risk of trade moving away from the U.S. dollar. One example is to introduce electronic Bills of Ladings, a critical document to acknowledge receipt of cargo, and upon which new trade finance, anti-money laundering, Know Your Customer products can be built that are denominated in U.S.-dollars.

4. **Risk: Shipping industry influence and weak government oversight**
   **Solution: Expand MARAD and the Federal Maritime Commission (FMC)**
   MARAD and the FMC require more resources, people and technologies to complete all of the complicated tasks related to managing, regulating and enforcing regulations within the U.S. maritime sector - as much as 10,000 staff and a 4X increase in budget to $4 billion for both agencies. This would still be over 4X lower than the considerably better resourced Federal Aviation Authority that performs the same role in aviation.

5. **Risk: Minimal U.S. representation during some strategic international discussions**

**Solution: Greater U.S. influence at IMO & global conferences**

The U.S. should have a strategic plan for how to ensure greater influence at key international maritime bodies and advocate for institutional reform to make such international bodies more effective. For example, securing the chair of the powerful environmental protection committee at the IMO that sets climate standards for the international shipping industry, but which opted out of the Paris Climate Accords.

6. **Risk: Underinvestment, vested-interests and foreign influence**

   **Solution: The U.S. Economic Security Program (ESP)**

   An equivalent program to the Maritime Security Program (MSP) and the Tanker Security Program (TSP) with a focus on Economic Security must be explored. The priority of the U.S. Economic Security Program should be to increase the amount of U.S.-controlled, ocean-going tonnage, engaged in international trade. This could be achieved by rapidly flagging-in purposefully-selected foreign-built tonnage into the U.S. Flag fleet, or, as some have suggested, by creating a 2nd U.S. Register (second U.S. maritime Flag). Second registries implemented by other nations have had mixed results. Incentives for rapidly flagging-in foreign-built ships should include favorable taxation or insurance conditions, or other benefits that go beyond cargo preferences to offset the price differential of operating a U.S.-flagged ship vs a cheaper foreign-flagged equivalent.

7. **Risk: Overexposure to risky business practices**
   **Solution: Global Maritime Risk Index (GMRI)**
   A Global Maritime Risk Index would act as a 'safety net' to protect against risky business practices (e.g., sanction violations). A global index applied to the international commercial fleet would analyze the business practices of ship operators, service providers and Flag States, and provide metrics about the likelihood that these entities might engage in risky business practices.

8. **Risk: Missed opportunities in the Blue Economy**
   **Solution: Effective communication of profitable maritime investments**
   The U.S. needs a holistic Blue Economy strategy, with supporting institutions and partnerships with the U.S. financial community to de-risk investments into this fast-growing new segment of the global economy (e.g., aquaculture, offshore windfarms, plastic alternatives, algae, short-sea shipping).

9. **Risk: Illicit trade and global supply chain security**
   **Solution: Intelligent Containerized Trade**
   Less than 2% of all containers are inspected as they enter the United States. The U.S. could become a world leader in intelligent containerization through the development of modern electronic seals – that would

replace the basic, single-use equivalents – and integrating sensors into containers, while encouraging data standards and interoperability between supply chain participants. This would help the U.S. CBP and USCG perform a greater number of data-augmented and risk-assessed container inspections.

10. **Risk: Anemic innovation in the U.S. maritime sector**
    **Solution: U.S. Maritime Economic Innovation Fund (MEIF)**
    The creation of a network of maritime innovation hubs will help the U.S. build the next generation of products and services, and grow the next cohort of industry leaders, in a similar fashion to the private space sector. A supporting Maritime Economic Innovation Fund (MEIF) would pool co-invested capital from Government and industry, and invest it into newly developed innovative maritime technologies, processes and assets.

11. **Risk: Misaligned taxes and inefficient maintenance of inland and coastal waterways**
    **Solution: U.S. Inland and Coastwise Waterways Authority (ICWA)**
    The U.S. needs to create an Inland and Coastwise Waterways Authority to boost inland waterway trade along its Maritime Highways. Much of the U.S. waterway systems are ineffectively maintained due to unfilled positions and ineffective coordination between local Government, the private sector and the U.S. Army

Corps of Engineers. A holistic and national Inland Waterways Authority (as exists in the EU, UK and India) would ensure efficient maintenance and more effective usage of funds being collected for this purpose (the Harbor Maintenance Tax, for example).

12. **Risk: Shipping, inflation and the cost of living**
    **Solution: Maritime Risk Register (MRR) & Economic Impact Barometer (EIB)**
    In the event of a major industry disruption, a Maritime Risk Register would aim to quantify what economic impact would be felt by all concerned parties. For example, how an escalated labor dispute shut down key West Coast ports and terminals. This would help decision-makers more effectively monitor and manage such risks.

13. **Risk: Underutilization of one of the most efficient forms of transportation**
    **Solution: Establish a Short-Sea Shipping Coalition (SSSC)**
    For the last three decades Short-Sea Shipping (SSS) has been described as the most promising innovation that could transform U.S. maritime transportation. The United States has some of the best river systems, inland waterways, and favorable coastlines in the world, and yet has not implemented a major Marine Highway Plan, or spent a noticeable amount of money on related initiatives. MARAD's 2023 budget included $10 million for U.S. Marine Highways, which is in contrast to the billions that most large countries in Europe and

Asia have successfully invested in Short-Sea Shipping over the last decade. To fully benefit from these and a range of other advantages, a U.S. Short-Sea Shipping Coalition (SSSC) should be created so that additional resources and funding is committed to SSS activities.

## ENERGY AND FOOD SECURITY

1. **Risk: Incorrect fleet blend to support U.S. Food and Energy Security**
   **Solution: The Flag-In Security Program (FISP)**
   A Flag-In Security Program would ensure that U.S.-flagged ships are available in the event of a national emergency and to maintain freedom of trade around the world. The Flag-In Security Program is designed to streamline the flag-in process and incentivize internationally operating, U.S.-owned energy and food companies to transition operations away from Flags of Convenience and instead use U.S.-flagged vessels. Reflagging into the U.S. registry has been streamlined for MSP and TSP ships, but not regular commercial ships. Within five years, this could include 50 LNG tankers, 100 oil tankers, 100 container ships and 100 dry bulk ships for the transportation of food.

2. **Risk: Distribution of transition and new maritime fuels**
   **Solution: Global Maritime Energy Security Map (GMESM)**
   The U.S. should create a Global Maritime Energy Security Map - an interactive map that takes input from

multiple sources, to accurately display the locations of globally available maritime energy stockpiles. The purpose would be to de-risk an orderly transition to a clean fuels future.

3. **Risk: Securing the correct maritime future fuels blend**
   **Solution: Establish MESS and MERC**
   A U.S. Maritime Energy Security Strategy (MESS) would aim to map out the available and proposed energy needs of the maritime sector, and then perform a detailed analysis on how those energy requirements will be secured (supply, storage, transportation and transmission/distribution). This Strategy should be formulated in close collaboration with a diverse array of stakeholders, coordinated by a Maritime Energy Research Coalition (MERC). Such a body could be hosted by the Department of Energy, Environmental Protection Agency and the DOD, and be guided by industry participants, university researchers with the input of the DOT and MARAD.

4. **Risk: Food spoilage across domestic and international supply chains**
   **Solution: U.S. Food Transportation Spoilage Scheme (FTSS)**
   A U.S. Food Transportation Spoilage Scheme (FTSS) would aim to map out where food spoilage occurs, with a particular focus on the maritime and cold-chain transportation links that are responsible for the transportation of food. Once problem areas are

identified, the scheme would actively work with a variety of public and private partners to reduce the risks of future spoilage, by deploying novel technologies, or by implementing new processes and procedures.

5. **Risk: Lack of investment in maritime infrastructure**
   **Solution: Maritime Capital Investment Fund (MCIF)**
   A MCIF would be a government Capital Investment Fund to support U.S. maritime projects during the decarbonized energy transition, and to support the secure distribution of U.S. food and food products. The U.S. Treasury could manage the fund much like it managed the post-COVID Capital Project Fund that provided $10 billion to states, territories and local governments to assist with the response to the public health emergency.

6. **Risk: Misalignment between Government initiatives and the private sector**
   **Solution: Annual Government and commercial alignment audits**
   An annual Blue Economy Summit should be created at which key agencies should present their strategic plans for Food and Energy security and align these with the private sector. This would help align various public and private stakeholders on common goals for key energy sources (e.g., wind, solar, hydro, tidal), as well as key food sources (e.g., seafood, algae).

7. **Risk: Food and Energy shipment protection**
   **Solution: Fund USCG expansion in regional hotspots**
   The USCG is deeply experienced in a range of activities, including interdiction and interception, boarding hostile vessels, and performing maritime search and rescue. The role of the USCG could be expanded to include regular patrols to be conducted in various maritime chokepoints and critical trade lanes.

8. **Risk: Lax standards of practice for commodity shipping**
   **Solution: Energy and Food Security Maritime Risk Register (EFS-MRR)**
   The EFS-MRR would be specifically designed to provide U.S. exporters and importers access to a ratified list of shipping providers, and include details about the risks involved with using those companies to move food, produce, commodities or energy.

9. **Risk: Cybersecurity threats affecting Energy and Food Security**
   **Solution: APT Threat-Modelling Program (APT-TMP)**
   Advanced Persistent Threats (APTs) are typically stealthy attackers - often nation state or state-sponsored - who gain unauthorized access to a system or network and remain undetected for an extended period, making them difficult to detect and causing a significant amount of disruption. An APT-TMP would conduct threat-modeling and assessment at a national level, with a

specific focus on shipping and maritime assets involved in energy and food distribution.

10. **Risk: Missed opportunities with U.S. Navy technologies and expertise**
    **Solution: U.S. Navy Technology Commercialization Accelerator (USN-TCA)**
    A U.S. Navy Technology Commercialization Accelerator would seek to identify U.S. Navy technologies (and operating procedures) that have a viable path to commercialization, and then work with industry collaborators to accelerate developing and integrating those solutions into the commercial maritime sector.

11. **Risk: Lack of U.S. leadership in the clean energy shipping revolution**
    **Solution: Produce scalable Small Modular Nuclear Reactors for commercial ships**
    The United States is in a unique position to pioneer the integration of nuclear propulsion into the global commercial maritime sector. Doing so, would decarbonize the industry, decrease running costs for operators, and also establish the U.S. as an undeniable leader in international commercial maritime affairs. Other countries may supply the hulls and superstructure but the United States is in a unique position to 'completely control the engine room'.

# CLIMATE SECURITY

1. **Risk: Lack of U.S. coordination with maritime climate risk initiatives**
   **Solution: Develop a holistic national Blue Economy Strategy supported with new Blue Economy Institutions and a National Maritime Climate Strategy (NMCS)**
   The U.S. could take a global leadership position in the Blue Economy, but needs a holistic Blue Economy Strategy to coordinate a joined-up approach across multiple Government agencies. Building the Blue Economy will also require new Blue Economy Institutions to ensure more effective ways to coordinate, regulate and promote the blue economy. For example, a National Maritime Climate Strategy could map out requirements and proposed solutions for major climate problems, and ensure that stakeholders are aligned with national climate objectives.

2. **Risk: Global fleet emissions are not accurately measured**
   **Solution: Global Maritime Emissions Map (GMEM)**
   A Global Maritime Emissions Map (GMEM) could map out the emission tracks of ships as they cross the ocean, and provides accurate data on which ship types, routes, and activities produce the most pollution. This would not just apply to $CO_2$, but also $NO_x$, $SO_x$, methane, Particulate Matter, black carbon and nuclear radioactivity. The ultimate goal of the GMEM would

be to quantify, and visually display the impact the shipping industry has on our shared marine environments.

3. **Risk: Port emissions from power-generating assets**
   **Solution: Expand the Clean Ports Program**
   The Department of Transportation (DOT) and Environmental Protection Agency (EPA) have committed $3 billion through the Clean Ports Program, to fund zero-emission port equipment and technology, and to help ports develop action plans to reduce air pollutants. This initiative should be expanded, so that it can be positioned to be a world-leading template for other ports across the globe.

4. **Risk: Incentivize the use of electric vessels and electric power**
   **Solution: Maritime Electrification Incentive Scheme (MEIS)**
   The Maritime Electrification Incentive Scheme (MEIS) will exist alongside the revised Clean Ports Program. A similar concept has been implemented in the EU and China. The MEIS would provide financial incentives and funding for the roll-out of shore-power systems, and would also encourage the installation of reciprocal power systems and hardware on vessels. The experiences of the automotive sector - e.g., as Tesla rolled out its 'SuperCharger' network, and as the automotive industry negotiated plug standardization - can be used to accelerate decisions around key port infrastructure and the hardware being used on ships.

5. **Risk: Sea level rise and extreme weather disrupting U.S. ports**
   **Solution: OctoPorts - Offshore, climate-secure cargo processing facilities**
   An OctoPort is a large, eight-sided, off-shore, cargo and commodity processing facility that complements the role of a traditional port facility. Once constructed in a U.S. shipyard, OctoPorts are floated out into position and anchored to the seafloor in a similar fashion as an oil and gas platform. A traditional port, attached to expensive static real-estate may never recover from a terrorist attack or airstrike, whereas an OctoPort can easily be replaced by a rapidly-constructed equivalent or supplied to other nations, built in the U.S. then installed in sovereign waters overseas and administered by U.S. operators. This would immediately improve port capacity in the nominated country, and given the OctoPorts ability for dual-use operations, would also perform a secondary role as an object of soft power projection.

6. **Risk: International shipping lanes require emission controls and security**
   **Solution: Navy Green Shipping Corridors (NGSC)**
   Green Shipping Corridors have been proposed for some time - including with more detail and 22 signatory nations at COP26 in 2021 - however have struggled in implementation. Some encouraging signs occurred across 2023, including the announcement in September of the formation of a Green Shipping Corridor across the Transpacific between the Port of Shanghai and the

Port of Los Angeles and Long Beach. The plan was developed with support from 'C40 Cities' - a global network of "nearly 100 mayors of the world's leading cities that are united in action to confront the climate crisis." The enhanced version of a Green Shipping Corridor would be a Navy Green Shipping Corridor (NGSC). A NGSG carries all of the advantages of a standard Green Shipping Corridor, but also implements oversight and protection from the U.S. Navy and Coast Guard. Users of the NGSC would pay for these protections via a transparently administered levy, which would be offset by reduced risks across the length of the voyage, along with other cargo and port preferences at each end of the NGSC that reduce overall operating costs.

7. **Risk: Lack of transparency about retailer and BCO shipping emissions**
   **Solution: Mandatory Emission Disclosure Scheme (MEDS)**
   Beneficial Cargo Owners (BCOs) and retailers often seek to transport goods using the lowest possible cost, and generally avoid disclosing shipping emissions. This can lead to 'just above the bar' compliance. The Mandatory Emission Disclosure Scheme (MEDS) will involve the collation and public disclosure of all transportation-related emissions of products from every U.S. retailer and BCO.

8. **Risk: Lack of standards for new-builds and overhauls**
   **Solution: Green Shipping Certification Program (GSCP)**
   Environmental and sustainability standards are required for new vessels that will be built over the coming decade, and also for vessels that are overhauled to comply with new standards. Class Societies - such as the American Bureau of Shipping - should be encouraged to incorporate new sustainability standards into the certification process.

9. **Risk: The global shipping industry will not meet climate targets**
   **Solution: Advanced Research Projects Agency - Maritime (ARPA-M)**
   The best mechanism to accelerate the creation of new technologies, manufacturing processes and production facilities will be to establish an entirely new, Public-Private Partnership (PPP) innovation incubator, the Advanced Research Projects Agency - Maritime (ARPA-M). ARPA-Energy, ARPA-Climate, ARPA-Health and ARPA-Infrastructure have been created to address major challenges in these respective fields. Given the essential nature of shipping to National, Economic, Energy & Food, Climate and Workforce Security, it is time that maritime had its own Agency.

# WORKFORCE SECURITY

1. **Risk: Poor public understanding of the role of shipping in the economy**
   **Solution: 'No Shipping, No Shopping' Campaign**
   A U.S.-led global awareness campaign would highlight the importance of shipping to the general public, consumers, producers and suppliers, while also supporting the work of seafarers.

2. **Risk: Numbers of available mariners unknown**
   **Solution: Qualified Available Mariner Audit (QAMA)**
   Numbers from MARAD and other official sources are often difficult to ascertain, and may not be entirely clear for the administrators and officials involved in either. A national Qualified Available Mariner Audit will allow these numbers to be better understood, and so they can be used to calculate shortfalls that may exist for crewing the RRF and other needed auxiliary services ships.

3. **Risk: Lack of qualified officers, SSO's and mariners for Sealift**
   **Solution: Expand USMMA and State Maritime Academies**
   The USMMA and SMA's enrollment and class sizes should increase to expand the available pool of mariners; for commercial activities, dual-use operations, and to maintain high levels of support for the U.S. Navy. Where possible, the State Maritime Academies should work with the USMMA to attract and

train students who are willing to commit to obligated service as well.

4. **Risk: Attracting the needed mariners to the U.S. merchant marine**
   **Solution: Appropriate Parity with U.S. Military Personnel**
   Since merchant mariners are critical to national security and perform duty overseas in support of national objectives, they should receive certain benefits granted to U.S. military personnel. These should include federal and state tax breaks when they work in hazardous duty areas designated by the Department of Defense that allow military personnel to exclude wages from federal and state taxation. Additionally, merchant mariners who are lawful permanent residents and have served the U.S. merchant marine for one year should be eligible for naturalization similar to a U.S. military person with the same status.

5. **Risk: Lack of command opportunities**
   **Solution: U.S. Merchant Marine Advanced Leadership Program (MM-ALP)**
   There is no defined career path 'from the deckplate to headquarters' for mariners serving in Military Sealift Command. This brings ambiguity to career positions, and stifles the chance of progressing beyond being a Port Captain or advising an area commander. Under the MM-ALP, Junior MSC mariners (2nd Mates or engineers) would be given the option to spend time ashore in MSC area commands, to communicate the

particular needs of merchant mariners to naval personnel.

6. **Risk: Reduced U.S. mariner competitiveness**
   **Solution: U.S. Mariner Benefits and Insurance Scheme (MBIS)**
   International fleets are reluctant to employ U.S. mariners because of a higher liability risk and therefore the potential for increased costs. Rather than asking U.S. commercial interests to take on this risk, one pathway would be for the U.S. Government (under MARAD) to agree with the main trade unions about how to cover the liability. This would mean commercial operators could employ U.S. mariners on similar commercial terms as crews from other countries, with stronger liability coverage provided by the U.S. Government. There are similar programs for other critical workforce groups for example the United Services Automobile Association that support veterans, and government-sponsored enterprise Fannie Mae. Group liability would be handled in tranches, or applied across the entire U.S. Merchant Marine. For example, to cover 50,000 U.S. merchant mariners with liability coverage of $100,000, would require an insurance bond of $5 billion.

7. **Risk: Lack of available support personnel and serving mariners**
   **Solution: Expand the 'Military to Mariner' Program**
   There are 200,000 military veterans who retire each year from every major service (Navy, Army, Air Force,

Coast Guard). 42% are officer rank, 52% are enlisted, and most will have skills that are highly relevant to maritime. Around 60% of retirees seek non-military work upon retirement, and a significant proportion might choose to join the U.S. Merchant Marine if there is a potential for career advancement and a recognition of prior military service and certification.

8. **Risk: Unknown numbers with mariners in conflict scenarios**
   **Solution: Advanced Maritime Contested Logistics Simulations (AMCLS)**
   AMCLS is an academic collaboration to obtain realistic calculations and to perform accurate simulations about the effect on the workforce of contested (logistics and geographic) domains. This involves using AI and computational intelligence to calculate various scenarios, including how many personnel are needed during a period of sustained conflict. These numbers will then be used to adjust the numbers required for training and deployment, and also directly inform talent acquisition and recruitment schedules.

9. **Risk: Lack of participation from industry**
   **Solution: Develop industry-sponsored Scholarship Programs**
   Industry-sponsored Scholarships will provide another avenue for students to be supported as they attend a Vocational School, COE or academy. Finding the right industry partners will make this more effective; not only does it provide needed funding to offset the students'

costs, but it also aligns the student with a potential future employer. Given that shipping is a truly global activity, partners should be sourced from every single industry vertical. For example, Nike is a major shipper of products all around the world, and could nominate to sponsor a student through a maritime training program.

10. **Risk: Reduced incentive to continue in the merchant marine**
    **Solution: Maritime Incentives & Rewards Program (MIRP)**
    This is a mature idea in the aviation sector - SkyMiles or AAdvantage - and has also been successfully deployed by major companies to support workers and increase staff morale. The MIRP offers a range of incentives to students and cadets for completing certain tasks, or being involved in certain activities. Implementing a reward system would positively impact job satisfaction and assist students to maintain a healthier work-life balance.

*This page is intentionally left blank.*

# REFERENCES


Alfaro, Joshua A. (2019) *Challenges Facing The U.S. Flag Revitalizing The U.S. Merchant Fleet Through A Shift In National Focus*, California State University Maritime Academy

Allied Market Research (2022), Luxury Yacht Market by Size Global Opportunity Analysis and Industry Forecast, 2022-2031

Alphaliner (2023), Top 100 Vessels - Global Analysis of The World's Commercial Container Fleet

American Maritime Partnership (2023), *The Jones Act a Line Of Defense Against China's Maritime Dominance*

American Petroleum Institute (2022), *Tankers: Fueling Americas Life*

Angevine, Robert G. (2011), *Hiding in Plain Sight—The U.S. Navy and Dispersed Operations Under EMCON, 1956–1972,* Naval War College

Ankara Centre For Crisis and Policy Studies (2023), *The Effects of New Technologies on The Russia-Ukraine Asymmetric War*

Arizona Submarine Veterans Perch Base (2000), *List of Submarine Classes of The United States Navy*

Armed Forces Communications & Electronics Association International (2023), *Putting Coalition at The Forefront Of JADC2*

Armstrong, Benjamin F. (2023), *21st Century Mahan*, Sound Military Conclusions for The Modern Era

Armstrong, Commander Benjamin (2021), *American Naval Dominance Is Not A Birthright*

Asif, Muhammad (2022), *Handbook of Energy And Environmental Security*

Association Of The United States Army (1991), *Operations Desert Shield And Desert Storm: The Logistics Perspective*

Australian Department Of Defense (2004), *Some Aspects Of Submarine Design Part 1. Hydrodynamics*

Australian Government, Department Of Foreign Affairs & Trade (2023), *AUSMIN - Australia-United States Ministerial Consultations*

Australian Government - Embassy USA (2023), *Australia And The United States*

Bader, Jeffrey (2020), *Meeting The China Challenge: A Strategic Competitor, Not An Enemy*

Barchamotore (2022), *How Many Boats There Are In The World, Where They Are, And Who Uses Them Most*

Barnard, Michael (2023), *And So It Begins: 1,000-Kilometer Route Yangtze Container Ship With Swappable Batteries,* Cleantechnica

Bentzel, Commissioner Carl W. (2023), *Recommendations On The Maritime Transportation Data System Requirements*, Federal Maritime Commission

Benway, Helen (2020), *Ocean Acidification Climate Analysis*, Woods Hole Oceanographic Institution

Berger, General David (2020), *Marines Will Help Fight Submarines*

Blasko, Dennis J. (2015), *China's Merchant Marine*

Bloomberg (2023), *The Messy, Booming Business Of Recycling Cruise Ships*

Bloomberg (2023), *US Commits Over $500 Million To Develop Sri Lanka Container Terminal*

Bloomberg (2023), *The Fed's Inflation Fight Faces A New Challenge: A Dry Panama Canal*

Boe, Mikal (2023), *Advanced Nuclear Power Could Transform U.S. Maritime Industry*, Maritime Executive

Brown, Hannah Story (2022), *Amidst A Record Supply Chain Crisis, What Is The Federal Maritime Commission's Capacity?* Revolving Door Project

Buzby, Mark H. (2022), *Merchant Mariner Shortage Has Gotten Worse, But A Partial Solution Is Available*

C40 Cities (2023), *Green Shipping Corridors*

Cancian, Mark F. (2021), *U.S. Military Forces In FY 2021: Navy*, Center For Strategic & International Studies (CSIS)

Cargill Global Fleet (2023), *Dry Bulk Carriers*

Carlisle, Rodney (2007), *The Attacks On U. S. Shipping That Precipitated American Entry Into World War I*

Carmel, Captain Stephen M. (2023), *The US Navy Needs Tankers: A Crisis In Capability*, Center For International Maritime Security (CIMSEC)

Carrière-Swallow, Yan, Pragyan Deb, Davide Furceri, Daniel Jiménez, Jonathan D. Ostry (2022), *How Soaring Shipping Costs Raise Prices Around The World*, International Monetary Fund

Castex, Admiral Raoul (1976), *Théories Stratégiques* (1878-1968)

CATO Institute (2018), *The Jones Act: A Burden America Can No Longer Bear*

CEM Specialists International (2022), *What Is Ammonia Slip?*

Center For International Maritime Security (CIMSEC) (2016) *China's Uniformed, Navy-Trained Fishing "Militia"*

Center For International Maritime Security (CIMSEC) (2018), *How The Fleet Forgot To Fight - Series*

Center For International Maritime Security (CIMSEC) (2021), *America Needs A Cabinet-Level Maritime Department*

Center For International Maritime Security (CIMSEC) (2021), *Clandestine Cargo: Hiding Sealift In Plain Sight*

Center For International Maritime Security (CIMSEC) (2021), *The Fourth Arm Of Defense: The U.S. Merchant Marine*

Center For Strategic & International Studies (CSIS) (2021), *Hydrogen: The Key To Decarbonizing The Global Shipping Industry?*

Center For Strategic & International Studies (CSIS) (2023), *U.S. EIA's International Energy Outlook 2023*

Center For Strategic And Budgetary Assessments (2015), *Deploying Beyond Their Means America's Navy And Marine Corps At A Tipping Point*

Central Intelligence Agency (CIA) (2022), Merchant Marine - Country Comparisons

Chambers, Sam (2022), *Up To 800,000 Seafarers Will Require Additional Training To Meet Decarbonisation Goals,* Splash24

China Aerospace Studies Institute (2022), *In Their Own Words: Science Of Military Strategy*

China Africa Research Institute (CARI) (2023), *From Contractors To Investors? Evolving Engagement Of Chinese State Capital In Global Infrastructure Development And The Case Of The Lekki Port In Nigeria*

China Dialogue - Ocean (2023), *Black Carbon: The 'Low-Hanging Fruit' For Cleaner Shipping*

China Maritime Studies Institute, U.S Naval War College (2022), *China Maritime Report No. 21: Commercial Shipping And Maritime Militia: The Logistics Backbone Of A Taiwan Invasion*

China Power (2023), *How Advanced Is China's Third Aircraft Carrier?*

Climate And Clean Air Coalition (2019), *Black Carbon And Maritime Shipping: The Long Road To Regulating A Short-Lived Climate Pollutant*

CNBC (2023), *Shipping Industry Could Lose $10 Billion A Year Battling Climate Change By 2050*

CNN (2023), *These May Be The World's Best Warships. And They're Not American*

Congressional Research Services (2010), *DOD Leases Of Foreign-Built Ships: Background For Congress*

Congressional Research Services (2023), *Navy Columbia (SSBN-826) Class Ballistic Missile Submarine Program: Background And Issues For Congress*

Coudert, Frederic R. (1921), *Comments On The Merchant Marine Act Of 1920*

Council On Foreign Relations (COFR) (2023), *Tracking China's Control Of Overseas Ports*

Cowden, Anthony (2022), *The Navy's Past - And Future: An Introductory Primer*

Cudahy, Brian J. (2006), *Box Boats - How Container Ships Changed The World*

Cybersecurity & Infrastructure Security Agency (CISA) (2023), *Critical Infrastructure Sectors*

Cybersecurity & Infrastructure Security Agency (CISA) (2023), *Sea Level Rise - Analysis And Report*

Dahlan, Nofri Yenita, Nurfadzilah Ahmad, Nur Iqtiyani Ilham, Siti Hajar Yusoff (2022), *Energy Security: Role Of Renewable And Low-Carbon Technologies*

Degnarain, Nishan (2020), *Calls For Global Shipping To Ditch Fossil Fuels And Meet Climate Go*als, Forbes

Degnarain, Nishan (2020), *Global Shipping's UN Climate Talks Fail Amid Threats Of A Walkout*, Forbes

Degnarain, Nishan and Stone, Gregory (2017), *Soul of the Sea in the Age of the Algorithm,* Leete's Press

Delaporte, Murielle (2023), *The Return Of Contested Logistics In The Direct Defense Of Europe,* Second Line Of Defense

Deloitte (2010), *Challenge To The Industry: Securing Skilled Crews In Today's Marketplace*

## REFERENCES


Department Of Homeland Security, United States Coast Guard (2018), *Flag State Control In The United States*

Department Of Homeland Security (2019), *The Defense Production Act Committee Report To Congress*

Disavino, Scott (2023) *U.S. Poised To Regain Crown As World's Top LNG Exporter*, Reuters

Donnellon-May, Genevieve (2023)*, China's Overseas Ports Acquisition Program,* Australian Institute Of International Affairs

Dushay, Molly (2023), *Maritime Workforce Forecasting and Assessment of Stakeholders*, MPSEC

Ebeling, Eric P. (2022), American Roll-On Roll-Off Carrier, *Testimony To Congress On The State Of The U.S.-Flag International Fleet*

Erickson, Andrew S. (2023), *Modern Chinese Maritime Forces,* Order Of Battle For World's Largest Navy, Coast Guard & Maritime Militia By Number Of Ships

Eurasia Review (2023), *Piracy On The Seas: The Great Security Challenge Of The 21st Century*

Federation Of American Scientists (2023), *Applying ARPA-I: A Proven Model For Transportation Infrastructure*

Filipoff, Dmitry (2023), *A Fleet Adrift: The Mounting Risks Of The U.S. Navy's Force Development*, Center For International Maritime Security (CIMSEC)

Foggo, Admiral James G. (2023), Usn (Ret.) *By Land And By Sea, Challenges Today And Tomorrow,* Harvard

Foggo, Admiral James G. Usn (Ret.) (2023) *The Us Navy Needs A Comprehensive Strategy To Support Future Fleet Design*

Food And Agriculture Organization Of The United Nations (FAO) (2006), *Food Security - Policy Brief*

Food And Agriculture Organization Of The United Nations (FAO) (2008), *The State Of World Fisheries And Aquaculture*

Ford, Rear Admiral Walter C. (1957), *The U. S. Merchant Marine And National Defense*

Freitas, Marcus Vinicius De (2023), *The Impact Of Chinese Investments In Africa: Neocolonialism Or Cooperation?*

Gady, Franz-Stefan (2015) *China Prepares Its 172,000 Commercial Ships For War*, The Diplomat gCaptain (2023), *ABS Launches Industry First Green Shipping Corridors Modeling And Simulation Service*

Getting To Zero Coalition, Global Maritime Forum (2022), *Annual Progress Report On Green Shipping Corridors*

Gilday, Admiral Michael M. (2020), Senate Armed Services Committee Subcommittee On Readiness, *Statement Of Admiral Michael M. Gilday, Chief Of Naval Operations On Current State Of Navy Readiness*

Gilday, Admiral Michael M. (2021), *Chief Of Naval Operations On The Posture Of The United States Navy*, House Armed Services Committee

Global Environment Facility (2023), *Areas Beyond National Jurisdiction (ABNJ)*

Goldman Sachs (2023), *The Rise Of Geopolitical Swing States*

Goldstein, Keith (2022) *The Global Impact Of Counterfeiting And Solutions To Stop It,* Forbes

Gosselin-Malo, Elisabeth (2023), *Ukraine Continues To Snap Up Chinese DJI Drones For Its Defense,* C4Isrnet

Gouré, Daniel (2001), *The Tyranny Of Forward Presence,* Naval War College

Government Accountability Office (GAO) (2018), *International Food Assistance - Analysis And Report*

Grady, John (2018), *U.S. Short Almost 2,000 Mariners To Supply American Forces In War,* USNI News

Grady, John (2023), *MARAD Head 'Not At All Confident' Ready Reserve Fleet Could Be Crewed In A Crisis*, USNI News

Greenwood, Jeremy and Emily Miletello (2021), *To Expand The Navy Isn't Enough. We Need A Bigger Commercial Fleet*

Greve, Paige (2019), *Careers Of The Future: The Jobs That Don't Exist Yet*

Grupp, George W. (1950), *The Economic And Military Importance Of Our Inland Waterways,* USNI Proceedings

Hamilton, Alexander (1791), *Report On The Subject Of Manufactures*

Hardman, Commander Paul (2023), *Maritime Trade Is Essential To The Indo-Pacific,* USNI Proceedings

Harvard Business Review (2023), *Batteries Included: Engineering A Way Out Of The Shipping Industry's Carbon Dependence*

Heavenrich, Sam (2022), The Neglected Port Preference Clause And The Jones Act

Henry, Lieutenant Shawn M. (2018), *'Military To Mariner' Program Bridges Merchant/Navy Gap,* USNI Proceedings

Hill, Malia Blom (2013), *The Sinking Ship Of Cabotage*, Capital Research Center

Hiller, Captain Todd M. (2020), *Strategic Sealift Officers Provide Critical Support,* USNI Proceedings

Holmes, James R., Toshi Yoshihara (2009), *Mahan's Lingering Ghost*

Holmes, James R. (2023), *Yes, The United States Needs A Real Maritime Strategy,* USNI Proceedings

Holmes, Kim R.,(2015), *What Is National Security?*

Hooper, Craig (2023), *Like It Or Not, New Nuclear Reactors Are Coming To The U.S. Waterfront,* Forbes

Hosanee, Nivedita M. (2009), *A Critical Analysis Of Flag State Duties As Laid Down Under Article 94 Of The 1982 United Nations Convention On The Law Of The Sea*

House Armed Services Committee (2018), *Mobility And Transportation Command Posture*

House Subcommittee On Coast Guard And Maritime Transportation (2022), *Cargo Preference: Compliance With And Enforcement Of Maritime's Buy American Laws*

Hwang, Jyhjong, Oyintarelado (Tarela) Moses (2022), China's Interest-Free Loans To Africa Uses And Cancellations

Infomaritime (2021), *World Merchant Fleet And Top 15 Shipowning Countries*

Institute For Demographic Research At The City (2007), University Of New York, *634 Million People At Risk From Rising Seas*

Institute For Energy Economics And Financial Analysis (2023), *U.S. On Track To Close Half Of Coal Capacity By 2026*

Intergovernmental Panel On Climate Change (2022), *Climate Change - Global Map Of Vulnerability*

International Chamber Of Shipping (2022), *Environmental Performance: Comparison Of CO2 Emissions By Different Modes Of Transport*

International Chamber Of Shipping (2023), *Shipping And World Trade: Global Supply And Demand For Seafarers*

International Monetary Fund (2023), *Fossil Fuel Subsidies Surged To Record $7 Trillion*

International Transportation Forum (2023), *Container Port Automation: Impacts And Implications*

International Transport Workers' Federation (2023) *IBF Deal Done: 250,000 Seafarers Pay Boosted By 6%*

International Water Association (2016), *What Role For Desalination In The New Water Paradigm*

Irion, Captain Alexander, Major Elle Ekman, And Captain Mitchell Ryan (2020), *Logistics Is A Shaping Factor*, USNI Proceedings

Jones, Bruce (2021), *To Rule The Waves - How Control Of The World's Oceans Shapes The Fate Of The Superpowers*

Jones, Bruce (2023), *Temperatures Rising: The Struggle For Bases And Access In The Pacific Islands,* Brookings

Judson Jen (2023), *US Army Has A 'Gigantic Problem' With Logistics In The Indo-Pacific,* Defense News

Kania, Elsa B. And Ian Burns Mccaslin (2021), *Learning Warfare From The Laboratory— China's Progression In Wargaming And Opposing Force Training*

Kardon, Isaac B. (2023), *China's Law Of The Sea*

Kardon, Isaac B. (2023), *China's Military Diplomacy And Overseas Security Activities*

Kardon, Isaac B. and Wendy Leutert (2023), *Pier Competitor - China's Power Position In Global Ports*

Katsos, George E. (2018), *The U.S. Government's Approach To Economic Security*

Kelley, Terry P. (1990), *Global Climate Change - Implications For The Navy*

Kennard, Harry (2023), *The Future Of Coal In The US Electricity System,* Center On Global Energy Policy

Kennedy, Conor (2023), *China Is Preparing Merchant RORO Ferries For Amphibious Warfare,* Maritime Executive

Kenney, Caitlin M. (2023), *Fewer Than 1/3 Of Navy's Amphibious Ships Are Ready To Deploy,* Defenseone

Kim, Lieutenant Jeong Soo (2023), *Use Allies In Shipyard Modernization,* USNI Proceedings

# REFERENCES


King, Colonel Kenneth Ervin (2007), *Operation Desert Shield: Thunder Storms Of Logistics: Did We Do Any Better During Post-Cold War Interventions?*

Konrad, John (2022), *Admiral, I Am Not Ready For War,* gCaptain

Konrad, John (2023), *Great Lakes Labor: Filipino Mariners Can Now Sail On Canadian Merchant Ships,* gCaptain

Konrad, John (2023), Logistics Wins Wars: A Deep Dive Into War In The Pacific, gCaptain

Konrad, John (2023), *Navigating The Information Fog Engulfing American Shipyards,* gCaptain

Konrad, John (2023), *Replenishing Controversy: The Us Navy's New Tanker Program,* gCaptain

Konrad, John (2023), *US Marine Corps Experiments Offshore,* gCaptain

Konrad, John (2023), *Without Waterways Biden's Climate Plan Will Waste Trillions,* gCaptain

Kumar, Shashi (2023), *U.S. Merchant Marine And World Maritime In Review,* USNI Proceedings

Lakhani, Nina, Aliya Uteuova And Alvin Chang (2021) *The True Extent Of America's Food Monopolies, And Who Pays The Price,* The Guardian

Latham, Andrew (2020), *Mahan, Corbett, And China's Maritime Grand Strategy*, The Diplomat

Lawhorn, Jeremy D. (2019), *Pursuing A Strategy For Yesterday's War*

Lawrence, Robert Z. and Robert E. Litan (1987) *Why Protectionism Doesn't Pay*, Harvard Business Review

Levinson, Marc (2006), *The Box - How The Shipping Container Made The World Smaller And The World Economy Bigger*

Llorca, Renato De Palma, Harlenn Dos Santos Lopes, Renato Da Silva Lima (2018), *Potential Effects Of Expansion Of The Panama Canal On Midwest Brazilian Soybean Logistics*

Lofgren, Eric, Whitney M. Mcnamara, Peter Modigliani (2023) *Commission On Defense Innovation Adoption Interim Report,* The Atlantic Council

Long, Lieutenant Madison L. (2023), *Information Warfare In The Depths: An Analysis Of Global Undersea Cable Networks,* USNI Proceedings

Luebke, Peter C., Timothy L. Francis, and Heather M. Haley (2023), *Contested Logistics Sustaining The Pacific War,* U.S. Navy Operations In World War II

Lynch, Justin (2015), *On Strategic Unpredictability,* Modern War Institute

Ma, Xinmin (2019), *China And The UNCLOS: Practices And Policies*

Mærsk McKinney Møller Center For Zero Carbon Shipping (2022), *Maritime Decarbonization Strategy: A Decade Of Change*

Mahan, Alfred Thayer (1890), *The Influence Of Sea Power Upon History: 1660–1783*

Mahan, Alfred Thayer (1902), *Retrospect And Prospect*; Studies In International Relations, Naval And Political

Manning, Dewry (2023) *Annual Review And Forecast Report*

Mantz, Lieutenant Commander Stephanie E. (2022), *Modernize Training For The U.S. Merchant Marine,* USNI Proceedings

Marine Benchmark (2020), *Maritime CO2 Emissions: Research Brief*

Marine Engineers' Beneficial Association (2017), *Support Full Funding For The Maritime Security Program*

Marine Insight (2022), Top 10 Largest Flag States In The Shipping Industry (2022)

Marine Insight (2023), U.S. To Transform India Into Naval Logistics Hub, To Expand Operations In Indo-Pacific And Counter China

Maritime Executive (2021), *Climate Activists Protest IKEA's Shipping Emissions*

Maritime Executive (2022), *First Vessel Purchased For U.S. Ready Reserve Under Renewal Program*

Maritime Executive (2023), *More Disruptions At SoCal Ports As PMA And ILWU Spar Verbally*

Maritime Executive (2023), *U.S. Navy Might Use Japanese Repair Yards For U.S. Warships*

Maritime Just Transition Taskforce (2022) *COP27: Shipping Decarbonisation Action Plan Launched To Upskill Global Seafaring Workforce*

Maritime Professionals (2021), *Amazon And IKEA Shipping Commitment Is Historic*

Markiewicz, Thomas R. (1983) *An Examination Of The Factors Involved In The Mobilization Of Strategic Sealift Assets*

Masters, Jonathan (2019), *Sea Power: The U.S. Navy And Foreign Policy,* Council On Foreign Relations (COFR)

Masters, Jonathan and Will Merrow (2023), *How Much Aid Has The U.S. Sent Ukraine?* Council On Foreign Relations (COFR)

Matsuda, David T. (2010), United States Department Of Transportation (USDOT) Maritime Administrator David T. Matsuda: *State Of The United States' Merchant Fleet In Foreign Commerce,* Sub-Committee On Coast Guard And Maritime Transportation United States House Of Representatives

Mccormick, David, Chris Brose, And Ryan Evans (2023), *Powering American Renewal With Innovation,* War On The Rocks

Mccown, John D. (2023), *The United States Needs A National Port Strategy* , Center For Maritime Strategy

Mckinsey & Company (2021), *Green Corridors: A Lane For Zero-Carbon Shipping*

Mercogliano, Sal (2023), *What Is Going On With Shipping?*

Methanol Institute (2016), *Methanol Gasoline Blends Alternative Fuel For Today's Automobiles And Cleaner Burning Octane For Today's Oil Refinery*

Miles, Franklin B. (1999), *Assymetric Warfare: An Historical Perspective*

Miller, Greg (2023), *Is Imo 2020 Shipping Regulation Worsening Global Warming?,* Freightwaves

Miller, Greg (2023), *Panama Canal Crisis Forces Us Farm Exports To Detour Through Suez,* Freightwaves

Miller, Greg (2023), *West Coast Dockworkers Making $200K Demand Higher Pay,* Freightwaves

Mizokami, Kyle (2018) *Navy Sub Repair Backlog Cost The Service $1.5 Billion,* Popular Mechanics

Mizokami, Kyle (2023), *Why A U.S. Destroyer Just Downed Drones And Cruise Missiles Over The Red Sea*, Popular Mechanics

Mongilio, Heather (2022), *Marine Corps Exceed Retention Goals Early, Hit More Than 100 Percent*, USNI News

Morales, Joseph (2018), *The Jones Act – The Real Natural Disaster: An Analysis Of The Merchant Marine Act Of 1920.*

Mordor Intelligence (2023), *SCUBA Diving Equipment Market Size & Share Analysis - Growth Trends & Forecasts (2023 - 2028)*

Morgan Stanley (2023), *Investing In The Blue Economy,* Institute For Sustainable Investing

Mosier, Richard (2022), *Distributed Maritime Operations – Becoming Hard-To-Find*, Center For International Maritime Security (CIMSEC)

NASA (2022), *Ocean Warming - Analysis And Data*

National Academy Of Public Administration (2021) *Organizational Assessment Of The U.S. Merchant Marine Academy: A Path Forward*

National Defense Transportation Association (2021), *Navy Develops Modular "CONSOL" Capability To Refuel Oilers At Sea*

National Oceanic And Atmospheric Administration (NOAA) (2013), *Currents And Marine Life*

National Oceanic And Atmospheric Administration (NOAA) (2022) *How Much Water Is In The Ocean?*

National Oceanic And Atmospheric Administration (NOAA) (2023), *How Many Species Live In The Ocean?*

National Security Archive (2023), *The U.S. Space Surveillance Network*

NATO Support And Procurement Agency (2016), *Products And Services,* Logistics Solutions

Nature (2021), *A Healthy Ocean Depends On Sustainably Managed Fisheries*

Nature (2021) *Global LIDAR Land Elevation Data Reveal Greatest Sea-Level Rise Vulnerability In The Tropics*

Naval Surface Warfare Center (2021), *Federal Agency Annual EEO Program Status Report*

NAVSEA (2021), *Campaign Plan To Expand The Advantage 3.0*

NEOM (2023) *'Port Of NEOM' Open For Business*

NPR (2023), *Businesses Face More And More Pressure From Investors To Act On Climate Change*

O'Brien, Robert (2022), *Chinese Sea Power: An Application Of Mahanian Determinants To The Conditions Of China*

Oceana (2022), *Marine Life Encyclopedia - Ocean Fishes*

Ovost, Gen. Jacqueline Van (2022), *American Shipyards Need Revitalization To Help Modernize Military Sealift Command,* USNI News

Ovost, Jacqueline D. Van (2023), *Sealift Or Sink: The Urgent Need To Renew U.S. Maritime Capacity*, Maritime Executive

Oxford University (2023), *Port Of Houston: Risks From Extreme Weather*

## REFERENCES


Park, Andrew I. (2023), *Renewed Security Relationship With The Philippines Presents An Opportunity To Washington,* Center For Maritime Strategy

Parker, Barry (2022), *Building Green Corridors For Shipping Will Take Teamwork,* gCaptain

Perry, Mark J (2017), *Why Protectionism Is Taken So Seriously*, Institute Of Free Trade

Peter G. Peterson Foundation (2023), *US National Defense: U.S. Defense Spending Compared To Other Countries*

Phillips, Ann C. (2023), *Hearing On "Shortage Of U.S. Mariners And Recruitment And Retention In The United States Coast Guard,"* Committee On Transportation And Infrastructure Subcommittee On Coast Guard And Maritime Transportation

Poling, Aidan (2023) *How A Fleet Of Private Satellites Can Help Secure The Us Military's Future,* The Atlantic Council

Ponars Eurasia (2022), *Russia's Icebreakers, North Sea Route, And Invasion Of Ukraine*

Port Of Houston (2023), *Trade Highlights And Performance Data*

Powell, Lane (2012), *The Harbor Maintenance Tax: What's It Really Doing To The U.S. Port Volumes And Imports; And What Should Be Done About It?*

Professional Mariner (2020), *Commercial Mariners Barred From Leaving MSC Ships During Pandemic*

Public Broadcasting Service (2020), *Who Made America? Containerized Shipping & Malcom Mclean*

Rand Corporation (2022), *The Problem Of Intra-Theater Lift: Moving Things Around In The Pacific Area Of Responsibility*

Rane Worldview (STRATFOR) (2008), *U.S.: Naval Dominance And The Importance Of Oceans*

Rane Worldview (STRATFOR) (2016), *The Geopolitics Of The United States, Part 1: The Inevitable Empire*

Rauworth, Michael J. (2017), *Probing The Mysteries Of The Jones Act*

Raymon, John M. (1963), *The Application Of Our Laws To Foreign Merchant Ships,* Pennstate Dickinson Law

Reagan, Michael (2010), *Maritime Workers And Their Unions,* Harry Bridges Center For Labor Studies

Reuters (2023), Iran Says It Had Court Order To Seize Chevron Tanker

Rickards, James (2022), *Sold Out: How Broken Supply Chains, Surging Inflation, And Political Instability Will Sink The Global Economy*

Riggs, Daniel (2021), *Re-Thinking The Strategic Approach To Asymmetrical Warfare,* Military Strategy Magazine

Ritchie, Hannah (2020), Food Transportation & Climate Change

Rodihan, Conor, Matthew R. Crouch, Ronald C. Fairbanks (2021), *Predictable Strategy And Unpredictable Operations: The Implications Of Agility In Northern Europe,* The Atlantic Council

Rogoway, Tyler (2019) *Vital Logistics Ships Will Be Without Critical U.S. Navy Escorts In A Major Conflict,* The Warzone

Ruiz, Alexander (2022), *U.S. Merchant Marine: A Heritage Worth Keeping, And A Matter Of National Security*

S&P Global Commodity Insights (2023), *Fossil Fuels 'stubbornly' Dominating Global Energy Despite Surge In Renewables*

Sadler, Brent D. (2022), *U.S. Navy: An Assessment Of U.S. Military Power,* Heritage Foundation

Sadler, Brent D. (2023),. *Look To Maritime Domain To Revive Failed U.S. Statecraft*

Sadler, Brent D. and Peter St Onge (2023), *Regaining U.S. Maritime Power Requires A Revolution In Shipping*

Safety4Sea (2018), *Drivers Of The 4th Industrial Revolution In Maritime Industry*

Schaefer, Brett (2023), *American Contributions To International Organizations Need Greater Scrutiny,* The Heritage Foundation

Schönander, Lars Erik (2023), *ZPMC And America's Ship-To-Shore Crane Industry: Recommendations For Improving Port Security,* Foundation For American Innovation

Schuler, Mike (2022), *Maersk Lines Up Ninth Partnership On Green Methanol Fuel Supply*, gCaptain

Schuler, Mike (2023), *Philly Shipyard Delivers First National Training Ship To MARAD,* gCaptain

Schwartzstein, Captain Joseph (202), *Bring Back The National Sealift Training Program,* USNI Proceedings

Seapower Magazine (2023), *Lawmakers Introduce Shipyard Act To Support National Defense Infrastructure*

Seapower Magazine (2023), *U.S. Marine Corps Activates First-Ever Marine Innovation Unit, Hosts Defense Innovation Roundtable Event*

Sempa, Francis P. (2014), *The Geopolitical Vision Of Alfred Thayer Mahan*

Setser, Brad W. (2020), *Five Points About U.S. Trade Over The Last Thirty Years*, Council On Foreign Relations (COFR)

Shahbakhsh, Mehrangiz, Gholam Reza Emad, Stephen Cahoon (2022), *Industrial Revolutions And Transition Of The Maritime Industry: The Case Of Seafarer's Role In Autonomous Shipping*

Sharma, Ishanee, Vrutang Shah, Manan Shah (2022), *A Comprehensive Study On Production Of Methanol From Wind Energy*

Ship It Zero (2021), *Shady Ships Report: Retail Giants Pollute Communities And Climate With Fossil-Fueled Ocean Shipping*

Si, Katherine (2021), *Chinese Crew Onboard International Vessels Top 120,000 In 2020,* Seatrade Maritime

Sinclair, Michael, Rodrick H. Mchaty, Blake Herzinger (2021), *Implications Of The Tri-Service Maritime Strategy For America's Naval Forces*

Singh, Lovedeep (2019), *The Metal Box That Transformed Global Trade: The Innovative Vision Of Malcom Mclean Behind The Container Revolution*

Smil, Vaclav (2019) *Electric Container Ships Are Stuck On The Horizon,* IEEE Spectrum

Smithsonian Institute (2017), *With Every Breath You Take, Thank The Ocean*

Stover, Dawn (2021) *Broken Record: The Planet Is Getting Hotter. And Hotter. And Hotter,* Bulletin Of The Atomic Scientists

Subramanian, Samanth (2022), *Forty Percent Of All Shipping Cargo Consists Of Fossil Fuels*

Sullivan, Dylan and Jason Hickel (2022), *Capitalism And Extreme Poverty: A Global Analysis Of Real Wages, Human Height, And Mortality Since The Long 16th Century*

Sweeney, Mike (2023), *Submarines Will Reign In A War With China,* USNI Proceedings

The Atlantic (2023), *The Age Of American Naval Dominance Is Over*

The Economist (2012), *The Third Industrial Revolution*

The Economist (2022), *China's Expanding Investment In Global Ports*

The Economist (2022), *Global Hunger Is Now More A Problem Of Price Than Availability*

The Economist (2023), *Global Food Security Index 2022*

The European Centre Of Excellence For Countering Hybrid Threats (2023), *Handbook On Maritime Hybrid Threats: 15 Scenarios And Legal Scans*

The Institute For Energy Economics And Financial Analysis Ieefa (2022) *U.S.: Booming U.S. Natural Gas Exports Fuel High Prices*

The International Council Of Clean Transportation (2017) *Greenhouse Gas Emissions From Global Shipping, 2013–2015*

The International Transport Forum (2019) *Maritime Subsidies Do They Provide Value For Money?*

The Navy League Of The United States (2021) *Legislative Path To A New Maritime Transportation Strategy*

The New York Times (2023) *Drought Saps The Panama Canal, Disrupting Global Trade*

The Washington Post (1984) *Navy Is Escorting Its Oil Tankers In The Persian Gulf*

The White House (2015) *Findings From Select Federal Reports: The National Security Implications Of A Changing Climate*

The White House (2022) *U.S.-Africa Partnership In Promoting Peace, Security, And Democratic Governance*

The White House (2022) *U.S. Innovation To Meet 2050 Climate Goals: Assessing Initial R&D Opportunities*

The White House (2023) *Australia-United States Joint Leaders' Statement – An Alliance For Our Times*

The White House (2023) *Biden-Harris Administration Announces New Actions, Hosts Inaugural ARPA-I Summit To Highlight The Next Generation Of Transportation Infrastructure Innovation*

The White House (2023) *Fact Sheet: The President's Budget For Fiscal Year 2024*

The World Bank (2022) *Food Security Analysis - Understanding Poverty*

The World Bank (2023) *Food Security Update: Global Market Outlook*

Thomas Heaton (2022) *'Ticking Ecological Time Bombs': Thousands Of Sunken WWII Ships Rusting At Bottom Of Pacific,* Pulitzer Center

Thompson, Loren (2021), *Dwindling U.S. Merchant Fleet Is A Crisis Waiting To Happen,* Forbes

## REFERENCES


Totten, Tyler (2023), *Procuring Modular Containerships For Flexible And Affordable Capability*, Center For International Maritime Security (CIMSEC)

Tuthill, Greg (2023), *Food Waste Mitigation Via Transportation,* Food Engineering

United Nations (UN) (2017) *Ocean Fact Sheet - Sustainable Development*

United Nations (UN) (2023) *Beyond Borders: Why New 'High Seas' Treaty Is Critical For The World*

United Nations (UN) (2023) *Percentage Of Total Population Living In Coastal Areas*

United Nations (UN) (2023) *Review - 2030 Agenda For Sustainable Development*

United Nations (UN) (2023) *Strengthening Of The Coordination Of Emergency Humanitarian Assistance Of The United Nations*

United Nations (UN) (2023) *United Nations Convention On The Law Of The Sea (UNCLOS)*

United Nations Conference On Trade And Development (UNCTAD) (1980) *Review Of Maritime Transport, 1980*

United Nations Conference On Trade And Development (UNCTAD) (2014) *Structure, Ownership And Registration Of The World Fleet*

United Nations Conference On Trade And Development (UNCTAD) (2022) *Global Merchant Fleet - Handbook Of Statistics*

United Nations Conference On Trade And Development (UNCTAD) (2022) *Maritime Profile: China*

United Nations Conference On Trade And Development (UNCTAD) (2022) *Maritime Profile: United States Of America*

United Nations Conference On Trade And Development (UNCTAD) (2022) *Merchant Fleets - Fact Sheet #14*

United Nations Conference On Trade And Development (UNCTAD) (2022) *Review Of Maritime Transport*

United Nations Conference On Trade And Development (UNCTAD) (2023) *Merchant Fleet By Flag Of Registration and By Type Of Ship, Annual*

United Nations Department Of Economic And Social Affairs Exploring (2022) *The Potential Of The Blue Economy*

United Nations Educational, Scientific And Cultural Organization (UNESCO) (1987) *The Third Industrial Revolution*

United Nations Educational, Scientific And Cultural Organization (UNESCO) (2022) *Indian Ocean Basin: Complete Guide*

United Nations Environment Program (2020) *Status Of Coral Reefs Of The World 2020*

United States Agency For International Development (USAID) (2023) *Usaid Food Assistance Overview*

United States Bureau Of Labor Statistics (2022) *Water Transportation Workers*

United States Bureau Of Labor Statistics (2023) *Shipping Prices, Import Price Inflation, and The COVID-19 Pandemic*

United States Bureau Of Transportation (2021) *National Maritime Day - Spotlight On Waterborne Shipping*

United States Coast Guard (USCG) (2015) *Maritime Security Program Fundamentals*

United States Coast Guard (USCG) (2017) *Major Icebreakers Of The World*

United States Coast Guard (USCG) (2020) *Sea Services On Vessels Measured Under Both The Regulatory Measurement System And Conventional Measurement System*

United States Coast Guard (USCG) (2023) *Eligibility Of American Samoans For A U.S. Merchant Mariner Credential*

United States Department Of Agriculture (USDA) (2019) *Importance Of Inland Waterways To U.S. Agriculture*

United States Department Of Agriculture (USDA) (2021) *Ag And Food Sectors And The Economy*

United States Department Of Agriculture (USDA) (2022) *Food Security - Household Food Security In The United States Report*

United States Department Of Agriculture (USDA) (2023) *Crop Production 2022 Summary*

United States Department Of Agriculture (USDA) (2023) *Determinants Of Refrigerated Container Provisioning For Agricultural Exports*

United States Department Of Defense (USDOD) (2022) *DOD, other Agencies - Climate Adaptation Progress Report*

United States Department Of Defense (USDOD) (2022) *National Defense Strategy (NDS)*

United States Department Of Defense (USDOD) (2023) *National Defense Science & Technology Strategy 2023*

REFERENCES

United States Department Of Energy (USDOE) (2023), *Maritime Decarbonization*, Office Of Energy Efficiency & Renewable Energy

United States Department Of Energy (USDOE) (2023) *Floating Offshore Wind Shot,* Office Of Energy Efficiency & Renewable Energy

United States Department Of Energy (USDOE) (2023) *Marine Energy & The Blue Economy,* Office Of Energy Efficiency & Renewable Energy

United States Department Of Homeland Security (2023) *FY2023 Budget In Brief*

United States Department Of State (2009), *Asymmetric Warfare: Definitions And Analysis*

United States Department Of State (2021) *U.S. Relations With Marshall Islands: Bilateral Relations Fact Sheet*

United States Department Of State (2022) *U.S. Relations With Palau*

United States Department Of The Air Force (2023) *Department Of Defense Fiscal Year (Fy) 2024 Budget Estimates*

United States Department Of Transportation (USDOT) (2022), *Supply Chain Assessment Of The Transportation Industrial Base: Freight And Logistics*

United States Department Of Transportation (USDOT) (2022) *Budget Estimates Fiscal Year 2023*

United States Energy Information Administration (USEIA) (2022) *Electricity Generation From Wind*

United States Energy Information Administration (USEIA) (2022) *Electricity In The United States*

United States Energy Information Administration (USEIA) (2023), *Natural Gas Imports And Exports*

United States Energy Information Administration (USEIA) (2023), *U.S. Liquefied Natural Gas Imports From Trinidad And Tobago*

United States Energy Information Administration (USEIA) (2023), *US Lng Export Analysis*

United States Energy Information Administration (USEIA) (2023) *What Countries Are The Top Producers And Consumers Of Oil?*

United States Environmental Protection Agency (EPA) (2022), *Power Plants And Neighboring Communities*

United States Environmental Protection Agency (EPA) (2023), *Nuclear Submarines And Aircraft Carriers*

United States Environmental Protection Agency (EPA) (2023), *United States Ports Initiative*

United States Geological Survey (2019) *All Of Earth's Water In A Single Sphere*

United States Government (USG) (1920), *Merchant Marine Act Of 1920* From Title 46 Of The U.S. Code

United States Government (USG) (1998) *Oversight Of The U.S. Role In The International Maritime Organization,* U.S. House Of Representatives, Subcommittee On Coast Guard And Maritime Transportation, Committee On Transportation And Infrastructure

United States Government (USG) (2017), *Code Of Federal Regulations - Title 46,* Shipping

United States Government (USG) (2021), *Title 46—Shipping (USCODE),* MSP Limit

United States Government Accountability Office (USGAO) (1981) *Maritime Subsidy Requirements Hinder U.S.-Flag Operators' Competitive Position*

United States Government Accountability Office (USGAO) (1991) *Strategic Sealift: Part Of The National Defense Reserve Fleet Is No Longer Needed*

United States Government Accountability Office (USGAO) (2015) *International Food Assistance: Cargo Preference Increases Food Aid Shipping Costs, Benefits Unclear*

United States Government Accountability Office (USGAO) (2022) *Actions Needed To Enhance Cargo Preference Oversight:* Report To Congressional Committees

United States Government Publishing Office 50 *U.S.C. United States Code, (2011) Edition Title 50,* War And National Defense

United States International Trade Commission (2022) *U.S. Seaports Face Elevated Risks In A Warmer World With Higher Seas*

United States Marine Corps, United States Navy, United States Coast Guard (2020), *Advantage At Sea: Prevailing With Integrated All-Domain Naval Power*

United States Marine Corps (USMC) (2023) *Installations And Logistics 2030*

United States Marine Corps (USMC) *Force Design 2030*

REFERENCES


United States Maritime Administration (MARAD) (2004), *Merchant Mariner Training To Meet Sealift Requirements: Report To Congress*

United States Maritime Administration (MARAD) (2004), *Report On Survey Of U.S. Shipbuilding And Repair Facilities*

United States Maritime Administration (MARAD) (2011), *Comparison Of U.S. And Foreign-Flag Operating Costs*

United States Maritime Administration (MARAD) (2012), *Voluntary Intermodal Sealift Agreement*

United States Maritime Administration (MARAD) (2016) *Rrf Training Ships, Special Mission Ships, Retention Ships*

United States Maritime Administration (MARAD) (2020), *Maritime Day Observance Also Recognizes Award Of Congressional Gold Medal To World War II Merchant Mariners*

United States Maritime Administration (MARAD) (2021) *Ready Reserve Force (RRF) Brochure*

United States Maritime Administration (MARAD) (2022), *Cargo Preference Laws*

United States Maritime Administration (MARAD) (2022), *Office Of Policy And Plans,* U.S. Trade Data

United States Maritime Administration (MARAD) (2022) *Maritime Security Program Fleet*

United States Maritime Administration (MARAD) (2022) *Navigating A Stronger Future: MSP And VISA*

United States Maritime Administration (MARAD) (2023), *Budget Estimates Fiscal Year 2024*

United States Maritime Administration (MARAD) (2023), *Educating The Maritime Workforce*

United States Maritime Administration (MARAD) (2023), *Number And Size Of The U.S. Flag Merchant Fleet And Its Share Of The World Fleet*

United States Maritime Administration (MARAD) (2023), *Office Of International Activities*

United States Maritime Administration (MARAD) (2023), *Vessel Inventory Report (Reports And Analysis Since July 1990)*

United States Merchant Marine Academy (USMMA) (2023), *U.S. Merchant Marine Academy Graduates 212 Officers In The Class Of 2023*

United States Merchant Marine Academy Alumni (2018), *Why Congress Funds USMMA And The Other Federal Service Academies*

United States Merchant Marine Academy Alumni (2018) *The U.S. Merchant Marine Academy History And Mission*

United States Military Sealift Command (2023), *U.S. Navy's Military Sealift Command - Fleet*

United States Navy, United States Marine Corps (2021) *Tentative Manual For Expeditionary Advanced Base Operations*

United States Navy (2022), *Joint Fleet Maintenance Manual COMUSFLTFORCOMINST 4790.3*

United States Navy Chief Of Naval Operations (2022), *CNO: Navigation Plan*

United States Navy Military Sealift Command (2020) *2020-2021 Handbook*

United States Transportation Command (USTRANSCOM) (2019), *Comprehensive Report For Turbo Activation 19-Plus*

United States Transportation Command (USTRANSCOM) (2019), *Military Surface Deployment & Distribution Command: Surface Warriors Unite,* Briefing Presentation

United States Transportation Command (USTRANSCOM) (2021) *Visa Executive Working Group (EWG) Meeting Minutes*

United States Transportation Command (USTRANSCOM) (2022), *United States Transportation Command Strategy*

United States Transportation Command (USTRANSCOM) (2022) *Visa Executive Working Group (EWG) Meeting Minutes*

University Of California Museum Of Paleontology (2022), *Understanding Global Change: Oceanic Oxygen Levels*

University Of Michigan Center For Sustainable Systems (2023), *U.S. Food System Factsheet*

Vandersmith, Midshipman First Class Owen (2023), *How Open-Source Intelligence Is Changing Warfare,* USNI Proceedings

Webert, Michael (2018), *Ownership And Control: A Red Herring In The Decline Of The Merchant Marine*

Werrell, Caitlin and Francesco Femia (2017), *Chronology Of Military And Intelligence Concerns About Climate Change,* Center For Climate & Security

# REFERENCES


Winegar, Lieutenant Samuel Heenan (2022), *The Eyes Of The Fleet: Distributed Maritime Operations In The First Island Chain,* USNI Proceedings

Woodruff, Matt (2018), *Our American Mariners – A Commodity Like No Other,* gCaptain

World Economic Forum (2016), *The Fourth Industrial Revolution: What It Means, How To Respond*

World Economic Forum (2023), *'Unprecedented Challenges': Drought At The Panama Canal Disrupts Global Trade*

World Meteorological Organization (2021), *State Of The Global Climate*

World Shipping Council (2023), *Liner Shipping: The Critical Pathways To Zero Carbon Shipping*

World Shipping Council (2023), *Liner Shipping - A Global, Competitive Industry*

World Trade Organization (2023), *Global Trade Outlook And Statistics*

Wylie, Captain J. C. (1957), *Why A Sailor Thinks Like A Sailor,* USNI Proceedings

Yoshihara, Toshi (2018) *Red Star Over The Pacific (Second Edition)*

Zhao, Pieter (2023), *Chinese Political Warfare: A Strategic Tautology? The Three Warfares And The Centrality Of Political Warfare Within Chinese Strategy*

# AUTHORS

## Rear Admiral James Watson (USCG, Ret.)

James Watson is currently an independent consultant providing business development services to maritime clients. He held the position of Senior VP of the American Bureau of Shipping Global Government Services, where he was responsible for the ABS's government market sector. Prior to this, Watson was President and COO for the ABS' Americas Division where he was responsible for all operations of the ABS in the Western Hemisphere. Before ABS, Watson served as Director of the Bureau of Safety and Environmental Enforcement at the US Department of Interior. In this role he provided regulatory oversight for energy exploration and production on the US Outer Continental Shelf. Watson also served as the US Coast Guard's Director of Prevention Policy for Marine Safety, Security and Stewardship, where his responsibilities included commercial vessel safety and security, ports and cargo safety and security and maritime investigations. He was designated as the Federal On-Scene Coordinator for the government-wide response to the Macondo incident in the Gulf of Mexico. Watson earned a Bachelor's of Science in Marine Engineering from USCGA in 1978. He received his Master of Science in Naval Architecture and his Master of Science in Mechanical Engineering from the University of Michigan in 1985. Watson earned an additional Master of Science in Strategic Studies at the National Defense University in 2001.

## Carleen Lyden Walker

Carleen Lyden Walker is the Chief Evolution Officer of SHIPPINGInsight, leveraging off her experience as a marketing and communications professional in the commercial maritime industry with over 40 years of experience. She specializes in identifying, developing and implementing strategic programs that position SHIPPINGInsight as the most effective forum for shipowners and solution providers to advance optimization and innovation in the maritime sphere. In 2015, Ms. Lyden Walker was appointed a Goodwill Maritime Ambassador by the International Maritime Organization (IMO). She is a member of WISTA (Women's International Shipping and Trading Association), the Connecticut Maritime Association, WIMAC (Women in Maritime Association, Caribbean) and is a Past-President of the Propeller Club Chapter of the Port of NY/NJ. She was also elected to the Board of the New Era Academy (Baltimore Harbor School). Ms. Lyden Walker is also CEO of Morgan Marketing & Communications, Co-Founder/CEO of NAMEPA, and Founder of both CARIBMEPA and the Consortium for International Maritime Heritage. In 2010 she was awarded the Certificate of Merit by the United States Coast Guard, and in 2014 a Public Service Commendation for her work on World Maritime Day and AMVER, respectively. In 2023, the USCG presented her with the Distinguished Service Medal.

## Rich Mason

A 25+ year veteran of technology titans such as AT&T, Lucent Technologies' Bell Labs, and Honeywell International, Rich Mason possesses deep expertise in the fields of cyber security, physical security, and enterprise resilience. His last corporate post was as Honeywell's Global Vice President and Chief Security Officer (CSO), a $130 billion Fortune 100 global conglomerate. Mason now leads Critical Infrastructure LLC, a boutique Virginia-based consultancy, where he combines his unique experience, a Honeywell Operating System (HOS) and Six Sigma mindset, and a relentless focus on innovation, trust, and resilience as business enablers. An engaging communicator, demonstrated practitioner and creative thinker, Rich is well-respected among his peers in the cyber, information, and physical security domains. He is vocal about how the practical application of theory should be present at all layers of an organization, and passionately challenges the idea of 'tick box' (vs actual) security. Mason is a is an active member of the George Mason University's National Security Institute (NSI) Cyber and Technology Center, a contributor within a US maritime security accelerator coalition, a former member of the Secret Service's New York Electronic Crimes Task Force, a graduate of the FBI's Executive Academy, and a retired member of the FBI's National Security Business Alliance Council (NSBAC) and Domestic Security Alliance Council (DSAC). An Alumni with honor from Michigan State University, Mason received his Criminal Justice bachelor's degree with a specialization in Security Management.

## Jonathan Kempe

Jonathan Kempe is an entrepreneur, founder, and technology strategist with over 23 years of professional experience across a broad array of disciplines. Jonathan has held a number of diverse roles over his working life: From senior positions in large corporations, founding and running several small businesses, holding trusted roles in nationally accredited NFPs and NGOs, and providing technical services to the Australian Defense Force sector. When running Sydney-based Verifai, Jonathan developed deep experience in global supply-chains, including the implementation of unique security solutions - involving PhySec, CyberSec, IoT, biometrics, and a range of communication standards - to solve practical problems related to theft and cargo tampering, and to provide tracking services for product provenance. Jonathan is well connected within the Australian and New Zealand business communities, has lectured in universities, and spoken at conferences across the world, and regularly contributes to industry advocacy efforts through the provision of unique insights, research and ideation. Jonathan now leads Source Consulting, an innovative strategic consultancy, based in New Zealand. He is passionate about solving global problems, loves to work alongside like-minded individuals, and is dedicated to building impactful solutions that positively transform the world.

## Nishan Degnarain

Nishan Degnarain is a Harvard-educated Development Economist addressing sustainability with fast-growing technologies. He is currently Co-founder and Managing Partner of *The ExO Organization*, a leading Silicon Valley technology and sustainability advisory firm. He has given keynote addresses to Governments, United Nations agencies, the IUCN, World Bank and IMF, and has worked with some of the biggest technology companies on breakthrough innovations for the ocean. Since 2013, Nishan has chaired the World Economic Forum's Global Agenda Council on the Ocean, a group of leading ocean experts from around the world that meet at Davos each year. He sits on several boards, and was previously on the Monetary Policy Committee of the Central Bank of Mauritius and helped establish the National Ocean Council for their newly created Ministry of Ocean Economy. Prior to this, Nishan worked at McKinsey and Company, the World Bank, the UK Prime Minister's Strategy Unit under Tony Blair, and as a broadcast journalist for the BBC. Nishan holds an undergraduate degree from the University of Cambridge and a postgraduate degree from Harvard University's Kennedy School of Government in International Economic Development. He is the author of *Soul of the Sea in the Age of the Algorithm* (2017), on how exponential technologies can heal our oceans, and has won several international awards, such as being recognized as a Young Global Leader by the World Economic Forum and winning the Economist's Ocean Economy Innovation Prize.

## Captain Anuj Chopra

Captain Anuj Chopra is an international executive, enterprise risk manager, and an ESG champion. He co-founded *ESGPlus LLC*, an international consulting firm focused on bringing sustainability, resiliency, efficiency, and independent board advisory to clients invested in a sustainable global maritime supply chain. Before his time at ESGPlus, Captain Chopra spent nearly a decade as a Vice President Americas of *RightShip*, negotiating high-level due diligence and compliance agreements in developing business across Americas. Prior to his time at RightShip, he served as the President of Anglo-Eastern Houston, with direct oversight of vessels visiting US ports, risk evaluation, and government relations. Captain Chopra began his seafaring career as a deck cadet, working his way up to Captain. He has commanded large bulk carriers and tankers and holds a Commonwealth Extra Masters Certificate of Competency, Shipping Management from the Indian Institute of Management, Ahmedabad, India, and ACUE Certification. Captain Chopra currently serves as a Fellow of The Nautical Institute (Chairperson of the U.S. Gulf Branch), is on the Board of Directors at the Houston International Seafarers Center, Member of NOAA FACA HSRP, Advisory Board member of Houston Maritime center, and is an Adjunct Professor for the Supply Chain & Logistics Technology program at the University of Houston, where he has served as a lecturer and teacher for more than 32 years.

## ABOUT *ZERO POINT FOUR*

Dive into *ZERO POINT FOUR*, a groundbreaking narrative developed by six maritime, ocean, and security experts, and spearheaded by retired U.S. Coast Guard Rear Admiral James Watson. The book explores how the U.S. - a maritime nation - finds itself on a precipice. After World War Two, over half the world's ocean-going commercial ships flew the U.S. flag. Today, it is less than 0.4% (*ZERO POINT FOUR*).

This meticulously researched work scrutinizes the U.S. maritime industry's significance to America through five 'Principles': National, Economic, Energy and Food, Climate, and Workforce Security. From shortages in military support vessels to threats against U.S. dollar-denominated trade, and from insufficient numbers of U.S. mariners for food and energy security to the urgent need for climate-resilient maritime operations, the book breaks each issue down to its root causes. The authors don't just identify problems but present a visionary 57-Point Action Plan to revolutionize the U.S. maritime sector and transform America to be a leader in the Blue Economy.

As the world grapples with uncertainty - pandemics, conflicts, and climate crises – America's reliance on a robust maritime sector has never been more crucial. *ZERO POINT FOUR* isn't just a call to action; it is a roadmap to a more secure, preeminent, and viable United States.

Made in the USA
Middletown, DE
14 February 2025

70916592R00282